Raja Yoga: Yoga of Meditation

Raja Yoga: Yoga of Meditation

A means for freedom from suffering

Based on the Teachings of Sri Swami Satchidananda

O. R. Krishnaswami

Dev Publishers & Distributors
New Delhi

Published by:
Dev Publishers & Distributors
2nd Floor, Prakash Deep,
22 Delhi Medical Association Road,
Darya Ganj,
New Delhi-110002
Phone : 011-4357 2647
e-mail: devbooks@hotmail.com
website: www.devbooks.co.in

NOTE

In this Text the words 'man,' 'he' and 'him' are used in a generic sense and refer to both men and women.

ISBN 978-93-81406-53-3
First published 2016

Printed in India

Contents

SECTION III **169**

SECTION IV **273**

Preface

This Text on Raja Yoga was assembled from the books and transcribed lectures of our Gurudev Sri Swami Satchidananda, liberally drawing from his Commentary on *Sutras of Patanjali*, *Living Yoga*, *Meditation, Pranayama* and *Guru and Disciple* and also from the teachings of the grand Master Swami Sivananda Maharaj, Sri Swami Vivekananda, and various other Saints. A large number of spiritual works of modern saints and learned scholars, which are listed under References for various Sections, were also consulted. I acknowledge my indebtedness to all of them. If there are any errors and faults, I am personally responsible.

This Text is a comprehensive one, covering all aspects of Raja Yoga with detailed guidelines for practicing the eight-stage Raja Yoga. Raja Yoga is Yoga of Meditation. It encompasses the teachings of all the different paths. It concerns itself with three realms – the physical, the mental and the spiritual. By practicing Raja Yoga regularly, an aspirant learns to control his thoughts, desires and emotions and thus purifies his mind and finally attains Self-realization. The Self-realized Yogi becomes free from sorrows and suffering and enjoys eternal peace and bliss. This is the ultimate goal of life.

The compilation of this work was entirely due to the grace of Our Gurudev Sri Swami Satchidananda Maharaj and the Supreme Lord. Indeed Sri Gurudev and the Lord worked through this humble soul. With deep devotion I dedicate this Text to the Lotus Feet of Sri Gurudev and the Lord for having made use of this soul as an instrument in their Hands.

May this Text inspire and serve the students of Yoga and guide them in their sincere practice for achieving the ultimate Purpose of Life.

O.R. KRISHNASWAMI

Satchidananda Ashram-Yogaville
October 31, 2013

Acknowledgement

I am deeply grateful to Sri Swami Satchidanada Maharaj who inspired and blessed me to edit this Text as an instrument in his hands.

I am indebted to the authors of the books listed under References and cited in footnotes, from whose thoughts I derived enlightenment.

I am thankful to Swami Murugananda who developed the library of Satchidananda Ashram and archived all of Gurudev Sri Swami Satchidananda's Satsangs on his computerized database of the SASTRI PROJECT, from which references to Sri Gurudev's teachings were taken.

I am grateful to Swami Karunanda who was pleased to review the first draft of this Text and offered very valuable suggestions for revising the script.

I am also thankful to my sons and daughter for having presented me with a new laptop computer and my third son for having procured several books for my study and reference.

I am grateful to the Administrative Council of Satchidananda Ashram-Yogaville, Buckingham, Virginia for having provided me with all facilites and support for working on this project.

I am also thankful to my family, which gave me love, encouragement and support for doing this work.

O. R. Krishnaswami

SECTION I

1.1: What is Yoga?

Introduction

Yoga is a spiritual science. It deals with a human being's quest for his true nature. He is essentially Divine, perfect and infinite. He is an embodied Self or *Atman*. The *Atman* is eternal, pure, and perfect. It is not subject to the limitations of time, space and causation. It is an infinite, omnipresent Spirit. However, as it is embodied in a human form with a body, mind and senses, the apparent person (or the lower self) is unaware of his real nature, his Divinity. He falsely identifies himself with his body, mind and senses, which, being part of *Prakrti* (Nature), are composed of matter, and hence are subject to decay and death.

Ignorant of his true nature, a human being is primarily concerned with the preservation of his body. Driven by the forces of Nature, he seeks happiness from worldly objects and sensual pleasures; he falls a prey to endless desires. He binds himself by the effects of his selfish actions, for every action there is an opposite equal reaction. Yoga helps the apparent person to cast off his ignorance and leads him to realize his true nature, namely, the eternal Self or Spirit. With such realization, Liberation is attained from the bondage of the effects of actions. Yoga is, thus, a means for Self-realization and Liberation.

The Meaning of the word 'Yoga'

The Sanskrit word '*Yoga*' was derived from its root '*Yuj*,' which means 'to join' or 'to unite.' What are the two things, which join together? Although the human soul or the *jivatman* is a facet of the Supreme Soul or *Paramatman*, the Divine Reality, and in essence both are the same, the *jivatman* has become subjectively separated from *Paramatman* or God. However, after going through an evolutionary cycle in the manifested universe, it becomes reunited with *Paramatman*. This *union* of *jivatman* with *Paramatman*, and the method through which this union is attained, both are called Yoga.. However, there is no absolute union of Atman with God (Brahman); the practice of Yoga enables the embodied soul to realize its true nature, namely, *Atman,* which is same as God. The false identification of the soul with the body, mind, senses and intellect is loosely described as the feeling of separation from God and also as the bondage of *jivatman.* As a culmination of Yogic practice, the *jivatman* sheds its false feeling of separation and bondage and becomes one with God or *Paramatman.* So in its technical sense, "Yoga" refers to that enormous body of spiritual values, attitudes, precepts and techniques (that have been developed in India over several millennia), which purify the mind and heart of a human being and enable him to realize his Divine nature.

It is the modifications or thought-waves of of the mind that stand in the way of *jivatman* recogmnizing its divine nature, Therefore, the great sage Patanjali of ancient India, who has codified the science of Yoga in his *Yoga Sutras*, defines Yoga as "the stoppage of the modifications of the mind." (1.2)[1]. He classifies the modifications into five kinds: (1) right knowledge, (2) misconception, (3) fancy or imagination, (4) deep sleep, and (5) memory. (1. 5 -11). These modifications can be stopped by persistent practice of Yoga and non-attachment (*vairagya*) (1.12). When the modifications of the mind are restrained and the mind becomes pure and focused on higher Self, the Yogi would become established in his own essential nature, that is, he attains Self-realization. Lord Krishna in the *Bhagavad Gita2* says,

> "Evenness of mind is called Yoga." (2. 48).

Evenness means a mind balanced in pairs of opposites such as pleasure and pain, praise and blame, profit and loss, and success and failure. Essentially it is the attitude of looking dispassionately at life without being ruffled by its ups and downs. The balanced state is another aspect of the purity of mind.

In another sloka (2. 50), Lord Krishna defines Yoga as "Perfection or efficiency in action." This refers to one branch of Yoga called *Karma Yoga* or Yoga of Selfless Action. In the *Chandogya Upanishad*,[3] efficiency is defined in a very beautiful passage, which says:

> "Whatsoever is done with knowledge, with conviction, and with deep thinking, that alone becomes supremely efficient." (I.1.10)

This means that one must have (1) the knowledge of the technical know-how of a particular subject, (2) faith in oneself and faith in the cause for which one is working, and (3) deep thinking about the subject so that one can get the best out of it.

The Paths of Yoga

There are many paths to the realization of the Self, just as there are many paths to the summit of a mountain. They primarily consist of *Karma Yoga* (the Path of Selfless Action), *Bhakti Yoga* (the Path of Devotion), *Jnana Yoga* (the Path of Knowledge), and *Raja Yoga* (the Path of Meditation). The word "Yoga" in a generic sense refers to all the different paths. The paths vary so as to suit the varying temperaments and capacities of human beings, but all the paths lead to the same goal of Self-realization. The different paths of Yoga are not mutually exclusive. They simply represent a difference of emphasis.

Karma Yoga

The Sanskrit word *Karma* means action. So 'Karma Yoga' means Yoga of Action. The tendency to perform action is innate in all beings, and none can remain inactive. For those who are particularly of an active temperament, what is required is not cessation from action but the proper control and direction of their activity. Work with attachment to its fruits binds the soul, but selfless work performed in a spirit of worship becomes a means for attaining freedom. Selfless action does not bind the doer, as he has no sense of doership or attachment to the fruits of his action. Sri Krishna says in the *Bhagavad Gita*:

> "One who does actions, offering them to the divine, and forsaking attachment is not tainted by evil, just as a lotus leaf is not tainted by water." (5.10).
>
> "Though ever engaged in actions, one, having taken refuge in Me (the Lord), attains to the eternal and immutable state of being by My grace." (18. 56).

The work that is offered to God becomes worship and Karma Yoga. Karma Yoga helps a person to live successfully and usefully in the world while remaining above it, unaffected by its *fetters,* as lotus leaves on the water.

Bhakti Yoga

This means Yoga of Devotion, a path of love and devotion to God. It is an intense longing and love for God. It enables the aspirant to constantly remember God. It purifies his emotions and elevates his mind to the consciousness of the Reality. He surrenders all his thoughts, words and deeds to the Lord and adores Him with an unflinching devotion. By the constant meditation of the Lord, the *bhakta* (devotee) imbibes into his own being the Divine attributes. The devotee yearns for union with his beloved Lord with all his heart. Worldly love does not satisfy this deep passion of the soul. The devotee's entire mind flows, as it were, in a continuous stream towards the Lord. The Lord is not a being dwelling somewhere in a far off heaven, but is seated in his own heart. In order to see Him and to feel His Divine presence he has only to look within. "The Lord," says Sri Krishna, "dwells in the hearts of all beings .

Take refuge in Him with all thy being; by His Grace you shall attain supreme peace and the eternal abode." (*Bhagavad Gita,* 18. 61,62). By total devotion and self-surrender to God, one can attain God or the ultimate Reality. Bhakti Yoga is simple and suitable for all those of an emotional nature.

Jnana Yoga

The word *Jnana* means knowledge. So Jnana Yoga is a Yoga of Knowledge. This path involves intense discrimination (*Viveka*). One with a contemplative mind tries to seek answer to the basic question: "Who am I? Am I a body or mind? If not, what else?" He discriminates between the real and the unreal, between the transient and the eternal. Such persistent discrimination and self-inquiry ultimately lead to Enlightenment or the Knowledge of Self. Ramana Maharishi, the great Indian sage of the twentieth century, was a great Jnana Yogi.

The seeker, who is having a philosophic turn of mind, is not satisfied with the little pleasures of the worldly life. He is eager to know his true nature and the Reality behind the phenomenal world. He does not feel any great attraction to the personal aspects of the Divinity. He yearns to attain to the Infinite, his true Self. Speaking of the followers of the path of knowledge, Sri Krishna observes in the *Bhagavad Gita*:

> "Those who have their intellect absorbed in That, whose Self is That, established in That, with That as their supreme goal, (they) attain to the highest Salvation, their impurities being cleansed by Knowledge." (5.17)
>
> "Relative existence, even here in this world, has been conquered by those, whose minds rest in evenness. As the infinite Self is even and without imperfection, they are established in It" (5.19)

Raja Yoga

This 'royal path' (*Raja*) is highly scientific. It is as old as human civilization. It is a Yoga of Meditation. The saint Patanjali codified it in his *Yoga Sutras*. Raja Yoga encompasses the teachings of all the different paths; it concerns itself with three realms – the physical, the mental and the spiritual. By practicing Raja Yoga regularly, one learns to control his desires, emotions and thoughts and thus to purify his mind, and finally to attain *Samadhi*, the state of Super-consciousness.(*See* 4.18 *Samadhi:* Meaning and Kinds, *below*)

The man of a contemplative bent of mind, endowed with

tremendous will power, wants to control the whole of Nature, external and internal. But spasmodic attempts at concentration will lead only to failure and moral depression. The restless mind is to be brought under control slowly and steadily through practice and renunciation. Speaking of the Yoga of Meditation, Sri Krishna says, "With the intellect steadfast, with the mind fixed on the Self, let the Yogi attain quietude little by little, without thinking of anything else. By whatever cause the restless, unsteady mind wanders away, let him, restraining it from wandering, bring it back under the control of the Self alone. Verily, supreme bliss comes to the Yogi, whose mind is perfectly tranquil, whose passions are quieted, who is free from impurities, and who has become one with the all-pervading Being." (*Bhagavad Gita*, 6.25–27). (For details, *See* 3.1 Raja Yoga, *below*)

Complementarity of Paths

The different paths of Yoga are not mutually exclusive. They are complementary to one another. An aspirant cannot really follow any one of these four paths to the exclusion of the rest; he may only lay greater emphasis upon one or the other. For instance, meditation is to be practiced as a discipline, no matter which path the aspirant may follow. Besides, the aspirant must cultivate discrimination and gain spiritual knowledge to practice even Bhakti Yoga and Karma Yoga. And even the aspirant who practices Bhakti Yoga or Jnana Yoga or Raja Yoga has to be active and perform actions without expecting their fruits or dedicate them to the Lord. Above all, every aspirant, irrespective of the path chosen by him, must have devotion to God or love for the Chosen Ideal. Thus in reality, there is a combination of Yogas in every aspirant's life, because perfection is attained only by developing all aspects of one's own personality – physical, mental, moral and emotional—i.e., by attaining an all-round or over-all spiritual growth.

In fact, one-sided development is fraught with dangers. Work sometimes becomes aimless and leads to mere restlessness. Yoga of Meditation at times degenerates into physical mortification and pursuit of psychic powers. Devotion often deteriorates into meaningless sentimentalism. Knowledge may also lapse into dry intellectualism and morbid inactivity. Hence there is a great necessity for combining the different paths in order to safeguard against the dangers of following one path to the exclusion of others. Let work be combined with meditation, and knowledge be tempered with devotion. Let us try to be equally established in all the Yogas and bring about a harmonious development of all our latent spiritual powers. This all-sided development of personality is the healthiest ideal for any spiritual aspirant to pursue.

This is why, in the teachings of the *Bhagavad Gita* and of Sri Ramakrishna, emphasis has been laid upon synthesizing all the Yogas in one's life. In the Integral Yoga Institutes established by Sri Swami Satchidananda, the apostle of peace, in the United States of America and other countries, this total approach is rightly called 'Integral Yoga.' 'Integral' means a synthesis or harmonious blending. Integral Yoga is a combination of Hatha Yoga, *Pranayama*, Bhakti Yoga, Karma Yoga, Jnana Yoga and Raja Yoga. It gives Yoga an affirmative and dynamic form. Its goal is complete self-integration. Action, devotion, wisdom and peace are equally important elements in such integration. Over-emphasis upon any one of them leads to lop-sided development and disturbs the balance of life.

All the above elements are inter-dependent and inter-related. Devotion in its full flowering is inseparable from wisdom and selfless action. Devotion is not subjection to overwhelming waves of emotion, but ever-expanding appreciation of the glory of the Spirit.

Devotion, in its spiritual essence, is an attribute of wisdom. It flows from the vision of the inter-dependence of all life and the oneness of all existence. It is the joyful expression of the soul freed from the bonds of selfishness.

Similarly, knowledge, in its full flowering, is inseparable from devotion and action. Knowledge is not an ivory-tower contemplation, but a comprehensive awareness of the nature of existence. It is the vision of oneness of all things and beings. It awakens the jnani to the timeless dimension of being.

In the same way, action is not a mere means to self-purification resulting in salvation. The liberated individual participates in the creative adventure of life. His action is a total and joyful self-giving at the altar of welfare of all beings.

Integral Yoga aims at the integral development of body, mind and soul, a balanced development of all different aspects – physical, vital, mental, moral, intellectual, intuitional and emotional aspects – of an individual's personality. Of course, an individual may lay greater emphasis on the practice of a particular path of Yoga. But the individual should be physically strong and healthy; he should have good control over the senses, mastery over the mind, and maintain emotional balance; he should have perfect morality and sharp intelligence; and he should lead a useful life of dedication and express his divine nature. The practice of Integral Yoga will yield such a balanced development and perfection and permanent peace and joy.

Yoga and Religion

Is there any relationship between Yoga and religion? Yoga is not a special form of religion. Every religion in its essence is a kind of Yoga in so far as it helps human beings in realizing God. But unlike the sectarian creeds and ritualistic observations, which erect barriers among human beings and create divisions in the name of God, Yoga stands for the spiritual oneness of all mankind, and it is a universal spiritual pursuit beyond all religions. Religions are different paths to the same destination, though people do not generally understand this. Anyone can practice Yoga, whatever may be his religious faith. The sacred scriptures of most religions contain references to Yogic methods. The *Vedas*[4] of Hinduism, the *Upanishads* and the *Bhagavad Gita*, the *Book of Genesis*[5], the *Book of Revelations*[6] and *Psalms*[7] contain many references to Yogic methods. The mystics of all religions of the world have practiced Yoga in one form or other.

The Universality of Yoga

Yoga is universal in its approach. It is a means for achieving ethical, moral and spiritual perfection, which is our original state. It dispels ignorance, develops universal outlook and love in the minds of those who practice it. Yoga enables them to perceive unity in the midst of diversity. The names and forms, thoughts, emotions, outlook, etc. vary but the *Atman* or Self within all beings is the same.

The *Isa Upanishad* declares:

> "He, who sees all beings in his Self, and his own Self in all beings, loses all fear." (I.6)
> Lord Krishna, in the *Bhagavad Gita* says,
> "He, who sees Me (Brahman) everywhere and sees everything in Me, never becomes separated from Me, nor do I become separated from him." (6.30)

Two Aspects of Yoga Science

The science of Yoga has two aspects, theoretical and practical. Theory can be learnt through books and scriptures, but the guidance of a *Guru* or teacher is needed for practicing Yoga. (*See* 3.2. *Guru* or Teacher, *below*). There are several methods, techniques and stages of Yoga. Only a *Guru* can see the capacity and temperament of the disciple and guide him in a way to bring out his own interest. He will systematically guide the student to practice properly the techniques of Yoga and enable him to reach the ultimate stage of perfection.

Yoga Science *vs*. Physical Sciences

Physical sciences study the external phenomena. They are based on sense perception and rational interpretations. Through physical sciences we gain knowledge about the external world – matter, energy, physiology of human beings and other living creatures, planets, stars, sun, flora and fauna, etc. But the physical sciences do not give us a complete understanding of the various forces shaping human beings and other beings. They do not give us any idea of our real nature and our inner world. Yoga science deals with this fundamental aspect of human beings. It is the soul of all sciences and all philosophies. It leads us to the highest source of knowledge – intuitive and experiential knowledge.

The ancient sages of India renounced worldly cares and pleasures in order to devote themselves to the pursuits of the highest knowledge. They practiced and perfected the techniques of Yoga and through its practice experienced the ultimate Reality. This direct knowledge has been handed down from *Guru* (teacher) to disciple in a long chain from ancient times to the present day. What has been experienced by the ancient sages through their internal search can be experienced by a sincere aspirant even today. (*See* 2.3 *Yoga:* An Internal Research, *below*). Yogic knowledge is, thus, scientific and practical. It is the spiritual science of being and becoming. Its methods and techniques have been tested and experimented by thousands of Yogis over centuries. They help a Yogic aspirant to go beyond the mind, and experience the Self or Spirit, which is his real nature.

Yoga, as an internal science, is primarily concerned with mental training. Its first objective is to control the restless mind and to bring it into focus on a point. When the aspirant goes deeper and deeper into the consciousness, he finally transcends the mind and directly experiences the ultimate truth, the Self or Spirit.

Yoga and Asceticism (*Tapas*)

In India asceticism (*Tapas*) came into existence as an independent tradition alongside Yoga. *Tapas* is a body of knowledge and techniques aimed at the transformation of ordinary consciousness. It is a Yoga-like practice. This ancient Sanskrit word '*Tapas*' is derived from the verbal root *tap* meaning "to burn" or "to glow." The word *Tapas* came to be applied to the rigorous spiritual self-discipline of austerities. The ascetic gets "burnt out" through austerities.

Tapas is a means to know Brahman. In the *Taittiriya Upanishad*, the teacher says to a student, who wanted to learn about Brahman: "Through *Tapas* seek to know Brahman. Brahman is *Tapas*." (3.3.1). The *Mundaka Upanishad* says: "He is the All-knowing, He is the All-wise, and His *Tapas* consists of knowledge." (1.1.9). "Of all the means employed to achieve objectives by disciplined means, *Tapas* alone is the most efficient one. . . . *Tapas* means the stilling of the senses and the mind. The concentration of the energies of the mind and the sense organs is supreme *Tapas*; that is, verily, superior to all *dharmas* (disciplines); that is called the supreme *dharma*" says the *Yajnavalkya Smrti*.

Tapas is generally pursued through the observance of celibacy (*bramacharya*) and the control of the senses (*indriyas*). Celibacy does not mean suppression of sexual energy. It is a sublimation of spiritual energy, which generates psychophysical effulgence (*tejas*), radiance and vitality (*virya*). It also generates *ojas* or numinous energy that charges the entire body-mind.

Tapas yields ecstatic status, vision of the God, even transcendental Consciousness and not least psychic powers (*siddhi*). The parallel development of *Tapas* and Yoga is documented in the two great ancient epics of India: the *Mahabharata* and the *Ramayana*. The *Mahabharata* relates many stories of such celebrated ascetic sages as Vyasa, Vishvamitra, Vashishtha, Bharadvaja and others. In *Ramayana* we come across stories of powerful demons like Ravana who witnessed their downfall by abusing their psychic powers acquired through severe *Tapas*.

Yoga spiritualized the earlier tradition of *Tapas* by emphasizing Self-realization over the acquisition of psychic powers. At the same time, it adapted many of the practices of *Tapas*. Celibacy is one of the five restraints (*Yamas*), which form the first step in the eight-step Raja Yoga. The sage Patanjali who codified the tradition of Yoga in his *Yoga Sutras* states that the Yogi who is grounded in celibacy gains vigor (*virya*) (2. 38). He also mentions *Tapas* as one of the five observances (*Niyamas*), the second step in Raja Yoga, and declares that through asceticism the body and its senses are perfected (2. 43). The tradition of *Tapas* has existed along side Yoga over centuries and continues to exist even today. (*See* 3.1 Raja Yoga, *below*).

Yoga and Renunciation (*Sanyasa*)

Though many facets of *Tapas* have been integrated into the practice of Yoga, Yoga is closer in spirit to another tradition called renunciation (*sanyasa*) of worldly life. Renunciation, as a way of life, seems to have entered the sphere of spirituality in India either during the Upanishadic Age or earlier.

There are four stages in life *(Asramas*), namely, *Brahmacharya* or the period of studentship, *Grihastha* or the stage of householder, *Vanaprashta* or the stage of the forest-dweller or hermit, and *Sanyasa* or the life of renunciation. These four stages regulate the human life. Renunciation can take place in two principal ways: formal renunciation and mental renunciation. Formal renunciation means giving up ordinary worldly life. One who renounces leaves every thing behind – wife, children, property, work, worldly ambitions and any concern for the future, and becomes a monk, seeking Self-realization. Mental renunciation means giving-up of all attachments and of the ego as well. The formal renunciation of worldly life without dispassion and non-attachment is a mockery. Such a renouncier is a hypocrite, says Sri Krishna, in the *Bhagavad Gita* (3.6). The formal renunciation with dispassion for worldly things enables the renouncier to concentrate on spiritual practices with total dedication.

An aspirant who seeks Self-realization through Yoga is expected to control the senses and give up desires for worldly objects and enjoyments, though not renounce the worldly life. So mental renunciation is necessary for Yogic practice. Purity of heart is essential for attaining Self-realization. The control of senses and dispassion is a means for purification of heart. "Blessed are those who are pure in heart, for they shall see God," says the Holy *Bible*[8].

1.2: The Purpose of Life and Yoga

Why do we live

What is the purpose of life? Why are we born as human beings? Do we merely exist until we die? Why do we suffer often and are happy some times? These and allied questions do arise in the minds of many of us at some time or other in our life. The tragedy is that they do not arise in the minds of most of us until we are rudely shaken by some terrible shock, loss or calamity.

The average person in the modern world is far too busy with the struggle for existence to find time for such thoughts about life. Like a long-caged bird that has forgotten its very birthright to soar into the sky, and struggles to remain in its cage, the average person is engrossed in ignorance.

We do not live for eating, drinking, sleeping and procreating, but we eat, drink and sleep for living. Swami Sivananda[9] used to sing: "Is there not a nobler mission than eating, drinking and sleeping? It is difficult to get a human birth. Therefore try your best to realize God in this birth."

Even miseries fail to awaken us. Since ages we have been going on adding to our ever increasing wants and desires, and we have created innumerable things for fulfilling them. We also aspire for position, power, control over others, name and fame. Do we live for meeting such endless wants? What is the underlying purpose behind such wants, and the restless activities performed for meeting those wants? The underlying purpose is to be happy.

Happiness

Happiness seems to be the main purpose behind all our aspirations and actions. Everyone in this world seems to be in search of happiness. Why do we want money and possession? Why do we want to learn and to earn? Why do we want position, power, beauty and strength? There is only one answer; ultimately we just want to be happy.

Does Happiness come from Outside

But are we finding the happiness? We chase the fleeting shadows of wealth, position and power. There are millionaires floating in affluence, with big palaces with all kinds of facilities and amenities, holiday homes in health and holiday resorts, a fleet of cars, hundreds of dresses, matching shoes and other accessories, high positions, prestige and so on. But do they enjoy peace and happiness? No, they have, in fact, greater worries, anxieties and stress than anybody else.

This is something like a race of running in a circle by a batch of people: one person overtakes the other; he, in turn, is overtaken by another. Everyone competes to overtake and run fast, but all of them remain at the same place. Thus life at present is becoming faster and faster due to the possessive tendency, but still it is encircled around the objects of the five senses.

Material wealth, no doubt, is necessary for a decent healthy living. Nevertheless it should come through honest means, and rich people should hold their surplus wealth as trustees, as emphasized by John Ruskin[10] and Mahatma Gandhi[11], and use it for the benefit of the needy people. Greediness and extravagance are not going to bring any happiness and peace.

Why do we run after material wealth, position, power and sensual pleasures? We all seem to be thinking that happiness is something to come from outside, from worldly objects and sensual pleasures, something to be grabbed from somewhere. The happiness that comes from outside is momentary and it is followed by manifold miseries. Every one of external things such as beauty, relationship, wealth, position, power, name and fame that give us some fleeting happiness is subject to change. Yet we go on aspiring for them as if we live for them.

What is that really happens

You just want to do something or get something to be happy. The very desire makes you unhappy until you get it fulfilled. But before the desire arose you were peaceful. Now the desire prompts you to take all the effort to get it satisfied. When you get the thing you wanted, the desire is fulfilled and the mind feels peaceful again. You may feel happy that your desire was fulfilled. You may think that the thing, which you got, brought the happiness. But what really happened was you just *regained* the mental tranquility that was there before the desire arose. The thing just satisfied your want, which disturbed your happiness.

Now you got what you wanted. You may feel happy; but immediately the fear of losing it comes in. You start worrying about it. So no permanent happiness can come from outside. In the *Yoga Vasishtha*[12] the sage Vasishtha asks,

> "What do people call happiness? Can it be found in the transitory objects of this world? All beings in this world take birth, only to die. And they die, only to be reborn! What is true happiness? Where can we find it?"

Permanent Happiness

Is there permanent happiness? Yes. There is permanent happiness. But it does not come from outside. It already exists within our heart. Our very real nature itself is peace and joy. Without realizing that, we are going on searching for it from outside things or experiences, and get entangled in a continuous stream of desires and face the consequent anxieties, worries, stress, disappointments, distress and dejection.

Ignorance of our Real Nature

We have made unprecedented progress in getting the knowledge of the external world. We have invented unimaginable devices, gadgets and equipments. We have even learnt to harness the atomic energy and to make powerful destructive devices. Indeed our recent achievements are tremendous. We have scaled the highest peak in the world, and delved deep into the bowels of the earth in search of gold, diamond, coal and oil. We have come to know what is in the bottom of the sea. We have revolutionized our communication system. We have landed on moon and sent unmanned craft to the mars. We are building space station and so on. But alas we do not know what we are, and what is our real nature! Are we the body-mind-senses complexes? No. We are not the body; we are not the mind; we are not the senses. They are only our external covers. We are really the eternal Self, the *Atman* within us. The *Atman* is the God within us. The *Atman* has neither form nor shape. It is Consciousness or Awareness. It is omnipresent. It is eternal peace and bliss. That is our real nature. The *Chandogya Upanishad* declares:

> "That which is the subtle essence, this whole universe has for its Self; That is the Truth; That is the Atman or Self; and That thou art (*Tat twam asi*)." (VI.8.7)

We are that *Atman*. We are infinite, immortal and ever pure. That is our true nature. *Kena Upanishad* proclaims:

"If one realizes It (Self) here (in this life), then is there truth. But if he knows It not, there is great loss." (II.5)

In an inspiring song, Swami Sivananda says,

> "Within you is hidden God. Within you is immortal soul. Kill the letter "I," die to live. Lead the Divine Life. Within you is the fountain of joy. Within you is the ocean of bliss. Rest peacefully in your own Atman. Drink the nectar of Immortality."

Why is, then, most of us are not aware of our real nature? Out of ignorance, we wrongly identify ourselves with our body-mind complexes, and concentrate on self-preservation and satisfaction of our endless desires. As wants are insatiable, we are always discontent and dissatisfied. We are restless and blindly cling to earthly existence. We are perverted, self-centered and selfish. We are ready to do anything to earn money and to satisfy our egoism. We do not hesitate to manufacture and sell toxic materials like cigarettes, liquors and meat that cause deadly diseases to our fellow beings. We sell powerful destructive weapons to countries, which fight one with another. We, at times, become so fanatic as to kill our fellow beings in the name of religion and ethnic difference. What is the outcome? The world is plagued with miseries, diseases, violence, strife and discord. "Even if a small fractional part of the human beings," says Swami Vivekananda[13], "can put aside the idea of selfishness, narrowness and littleness, this earth will become a paradise tomorrow."

Know thyself

What is the way out? "Know thyself" is the answer. A Sophist approached one of the Wise Men of ancient Greece, and thought to puzzle him with the most perplexing questions. But the Sage of Miletus was equal to the test. He replied to them all, without the least hesitation yet with the utmost exactitude.

1. What is the oldest of all things?
   "*God*, because He has always existed."
2. What is the most beautiful of all things?
   "*The Universe*, because it is the work of God."
3. What is the greatest of all things?
   "*Space*, because it contains all that has been created."
4. What is the most constant of all things?
   "*Hope*, because it still remains with man, after he has lost everything else."
5. What is the best of all things?
   "*Virtue*, because without it there is nothing good."
6. What is the quickest of all things?
   "*Thought*, because in less than a second it can fly to the end of the universe."
7. What is the strongest of all things?
   "*Necessity*, which makes man to face all the dangers of life."
8. What is the easiest of all things?
   "To give advice."

But when it came to the ninth question our sage pronounced a paradox.

9. What is the most difficult of all things?
   The Miletian sage replied:
   "To know thyself!"

How can we know ourselves? Is it a mere intellectual knowledge that we need? Modern psychology may explain many of the functions of the mind and make interesting guesses; but it is a study of the mind as an object. That does not help us to know ourselves. Realized sages and saints who have completely mastered the secrets of life tell us that for the pursuit of true peace and joy we have to take our thoughts and vision away from the vanishing objects of the external world, and instead to turn inward and go deep into the recesses of our mind, and find the immortal Self, the very source of our existence and everlasting peace and joy. Great saints and sages throughout the ages realized the Self within and thus attained immortality. But most of the rest of us are busy with worldly pursuits and are waiting for the tide to rise. But of course none of us would be lost. Life has a goal. Even if it takes hundreds of lifetimes, evolution itself will carry us to the fulfillment of the life's goal of Self-realization.

Here we have a uniquely human choice: shall we wait for millions of years, knocked about in the painful process of evolution, until we finally enter the sea of eternal joy? Or shall we try to enter it now in this very lifetime, by taking our personal evolution into our own hands? Whatever be our condition, this is something that can be done by everyone of us through the practice of Yoga.

Yoga places this loftiest goal before us and gives us the means by which that goal can be achieved. No matter how far the technology advances, without this overriding supreme goal in life, it is not possible to get where you want to go. With a goal, even if you wander, you always know how to regain your course; without a goal, you never even know where you are. The *Chandogya Upanishad*, one of the oldest *Upanishads* composed several thousand years ago, declares:

> "The Self within the body does not grow old and does not die when body dies." (8.1.5)
> "It is this Self that one should seek and know. He, who has found out and knows that Self, has attained all the worlds, and all desires." (8.7. 1)

When that higher knowledge – enlightenment – dawns, it destroys our ignorance like sunrise dispels darkness. Then we experience our own true Self, the *Atman* within. In the *Bhagavad Gita* Lord Krishna says,

> "To those whose ignorance is destroyed by the Knowledge of Self, like the sun, the Knowledge reveals the Supreme (Brahman)." (5.16).

This Knowledge of Self is pure knowledge. In the *Bhagavad Gita*, Lord Krishna says again,

> "That by which one sees the same indestructible Reality in all beings, not separate in all the separate beings, know that knowledge is pure." (18.20).

The attainment of the Knowledge of Self is the ultimate purpose of life. Only human beings like us can attain this knowledge. How is this pure knowledge attained? The answer of the *Upanishads* is quite definite. *Atman*, the mystery of our life, the light of our soul is something beyond reason, and therefore it can never be attained by reason alone. The *Katha Upanishad* declares:

> "Not through instruction is the Self attained, nor by the intellectual power, nor even through much hearing. It is to be attained only by one whom the Self chooses. To such an one the Self reveals Its own nature." (I.2.23)
> "Not through deep knowledge can the Atman be reached, unless evil ways are abandoned, tranquility is maintained, and the mind is concentrated and composed." (I.2.24)
> "The Self though hidden in all beings, is invisible, but can be

seen by those subtle Seers through their sharp and subtle intelligence." (I.3.12)

The realization of the Self is described as *Mukti* or Liberation or Self-realization. This is the goal of life. Shankaracharya (eighth century AD)[14] says, "A man is born not to desire life in the world of senses, but to realize the bliss of a free soul in union with God." Yoga is the means through which this goal is reached. It is the self-training for Self-realization, which is a state of eternal peace and joy. Then one sees that the *Atman* or God in himself is the same God in all beings. He crosses the ocean of life and he is liberated from bondage, and enjoys the eternal peace and joy.

The Aim of Yoga

In the West, Yoga is regarded merely as a unique system of physical culture. Indeed Hatha Yoga contributes to sound physical and mental health. Yoga postures exert a profound and salutary influence upon the internal vital organs of the body. *Pranayama* regulates the flow of vital energy and makes the mind calm and serene. Yoga promotes overall well-being. But these are not ends in themselves. The real aim of Yoga is the attainment of the highest goal of Self-realization.

The physical part of Yoga improves our health, frees us from tensions and diseases and confers a state of well-being. The spiritual aspect of Yoga enables us to acquire progressively increasing control over our mind and our emotions. Yoga, by generating, promoting and preserving inner harmony, confers freedom from psychosomatic disorders of the body and the mind and ensures good adjustment. Physical well-being, mental relaxation, peace of mind, purity of heart, brilliance of intellect and illumination of the soul are some of the fruits of Yoga. It does not disturb one's religious faith but strengthens it. (For details, *See* 4.14 Meditation and Health, below,). Yoga enables us to purify our heart and mind. It enables us to come face to face with our own Self, which is the Self of all.

1.3: History of Yoga Pre-classical Period

Origin of Yoga

Yoga is as ancient as human existence. The earliest beginnings have been lost in the obscurity of ancient Indian pre-history. The *Bhagavad Gita*, which was supposed to have been composed during the third or second millennium BC, speaks of Yoga as being archaic. It declares:

> "This, handed down thus in regular succession, the royal sages knew. This Yoga, by a long lapse of time, has been lost here, O Arjuna." (4.2)
>
> "That same ancient Yoga has been today taught to thee by Me, for thou art My devotee and friend. It is the supreme secret." (4.3)

These verses indicate the antiquity of Yoga and how it was handed down in regular succession from teacher to pupil. As time progressed much was added, much was changed by experimentation, and in due course it was developed into a scientific psycho-spiritual system in ancient India. During that time, very wise people began to explore the true nature of human beings by asking such fundamental questions as "Who am I?" "What is the purpose of life?" In order to find the right answers, the ancient sages experimented with various approaches to Self-Knowledge, and discovered some definite methods of Yoga. The *Svetasvatara Upanishad* says,

"By Meditating on the Lord, by uniting with Him, by reflecting on His being more and more, one becomes totally free from the Illusion (*Maya*) of the world." (I.10)

The knowledge so experienced was passed on from teacher to student in the oral tradition. This knowledge was realized not only in depths of forests or caves by sages but also by persons who led the busiest life – ruling monarchs who had to command armies, to sit on thrones and take care of the welfare of millions. In various *Upanishads* this is indicated. For example, Shvetaketu, the son of a sage, was taught by Pravahana Jaivali, the king of the Panchalas. Similarly, sages sent their sons to the royal sage King Janaka for learning. The *Bhagavad Gita*, which is the essence of *Upanishads*, was taught to Arjuna by Lord Krishna in a battlefield. Hence Krishna's statement "royal sages knew." (4.2).

Indus Civilization

The earliest archaeological evidence for the practice of Yoga in ancient India is afforded by the magnificent Indus Civilization of India, discovered in the early 1920s during the Archaeological Survey conducted by Sir John Marshall. This civilization was one of the great civilizations of antiquity. It flourished in the fourth or third millennium BC.

The survey found a number of soapstone seals that show horned deities seated in the posture of Yogic Meditation. Scholars are of the view that Yoga antedated the invasion of Sanskrit-speaking Aryans. Scholars are inclined to believe that the peace-loving Indus people spoke an archaic form of Dravidian language, and that after the destruction of their civilization they migrated to the southern part of the peninsula. The invaders were ultimately absorbed by the land and the native cultures. It is clear from the *Rig Veda* that, after the fall of the great cities of Indus Civilization, the Vedic tribes gradually assimilated many of the notions and customs of the non-Vedic native population. This is reflected in the language of the *Rig Vedic* hymns, which contain many non-Sanskrit words. At any rate, the archaeological finds have demonstrated that Yoga was dated to a period earlier to the Vedic period. (George

Feuerstein, Yoga: *The Technology of Ecstasy*, 1989, p.102).

Yoga in *Vedas*

The earliest literary evidence is found in the *Vedas*, the ancient Sanskrit scriptures of India. They consist of the eternal truths revealed by God to the ancient *rishis* (seers) of India. They are held to be eternal and divine in origin. They were handed down orally, direct from teacher to disciple. They are considered as *Srutis*, which means "what is heard." Eventually they were committed to writing. The word *Veda* means knowledge. So the *Vedas* teach the knowledge of God and lay down work (sacrificial rites and secular duty) as a means to that knowledge. They are divided into four major parts, namely, *Rig, Sama, Yajur* and *Atharva*. "The *Rig Veda,*" says Max Muller, "is the most ancient book of the world." Each of the *Vedas* consists of two main divisions: the work portion and the knowledge portion.

The work portion of the *Vedas* is subdivided into *Samhitas, Brahmanas* and *Aranyakas*. The *Samhitas* are collections of *mantras* or hymns in praise of personal gods. The *Brahmanas* contain the descriptions of the methods of using the *mantras* in sacrificial rites, and the duties and rules of conduct. The *Aranyakas* (forest treatises) give philosophical interpretations of the rituals. They are intended for the hermits who prepare themselves for taking *sanyasa* (monkhood).

The knowledge part of the *Vedas* is known as *Upanishads* or Vedanta (the end of *Vedas*). (For details, *see* the next subheading in this chapter).

The Vedic hymns were expressions of the deep spirituality of the Vedic settlers. The proto-type of Yoga of the rishis contains many elements characteristic of later Yoga: concentration, watchfulness, austerities, regulation of the breath, and visionary experience.

According to Jeanine Miller, the meditative practice in Vedic times displays three distinct but overlapping aspects, which she calls *Mantra* Meditation, Visual Meditation and Absorption (*Samadhi*). In *Mantra* Meditation, a sacred *mantra* is repeated.

In Visual Meditation a particular deity is envisioned. Absorption is the highest meditative stage in which the seer explores the great cosmic mysteries. Meditation culminates in illumination, the vision of "eternal light." (*The Vedas: Harmony, Meditation and Fulfillment*, London: Rider, 1974, p. 97).

Of the 1028 hymns of the *Rig Veda*, five are of special relevance to Yoga. The first is the *nasadiya-sukta*, often called the hymn of creation (X.129). This cosmogonic hymn foreshadows the later metaphysical speculations of the Samkhya Philosophy that is closely allied with Yoga. Cosmogony is concerned with the origin of the universe.

The second hymn (X.72) is another cosmogonic speculation, addressing to the riddle of how the universe came into existence. The third is the *Purusha-sukta*, hymn of man (X.90). Of the various cosmogonic hymns, this hymn is one of the most striking. In the first verse, the primeval *Purusha* is said to have pervaded the entire creation and extended beyond it. This is meant to suggest that the Creator transcends His creation. A more elaborate version of this hymn is found in the *Atharva Veda* (XIX.6).

The fourth hymn is I.164 (*Atharva Veda,* IX.9 –10). This composition is a collection of profound mystical riddles. The sixth verse, for instance, raises the question of the nature of the human Self or *Atman*. It is the controller of the body; it is unborn and is yet the cause of the manifested universe. Two famous verses 20 – 22 of the fourth hymn I.164 speak of two birds that occupy the same tree; one is said to eat its fruits, while the other merely looks on. The tree represents the body. The onlooking bird is the supreme Self beyond the realm of nature, and the other bird is the individual embodied soul, which enjoys the fruits of actions and enmeshed in worldly life.

In verse 46 of the same hymn we find the oft-quoted statement: The truth is one, the sages call it by many names.

The fifth hymn (X.136) is known as the *keshi-sukta*, hymn of the longhaired one. Here a non-Vedic ascetic is eulogized. This hymn refers to the practice of breath control (*Pranayama*).

What we find in the Vedic era is a fairly developed body of

lofty ideas and practices centering on Meditation and contemplation of the Divine Mystery.

The *Atharva Veda* contains references to immortal Self, three *gunas*, *Pranayama*, initiation, spiritual practice, non-dualism and so on. The *Vratya khanda* (XV) speaks of a community called *Vratyas* who laid the foundation of Yoga and Samkhya[15].

Some of the other references to Yoga in the *Vedas* are:

> "O self-illumined Lord, . . . O Consciousness Supreme, grant that we may ever engage in the practice of Yoga to please Thee, and may we ever be devoted to Thee." — *Yajur Veda*
>
> "He who supports within Himself the heavenly bodies, the earth and all that it contains, . . . May we, with devotion and purpose, offer adoration to that most desirable One, so that we may attain to union with Him." — *Rig Veda*
>
> "Ye men! Let us unit to offer perpetual devotion to the Lord, the Creator of the Universe, . . . The learned Yogis, having attained the state of Conscious immortality, abide in Him who is free from all suffering, and who is Bliss Absolute. That Lord is our Guru, our Sovereign and the source of Justice." - *Yajur Veda*
>
> "The learned who are engaged in the good of others day and night,
> whose souls are decorated with Divine knowledge, attain immortality and liberation." — *Yajur Veda*
>
> "The mind, which, when engaged in the practice of Yoga and devotion, acquires the knowledge of the past, future and present through which the laws of the world are known. May that mind ever think of the good of all beings!" —*Yajur Veda*

Yoga in Upanishads

The word "*Upanishad*" is derived from "*upa*" (near), "*ni*" (down) and "*sad*"(to sit), i.e., sitting down near..Groups of students sit near the teacher to learn from him the sacred doctrine. In the quietude of forest hermitages the *Upanishad* seers pondered on the problems of the deepest concern and communicated their knowledge to fit students sitting before them.

The *Upanishads* are the concluding portions of the *Vedas*. They represent the central aim and meaning of the teaching of the *Vedas*. They contain the essence of the *Vedas*. They are rich in profound philosophical thought. "In the whole world," says Schopenhauer, the renowned philosopher of the West, "there is no study so beneficial and so elevating as that of the *Upanishads*. They are products of the highest wisdom. They are destined, sooner or later to become the faith of the people."

The *Upanishads* are metaphysical treatises replete with intuitions of universal truths. The inner direct, intuitive and mystical experiences of the ancient seers of India are embodied in these sublime treatises. They contain the eternal Divine knowledge of Brahman, and show the pathway to Self-realization.

They provide us with a complete chart of the unseen Reality. They give us the most intimate and convincing light on the secret of human existence, and formulate, in philosopher Deussen's words, "philosophical conceptions unequaled in India or perhaps anywhere else in the world." They tackle every fundamental problem of philosophy. Their ideas not only enlighten our minds but also stretch our souls.

The literature of *Upanishads* has been growing from early times. The Indian tradition puts their number at one hundred and eight. The principal *Upanishads* are said to be ten. Shankaracharya commented on eleven, namely, *Isa, Kena, Katha, Prasna, Mundaka, Mandukya, Taittiriya, Aitareya, Chandogya, Brahadaranyaka* and *Svetasvatara*. They represent the Vedanta Philosophy in its pure original form, and are the earliest philosophical compositions of the world.

As almost all the early literature of India was anonymous, the names of the authors of the *Upanishads* are not known. Some of the chief doctrines of the *Upanishads* are associated with the names of renowned sages such as Aruni, Yajnavalkya, Balaki, Svetaketu and Sandilya.

As a part of the *Vedas*, the *Upanishads* belong to *Srutis* or revealed literature. They are timeless. Their truths are said to be breathed out by God or perceived by the seers. They are the utterances of the sages who speak out of the fullness of their illumined experiences. They are said to be a direct disclosure from the Divine. The truths revealed to seers are verified not only by logical reason but also by personal experience.

According to the *Upanishads* there is one single Reality and it is *Brahman*. The Reality of Brahman is based on facts of spiritual experience. Brahman is the Reality of the real, the source of all existing things (*Brahadaranyaka Upanishad*, 2.1.20).

The *Taittiriya Upanishad* concludes that the absolute Reality is Truth (*Satyam*), Knowledge (*Jnanam*), Infinity (*Anantam*). Brahman is the source of all other beings. Brahman, the first principle of the universe, is known through *Atman*, our inner Self. The *Svetesvatara Upanishad* declares:

The Self, which pervades all things as butter is contained in milk, which is the root of self-knowledge and austerity (*Tapas*), that is the Brahman, the highest mystic doctrine." (I.16).

The *Katha Upanishad* says,

> "Not within the field of vision stands this form. None can see It (Self) with the physical eyes. but by heart, by thought, by mind apprehended. They who know It become immortal." (II.3.9)

We cannot see *Brahman* with our physical eyes. Yet we can apprehend It through the concentrated focus of mental power.

The *Upanishads* contain important conceptions peculiar to Yoga and its ally Samkhya Philosophy. The Upanishadic sages have adopted meditative practice as the chief means of obtaining transcendental knowledge. Yajnavalkya states in the *Brahadaranyaka Upanishad*:

He who breathes in with your inhalation (*prana*) is the Self of yours, which is in all things. He who breathes out with your exhalation (*apana*) is the Self of yours, which is in all things. He who breaths out with your diffused breath (*vyana*) is the Self of yours, which is in all things. He who breathes up with your up-breath (*udana*) is the Self of yours, which is in all things. He is your Self, which is in all things." (III.4.1)

When being asked how the Self is to be conceived, Yajnavalkya continued:

> "You cannot see the Seer of seeing. You cannot hear the Hearer of hearing. You cannot understand the Understander of understanding. He is your Self, which is in all things. Everything else perishes." (3.4.2)

This passage epitomizes the essence of the *Upanisadic* mystic teachings that were passed on from Self-realized sages to disciples by word of mouth. The transcendental source of the universe is identical with the transcendental core of the human beings. That is, Brahman equals Atman. That supreme Reality cannot be described. It must simply be realized. Upon realization, the Self will be found to be infinite, eternal, free and blissful.

How can the Self be realized? The *Upanishadic* sages emphasized the need for renunciation, intense contemplation and discrimination between the real and the unreal – all sustained by a burning desire for Self-realization and an intention to transcend the ego.

The *Upanishads* speak not only of the glory of the Self and the means of realizing It, but they also contain a great mass of other teachings including the cycle of births and deaths governed by the moral Law of Karma, and the esoteric means by which the world of change and the endless rebirth can be transcended.

Isavasya Upanishad. This is one of the classical *Upanishads*. It prescribes two paths: the path of renunciation or Jnana Yoga for renunciates, and the path of Action or Karma Yoga for others.'

> "The Atman moves, and moves not. It is far and is near; It is within all, and it is outside all."
>
> " He who sees all beings in the Self (Atman) and the Self in all beings, has no fear from anything."
>
> "When one who knows all beings have become one with his own Self, and sees this Oneness, then what delusion and what sorrow can be to him?" (5-7)

Kena Upanishad. It belongs to *Sama Veda. Kena* means "by whom." It deals essentially with the nature of Brahman and the Knowledge of Self. It explains how one can realize the Brahman by transcending the mind and senses. In its fourth part, the methods of Meditation on Brahman and the fruits of Meditation are explained.

> "There the eyes go not, speech goes not, nor the mind; we know not, we understand not, how one can teach this." (I.3)

Since Brahman is not reached by the senses or the mind, we do not know of what nature It is. We are therefore unable to understand how anyone can explain that Brahman to a disciple.

> "It is indeed above the known and also It is above the unknown. Thus we have heard from the ancient sages who have explained It to us." (I.4)

It is indeed above the known and unknown, but It is not unknowable. Verse 6 says, "that, verily, is Brahman, know thou," implies that Brahman is not beyond our apprehension. But we cannot know It by logic; we have to experience It. "Those who know do not speak; those who speak do not know." – *Tao Te' Ching, 56*

> "That which cannot be expressed through words, but That by which words are spoken, know that alone is Brahman, not what people here adore." (I.5)
>
> "If here a person knows It, then there is Truth, and if here he knows It not, there is great loss. Hence seeing It in all beings, the wise become immortal." (2.5)

The wise person sees the same Brahman in every being, and attains immortality.

Katha Upanishad. In this beautiful *Upanishad*, the eternal truths are given in a narrative form. This *Upanishad* is considered to be the oldest one that deals explicitly with Yoga of Self (*Adhyatma Yoga*). In it the way to attain Self-realization is fully treated. There are some passages common to this *Upanishad* and the *Bhagavad Gita*. This *Upanishad* declares:

> "Realizing through self-contemplation, the primeval God, difficult to be seen, deeply hidden, set in the cave (of the heart), dwelling in the deep, the wise leaves behind both joy and sorrow." (I.2.12).
>
> "The knowing Self is never born; nor does It die at any time. It sprang from nothing and nothing sprang from it. It is unborn, eternal, abiding and primeval. It is not slain when the body is slain." (I.2.18).

The Self is the inner reality of each person. It is without a cause and is changeless. When It knows itself as the Spirit, It realizes Its true nature.

> "This Self cannot be attained by instruction, or by intellectual power, or even through much hearing. It is to be attained only by the one whom the (Self) chooses. To such a one the Self reveals Its own nature." (I.2.23)

In a sense all life is from God, all prayer is made by the help of God's grace. However the heights of contemplation, which are scaled by a few, are attributed in a special degree to divine grace. If a person becomes aware of God's presence in the Self, it is due to God's working in the Self. The spiritual aspirant, of course, has to undergo the necessary preparation for the God's grace.

In Section 3 of Chapter I of *Katha Upanishad,* the process of Self-realization is explained by the famous parable of a chariot:

> "Know the Self as the Lord of the chariot and the body as, verily the chariot; know the intellect as the charioteer, and the mind as the reins." (I.3.3).
>
> "The senses, they say, are the horses, the sense-objects the

paths; the soul associated with the body, the senses and the mind, the wise men declare, is the enjoyer." (I.3.4).

The Atman (Self) is compared to the owner of a chariot, the body being the chariot, intellect *(manas)* is the driver, the horses are said to be the senses, the mind is the reins by which the intellect controls the senses.

> "He who has no understanding, whose mind is always unrestrained, his senses are out of control, as wicked horses are for a charioteer." (I.3.5).
> "He, however, who has understanding, whose mind is always restrained, his senses are under control, as good horses are for a charioteer. (I.3.6).
> "He, however, who has no understanding, who has no control over his mind (and is) ever impure, reaches not that goal, but comes back into mundane life (*samsara*)." (I.3.7).
> "He, however, who has understanding, who has control over his mind, and (is) ever pure, reaches that goal from which he is not born again." (I.3.8).
> "He, who has the understanding for the driver of the chariot and controls the reins of his mind, reaches the end of the journey, the supreme abode of the All-pervading." (I.3.9).

The *Katha Upanishad* also indicates the order of the spiritual practices as a progression of seven stages.(I.3.10 and 11). From the sense world where the senses reveal their objects, we pass to the dream world where the mind operates independent of the senses. From the latter we pass to the world of dreamless sleep where the unmanifest *Prakrti* (Nature) becomes the Divine mother. Those who are absorbed in *Prakrti* have the bliss and freedom of dreamless sleep, but it is not the illuminated freedom that we seek. For that we must go to the *Purusha* (Self) who is the source of all. Only when the Yogi goes deep inside, withdrawing from senses, sense-objects, mind, intellect and the unmanifested *Prakrti*, he could know his own Self. It is the transcendental Self that is the goal of the Yogi's spiritual practice. But this sacred effort begins very humbly. This is clear from the definition of Yoga furnished in the Second Chapter:

> "When the five senses together with the mind cease (from their normal activities) and the intellect itself does not stir, that, they say, is the highest state." (2.3.10).
> "This they consider to be Yoga, the steady control of the senses. Then one becomes undistracted; for Yoga comes and goes." (2.3.11).

Yoga means the state of inner tranquility when the senses are controlled and the mind becomes still, then one can begin to discover the wonders of the inner world, the vast horizons of Consciousness. This is a precondition for getting the Divine grace.

The teachings of the *Katha Upanishad* thus represent an important milestone in the tradition of Yoga. In its beautiful poetry, we find expressed some of the fundamental ideas underlying Yogic practice.

Prasana Upanishad. This belongs to the *Atharva Veda*. This contains six questions and their answers and hence its name "*prasana*" that means inquiry. Along with *Mundaka* and *Mandukya Upanishads* it lays great stress on the sacred syllable OM, the *pranava.*

Mundaka Upanishad. This belongs to the *Atharva Veda*. This is intended for the monks. Hence the name *Mundaka* or "shaved one." This *Upanishad* teaches the highest knowledge of Brahman, and explains how it is related to salvation as a means to its end. The individual soul attains liberation through the knowledge of Brahman. Just as the rivers, when flowing into the ocean, become one and the same with it, so also one who knows Brahman becomes One with Brahman. (3.2.9)

Mandukya Upanishad. This *Upanishad* belongs to the *Atharva Veda*. It contains only twelve verses. It is said that even if one cannot study all the 108 *Upanishads*, one can still attain Liberation, if he delves into the *Mandukya*, because it contains the essence of the *Upanishadic* wisdom. Gaudapada, teacher of Shankaracharya's teacher, wrote his famous *Karika* on this *Upanishad*, which is the first systematic exposition of Advaita Vedanta. Shankaracharya has commented on both the *Upanishad* and the *Karika*.

The *Mandukya Upanishad* gives an exposition of the principle of AUM as consisting of four elements, a, u, m and the the "m" sound. They refer to the four states of waking, dream, dreamless sleep and the state of the transcendental Consciousness (*turiya*). The last alone is all-inclusive and ultimately real, and it is the Lord of all. In the waking state we are bound by the fetters of senses of perception and desires. In the dream state we have a greater freedom as the soul makes a world of its own, out of the materials of the waking world. In dreamless sleep, the soul is liberated from the empirical world, and enjoys bliss. In the fourth "*turiya*" state the soul becomes One with Brahman, being free from all phenomenal relationship. Brahman is a pure being beyond all word and thought. Where there is no duality, there is no fear. So the fourth state is a fearless condition. This Yoga is synonymous with Jnana Yoga in its highest form. As such it represents the crowning achievement of the entire non-dualist tradition of the *Upanishads*.

Taittiriya Upanishad. This belongs to the *Yajur Veda*. It is divided into three sections. The second and the third sections deal with the knowledge of the Supreme Self. The most peculiar teaching of the *Taittiriya* is the doctrine that everything is to be looked upon as food (*anna*). This idea refers to the inter-connections of all things, the chain of life, and to the sacrificial nature of all forms of life. The *Taittiriya Upanishad* declares:

> "He who is here in a human being, and He who is there in the sun, He is the One. He who knows this, on departing from this world, reaches the Self consisting of food, reaches the Self consisting of mind, reaches the Self consisting of life-force, reaches the Self consisting of mind, reaches the Self consisting of Consciousness, reaches the Self consisting of bliss." (2.8.1).

This verse hints at the Vedantic doctrine of five sheaths (*pancha kosha*):

1. The food sheath (*annamaya kosha*), the physical body
2. The vital air sheath (*pranamaya kosha*)
3. The mental body (*manomaya kosha*) consisting of the mind and the five senses of perception
4. The intellectual sheath (*vijnanamaya kosha*)
5. The bliss sheath (*anandamaya kosha*) consisting of the bliss experienced by a person during the deep-sleep state

Each of the five sheaths apparently "covers" the *Atman* that is not perceived in its true nature, because of the identification with the elements corresponding to the sheaths. *Atman* is realized by one who transcends all the five sheaths.

Aitareya Upanishad. This *Upanishad* forms part of the *Rig Veda*. It teachings are: the whole universe is the manifestation of Brahman; the individual Self is identical with the Supreme Self; and the goal of life lies in the realization of the unity of the individual Self with the Supreme Self. The end attained by this realization is immortality.

One should become a renouncer to practice the Knowledge of Brahman, as it is difficult to practice it without absolute renunciation. A renouncer can devote the whole time in study and Meditation. The practice of Meditation on the Self cannot be pursued with intense vigor and devotion without relinquishing the concern of life.

The *Aitareya Upanishad* is of interest because of its ancient cosmogonic material. This work opens with the creation of the world:

> "The Self, verily, was (all) this, One only, in the beginning. Nothing else whatsoever even winked. He thought, 'Let me now create the worlds." (I.1.1).

First the Self created the material elements. Then the Self created the various functions such as hearing and sight, which joined with the human form. Next the Self created food for all creatures. As the final act of the process of creation, the Self enters the human body through the saggital suture of the head

Chandogya Upanishad. This belongs to the *Sama Veda.* It commences with elaborate mystical speculations about the sacred syllable OM:

> "... As all leaves are held together by a stalk, so are all words are held together by OM. Verily the syllable OM is the whole universe." (2.23.3).

In his commentary on this *Upanishad*, Shankaracharya, the great profounder of Vedantic non-dualism, observes that OM is the most appropriate name of the Divine or transcendental Reality. A boy Svetaketu wanted to know the supreme Knowledge. His father explained this to him with the examples of a seed, and salt placed in water. From the very essence in the seed, which we cannot see, comes the vast banyan tree. Similarly, salt dissolved in water cannot be seen. In the same way we cannot see the Cosmic Spirit. That is Reality. That is Truth. Thou art That.

This *Upanishad* answers the fundamental question "Who am I?" through the story of Indira, the king of celestial beings, and Virochana, the chief of demons. A human being is not the finite body, mind and senses, but the infinite Atman that dwells in his heart.

BrhadaranyakaUpanishad. This is the oldest of the early *Upanishads*. It is recognized as the most important of the *Upanishads*. It consists of three sections. The first section expounds the teaching of the basic identity of the individual Self and the Universal Self. The second section provides a philosophical justification for the teaching, and the third section deals with the methods of spiritual practices to be followed: hearing the teaching (*sravana*), logical reflection (*manana*) and contemplative Meditation (*nididhyasana*).

In the *Brahadaranyaka Upanishad*, the origin of the universe is said to spring from the One Being, the Absolute Brahman or the

Supreme Spirit. The realization of this One Being is the true goal of life. When the Brahman is realized, then everything else becomes known. The sage Yajnavalkya illustrates this point strikingly:

> "As a spider moves along the thread, as small sparks come forth from the fire, even so From the Self come forth all breaths, all worlds, all divinities, all beings." (2.1.20)
>
> "As a lump of salt thrown into water therein becomes dissolved, no one can see it, because from wherever one may take it, it tastes saline. So verily the Supreme Being, infinite and limitless, is nothing but pure Consciousness." (2.4.12).

Where there seems to be a duality, there one sees another, one hears another, and one knows another. But when all has become Self, how and whom could one see? How can the Knower be known? The Self is nothing that could be pointed to in the finite world. A steady practice of discrimination between the real and the unreal awakens in the Yogi the will to renounce everything in the world of change. Discrimination and renunciation ultimately lead to the realization of the Universal Self.

Svetasvatara Upanishad. This Upanishad belongs to *Yajur Veda*. This is one of the most beautiful creations. It gets its name from the sage who taught it to his disciples. It deals with Karma Yoga and Jnana Yoga. It is theistic in character and identifies the Supreme Brahman with Rudra who is being conceived as the material and the efficient cause of the world. The elements associated with theism – Personal God and devotion to Him – are prominent in this *Upanishad*. Terms that were used by the later Samkhya Philosophy occur in this *Upanishad*, but *Prakrti* (Nature) is not an independent entity. It belongs to the Self of the Divine. This *Upanishad* teaches the unity of the souls and the world in the One Supreme Reality:

> "Those who were devoted to the Yoga of Meditation and contemplation saw the self-power (*atma-shakti*) of Divine hidden in its own qualities. He is the One who presides over all

these causes from time to the soul." (I.3).

"The Lord (*Isha*) supports all this universe, composed of the perishable and the imperishable, the manifest and the unmanifest and the individual soul (which is), not being the Lord, is bound because of its being an enjoyer. But on knowing God, (it) is released from all fetters." (I.8).

"What is perishable is *pradhana* (primary matter). What is immortal and imperishable is *Hara* (the Lord). Over both the perishable and the soul the One God rules. By meditating on Him, by uniting with Him, by reflecting on His being more and more, there is complete cessation from the illusion (*Maya*) of the world." (I.10).

"By knowing God, there is a falling off of all fetters; when the sufferings are destroyed, there is cessation of birth and death. By meditating on Him, there is the third state; on the dissolution of the body, Self, being alone, all its desires are fulfilled, and it becomes One without a second." (I.11).

This verse describes the different sides and stages of liberation. Negatively, it is freedom from the cycle of births and deaths; positively it is Oneness with Isvara so long as there is the manifested world, and it is Oneness with the Brahman when the manifested world ceases to exist.

The *Svetasvatara* recommends Meditation by means of the recitation of the sacred syllable OM, called the *pranava*. The meditative process is described as a kind of churning by which the inner fire is kindled, leading to the revelation of the Self's splendor. The pre-requirements of right environmental conditions, correct posture, regulation of *prana* (*Pranayama*) and concentration are suggested.

When the mind is stilled, all kinds of internal visions can appear, which must not be confused with God-realization. Among the first signs of successful Yoga practice are lightness, health, steadiness, clearness of complexion, pleasantness of voice, agreeable odor and scanty excretions. This suggests the transmutation of the body into a body "fashioned out of the fire of Yoga." But the supreme goal of this Yoga is the realization of the transcendental Self. That realization is not a mere visionary state, nor an experience, for experience presupposes experiencing subject and the experienced object. Enlightenment is that condition of being, in which the subject and the object fuse into One. It is the immortal state.

> "Where fire is kindled (or churned out), where the wind is directed, where the soma juice overflows, there the mind is born." (2.6).

Fire stands for Knowledge of the Self. This supreme knowledge is churned out by the study of scriptures under a competent teacher and by constant Meditation on Brahman, the Absolute. Churning represents Meditation. The control of air refers to the practice of *Pranayama*. When one performs actions selflessly, and offers the actions and their fruits to the Lord, then he experiences immense joy and exhilaration of spirits. This is drinking *soma* juice. In this verse the synthesis of Jnana Yoga, Raja Yoga and Karma Yoga is recommended. Karma Yoga will purify the mind; Raja Yoga will steady the oscillating mind; and Jnana Yoga will remove the veil of ignorance.

> "Let us love the ancient Brahman by the grace of *Savitri* (the Sun). If thou attain thy source (Brahman), there thy work will no longer bind thee." (2.7).

This verse treats of Bhakti Yoga. Without *Bhakti* (devotion) you cannot attain the Grace that is essential for attaining the knowledge of Brahman. When one attains the Brahman, he is not bound by his former actions. The fire of knowledge burns the seeds of *karmas*. Hence the sage does not take rebirth.

Kausitaki Upanishad. This contains a detailed exposition of the doctrine of rebirth and a description of the path to the "World of the Absolute." It also includes a long discourse on the life force as being identical with the Absolute. One verse reads as follows:

"Life is *prana, prana* is life. As long as *prana* remains in this body, so long is there life. For indeed, through *prana*, one obtains, even in this world, immortality." (3.2).

Maitrayaniya Upanishad. This *Upanishad* belongs to *Yajur Veda*. In it the sage Sakayanya teaches the king Brihadratha the mystery of the Great Self and the individual soul (elemental self). The individual soul is affected by the good and bad effects of actions, by the pairs of opposites like pleasure and pain. It is subject to the cycle of births and deaths. But it can realize the Supreme Self through study, austerity, recitation, Meditation on OM and the pursuit of one's own duty. Sakayanya speaks of this realization in terms of becoming One with the Supreme Self. Then the sage expounds the six-fold Yoga:

"This is the rule for achieving this (Oneness): control of the life-force (*Pranayama*), withdrawal of the senses, Meditation, concentration, contemplative inquiry, and absorption (*Samadhi*), (This is) said to be the six fold Yoga. When, by this (Yoga) he beholds the gold-colored maker, the Lord, the Person, the Brahma source, then the sage, shaking off good and evil, makes everything into Oneness in the Supreme Indestructible." (6.18).

This *Upanishad* is still more specific. It mentions the central channel, *Sushumna Nadi* along which the life force (*prana*) must rise upward from the base of the spine to the crown of the head. This process is accomplished by joining the breath, the mind, the senses, and the sacred syllable OM.

The *Maitrayaniya* contains many fascinating ideas, hinting at practices that suggest a further advance in the development of Yoga, and thus prepared the ground for saint Patanjali's classical formulations.

1.4: History of Yoga: Yoga in Epics

Yoga in Epics

India's two great epics are the *Ramayana* of Valmiki and the *Mahabharata*. No single literary creation has more influence on the lives of millions of people in India and Southeast Asia than the ancient epic *Ramayana*, the story of Sri Rama.

Ramayana. The significance of the *Ramayana* for the students of Yoga lies in the moral values it promulgates so vividly. It can be regarded as a consummate treatise on what are known in Yoga as the restraints (*Yama*) and moral observances (*Niyama*). The *Ramayana* extols virtues like righteousness (*dharma*), non-harming, truthfulness and austerity. It also serves as a great illustration for Karma Yoga, the Yoga of Selfless Service. Sri Rama's brother Lakshman, and his devotee Hanuman are illustrious Karma Yogis.

The *Ramayana* also illustrates how Yogis who misuse psychic powers acquired through intense *Tapas* (austerities) destroy themselves. Ravana and his associates had acquired enormous psychic powers through intense Yogic practices, but they are demons and applied their powers for mean selfish purposes and for causing untold miseries to innocent people including celestials. They were killed in the war with Sri Rama, the embodiment of righteousness and Divine qualities.

Yoga Vasishta. This is a continuation of the *Ramayana*. This philosophical work of about 32,000 verses is the earliest detailed work on Yoga and Vedanta. It contains the teachings of the sage Vasishta to the young prince Rama. It is a lasting monument to the wisdom of non-dualism. The spiritual path outlined in the *Yoga*

Vasishta is essentially Jnana Yoga, and it is similar to the *Buddhi* Yoga taught in the *Bhagavad Gita*, where action and knowledge are blended harmoniously. The genuine Yogi, according to Vasishta, is free from the push and pull of passionate attraction and aversion. Such a Yogi looks at a lump of gold and a pile of rubbish with the same equanimity.

It is the human mind that creates bondage and liberation. The mind is compared to a madman with thousand hands, who constantly beats himself. The mind is galvanized by the vibration of the lifeforce (*prana*) circulating in the body. Control of the *prana*, Concentration and Meditation are the means for quieting the mind and transcending the compelling force of desires.

Vasishta's Yoga comprises seven stages:

(1) eagerness to know the truth,
(2) deepening of study and contact with holy people,
(3) refinement of thinking,
(4) dispassion or nonattachment,
(5) quiescence of the mind,
(6) recognizing the illusion of the world and the reality of the Self, and
(7) Liberation or abiding in pure Consciousness (Self).

The Yogi who has realized the Self is liberated while living. Enlightenment is ego-transcendence in every moment regardless of whether the body-mind is active or otherwise.

> "Just as there is butter in every kind of milk, the Supreme abides in the bodies of all things."
>
> "The perverted intellect, who considers himself as the body, is verily confined in it, but when he knows himself to be identical with the taintless Self, he is liberated."
>
> "With boundless patience, courage and service, carry on your meditation and self-study, and worship God in holy Yoga."
>
> "True worship consists in inward Meditation alone, and in no outer form of worship, therefore, apply your mind to the adoration

of the Universal Spirit by meditating within yourself."

Mahabharata. The second epic *Mahabharata* is a magnificent and invaluable treasure house of mythology, religion, philosophy, ethics, customs and information about kings and sages. It comprises about 100,000 stanzas. The nucleus of the epic is the strife between the righteous Pandavas and their cousins, wicked Kauravas. Ultimately truth prevails.

The *Mahabharata* is an encyclopedia of Hindu righteousness. It contains noble moral teachings, useful lessons of all kind, many beautiful stories and episodes, discussions, parables and dialogues that set forth the principles of morals and metaphysics.

Yoga and Samkhya loom large in the philosophy of this epic. Both traditions have their taproots in the pre-Buddhist period. The most significant materials on Yoga are found in the famous *Bhagavad Gita* and the *Moksha Dharma* Section, which form part of the sixth and the twelfth Books of *Mahabharata.*

Bhagavad Gita. The *Bhagavad Gita* or Song Celestial is part of the epic *Mahabharata*. It is a dialogue between the Incarnate Lord Krishna and his friend and disciple Arjuna, one of the Pandava brothers. This immortal conversation is the climax of the story of *Mahabharata*. The *Bhagavad Gita* contains the cream of the *Upanishads*. It is a universal gospel. It is of great importance to the Yoga tradition. It teaches the Yoga of Knowledge of Self, Yoga of Meditation, Yoga of Knowledge, Yoga of Action, Yoga of Self-control and Yoga of Devotion.

Aldous Huxley calls this ancient work as "the most systematic statement of the perennial philosophy." The *Gita* is the first successful attempt in human cultural history to work out a complete philosophy of life, reconciling the secular and sacred, work and worship. Even though *Gita* is an ancient scripture composed several thousand years back, it is relevant to all times and to all people.

The central message of *Gita* is the harmonization of worldly life and spiritual life. Its gist is found in the following sloka:

"Perform your duty, O Arjuna! being steadfast in Yoga,

> abandoning all attachment and balanced in success and failure. Such evenness of mind is called Yoga." (2.48)

This emphasizes the important requirement of Yoga, namely, a steady mind, balanced in success and failure, pleasure and pain and other pairs of opposites.

In order to attain enlightenment, Lord Krishna declares, one need not forsake the world or one's responsibilities. Renunciation of action is good by itself, but better still is renunciation in action. This is the celebrated ideal of inaction in action (*Niskarmya Karma*), which is the basis of Karma Yoga. Life in the world and spiritual life are not in principle inimical to each other; they can and should be cultivated simultaneously. Such is the essence of an integrated life. Lord Krishna taught *Gita* to Arjuna in the battlefield of Kurkshetra. It symbolizes the eternal battle raging within the mind of every one of us – a battle between good and bad, virtue and vice (*dharma* and *adharma*). Arjuna represents the individual soul; the charioteer represents Lord Krishna, the Divinity within our heart; the chariot represents the body; the horses represent the five senses; and egoism, mental impressions, desires, likes and dislikes, lust, anger, greed, jealousy, pride, hypocrisy, etc. are our enemies. In this battle the message of Gita will ever remain as an unfailing guide to the individual souls.

Some of the slokas pertaining to Yoga are as follows:

> "Endowed with wisdom (evenness of mind), one casts off in this life both good and evil deeds; therefore devote thyself to Yoga. Yoga is perfection in action." (2.50)
>
> "There is no knowledge of the Self to the unsteady, and to the unsteady no Meditation is possible; and to the unmeditative, there can be no peace, and to the person who has no peace, how can there be happiness?" (2.66)

One who cannot focus his mind in Meditation cannot acquire the knowledge of the Self. The mind must succeed in stilling the clamor of the senses and it must become pure, steady and still.

This is the inner condition which spiritual seekers have attained and realized God, the inner most Self of all. Sloka 4.10 of the *Gita* affirms this truth:

> "Freed from attachment, fear, and anger, absorbed in Me, and taking refuge in Me, purified by the fire of knowledge, many have attained to My Being."
> "When one is not attached to the sense-objects or to actions, having renounced all thoughts (desires), then he is said to have attained to Yoga." (6.4)
> "Thy right is to work only, but never to its fruits. Let not the fruits of action be thy motive, nor let the attachment be to inaction." (2.47)

Actions performed with the expectation of reward bring bondage. It is the desires and attachments that are responsible for bondage and the consequent rebirths.

> "He who does all actions for Me, who looks upon Me as the Supreme, who is devoted to Me, who is free from attachment, and who bears no enmity toward any creature, comes to Me." (11.55)

This verse contains the essence of the philosophy of the *Gita*. When we perform actions as offering unto the Lord, we will attain purity of our heart and eventually Self-realization.

> "To those whose ignorance is destroyed by knowledge of the Self, like the sun, knowledge reveals the Supreme (Brahman)." (5.16)
> "The Yogi, who is self-controlled and peaceful, is balanced in cold and heat, in joy and sorrow, and in honor and dishonor." (6.7)
> "The Yogi who is satisfied with the knowledge of the Self, who has conquered the senses, and to whom a clod of earth, a piece of stone and gold are the same, is said to be harmonized." (6.8)

> "He who regards well-wishers, friends, foes, the indifferent, neutrals, the hateful, relatives, the virtuous, and the vicious all alike, excels (among the Yogis)." (6.9)

To the right Yogi the virtuous and the sinful and all others are but manifestations of Brahman Now the *Gita* gives the procedure of the Yogic practice

> "The Yogi should endeavor constantly to keep the mind steady, remaining in solitude, with the mind and the body controlled and without expectations and greed." (6.10)

The Yogi, who treads the path of renunciation, has to practice meditation in a solitary place like a cave in the mountains, and he has to renounce mentally and externally all possessions and desires. A householder with spiritual inclinations can practice meditation in a solitary and quiet room in his house or in any other solitary place. He should lead his life with dispassion and non-attachment.

Then *Gita* prescribes the seat and the posture for practicing meditation.

> "The Yogi has to sit firmly on a clear spot, neither too high nor too low, consisting of *kusha* grass, over it deer skin and on the top a folded cloth." (6.11)
>
> The Yogi has to sit in a naturally clean spot as the bank of a river or make the place clean wherever he wants to practice meditation.
>
> "Keeping his chest, neck and the head straight and steady, without looking around, let him look as if he is gazing at the tip of the nose." (6.13)

In this verse, the meditative posture is described. Unless the body is steady, the mind will not become steady. Sitting erect will facilitate the flow of Divine energy (*Kundalini*) upward through the subtle nerve-channel called the *Sushumna Nadi* from the base of spine.

> "Thus seated with controlled mind and senses, having made the mind one-pointed, practice Yoga for the purification the mind." (6.12)

The verses 6.14 and 15 stress the importance of keeping the mind serene, controlled and balanced, observance of celibacy in order to conserve energy, and fixing the thought on the Lord with an awareness of the goal of God-realization or Self-realization. When the Yogi controls the modifications of the mind, he attains the supreme peace of the Eternal, which culminates in Liberation.

> "Yoga is not possible for him who eats too much, nor for him who does not eat at all; nor for him who sleeps too much, nor for him who is sleeplessly awake." (6.16)
>
> "Yoga destroys sufferings for him who is always moderate in eating and recreation, who is moderate in his activities, and equally moderate in his sleep and wakefulness. (6.17)
>
> For the practice of Yoga moderation in eating, sleeping, working and recreation is necessary. Extremes in these activities should be avoided.
>
> "As a lamp flickers not in a windless place, the Yogi, who controls his mind, remains focused on the Self." (6.19)
>
> "When the mind, controlled by the practice of Yoga, attains to quietude, and when, seeing the Self by the Self, the Yogi is satisfied in his Self; where he experiences absolute bliss through subtle intellect and wherein established, he swerves not from the Truth; where no other gain is considered greater, and where he is not moved even by the greatest sorrow. That state which is free from misery is Yoga. This Yoga should be practiced with determination and with an undesponding mind." (6.20–23)

What a beautiful description of Yoga!

> "And completely casting off all desires born of one's imagination and restraining by his mind the senses running on all sides; step by step, gradually, let the mind attain tranquility by the

intellect held firmly. Fix the mind on the Atman alone and let no other thought occupy it." (6.24–25)
"From whatever cause the restless, unsteady mind wanders away, from that let him restrain it and bring it towards the Self alone." (6.26)

The above Slokas 20 to 26 describe the process of Yoga. The Yogi has to bring back the mind to the point of concentration repeatedly, when it runs towards external objects.

The results experienced by a Yogi are given in the next two Slokas.
"Supreme peace descends on this Yogi who has attained quietude of mind, devoid of all passions. He becomes one with Brahman itself, and evils never taint him." (6.27)
"Thus striving incessantly, the Yogi bereft of all taints easily attains infinite bliss born of oneness with Brahman." (6.28)

Now the *Gita* gives the unique result of this Atma Yoga, which Patanjali did not conceive. Self-realization takes one to the acme of *Viswatmabhava* (Oneness of Atma with the whole universe). This is stated in the next four verses.

"The Yogi absorbed in his Yoga sees the Self abiding in all beings and all beings in his Self. He sees the same everywhere." (6.29)
"He, who sees Me (Lord) everywhere and everything in Me, never becomes separated from Me, nor do I become separated from him." (6.30)

In this verse the effect of the vision of oneness or unity of Self has been stated. Shankaracharya calls this *Samyak Darsana* (correct Insight).

"Established in Unity, the Yogi, who worships Me as residing in all beings (as their very Self), ever dwells in Me whatever his mode of living may be." (6.31)
"He who, through the Oneness of the Self, sees equally

everywhere, be it pleasure or pain, is regarded as the highest Yogi." (6.32)

The Yogi sees that whatever is pleasure or pain to himself is also pleasure or pain to other beings. He thus sees equally everywhere.

Slokas 18.65 and 66 sum up the essence of the entire *Bhagavad Gita*:

> "Fix your mind on Me, worship Me, dedicate every action to Me, and surrender yourself to Me. Then you will certainly come to Me. I promise you this because you are my devotee." (18.65)

Each phrase indicates one of the paths of Yoga. "Fix your mind on Me" – Raja Yoga; "Worship Me" – Bhakti Yoga; "Dedicate every action to Me" – Karma Yoga; "Surrender yourself to Me" – humility; "Come to Me" – Jnana Yoga. Integrate all these kinds of Yoga into your life in order to attain the goal of your life.

> "Renounce all duties (*dharma*), take refuge in Me alone. I will liberate you from all sins; grieve not" (18.66)

The statement "Renounce all duties" does not mean giving up your duties. Your body and mind do things according to your nature, but the real "you" (Self) does not act, just watches as a silent observer. Let things happen through your body and mind, but do not identify yourself with those things. You are not the actor, nor the agent. The Cosmic force functions through your body and mind; the fruits of the actions belong to the Cosmic force. <u>You</u> are not affected by the actions. Just take refuge in the Cosmic Reality that will take care of you and take you beyond sufferings and sorrow; that is, *you* attain eternal Liberation, peace and bliss.

Moksha-Dharma. Next to the *Bhagavad Gita*, the most significant materials on Yoga in the *Mahabharata* are found in the *Moksha-Dharma* Section. This section comprises Chapters 168–353 of the Twelfth Book. *Moksha-Dharma* gives important details about the "epic" forms of (or Pre-classical) Samkhya Philosophy and Yoga. Both traditions have their specific theoretical frameworks and they are distinctively theistic. The Epic Yoga is based on solid moral foundations. It instills such virtues as truthfulness, humility, non-possessiveness, harmlessness, forgiveness and compassion. Lust, anger, greed and fear are listed as the Yogi's greatest enemies. Doubt, discontent and psychic powers are deemed to be severe obstacles on the spiritual path. Withdrawal of senses from the external world, Concentration and Meditation are considered to be the primary means of Yoga.

Ethical Literature (*Dharma Shastra*)

Elements of pre-classical Yoga[16] are also found in the ethical literature known as *Dharma Shastra*. The higher spiritual life can blossom only when it is founded on morality. Therefore there are many references to Yoga in the manuals on ethics and law, which regard Liberation as the highest possible virtue. The *Manu Smriti*, an important work of pre-Christian era on morality and law, recommends *Pranayama*, Concentration and Meditation for combating such undesirable emotions as anger, avarice and jealousy. Similar statements are found in the *Baudayana Dharma Sutras*, an important juridical work of the same period.

There is a quotation of a verse in *Apastamba Dharma Sutras* of fourth century BC, which states that all taints of character can be eliminated through the practice of Yoga.

The *Yajnavalkya Smirti* describes the entire Yogic process – from assuming the right posture, to withdrawing senses from external objects, to performing *Pranayama*, Concentration and Meditation. What is clear from these ethical literatures is that Yoga was already an integral part of India's cultural and moral life in pre-Christian era.

1.5: History of Yoga: Classical and Post-classical Period

CLASSICAL PERIOD

Patanjali's *Yoga Sutras*

The sage Patanjali codified the teachings on Yoga into the *Yoga Sutras*. This script represents the culmination of the long development of the system of Yoga. It consists of 196 sutras in four *padas* or parts. The first part treats of the nature, aim and forms of Yoga, the modifications of the *chitta* or mind-stuff and the kinds of *Samadhi* and the methods of attaining them; the second part deals with Kriya Yoga as a practical means of attaining *Samadhi*, causes of suffering, cessation of suffering, three *gunas*, the eight limbs of Yoga and their practice; the third part gives an account of the inward aspects of Yoga and the supernatural powers which manifest themselves during the practice of Yoga; and the last part deals with the nature and forms of Liberation (*Kaivalya*), the reality of the transcendental Self and attaining Liberation. The *Yoga Sutras* is a scientific treatise on Raja Yoga. (For details, *see* 3.1 Raja Yoga, *below*).

Yoga is intimately allied to the Samkhya Philosophy. (For details, *see* 1.7 *The Philosophical Basis of Yoga:* (b) *Samkhya Philosophy, below*). For all practical purposes, Samkhya and Yoga may be treated as the theoretical and practical sides of the same system. Yoga mostly accepts the metaphysics and the epistemology of the Samkhya. It shows the practical path for attaining discriminative (intuitive) knowledge that alone leads to Liberation. Yoga accepts the three sources of knowledge – perception, inference and testimony – of the Samkhya, and also its twenty-five metaphysical principles. But unlike the Classical Samkhya, Yoga believes in God as the highest Self, distinctive from other selves.

Commentaries on *Yoga Sutras*

Sutras (aphorisms) are terse and laconic. The *Rishis* (Seers) have condensed their thoughts in the aphorisms. It is very difficult to understand them without the help of commentaries. Hence there arose many commentaries on *Yoga Sutras*. The oldest extant commentary on the *Yoga Sutras* is the *Yoga Bhashya* (exposition on Yoga) by Vyasa. This work holds the key to many of the more enigmatic aphorisms of the *Yoga Sutras*.

The next available commentary is Shankara Bhagavatpada's *Vivarana* on the *Yoga Bhashya*. It is a remarkable original work. Its author, according to tradition, is the great saint Shankaracharya (eighth century AD)

Vacaspati Mishra's (ninth century) commentary known as *Tattva Vaisharadi* (Clarity of Truth) offers many useful clues to some of the more difficult passages of the *Yoga Bhashya*.

In the eleventh century the famous Persian scholar Al-Biruni translated the *Yoga Sutras* in Arabic, which has exercised a lasting influence on the development of Persian mysticism.

The next important commentary is *Yoga Varttika* by Vijnana Bhikshu (sixteenth century), a renowned scholar. He interpreted Yoga from a Vedantic point of view. In recent centuries many commentaries were written both in Sanskrit and in English.

Srimad Bhagavatam

This magnificent scripture depicts the heroic life of Lord Krishna and the stories of sages, devotees and kings. No other scripture, except the *Bhagavad Gita*, has enjoyed such widespread popularity through centuries. In Indian devotional literature *Bhagavatam* is pre-eminent for its philosophical depth, devotional exuberance and literary beauty.

Yoga is mentioned in many passages of *Bhagavatam*. It

reconciles, like *Bhagavad Gita*, Yoga of Devotion, Yoga of Knowledge, and Yoga of Action. "Yoga is fried in the butter of Knowledge," says Sri Ramakrishna, "and steeped in the honey of Love." *Bhagavatam* accepts Patanjali's eight limbs of Yoga, but rejects his dualistic philosophy.

Of particular interest for the Yoga student is the Book XI known as the *Uddhava Gita*. In it Lord Krishna expounds the Yoga of Devotion to His disciple Uddhava.

Perhaps the most extraordinary teaching of the *Bhagavatam* is the Yoga of hatred. According to this Yoga, a person who thoroughly hates the Divine can achieve God-realization as readily as one who deeply loves the Lord. Sage Narada, frequent speaker for the *Bhagavatam* teaching, expresses it thus:

> "All emotions are grounded in the erroneous conception of 'I' and 'mine.' The Absolute, the Universal Self, has neither 'I' sense nor emotions. (7.1.23)
>
> "Hence one should unite (with God) through friendship or enmity, fearlessness or fear, attachment or love. (The Divine) sees no distinction whatsoever." (7.1.25)

Kamsa reached God through fear, and Shishupala through hatred. The idea that hatred can turn out to be a pathway to God, though shocking apparently, is a logical consequence of the ancient esoteric doctrine that we become whatever we meditate upon.

POST-CLASSICAL PERIOD

Most of the Yoga teachings that emerged after Patanjali's time did not adopt his dualistic metaphysics of *Purusha* (Self) and *Prakrti* (Nature). Those teachings can be referred to collectively as Post-classical Yoga. They adopted the Vedantic non-dualism.

The post-classical literature of Yoga is most diversified and richer in content than the pre-classical literature. It includes *Puranas, Saiva Agamas* (Traditions) of the Saivism, one of the main branches of Hinduism, *Vishnu Samhitas* (Collections) of

Vaishnavism, another main branch of Hinduism, and *Tantras* (Looms) of the Shakti worshippers.

Puranas

These are ancient narratives that deal with the origin of things. They contain, among other things, brief treatment of Yoga and numerous fascinating stories about aspirants and masters of Yoga. The *Markandeya Purana* speaks in detail about the qualities of an aspirant of Yoga and also about the environmental conditions necessary for success in the Yogic practice.

The *Linga Purana* describes Patanjali's eight-stage Yoga and the obstacles to be overcome. The *Agni Purana* contains extensive information about *mantra* recitation, *Mudras* (hand gestures), *yantras* (mystic diagrams), *Pranayama* and Patanjali's eight-stage Yoga.

In the *Garuda Purana* an important place is assigned to the eight-stage Yoga and also to *Bhakti Yoga* and *Tantric Yoga*.

The voluminous *Shiva Purana* deals with five types of Yoga including *Mantra Yoga* and *Maha Yoga* (Great Yoga), which is the contemplation of Lord Shiva without any restricting conditions.

The *Puranas* thus contain records of various Yogic practices. Some of them follow Patanjali's model. However, what distinguishes them from Patanjali's tradition is that they propose a single ultimate principle, the Self or God. Many of the *Puranas* are available in English translations. The fund of myths and legends preserved in the *Puranas* is a perennial source of inspiration to the Yoga students.

The *Agamas*

These are theological treatises and practical manuals of Divine worship. They include the *Tantras*, *Mantras* and *Yantras*. These are treatises explaining the external worship of God. They also give elaborate details about ontology and cosmology, liberation, devotion, meditation, philosophy of *Mantras*, mystic diagrams, etc.

There are *Agamas* for each of the three chief sections of Hinduism, namely, Saivism, Vaishnavism and Saktism. The *Saiva*

Agamas glorify God as Siva and have given rise to an important school of philosophy known as Saiva Siddhanta. The *Vaishnava Agamas* glorify God as Vishnu. The *Sakta Agamas* or *Tantras* glorify God as Sakti or the Mother of the Universe.

Darsanas

Darsanas are Schools of Philosophy based on the *Vedas*. They appeal to the intellect, while the Epics, Puranas and Agamas appeal to the heart. The word *darsana* means "the vision of truth." The chief Hindu philosophical systems are Nyaya, Vaisesika, Samkhya, Yoga, Mimamsa and Vedanta. Each of these *Darsanas* holds a holistic approach toward life, aiming at a direct experience of the Ultimate Reality and Truth. Yoga is closely related to the Samkhya Philosophy and Vedanta. (For details, *see* 1.6 The Philosophical Basis of Yoga: (a) Vedanta or Advaita Philosophy, and 1.7 The Philosophical Basis of Yoga: (b) Samkhya Philosophy, *below*)

Shankaracharya

Shankaracharya (eighth century) is one of the greatest sages in the history of Yoga. He made great contributions to the philosophy of Vedanta and Yoga. His major writings were his commentaries on twelve individual *Upanishads*, on *Bhagavad Gita* and on the *Vedanta Sutras*. He also wrote independent mystical poems such as *Viveka Chudamani* (Crest Jewel of Wisdom), *Aparokesha-nubhuti* (Direct Experience of Reality), *Atma Bodha* (Knowledge of the Self), and *Vakyavritti* (Explanation of the Text). As a great sage and a Yogi, he handled difficult metaphysical questions with relative ease and simplicity. The world is fortunate that almost all his writings are now available in English translation.

The Southern Saivism

The Southern Saivism favors a qualified monism that, in practice, is dualistic with Lord Siva on the one side and the devotee on the other. This is epitomized in the devotional songs of such great saints as Appar, Sundarar, Manickavasagar and Thirujnana Sambandar. The Sekizhar's *Periapuranam,* which tells the life stories of sixty-three *Nayanmars* (Saiva Saints), is a great literature on Bhakti Yoga.

The famous *Thirumantiram* of the great Sage Thirumular is an extraordinary scripture on Yoga, devotion, Tantric practices and *gnosis* (jnana). It is a unique scripture of 3000 verses spread over Nine Tantras. Tantra Three describes the procedure of eight-limbed Yoga and special types of Yoga such as *Kecari Yoga* (the Supreme state of Yogic Bliss) and *Chantra Yoga* (Yoga for achieving immortality). Thirumular discusses Yoga more fully than Patanjali. Tantra Four deals with *Mantras* and *Yantras*. Tantra Seven among other things deals with Kundalini Yoga. Tantra Nine presents a picture of the Divine Vision. (*See* Thirumular, *Thirumantiram* (with English Translation and Notes), Madras: Sri Ramakrishna Math, 1991)

The Northern Saivism

The Northern Saivism leans toward a non-dualist interpretation of Reality. At the beginning of the ninth century the Kashmiri adept Vasagupta discovered the *Shiva Sutras*, a digest of the earlier Agama teachings. This is a treatise on Yoga. The commentaries on the *Shiva Sutras* contain invaluable materials on *Pranayama*.

Samhitas

These are the religious works of the Vaishnavas. They are corresponding to the *Saiva Agamas* and the *Tantras* of the Sakti worshippers. The emphasis of the teachings of the *Samhitas* is on ritual worship and a moral way of life. The *Vishnu Samhita* introduces a six-step Yoga. But many other *Samhitas* recommend Patanjali's eight-step Yoga.

The devotional Tamil poems of *Alvars* (Vaishnava saints) sparkle with passionate love for the Divine. The *Alvars* were steeped in devotion to Lord Krishna, a full incarnation of the Lord Vishnu. Their "rapturous passions are like a whirlpool that eddies through the very eternity of the individual soul." The *Alwars* in their ecstatic delight visualize God everywhere.

The *Gita Govinda*, Sanskrit poems of Jayadeva of Bengal

(North-eastern part of India), is a profound allegory of the love between the Personal God and the human Self.

The works of Vaishnava preceptors include *Yoga Rahasya* (Secret Doctrine of Yoga) by Nathamuni, *Siddhi Traya* (Triad of Perfection) by Yamuna, and the great Ramanuja's works expounding the philosophy of qualified nondualism.

Yogic teachings also played a role in the works of other great Vaishnava preceptors – Madhva (1238-1317), Nimbarka (mid-twelfth century) and the ecstatic Krishna Caitanya (1486-1533). These teachers are great exponents of Bhakti Yoga.

Universality of Yoga

Though the practice of Yoga originated in India, Yoga is not confined to India. It has spread out to various other countries. A school of Meditation was established by Indian monks in Egypt around the third century BC. Later the doctrines and practices of Yoga were carried to China and thence to Japan by Buddhist missionaries. (*See* 4.5 Meditation Traditions, *below*). The mystics of all major other faiths such as Buddhism, Jainism, Judaism, Christianity and Islam have attained a direct insight into the nature of Reality. Thanks to Sri Ramakrishna Vedanta Centers established by Swami Vivekananda in Western countries, and Yoga Centers established by great Indian Yogis of twentieth century in various parts of the world, Yoga is taught and practiced today by people belonging to various faiths all over the world, and it is bringing about a World-wide spiritual renaissance today.

1.6: The Philosophical Basis for Yoga: (a) Vedanta or Advaita

Introduction

Philosophy, in its widest sense, means "love of knowledge." The Sanskrit word for philosophy is *darsana* that means "the vision of truth." Indian philosophy deals with the knowledge of truth. It tries to seek answers to such fundamental questions as "what is the true nature of a human being? What is the purpose of life? What is the nature of this world in which we live?"

Practical Guide. Indian philosophy is not a mere metaphysical speculation or intellectual pursuit like the Western philosophy. It is a practical guide to the daily life. Its insights were directly experienced by ancient sages of India. Its ideas and theories are not limited to any particular era, culture or group. They are universal and meant for one and all.

Holistic and Multi-discipline. Indian philosophy is much more comprehensive than Western philosophy. It is an integration of several disciplines like metaphysics, epistemology, logic, axiology, aesthetics, ethics, sociology, psychology and physiology. In the West different aspects of every problem are studied by separate disciplines. But the Indian philosopher studies each problem from all possible approaches. This tendency denotes the synthetic or the total outlook of the Indian philosophy. It holds a holistic approach toward life, aiming at a direct experience of the ultimate Reality and Truth. The ultimate Truth can be experienced not merely by a chosen few, but, under right conditions, by all human beings.

Modern human being knows much about the external world but knows nothing about his real and internal nature. Prompted by external clamors and sophistication he seeks peace and happiness from external objects and sensual enjoyments, and consequently suffers from emotional problems and several psychosomatic diseases. This is due to a lack of a philosophy of life. Life, without a guiding philosophy, is like a castle built on the sand. Indian philosophy provides an effective philosophy of life and opens the door to eternal peace and joy.

The Systems of Indian Philosophy

The Schools of Indian philosophy are divided into two broad groups: orthodox and heterodox. To the first group belong the six chief philosophical systems, namely, Nyaya, Vaisesika, Samkhya, Yoga, Vedanta and Mimamsa. These are regarded as orthodox because they accept the authority of the *Vedas*. The chief three heterodox systems are the Carvakas, the Buddhism and the Jainism. These do not believe in the authority of the *Vedas*. However they do believe in the authority of their own spiritual leaders and founders.

Though the different Schools hold different views, each School took care to learn from the views of all others; and they did not come to any conclusion before considering thoroughly what others had to say and how their points could be met. This catholic spirit of treating rival positions with consideration was more than rewarded by the thoroughness and perfection that most of the Indian Schools attained.

Nyaya. This is a system of logic that forms the basis for scientific inquiry and rules of debate used by other systems.

Vaisesika. This system concerns itself chiefly with logic, physics and chemistry.

Samkhya. This is a dualistic School that sees two primary constituents of the universe–Nature and Consciousness.

Yoga. This is essentially a system for the practical application of the Samkhya theory.

Mimamsa. This system emphasizes the use of ritual, worship and ethical conduct to achieve salvation.

Vedanta. This deals with the concept of consciousness as the Reality or substratum underlying all forms of manifestation.

There is a gradual progression from concern with the scientific methods for investigation of the material aspects of the universe to concern with the duality of the universe in terms of matter and consciousness, and finally, in Vedaṅta to a concern with the essential nature of consciousness itself.

The Nyaya, the Vaisesika, the Samkhya and the Carvaka have based their theories on ordinary human experience and reasoning. But on matters such as God, Liberation, etc. ordinary experience is not dependable. Philosophy must depend for these on the experience of saints and seers who have a direct realization of such things. The authority or the testimony of reliable persons and scriptures thus forms the basis of philosophy. The Mimamsa and the Vedanta Schools follow this method. Even the Buddhism and the Jainism depend mostly on the teachings of their prophets.

Advaita Vedanta (Non-dualism)

The intellectual basis of Yoga is furnished by the Vedanta, a system of thought that draws its inspiration from the metaphysical reflections of the great Seers (*Rishis*) of the *Upanishads*. The word "*Vedanta*" means "the end of the *Vedas*." The Vedanta was developed from the *Upanishads* that constitute the culmination of the Vedic thought. An ancient scripture called the *Brahma Sutras* deals with the doctrine of Vedanta. The *Brahma Sutras* was composed in 555 sutras by Vyasa also known as Badarayana, a great saint of ancient times. It systematizes the teachings of the *Upanishads*. The *sutras* consist of two or three words each, and so cannot be understood without a commentary. The different commentators have given different interpretations in the light of their own preconceived opinions. The chief commentators are Shankaracharya, Ramanuja and Madhva. Each of them became the founder of a particular School of Vedanta.

The most common question on which the Schools of Vedanta vary is: What is the nature of the relation between the Self (*jiva*) and Brahman (God)? Shankaracharya holds that the two are absolutely identical. This view is known as Monism or Non-dualism (*Advaita*). Ramanuja holds that the *jiva* and Brahman are related as a part and the whole. This view is called Qualified Monism (*Vaistadvaita*). Madhva holds that the Self and God are two different entities. This view is called Dualism (*Dvaita*).

None of these three Schools agree with the Nyaya, the Vaisesika, the Samkhya, the Yoga and the Buddhism regarding the theory of the manifestation of the universe. Vedantins do not consider the universe as the transformation of an unconscious *Prakrti*. They hold that without the guidance of the conscious principle, an unconscious matter could not produce this world, which adheres to certain rules and laws. Such order and regulation, they argue, cannot be the attributes of an unconscious principle.

The Schools of Vedanta also unanimously agree on the existence of God. God's existence can be established only through direct experience or by testimony.

Sankaracharya's Monism or Advaita Vedanta

Pure Monism originates from the *Upanishads*. Shankaracharya (eighth century) was the first philosopher to establish a formal School of *Advaita* Vedanta. He based his theory on the *Upanishads*, the *Brahma Sutras* and the *Bhagavad Gita*. He wrote profound commentaries on these three scriptures. He also produced many other works that are great contributions to the Philosophy of Vedanta. The main topics of this philosophy are: the Self (Atman), the Supreme Consciousness (Brahman), Cosmic Illusion (*Maya*), the universe, God, human life and Liberation.

Self: The Self within us is pure Consciousness. It is different from the body, the senses, the mind and the intellect that are the outer covers or sheaths. It is beyond time, space and causation. It is an absolute Reality that has no beginning and no end. It is also known as Atman. The Self of a human being is identical with the Self of all beings and therefore with Brahman.

Brahman: Brahman is the ultimate Truth. It is all-pervading self-illumined Consciousness. It is the unaffected and unchanging Absolute. Brahman is the only Reality. Nothing exists apart from Brahman. Then what is this universe with diverse phenomena? The universe is the projection of *Maya*. Because *Maya* veils the

Truth, the individual self misconstrues both the world and itself as different from Brahman.

Brahman and the Universe.
The manifested universe is called *Jagat* (the ever-moving), because its nature is a continual state of flux. That which is changing implies something that is changeless. Change signifies flow or movement against an unchanging background. Otherwise no change would ever be recognizable. The world is a changing phenomenon against the background of the changeless Brahman.

What is the relation between the world and Brahman? Shankaracharya answers this question using a classical simile of Vedanta. A peasant, returning one evening from the field, sees a snake coiled up in a corner of his hut. He is terribly afraid until he goes nearer to it with a lamp and finds the 'snake' to be a harmless rope. His fear is due only to his superimposition (ignorance) of the true nature of the snake on a harmless rope. In the same way the world of phenomenal names and forms is a superimposition on the underlying reality, Brahman. By the light of the lamp the peasant discovers the reality, and his fear and anxieties disappear. In the same way the light of Self-Knowledge gives a realization of the real nature of Brahman and the unreality of world, and thereafter all sorrow and suffering ends.

Brahman and the Individual Soul. Brahman and the individual soul are one and the same. Brahman is the only One reality; everything else is Its manifestation. The purpose of Yoga is to enable us to realize the identity between Brahman and our individual souls. It is by finding Brahman within ourselves that we fulfill the purpose of life. In the *Bhagavad Gita*, Lord Krishna exhorts Arjuna:

> "Therefore, with the sword of knowledge (of the Self) cut asunder all doubts, born of ignorance about the Self residing in the heart, and resort to Yoga." (4.42)

The Nature of the Self. We do not know our true nature. Just as the illusory snake is superimposed on the rope, an illusory personality is superimposed on the real Self or Atman. Thus we think of ourselves as other than what we are; our real Self is obscured by the cocoon of our false identification with the body, mind and senses, which is spun over it, and we imagine ourselves to be limited individual souls (*jivas*). For instance, one may describe himself as an Asian-American, aged thirty years. These are all attributes of the body. His body, thoughts and feelings go on changing. But the changeless thing (Atman) within him is essentially unconnected with those changes. It is their witness in the same sense as a lamp hanging from the center of a room witnesses and illumines whatever goes on in the room. The Atman within is the witness of the activities of the body and mind.

Self or Atman–One Only. There is only one Self, not a multiplicity of different selves as commonly believed. A light shining through a number of prisms refracts as different colors peculiar to each of the prisms. In reality it is nothing but light, but it appears to take on the characteristics of the medium through which it is refracted. Similarly, an individual soul (*jiva*) is in reality nothing but the Self or Brahman, but it appears to take on the limitations and characteristics of each personality and body in which it is refracted. The one Self, refracting through the medium of different personalities, comes to be regarded as many selves, but this is a mistake. The Oneness of the Self is realized in the deep spiritual experience that may be termed Super-consciousness that supersedes the ordinary waking state. In a dream, one may see that a voracious tiger is fast approaching him. It appears real at that time. It is only when the dreamer suddenly wakes up, he recognizes it as a dream. The Vedanta holds that all sufferings and miseries are due to the false belief that something exists other than one's Self, and that on "waking up" to the Truth, the anxieties and sorrow arising out of this false belief come to an end. To a knower of the Self there is nothing outside himself, which can be a cause of fear or suffering. The *Isha Upanishad* says:

"When one knows that all beings have become one with his

own Self, then what delusion and what sorrow can be to him who has seen the Oneness?" (7)

When an individual realizes this unity, he becomes liberated from sorrow, which is the product of duality. When the Self of the perceiver becomes all things, there can be no source of disturbance or anxiety. The vision of all beings in the Self and of the Self in all beings is the foundation of freedom and joy.

In the *Taittiriya Upanishad*, Brahman is described as "that fundamental Reality from which the world of beings is born, by which it is supported, and in which it finally dissolves." (3.1.1). Shankaracharya accepts the fact of the world from the standpoint of ordinary experience; he does not assert its complete unreality. The universe comes into being, is sustained, and passes away like thoughts that arise at the surface of the mind and then sink back into the subconscious. Brahman is the sole cause of the world and the world is real only in so far as it is Brahman. The dream is only real in so far as it is a part of the dreamer's consciousness. He is not affected by the changes that take place in the dream. So also God is not affected by the changes that take place in Its manifested universe.

Maya. If Brahman, the Reality, is non-dual and One-without-a-second, how does the experience of the manifold world ever come about? This illusion is due to *Maya*. It is due to *Maya* that an apparent distinction exists between the world, the individual souls and the Personal God (*Isvara*). *Maya* is an inherent power (*Shakti*) of Brahman. With His power of *Maya*, Brahman has projected the appearance of the world as time-space-causation. To seek to learn when time began is a philosophical absurdity. Being itself a product of *Maya*, the intellect can no more fathom the mystery of the origin of *Maya* than a son can be present at his father's christening.

It is *Maya*'s nature to conceal and to imprison the soul (*jiva*) by a web of ignorance; hence a synonym for *Maya* in the Vedanta is *ajnana* (ignorance). *Maya* is indescribable, because it is neither real nor unreal.

Ultimately all projections of the *Maya* are unreal, being illusory in nature. The universe is only an appearance. As long as one mistakes a rope for a snake, he is frightened and reacts to the rope exactly as if it were a real snake. But when one realizes that it is a rope and not a snake, he may laugh at his own folly. Likewise, as long as one is engrossed in the ignorance, the world is quite real. But when true knowledge arises, the world does not exist independently from the cause, Brahman.

The illusion or ignorance can be eliminated by obtaining wisdom through the practice of contemplation and Meditation, and devotion to God. When the veils of ignorance are removed, then the *jivatman* realizes its own essential nature – Existence-Knowledge-Bliss (*Satchidananda*). This realization of the Truth that already abides within is called Liberation.

Personal God (Isvara). The state in which Brahman is consciously associated with *Maya* to manifest the universe is called *Isvara* (Personal God). The intellect cannot perceive the formless Brahman, but it can have an idea of *Isvara. Isvara* is the highest reading of Brahman by the human mind. It is *Isvara* who incarnates on earth from time to time to re-establish righteousness (*dharma*). Rama, Krishna, Buddha, Jesus Christ and similar others have been incarnations of God on earth.

Worship of the personal God is a great help in all stages of Yoga. It opens the heart to His light. Ultimately the worship of *Isvara* is transformed into the realization of the unconditioned Brahman beyond *Maya* and without attributes. The *Mundaka Upanishad* says:

> "The wise see That which is beyond perception, which is incomprehensible,
> which has no origin,which is free from all properties, which has neither the sense of hearing nor the sense of perception, which has neither hands,
> nor feet, which is eternal, manifest in diversity, and the source of all beings." (I.1.6)

The Link between the Microcosm and Macrocosm.

An important thesis of Vedanta is that what is observed in the microcosm, the individual, is also reproduced in the cycles of the macrocosm, the universe. For instance, an individual's mental activity starts at the dawn of the day, continues until the evening, when it is absorbed in the subtle layer of consciousness during dreamless sleep. The thought process is also a similar process working on a yet smaller scale. A thought rises in the mind, it is retained by it for a short time, and it eventually falls back into the sub-conscious. In the same way the universe, in which we now live, has come into manifestation, will remain in existence for a certain period, and will then be withdrawn into the undifferentiated state of *Maya*, which is the causal aspect of God.

Ramanuja's Qualified Non-dualism

Ramanjua (eleventh century), a great saint of South India, fixes his attention on the world, the Self and God. For him all these are real, but the world and the selves depend on God. While Brahman is eternally free from all imperfections, matter is unconscious, and the individual selves are subject to ignorance and suffering prior to release. God, selves and the world are part of Brahman. Brahman is the controlling power of the body, the world and *jivas* (embodied souls). Apart from Brahman they is nothing. Ramanuja's theory, therefore, is non-dualism with a difference, namely, that the one Brahman has two forms: selves and matter. Ramanuja admits the individuality of selves and holds that the Supreme Brahman is a person. He stresses devotion to Him.

Salvation. Salvation, according to him, is not the disappearance of the Self, but its release from the limiting barriers. The Self cannot be dissolved into God. The released Self has a permanent intuition of God. Its essential nature, which is obscured by ignorance and desires in the state of bondage, is manifested in the state of release.

Madhva's Dualism

Madhva (1197-1276), a Vaishnava saint, holds that God, selves and the world exist permanently, but the latter two are subordinate to God and dependent on Him. Brahman or God possesses all perfection, and is identified with Vishnu. The Supreme directs the world. He is endowed with a supernatural body, and He is transcendent to the world as well as immanent in it, since He is the inner ruler of all selves.

Everything – a Living Organism. For Madhva, everything on earth is a living organism. The Self is not an absolute agent, since it is of limited power and is dependent on God. It is, by nature, blissful, though it is subject to pain and suffering as a result of its connection with a material body due to its past karma. So long it is not freed from impurities, it wanders about in changing forms of existence. No two selves are alike.

God cannot be approached directly. *Vayu* (air) is the mediator. The Divine will is supreme. It sets human beings free or casts them into bondage. Salvation, for Madhva, consists in the perpetuation of the individual Self in the condition of release, where the Self takes delight in the adoration and worship of God.

Ethical Discipline. Although Self-Knowledge, and not ethics, is the goal of life, ethical discipline is considered essential for the realization of that goal. Ethical discipline enables us to control our senses and minds, and thus to attain non-attachment and selflessness, which are essential for the attainment of spiritual vision. It is the desires and attachments that agitate our minds. The Self can only be realized when the mind is serene and unagitated by desires. A verse of the *Katha Upanishad* sums it up:

> "When all desires dwelling in the heart are destroyed, then the mortal becomes immortal and he attains Brahman even here in this life." (2.3.14)

The *Bhagavad Gita* and Patanjali's *Yoga Sutras*, and other scriptures like *Thirukkural*, an ancient ethical literature in Tamil (an ancient language of India) give detailed ethical instructions, which accord with the similar teachings of Christianity, Buddhism and other great religions. (*See* 3.4 Yama and 3.5 *Niyama, below*)

Action (Karma). Action is the key to the ethical life. We cannot avoid action even for a single moment. Even breathing and thinking are actions. "As a person thinks, so he becomes" is the maxim of Yoga. Thoughts materialize in actions and shape not only our character but also our future. The Law of Karma is very precise. For every action there is an equal reaction. We reap what we sow. To this extent we are architects of our fate. Our present life is the result of our previous actions in this and many past lives, while the reactions of those actions and new actions determine our future lives. Selfless action and self-surrender to God release us from the bondage of karma.

Death and Reincarnation. The soul returns to the world in a new body after death and will continue to do so until it reaches the end of spiritual evolution called Liberation (*Moksha*). The *Bhagavad Gita* says:

> "Just as a man casts off worn-out clothes and puts on new ones, so also an embodied soul leaves its worn-out body and enters a new one." (2.22)

After death, the physical body returns to its constituent elements. On leaving the body after death, the soul may go to Heaven or Hell to experience the effects of good or bad actions, but Heaven or Hell is a temporary state. When the karmic merit or demerit that has warranted that experience has been exhausted, the soul takes birth once again in a body.

Liberation. The process of birth, death and re-birth is not endless. It lasts only so long as a person has not consciously realized the Self. The birth in a human form is the highest form of birth. It marks substantial progress in the spiritual evolution of the soul, which has earlier had innumerable plant and animal bodies. It is with the human body and mind, and only with this instrument, that the soul can be liberated from the bondage of *Maya*. The soul's Liberation is often described as Self-realization. This term does not imply knowing something new but rather recognizing what is already a fact.

Once a lion cub was left in the forest soon after birth when its parents were shot by a party of hunters. The cub grew up with a flock of wild sheep. Since it saw nothing but sheep around it, it thought itself to be a sheep. One day it caught sight of its reflection in a clear pool of water. Giving a roar for the first time in its life, it threw off its meekness and knew itself to be a king of the jungle. The Yoga says that a human being is like that lion cub. He is ever the Self or Brahman, but imagines himself to be a helpless individual doomed to a life of suffering and frustration, only occasionally relieved by some brighter moments. At any time he can see his reflection in his purified and peaceful mind and realize the lion-like majesty of his Self. At the right moment, the teacher will say to him: "*Tat tvam asi*, That thou art. Thou, the individual soul, is in fact the supreme Reality (Brahman)."

1.7: The Philosophical Basis of Yoga: (b) Samkhya Philosophy

Introduction

The Samkhya Philosophy was expounded by the sage Kapila during the seventh century BC. The *Samkhya Pravacana Sutra*, which is now not available, is attributed to him. The earliest available text is the *Samkhya Karika* of Isvarakrsna of the third century AD The Samkhya is a philosophy of dualistic realism. It admits two ultimate realities:

> Purusha *(Spirit or Self) and the unconscious* Prakrti *(primordial matter or Nature).*

Purusha and *Prakrti*

Purusha is ever pure and ever free, but it becomes subject to pain and pleasure when it forgets its true nature and identifies itself with *Prakrti*. *Purusha* consists of multiple selves. *Prakrti* is both the material and the efficient cause of the world. It is composed of three *gunas* (modes or forces) – *sattva* (light), *rajas* (activity) and *tamas* (lethargy). It is active and ever changing, but blind and unintelligent. In contact with the conscious and intelligent *Purusha*, *Prakrti* evolves the world. The Samkhya holds that the mere presence of *Purusha* is sufficient to move the *Prakrti* to act, although *Purusha* itself remains unmoved. Similarly it is due to the reflection of the conscious *Purusha* on the unconscious intellect (*manas*), the cognitive and other psychical functions are performed by the latter. But how the mere presence of *Purusha* can be the cause for changes in *Prakrti* is not clearly explained. Further the multiplicity of *Purusha* is proved with reference to the differences in the nature, activity, birth and death and sensory and motor endowments of different living beings. But all these differences pertain not to the Self as pure consciousness but to the bodies associated with it. The pure consciousness in all beings is the same. According to the Vedanta, there is only One Reality, namely, Atman and everything else – including *Prakrti* – is Its manifestation. The Vedanta thus carries the process of idealization to a further stage that alone can be the ultimate stage.

The Theory of Causation

The evolution of the universe is explained on the basis of a theory of causation known as *satkaryavada.* This means the effect exists in its material cause in potential form prior to its production. There can be no production of a thing that is previously non-existent potentially in its material cause. The Samkhya system holds that the entire world, including human body, mind, senses and the intellect are the manifestations of *Prakrti*.

Prakrti and *Gunas*

Prakrti is neither an atomic substance nor consciousness. It is a mere balanced combination of three *gunas* (forces): *sattva, rajas* and *tamas. Sattva* (goodness or purity) is potential consciousness; *rajas* (passion) is the source of activity, and *tamas* (dullness or inertia) is the source of resistance to activity. The three *gunas* are not the attributes of *Prakrti*. They are the constituent components of *Prakrti*. All things including human beings, as products of *Prakrti*, consist of the three *gunas* in different proportions. The three *gunas* are intertwined like three strands of a rope that binds the soul to the world. The varied interaction of the *gunas* accounts for the variety of the world. When there is equilibrium, there is no action. When there is a disturbance of the equilibrium, the process of evolution begins.

Prakrti is unconscious. Its evolution can take place only through the presence of conscious *Purusha*. The presence of *Purusha* excites the activity of *Prakrti*, and, thus, upsetting the equilibrium of *gunas* in *Prakrti*, passively starts the process of evolution.

Evolution of the Universe

At the advent of a new cycle of creation, *Prakrti* is roused from its slumber by the transcendental influence of *Purusha*. As a consequence of this, the equilibrium state of *gunas* is disturbed, and the *gunas* begin to vibrate. This primeval vibration releases a tremendous energy (big bang) within *Prakrti*, manifesting the universe in twenty-four stages.

The first evolute of *Prakrti* in the process of evolution is *mahat*, the cosmic intellect. It is great in space as well as in time. Hence the name "*mahat*" that means "great one." The individual counterpart of this cosmic state *mahat* is called *buddhi*, the intellect.

From *mahat* evolves *ahamkara,* the sense of I-ness or ego. It is more developed than *mahat*. As differentiation and further differentiation go on in a descending order, the effects, one after another, become more and more developed and subtle. The sense of "I" separates one's individual self from all others and creates an individual entity.

The five senses of perception (hearing, seeing, tasting, smelling and touching) and the five senses of action (verbalization, apprehension, locomotion, excretion and procreation) and the mind arise from *sattvic ahamkara.*

From the *tamas*ic *ahamkara* the five subtle elements called *tanmatras* are derived. They consist of sound, touch, color, taste and smell. *Rajas*ic *ahamkara* does not give rise to any new evolute. It only excites the other two *ahamkaras* to function.

The ears, eyes, tongue, nostrils and skin are the corresponding physical organs of senses of perception. The mouth, arms, legs, and the organs of excretion and procreation correspond to the senses of action. These physical organs are not the senses; rather they are given powers by the senses. The sense organs come into contact with the objects and are modified into the shape of the respective objects as they are. This is the only function of the sense organs. Each of the organs of action has gotten its special function that cannot be performed by any other. Mind is both a sensory and motor organ. The sensory and motor organs can operate only through the mind. The mind, the ego and the intellect are called the internal organs, while the five senses of perception or cognition and the five senses of action are called the external organs. The three internal and the ten external organs are collectively called the thirteen organs (*karanas*) in the Samkhya Philosophy.

In the final stage, from the five subtle elements evolve the five gross elements of ether (*akasa*), air, fire, water and earth with one, two, three, four and five attributes respectively (*Samkhya Karika*, 22 and 28). Thus the gross element of ether (or space) with its attribute of sound evolves from the subtle element of sound. Similarly, the gross element air with its attributes of sound and touch evolves from the subtle element of touch, and so on. Finally, the gross element of earth with all the attributes of sound, touch, color, taste and smell evolves from the subtle element of smell.

Thus the total elements are twenty-five, namely, *Prakrti* (cause only), *Purusha* (neither cause nor effect), *mahat, ahamkara*, the five senses of perception, the five senses of action, the mind, the five subtle elements, and the five gross elements. These are the twenty-five basic principles (*Tattvas*) of the Samkhya Philosophy.

The purpose of Evolution

The purpose of evolution is twofold. The first is the purpose of *Prakrti*, namely, becoming the object of enjoyment of *Purusha*. But *Purusha* is a passive observer so it cannot directly enjoy *Prakrti*. It indirectly enjoys *Prakrti* when it experiences the pleasurable and painful images presented to it by the intellect. This is possible only when *Prakrti* reveals itself to the *Purusha* in and through its various manifestations. This revelation of itself to the *Purusha* is the purpose of *Prakrti*.

The second is the *Purusha*'s purpose of freeing itself from the clasp of *Prakrti*. Though it is attributeless, it ascribes pleasure, pain and other properties of *Prakrti* to its own Self, and thus appear to become affected by them. Due to its constant association with the *Prakrti*, it fails to discriminate its own Self from *Prakrti*. But when discriminative knowledge dawns, it realizes its true nature and withdraws itself forever from the association of *Prakrti*. This is called Liberation.

The Sources of Knowledge

The Samkhya Philosophy accepts only three independent sources of valid knowledge, namely, perception, inference and testimony. The other sources of knowledge like comparison, postulation and non-cognition are included under these three sources, and not recognized as separate sources of knowledge.

Perception is the direct cognition of an object through its contact with a relevant sense. For example, we perceive an object like a table when it comes within the range of our vision.

Inference means knowledge derived through the observed relationship between two things. It is the knowledge of a non-observed thing through a related perceived thing. For example we infer fire on a hill from the perception of smoke on it.

Testimony consists of authoritative statements made by trustworthy persons, and gives the knowledge of objects that cannot be known by perception and inference. The nutritionist's statements regarding vitamins, and the scriptural statements about God and immortality are examples of testimony.

The Ethics of the Samkhya

Life on earth is a mixture of pleasure and pain, and even pleasure ultimately ends up in pain or suffering. The suffering is of three kinds. The first is the suffering arising out of intra-organic causes like bodily disorders and mental afflictions. The second is the suffering arising out of extra-organic causes like other human beings, animals, plants, insects, etc. Instances of this kind are injury caused by another person, murder, snakebite, prick of thorn and so on. The third kind of suffering arises out of extra-organic supernatural causes like thunderstorm, cyclone, earthquake, etc.

All the blessings of modern science and technology give us only temporary relief from pain or suffering. They do not assure a total and final relief from all the ills to which our mind and body are subject. What is the ultimate cause of suffering? *Purusha* (Self) is ever pure and free. But it experiences misery due to its association with the *Prakrti*. Due to ignorance it identifies itself with the body and the mind, the effects of the *Prakrti*. It is the mind and body that are subject to pain and suffering. It is the lack of discrimination between the eternal Self and the mortal body and worldly objects that is the cause of our bondage and suffering. Once discriminative knowledge dawns, we realize our true nature and attain Liberation. But discriminative knowledge is not theoretical. It is the outcome of the practice of virtue and Yoga. The Yoga system constitutes the practical side of the Samkhya Philosophy; it enumerates and elaborates the practical methods that lead to the discriminative knowledge and thus to Liberation.

Bondage and Liberation

Bondage and Liberation pertain to the intellect. Bondage arises when non-discrimination exists and the intellect goes after worldly experiences, and Liberation arises when constant discriminative knowledge prevails. The attainment of Liberation means just the clear recognition of the Self as a reality beyond time and space, and above the mind and the body. It is absolute freedom from all suffering. It is the ultimate goal of our life.

The Concept of God

There is a great controversy among the Samkhya philosophers regarding the concept of God. The original Samkhya was monistic and theistic. But the classical Samkhya, perhaps under the influence of Jainism and early Buddhism, became atheistic. The earliest available text, the *Samkhya Karika* does not discuss the existence of God. This led scholars to believe that early Samkhya did not accept the existence of God. They argued against the existence of God. There is no doubt that the world must have a cause. But God or Brahman cannot be the cause of the world. God is said to be the eternal and immutable Self; and what is unchanging cannot be the active cause of anything. In the presence of *Purusha*, the ever-changing *Prakrti* is enough for creating the universe. However, later developments in the Samkhya clearly indicate the acceptance of the existence of God. The later philosophers point out that in metaphysical discussions, it is very difficult to explain the nature of the universe and of *Purusha* without accepting a Supreme Being. The existence of God is supported by reason as well as by the scriptures.

1.8: The Yoga Philosophy

Introduction

Yoga is as old as humanity. It was practiced by Yogis and sages since ages. Its value is lauded in the Indian scriptures of the *Vedas* and the *Upanishads*, and in the Epics and Puranas. (For details, *See* 1.3 History of Yoga: Pre-classical Period, 1.4 History of Yoga: Yoga in Epics, and 1.5 History of Yoga: Classical and Post-classical Period, *above*). The importance of Yoga as a means of realizing the ultimate Reality has been recognized by all the important Indian systems of philosophy. Yoga Philosophy is an invaluable gift of the great sage Patanjali who codified the system of Yoga several thousand years ago. His work known as *Yoga Sutras* is the first work of this School of Philosophy. Vyasa's *Yoga Bhasya* is the oldest commentary on the *Yoga Sutras*. Bhojaraja's *Virtti* and *Yoga Maniprabha* are very simple and popular works on the Yoga Philosophy. Vijnanabhiksu's *Yogavartika* and *Yogasara Sangraha* are other useful manuals of the Yoga system.

Yoga is not a theory, but a practical method for attaining Self-realization. Yoga means the cessation of mental modifications, and the union of an individual soul with the Cosmic Spirit or Consciousness. It is closely allied to the Samkhya system. The Yoga Philosophy mostly accepts the epistemology and metaphysics of the Samkhya Philosophy, but unlike the Samkhya, it believes in God.

Eightfold holistic System

The Yoga system prescribes an eightfold holistic system of practice for controlling the modifications of the mind, and for attaining Self-realization. The eight steps are: *Yama* (restraint), *Niyama* (observance or moral code), *Asanas* (physical Postures), *Pranayama* (regulation of *prana*), *Pratyahara* (withdrawal of senses), *Dharana* (Concentration), *Dhyana* (Meditation) and *Samadhi* (Absorption in Superconsciousness). The individual seeker ultimately realizes his true Self or pure Consciousness. Practicality is the main characteristic of Yoga Philosophy.

Samkhya and Yoga: Similarities

The Samkhya Philosophy and the Yoga Philosophy are very much inter-related, and do not vary in their essentials. The Yoga is the application of the theory of the Samkhya in practical life. It mostly accepts the epistemology and metaphysics with 25 principles (*See* 1.7 The Philosophical basis of Yoga: (b) The Samkhya Philosophy, *above*). The Samkhya lays greater stress on the discriminative knowledge as the essential condition of Liberation, whereas the Yoga lays down a systematic practical method of attaining the discriminative knowledge. By practicing Meditation and its prerequisites, the mind is progressively stilled and purified and thus becomes fit for experiencing the transcendental Spirit or Superconsciousness. Both the Samkhya and the Yoga may be considered as the concave and convex sides of the same sphere.

According to the Samkhya, the sources of knowledge are perception, inference and valid testimony. The Yoga accepts these means of knowing. The Sutra 1.7 of the *Yoga Sutras* says: "Direct perception, inference and revealed authority are the valid proofs."

Differences

The Concept of God. The main difference between the Samkhya and the Yoga lies in their treatment of the concept of God. The earliest available text *Samkhya Karika* of the Samkhya system does not discuss the existence of God. The absence of such discussion led scholars to believe that early Samkhya did not accept the existence of God. However the later developments in the Samkhya clearly indicate the acceptance of the existence of God.

The Yoga, on the other hand, gives a prominent place to *Isvara* or God. *Isvara* is described as a special *Purusha* not affected by afflictions, actions, their fruits and the domains of their accumulated impressions. (*Yoga Sutras*, 1.24). The Yoga system also regards devotion to God or surrender to God (*Isvara-pranidhana*) as a means for quickly attaining *Samadhi* (1.23). Surrender to God is also considered as one of the three preparatory requirements for the practice of Yoga, the others being purification (*Tapas*) and self-study (2.1). It is also one of the *Niyama*s to be observed for the practice of Yoga (2.32).

The Twenty-three Evolutes. According to the Samkhya, in the process of the evolution of the universe, the *mahat* (intellect) is the first product of *Prakrti*. From *mahat* arises *ahamkara* (ego); from the *sattvic* aspect of *ahamkara* evolves the mind, the five senses of perception and the five senses of action; and from the *tamas*ic aspect of *ahamkara* evolves the five subtle elements, and from the subtle elements the five gross elements.

The Yoga Philosophy gives alternate explanatory titles to the above twenty-three evolutes as follows (*Yoga Sutras*, 2.19):

Prakrti : *Alinga*, without a distinguishing mark

Mahat : *Linga-matra*, merely a mark, but with no distinguishing features

Ahamkara and 5 subtle elements : Six *avisesas* or non-specific intermediate links between *mahat* and the final sixteen evolutes

Mind, 5 cognitive senses, 5 active senses, 5 gross elements : } *Visesas* or specific final sixteen products

It is generally thought that the idea of evolution is a new contribution made by science to modern civilization, and Darwin is considered to be the father-of this idea. This is not really correct. The idea of evolution has come down to us in one form or another from the earliest times. Patanjali has put the fundamental idea underlying the theory of evolution in One *sutra*: The contact of

Purusha with *Prakrti* is the means of realizing by the *Purusha* of his true nature, and of unfolding the powers latent in both. (*Yoga Sutras*, 2.23). He has brought into this generalization the most important aspect of evolution, which is missing in the modern scientific theory.

According to the modern theory there is an evolutionary transformation in the physical forms of species in their effort to adapt themselves to the changing environment. The mere evolution of form would be a meaningless process without an evolution in life. Yoga emphasizes the total evolution that leads to the gradual unfoldment of consciousness and to the increase in the efficiency of the vehicle as well. By studying the kingdoms of vegetables, animals and human beings, we find that there is a remarkable increase in the degree of unfoldment as we pass from one kingdom to another. Along with that we find that the vehicle also becomes more and more complex and efficient for the expression of the unfolding consciousness. When we compare the brain of a snail with that of a monkey and again with that of a highly civilized human being, we find that there is a tremendous development in the capacity of the vehicle to manifest the latent powers in the consciousness. The mental and spiritual powers exhibited by a highly intellectual person of today are nothing when compared to the psychic powers of an advanced Yogi. It is in the invisible realms of the mind and the spirit that the evolution produces its most magnificent results and the astounding powers of the *Purusha* find their main expression.

The powers of *Prakrti* refers to the capacity of the vehicle to respond to the demands of Consciousness. The powers of the *Purusha,* on the other hand, refer to the powers of Consciousness to function through the vehicles. As *Purusha* is pure Consciousness and Consciousness is eternal, there cannot be any evolution of his powers in the normal sense of the word "evolution." But Consciousness has not only to manipulate and control Its vehicles with increasing efficiency, but has also to transcend them. This is what Self-realization aims to accomplish.

Mind. In the Samkhya, the mind is categorized into three parts, lower mind, ego and intellect. In the Yoga, the mind is studied holistically and the term *chitta* is used to denote the mind-stuff. It is all-penetrating and it includes the unconscious or lower mind, active mind (*manas*), intellect and ego, that is, the entire inner organ (*antakarana*). All psychical states are the qualities (*dharmas*) of this organ. They arise out of impressions (*samskara*) of the past thoughts and experiences that cling to the psychical organ. *Chitta* undergoes modifications when it is affected by the worldly objects through the senses.

The involvement of the soul in the world of objects and desires is deep and complex. The soul, as pure awareness, has no power of its own to gain insight regarding its involvement or to struggle against its unhappy entanglement in the miseries of the world. The soul is dependent upon the *chitta* (mind), which is part of the body (*Prakriti*), for the effort required to free both mind and soul from suffering (*See* 2.9 Freedom from Suffering, *below*). Mind is caught paradoxically in a double predicament. First, in seeking to rid both itself and soul from desire, it must desire to be desireless. This very desire for freedom from desire becomes an all-consuming desire, and thus the most difficult of all the desires to be overcome. Second, in seeking to free the soul from its association with body, the mind must consciously seek to surrender its own awareness, for when the soul leaves the body, the mind ceases to be conscious. Self-awareness ceases and the mind itself devolves into an unconscious latent lifeless state. Yet, so long as the soul mistakenly identifies itself with body, and so long as the mind mistakenly believes its borrowed awareness as its own, both are deluded. Enlightenment, freedom from delusion, is better for both. The bound soul may undergo reincarnation innumerable times because it remains attached to a subtle body where karmic effects require other lives in which to work out its fate. But through the successful practice of Yoga once the soul experiences Self-Knowledge and thus achieves final Liberation, it is freed from further re-births.

When the soul (*Purusha*) regains its isolation or freedom from all disturbing association with the body, its own integrity is restored. The soul becomes the Self or the ultimate Reality. The freed soul has no memories and no desires and nothing to cause it to become again involved in the miseries of bodily life.

Subtle Body. According to the Samkhya, there are two bodies in a living being, namely, a subtle body and a gross body. The subtle body is an eighteenfold body and it is made up of the intellect, the ego, the mind, the five senses of perception, the five senses of action and the five subtle elements. It leaves the gross body at the time of death, transmigrates and undergoes a series of rebirths impelled by the karmic effects (the effects of past actions).

In the Yoga Psychology there is no subtle transmigrating body. As *chitta* is all-pervasive, a subtle body is unnecessary.

Suffering. The Samkhya holds that there are three kinds of suffering. They are:

1. *Adhyatmika*: Mental and physical suffering arising out of organic causes such as anxiety, depression and other mental and bodily disorders.

2. *Adhibhautika*: Suffering and pain arising from extra-organic causes like other human beings, beasts, thorns, etc.

3. *Adhidaivika*: Suffering caused by deities, planetary influences and other natural forces such as heat, cold, flood and earthquakes.

TheYoga Philosophy,on the other hand, classifies the causes of suffering or affliction into—

1. Ignorance (*avidya*): Considering non-eternal as eternal, not-self as the Self, and the impure as pure.
2. Ego or I-ness(*asmita*): The false notion of the Self as identical with body-mind complex.
3. Attraction (*raga*): Liking for things which give pleasure.
4. Aversion (*dvesa*): Aversion to things which cause pain.
5. Fear of death (*abhinivesha*): Clinging to life. (*Yoga Sutras*, 2.3-9).

The Means of Liberation. The Samkhya suggests that the *Purusha* can attain Liberation by means of discriminative knowledge. When the *Purusha* realizes that it is different from the *Prakrti*, and that it is pure Consciousness, then it attains Liberation.

On the other hand, according to the Yoga Philosophy, Self-realization can be attained through the perfect discipline of the will and the control of the mental states through an intensive and regular practice of moral codes, sense control and Meditation. Through the systematic practices of Yoga, the influence of the mind on the soul ceases and its activity can no more ensue. Thus the bond between the mind and the soul is untied. The soul, then, exists alone by itself in its true form, unaffected by any worldly thing and thus is Liberation achieved.

Conclusion

The categories of the Samkhya Philosophy are employed more in the Yoga Philosophy. Hence it is often referred to as the Samkhya-Yoga. The Samkhya Philosophy has its own independent existence, and does not refer to much of the practical system of Yoga. But the Yoga Philosophy does depend on the main aspects of the Samkhya system, but it gives them a new interpretation. It does not thereby lose its independent existence as a separate system of philosophy, particularly in the sphere of psychology and the doctrine of Liberation.

1.9: Three *Gunas*

Scientific Basis

The theory of *gunas* is one of the fundamental doctrines of Hindu Philósophy. The whole structure of the manifested universe is considered to rest on the three *gunas*: *sattva*, *rajas* and *tamas* (*Yoga Sutras*, 2.18). All the objects of perception are the result of the play of the three *gunas*. Even the working of the mind through which we try to comprehend their nature depends upon their interplay. There is some scientific basis for this doctrine.

The physical phenomena around us are based on three fundamental principles connected with motion. They are:(1) vibration that involves rhythmic motion of particles, (2) mobility or non-rhythmic motion of particles, and (3) inertia that involves relative position of particles. The cognition of visual phenomena depends upon the presence of light vibrations; auditory phenomena depend upon sound vibrations; and the sense of heat, etc. depends upon the impact of moving atom and molecules on the skin. The sensations of taste and smell depend upon the action of chemical substances on the membranes of the palate and nose. In every case vibration, mobility or inertia is at work and determines the nature of the perceived phenomenon. The articles whose motion determines the phenomenon are, according to science, combinations of protons, neutrons and electrons of atoms. The scientists have discovered that mass and energy are interconvertible. Therefore the ultimate basis of the manifested universe is nothing but motion or energy, and every article is a combination of three properties: wave motion, action and position. Since these are also the ideas associated with the nature of the three *gunas*, science has to a certain extent corroborated the theory of *gunas*.

Pervasiveness of *Gunas*

All the objects of the universe possess these *gunas*. The *Bhagavad Gita* says,

> "There is no creature on earth or in heaven among the gods, which is free from the three *gunas* of *Maya*." (18.40)

Everything in the world is pervaded by the *gunas* and can be classified according to the predominating *guna*.

Nature of *Gunas*

Sattva, *rajas* and *tamas* are distinct. Yet they function in coordination with one another. The nature of *sattva guna* is peace, and serenity; that of *rajas* is activity, sensuality, desire, attachment and enjoyment; and that of *tamas* is slothfulness, inertia, confusion, delusion and ignorance. When one of the *gunas* is dominant, the other two remain subdued. A Yogic aspirant should always be vigilant and see that *tamas* and *rajas* remain tamed with the help of *sattva* so that he can continue to march on the path of Yoga undisturbed and undistracted. In order to accomplish these, earnest effort should be made, and he should meditate regularly.

The following table, though incomplete, illustrates the manifestations of the three *gunas* in the outer world and in the inner world of the mind:

Sattva	*Rajas*	*Tamas*
External World	Light	Life
Darkness		
Balance	Force	Mass
Order	Movement	Inertia
Mind		
Happiness	Desire	Fear
Equanimity	Restlessness	Laziness
Balance	Passion	Carelessness
Calmness	Anger	Stupidity

The state of society and international relations simply reflect the inner conditions of human beings. Wars and strife are the externalization of inner conflicts. The welfare of society and the harmonious and friendly relations between nations depend more upon persons establishing inner harmony in their own minds by the cultivation of *sattva*.

Sattva

Sattva is purity, harmony and goodness. It is stainless and luminous. It produces knowledge and happiness. It enlightens the intellect. When *sattva* is predominant, one remains serene and happy. A sattvic person cultivates fearlessness. He is endowed with discrimination between real (*sat*) and unreal (*asat*). He enjoys peace of mind, inner harmony and tranquility. He controls senses; he performs selfless service; he has no attraction for the objects of senses. He is humble, pious, generous, merciful, forbearing, loving, caring and sharing. He practices ethical discipline. He remains in a state of peace and joy.

Sattva guna is full of delight; it is enlightening and very helpful for maintaining mental and emotional equilibrium.

Rajas

Rajas is passion or activity and ambition. It pleases the mind and keeps alive the passions. It creates attachment (*raga*) or aversion (*dvesa*) toward the objects of the world. A *rajas*ic person is full of cravings and desires. He is forced to act for their fulfillment. He becomes attached to those that help him to fulfill his desires and hates those that stand in his way. He runs after sensual pleasures and his desires become insatiable as a flame fed by oil. He is egoistic. He possesses the sense of "I and mine." He is ever greedy and restless. The more he acquires, the more passionate and greedy he becomes. Desires multiply. Nothing gives him satisfaction. He loses his power of discrimination. He runs after name, fame and comforts, and involves himself in endless activities. He has no peace of mind. He is attached to action and its fruits. He uses others as tools for his own self-aggrandizement. He is motivated by selfishness and binds himself by *karmas* or effects of his selfish actions.

*Rajas*ic mind likes certain persons, objects and places now, and after some time it becomes disgusted with them, and wants new persons for company. It finds pleasure in sight-seeing, and visiting new places. It always wants new sensations and variety. It is proud, egoistic, greedy and jealous. It makes a person constantly active and restless. It has a tendency to look into the defects of others. It also remembers the bad deeds or wrongs done by others and forgets easily their good acts. These tendencies intensify hatred and cause frequent disturbances in mind. *Rajas*ic mind always remains unsatisfied and seeks new sources of pleasure. It has no compassion for others' sufferings. These tendencies can lead to hypertension and many other diseases.

It is *rajas*ic mind that splits, separates and divides. It is under the sway of unconscious habits of wrong doings. Criminals when interrogated confess that they knew that they should not have acted in the way they did, but that they committed their offenses out of habit. It is *rajas* that led them to commit serious crimes.

Intense *rajas* takes sattvic turn. Dacoit Ratnakar became the sage Valmiki. Jagai and Madhai, who were intensely *rajas*ic and pelted stones at Lord Gouranga, a great saint, became his first disciples. *Rajas* can thus be transformed into a creative and constructive force.

Tamas

Tamas means sloth and inertia; it produces ignorance and destroys the sense of discrimination. It creates delusion, and so one cannot decide things on time. Thus it leads one to inaction. A *tamas*ic person is thoughtless and ignorant. He is negligent and indolent. He forgets everything. He completely identifies himself with the body and begins to fight with people if they speak ill of him. He has no sense of proportion and no sense of balance or poise.

A *tamas*ic person remains in a state of sleepiness and lethargy, and in such a state of mind he goes through negative withdrawal. For him life is full of gloom; he does not experience joy or delight.

Such a person becomes fat and flabby and is prone to disease. *Tamas* leads one to many illnesses; *tamas*ic person becomes passive and suffers from all the diseases related to passivity. He does not want to move; he remains in a semi-conscious state. He is controlled by negative emotions. He is depressed, dependent and helpless. Life becomes burdensome for him.

Gunas and Actions (*Karmas*)

There is an intimate connection between the *gunas* and *karmas*. It is the *guna* that goads one to do action. Self is actionless, a silent witness. It is the body and mind that act. *Sattvic* person performs virtuous deeds without attachment to their fruits. He dedicates them to God or His manifestations. *Sattva* facilitates Yoga practice and helps one to become liberated from the bondage of karma.

*Rajas*ic person performs actions with selfish motives and his actions lead to pain and suffering. He remains haunted by the fear of death. He seeks wealth by all means. He works for his own glory, fame and self-aggrandizement. The *tamas*ic person remains in the darkness of ignorance. He depends upon others for everything.

Gunas and Rebirth

If a person dies when the *sattva guna* remains predominant, he takes birth in the homes of wise parents. But one who casts off his body in *rajas* is reborn in a family of pleasure-seekers. If *tamas* is predominant when one drops off the body, he is reborn in a dull, lazy and desolate family.

Gunas and Spirituality

The qualities of *sattva*, *rajas*, and *tamas* constantly intervene in human life. When *sattva guna* enables the light of knowledge to be dawn, one becomes a sage. When *rajas* predominates, the desire for enjoyment victimizes the human mind. One then loses all senses of discrimination and one indulges in sensual enjoyment. When *tamas* predominates, one becomes dull and lazy and does nothing creative and useful.

From *sattva* arises knowledge, from *rajas* desire is born, and from *tamas* arises ignorance. A sattvic person marches upward toward liberation; a *rajas*ic person remains in the middle; and a *tamas*ic one moves downward under the influence of base qualities.

In the first step in the spiritual journey, a Yogic student should not allow the *tamas*ic quality to raise its head. He should prevent his mind from going to the grooves of negativity and passivity. Failure and lack of confidence in life lead one to such a negative state.

In the next step the student should learn not to look for objects of pleasure. Sensual enjoyment robs his inner vitality that is the very basis of human unfoldment. Taming and keeping *tamas* and *rajas* under control, he should cultivate *sattva guna*. Without establishing *sattva guna* as the predominant quality, progress in Yogic Meditation cannot be achieved.

When one breathes primarily from the left nostril, *tamas* holds sway; when he breathes through the right nostril, a *rajas*ic state is evident; and when the breath flows equally through both nostrils, he is in a *sattvic* state. With the help of *Pranayama* practice he can balance the breath and establish coordination between the mind and breath. Then the mind prefers to meditate.

After cultivating *sattva guna* the student progresses to the final state. When he realizes the Self, he goes beyond *all* the *gunas* and nothing affects him. His vision, then, remains unalloyed and pure.

Transcending the *Gunas*

One, who has totally dedicated oneself to the Supreme Lord with one-pointed devotion, transcends the *gunas* and becomes fit to attain Brahman. The Supreme Lord is the final abode.

The seer knows that only *gunas* are the agents of action and that Self is not the doer. Knowing that the Self remains above the *gunas*, unaffected, he is well established in the Supreme Self. The body functions because of the three *gunas*, but the sage is free from the identification with body consciousness. Therefore he is freed from the cycle of births and deaths, and misery. He enjoys immortality.

The sage who has transcended the *gunas* neither likes nor hates *gunas*. He does not respond to them. He remains neutral as a non-involved observer. He remains balanced in pain and pleasure. To him a lump of clay and a piece of gold, praise and blame, honor and dishonor, friend and foe all are the same. He has no attachments.

When Liberation is obtained, the *Purusha* becomes established in the state of Self-realization, and he becomes free from the modifications of the *gunas*. (*Yoga Sutras*, 4.32)

1.10: References for Section I

1. Bahm, Archie J., *Yoga: Union with the Ultimate*, New York: Frederick Ungar Publishing Co., 1961
2. Brunton, Paul, *The Secret Path*, New York: E.P.Dutton and Co., 1935
3. Chatterjee, Satischandra and Dhirendra Mohan Datta, *An Introduction to Indian Philosophy*, Calcutta: University of Calcutta, 1984
4. Chaudhuri, Haridas, *Integral Yoga: the Concept of harmonious and Creative Living*, Wheaton,Ill.: The Theosophical Publishing House, 1974
5. Deshpande P.Y., *Authentic Yoga,* Bombay: B.I. Publications, 1979
6. Feuerstein, George, *Yoga: The Technology of Ecstasy,* Los Angeles: Jeremy P. Tarcher, 1989
7. Hari Prasad Shastri, *Yoga*, London: W and G Foyle Ltd., 1958
8. Juan Mascaro, The *Upanishads*, London: Penguin Books, 1965
9. Mircea Eliade, *Yoga: Immortality and Freedom*, Princeton: Princeton University Press,1973
10. Mishra, Ramamurti S., *Fundamentals of Yoga,* New York: Harmony Books, 1987
11. Radhakrishnan S., and Charles A. Moore, ed., *Indian Philosophy,* Princeton: Princeton University Press, 1973
12. Radhakrisnan S., trans., *The Principal Upanishads,* London: George Allen and Unwin,1969
13. Roy Eugene Davis, *Our Awakening World,* Lakemont: CSA Press Publishers, 1987
14. Shankaracharya, *Aparokshanubhuti* (The Direct Experience of Reality), tr., by Hari Prasad Shastri, London: Shanti Sadan, 1959

15. Swami Abhedananda, *Yoga: Its Theory and Practice,* Calcutta: Ramakrishna Vedanta Math, 1967
16. Swami Chidananda, *The Philosophy, Psychology and Practice of Yoga,* Shivanandanagar: The Divine Life Society, 1984
17. Swami Krishnananda, *Yoga as a Universal Science*, Shivanandanagar: The Divine Life Society, 1983
18. Swami Rama, *Choosing a Path*, Honesdale, PA: The Himalayan International Institute of Yoga Science and Philosophy
19. Swami Rama, *Lectures on Yoga*, Honesdale, PA: The Himalayan International Institute of Yoga Science and Philosophy, 1983
20. Swami Rama, *Perennial Psychology of the Bhagavad Gita,* Honesdale, PA: The Himalayan I. Institute of Yoga Science and Philosophy, 1994
21. Swami Ranganathananda, *The Message of the Upanishads*, Bombay: Bharatiya Vidya Bhavan, 1987
22. Swami Satchidananda, *Living Gita*, Yogaville: Integral Yoga Publications, 1995
23. Swami Satchidananda, *Introduction to Integral Yoga,* Yogaville: Satchidananda Ashram, 1975
24. Swami Satchidananda, *Sutras of Patanjali,* Yogaville: Integral Yoga Publications, 1990
25. Swami Sivananda, *The Bhagavad Gita*, Shivanandanagar: The Divine Life Society, 1989
26. Swami Venkatesananda, *Stop that Sorrow before It gets You*, South Fremantle: Integral Yoga Association of Western Australia
27. Swami Venkatesananda, *Lectures on Raja Yoga*, Elgin, S. Africa: the Children Yoga Trust, 1972
28. Swami Vivekananda, *Advaita Vedanta,* Calcutta: Advaita Ashrama, 1989
29. Swami Vivekananda, *Practical Vedanta*, Calcutta: Advaita Ashrama, 1987
30. Swami Vivekananda, *Raja Yoga,* New York: Ramakrishna Vivekananda Center, 1973
31. Taimni I. K., *Man, God and the Universe,* Wheaton, Ill.: The Theosophical Publishing House, 1974
32. Taimni I. K., *The Science of Yoga,* Wheaton, Ill.: The Theosophical Publishing House,1975
33. William James, *The Varieties of Religious Experiences,* New York: The Modern Library, 1994
34. Wood, Ernest, *Yoga,* London: Penguin Books, 1973

35. Yogashakti Saraswati, *Yoga Sadhana,* Bombay: Wilco Publishing House, 1972
36. Zimmer, Heinrich, *Philosophies of India,* Princeton: Princeton University Press, 1974

SECTION II

2.1: Yoga Psychology I

Introduction

Yoga Psychology is as old as civilization. It was developed by saints and seers of India thousands of years ago. Later it was adapted by Buddhist monks in India, China and Japan. Yoga Psychology is a search for knowledge about oneself. Its mode of inquiry is inward Concentration and experiential. (*See* 2.3 Yoga: Internal Research, *below*). It is a practical psychology. It is an attempt to forge a systematic understanding of one's own Self. Yogis apply it to discipline their own minds, control their senses and purify their hearts in order to attain a more ideal state of being (Goleman,1988, pp.114–15).

The Eastern Yoga Psychology postulates an ideal and supreme mode of being. Anyone who seeks with diligence, dedication and perseverance can attain it.

hrough intensive Yogic practices one can experience the supreme Reality, Knowledge of Self. The path to this transformation involves a far-reaching unfoldment of consciousness, and the main means to attain it are Yoga of Meditation (*Raja Yoga*), *Bhakti Yoga, Jnana Yoga* and *Karma Yoga*.

There is no model for such a radical transformation of consciousness in Western Psychology. It is about a hundred years old, and that level of human development over-reaches the vision and goals of Western Psychology (Goleman, 1988, p. 139).

Yoga Psychology's Inroads into the West

Even though the majority of American psychologists were ignorant of the Eastern psychologies till recently, Western thinkers, since the time of the Greeks and Romans, have been influenced by Eastern philosophies. Plotinus (AD 205-70)[17] was one of the early philosophers whose thoughts closely paralleled the psychological views of the Eastern thinkers of his day. Plotinus went to Persia and India in AD 242 to study their philosophies. His ideals became the hallmark of Christian mystics for centuries thereafter. Plotinus's version of ecstasy reflects the doctrine of such classical Indian texts as Patanjali's *Yoga Sutras* (Goleman, 1988, pp. 150-51).

With the rise of the natural science, the positive approach came to dominate Western science and philosophy. Western Psychology has its roots in the positivist tradition. Hence the early psychologists turned mostly to concerns other than those of the religious mystics. One rare exception was William James (1842-1910), America's most prominent nineteenth century psychologist. He was keenly interested in religion, both Eastern and Western. He befriended Swami Vivekananda of India, who toured America after speaking at the First World Congress of Religions in 1893 at Chicago. The work of James entitled "*The Varieties of Religious Experiences*" remains a classic on the psychology of religion.

Among the modern personality theorists, Carl Jung was probably the most knowledgeable about Eastern psychologies. Despite his familiarity with the psychologies of the East, Jung was critical of Europeans who tried to apply Eastern teachings to themselves (Jung, C.G., "Psychology and Religion: West and East," in *Collected Works,* Vol. 11, Princeton University Press, 1958). However, Jung did not reject the goal of the Eastern psychologies; he simply objected to their method as unsuited to the Western mind.

The Eastern Psychologies have made their greatest inroads in the West through their influence on the holistic outlooks of such theorists as Angyal and Maslow, the humanists Buber and Fromm, existentialist Boss, and the wave of "transpersonal" psychologists (Tart, Charles, ed., *Transpersonal Psychologies*, New York: Harper and Row, 1976). Maslow read extensively Eastern literature; Buber, Fromm and Boss have had contacts with Eastern teachers.

Medard Boss was invited to lecture on psychology in India, where he had an opportunity to meet with Indian holy men who impressed him deeply. (Boss, *A Psychiatrist Discovers India*, London: Oswald Wolff, 1965). Boss returned with the conviction that in the light of the teachings and behavior of the Eastern masters, the methods and aims of Western Psychotherapy were inadequate.

Alan Watts did much to bring the Eastern teachings to the awareness of Western psychologists as a guest lecturer at numerous medical school hospitals and psychiatric institutes, and in a series of books, most importantly, *Psychotherapy: East and West*, New York: Pantheon, 1961.

Abraham Maslow's book was published posthumously and it indirectly carried Watt's work a step further (*The Farther Reaches of Human Nature*, New York: Viking Press, 1971).

A close collaborator of Maslow, Anthony Sutich founded *Journal of Transpersonal* Psychology in 1969. This journal has become the forum for psychologists most open to studying and borrowing from the Eastern psychologies.

Charles Tart, a major investigator of altered states of Consciousness (1969) edited a pioneering collection of these Eastern theories in *Transpersonal Psychologies* (New York: Harper and Row, 1976) to serve as guides to Western Psychologists.

Ken Wilber and others published a book, *Transformations of Consciousness* (Boston and London: New Science Library, 1986). This is a pioneering effort in the most sophisticated integration of psychologies of East and West.

Non-dualistic Approach to Body and Mind

The philosophical line of thought from Plato to Descartes has emphasized a split of human nature into two distinct parts, mind and body. The "mind" through reason, will and thought has been interpreted as involving volition – consideration of an alternate course of action. The "body" has been considered as an "automaton," going on about its processes, making adjustments automatically, that is, it is not subject to high level control or alteration.

The "involuntary" nervous systems are beyond the possibility of conscious alteration. But there are strong indications that these Western distinctions between voluntary and involuntary components of human constitution are not at all valid. Yogis find that it is possible to consciously alter physiological processes through the practices of Meditation. Nobody is conscious of the internal organs of the body, the breathing, heart beating, digestion, etc. None of us can control the heart; it goes on its own way. But by Yogic practice one can bring even the heart under control. Nearly every part of the body can be brought under control. Physiological studies confirm this Yogic claim and indicate that there is much more voluntary control over our involuntary activity than we had thought possible.

The series of investigations that Bykov and his co-workers began in Russia in 1924 provide evidence that the autonomic nervous system is only *relatively* autonomic and is subject to voluntary control, if the situation is set up appropriately. Their work indicates that there is a far greater degree of modifiability of the heart, liver, spleen, kidneys, blood flow, etc. than supposed. It also shows that the division some have made between mind and body – mind as a process of reason and will, and body as an automaton – is false. The original explorations of Freud and Breuer on hysteria point in the same direction. The work of Neal Miller and Leo DiCara of Rockfeller University also confirms the possibility of voluntary alteration of physical process. (*Science*, 163 (1969), 434-45 and *Scientific American*, Jan 1970, 30-39).

Joe Kamiya, Joseph Hart and Charles Tart of the California University, B. Brown and many others have confirmed the voluntary alteration of the brain's electrical, beta and theta activities.

Elmer Green of the Menniger Foundation (1970), David Shapiro and his associates at Harvard University have shown that humans can alter their blood pressure at will (*Science*, 163 (1969), 588-90).

The older spiritual psychologies are thus rich sources of information for contemporary psychology, and a new and extended view of the human capacity is emerging from the blend of contemporary and older psychologies. The older psychologies are the precursors of the modern analysis of the interactive nature of awareness. They also offer alternative conceptual models for human behavior. Their centuries-old non-dualistic approach to mind and body has only recently been accepted by science. They also offer techniques for altering awareness and the "involuntary" aspects of nervous and glandular activity which Western science has for a long time ignored.

Mind and Body

Yoga Psychology has found the body-mind as one complex. The mind is a subtle counterpart of the physical body; the physical body is the manifestation of the mind; so when the mind becomes tense, the body becomes tense, and when the mind is relaxed the body is also relaxed. The face is the index of the mind. Thoughts, emotions and sentiments produce very noticeable expressions on the face.

The mind and the body are intimately connected. The mind acts upon the body, and the body reacts upon the mind. A pure, healthy mind gets a healthy body, because thoughts are the primary cause of all the ills of life. Violent fits of anger, for instance, seriously damage the brain cells, inject poisonous chemicals into the blood, produce shocks in the nervous system and drain away energy and vitality. But the pains and sufferings of the physical body are actually secondary to the diseases of the mind. On the other hand, if unwanted and undesirable thoughts are controlled, all diseases will disappear. It is possible to control undesirable thoughts, emotions and feelings through Yoga practices.

Analysis of Mind

Modern science is confirming the ancient wisdom by recognizing the supremacy of mind as the determinant of health and welfare. However, modern medical science and Western psychology are severely limited by their emphasis on physical determinants, and have not much to offer in explaining the impact of the mind and emotions on the body. But Yoga science has given us a detailed analysis of the mind and its various functions (*See* 2.4 and 2.5: Mind and Its Analysis I and II, *below*).

Negative emotions like fear, anger, hatred, jealously and frustration lead to stress-related diseases. A high percentage of our diseases is psychosomatic and their primary causes are our thoughts, attitude and beliefs. The way in which we react to our environment results in internal physiological changes that cause diseases. The practice of Yoga transforms the negative emotions into positive emotions of love, joy and peace. Positive emotions bring balance and harmony to mind and body.

Awareness: A Stream

Awareness is a continuous flow like a stream. William James in his *Principles of Psychology* (New York: Dover Publications, 1950) considered awareness as a stream, continuously flowing like a river, continuously changing direction.

Our thoughts are in constant change. Awareness shifts from one aspect of the stimuli surrounding us to another, to a thought of the past, to a bodily sensation, to a change in external stimulation, back and forth. The stream carves its own new path continuously. The more recent and precise analysis is that awareness is a simplification and a construction.

A similar characterization of awareness was offered by Swami Vivekananda. He compared mind to a "drunken monkey." The mind jumps from one random thought to another like a monkey. Saints and sages of ancient time in general have characterized consciousness in terms similar to those of modern psychology (Naranjo, Claudio and Ornstein, Robert E., 1972, pp. 190–91).

Turning Off Awareness

Practices of Meditation, chanting, repeating a *mantra*, counting breath, etc., are not exercises in reasoning or problem solving, but rather exercises in restriction of attentiveness. All the practices are aids in focusing awareness on a single object. When this is achieved, the awareness of the external environment diminishes and "turns off" for a period of time. Meditation is a practical technique. It uses an experiential knowledge of the structure of our nervous system to "turn off" awareness of the external world and to produce a state of blank-out or darkness, the "void," the cloud of unknowing. The techniques of concentrative Meditation are not mysterious or exotic, but are simply a matter of practical applied psychology. The studies made by psychologists on Yoga Meditation showed that during the Meditation and during the withdrawal there was no response in the Yogi's brain to external stimuli. In fact, in Yoga, the aim is to leave the "illusion," to stop identifying with the external world. (Naranjo, Claudio and Ornstein, Robert E., 1972, pp. 168–69).

The Classical Yoga literature states that a Yogi in a state of *Samadhi* is oblivious to external stimuli, but he does not lose awareness. The studies of Anand and others made in India in 1961, and of Kasamatsu and Hirai made in Japan in 1969 confirmed these classical hypotheses. (Anand, B. K., and others, "Some aspects of EEG Studies on Yoga," *EEG and Clinical Neurophysiology*, 13 (1961) pp. 452–56; Kasamatsu, A., and Hirai, T., "An EEG Study on the Zen Meditation," in *Altered States of Consciousness*, edited by C. Tart, New York: Wiley, 1969).

This state of insulation from the external world has some consistent after-effects on awareness. The meditator sees the world "fresh," and sees everything "glowing" or illuminated.

Ordinary Awareness: A Personal Construction

We normally consider that the single function of our sensory systems is to gather information about the world: We see with our eyes, and hear with our ears. Gathering information is certainly a major function of sensory systems, but they also act in a just opposite way. Our ordinary awareness of the world is selective and is restricted by the characteristics of sensory systems. Many philosophers have stressed a similar view, but only recently precise physiological evidence has been available. Huxley and D.C. Broad (the eminent Cambridge philosopher) have elaborated on Bergson's general view of the mind as "reducing valve." In *the Doors of Perception and Heaven and Hell*, Huxley quotes D.C. Broad:

"The function of the brain and nervous system is to protect us from being overwhelmed and confused by this mass of largely useless and irrelevant knowledge, by shutting out most of what we should otherwise perceive and remember at any given moment, leaving only that very small and special selection that is likely to be practically useful."

Modern work in psychology and physiology supports the same general view that ordinary awareness is a personal construction. If awareness is a construction and not a "registration" of the external world as normally assumed, then by altering the nature of the construction process, our awareness can be changed.

Sounds, electricity, light waves, magnetism, smell, chemical and internal electrical impulses, thoughts, internal muscular sensation, all constantly bombard us. How do we ever achieve a stable consciousness in the face of all this fantastic amount of stimulus?

There are two major ways in which we "make sense" out of the world. First, we use our sensory systems to discard and to simplify the incoming information, allowing only a few of the possible dimensions of sensation into our awareness.

Second, we further sort out the amount of information that does come along a very limited number of dimensions, out of which we construct our awareness. Each sensory organ is equipped physiologically to receive information only within certain limits. We would not expect our ears, for instance, to respond to the taste of sugar candy. Sensory systems by "design" reduce the amount of useless and irrelevant information. Their function is not only to gather information but to select and discard it.

There are thus similarities between the spiritual and modern psychologies of consciousness. Both stress that our awareness of the environment is a process of selection and categorization, that our sensory system serves the purpose of discarding much of the information that reaches us, and that we finally construct our awareness from the heavily filtered input.

The clear message of Patanjali's *Yoga Sutras* is that we, human beings, are not the mind, but far beyond the level of the mind. The true state of our being is covered by all sorts of wrong ideas, ignorance, distorting pressures of attachment, aversion, greed, anger and lust. So the first step toward the recognition of the Self within us is to withdraw from those things that delude us. When we achieve this, we achieve perfect alignment of our inner being and our external reality, and live in perfect harmony with all.

2.2: Yoga Psychology II

Integration of the Psyche

Modern psychology works toward integration of the psyche at the level of conscious mind. It tries to get in touch with the subconscious material, raise it to the level of conscious mind and deal with it there. But Yoga aims at the central core, and completes the process by which all the levels of consciousness are realized and harmonized.

Millennia before Freud, Yoga Psychology recognized a four-fold division of psyche into the mind, ego, intellect and subconscious, all encompassed by the Inner Self. (*See* 2.4 and 2.5 Mind and its Analysis-I and II, *below*). Yoga actually makes assimilation of the dark and alien contents of the subconscious easier by showing us the perfect Self from which it springs.

Purusha's Awareness of Mind's Modifications

Studies in psychology have shown that the mind is frequently modified by external objects even though it is not aware of them at the time. The recovery of such impressions later from the mind by hypnotizing the person is a proof for this finding. The modifications of the mind are always known to the *Purusha* (Self), because it is eternal (*Yoga Sutras*, 4.18). Only a changeless, eternal consciousness can provide a constant background for the continuous modifications of the mind. A cinema picture cannot be projected on a screen that is changing constantly.

The *Purusha*, being the ultimate consciousness, is aware of the mind's modifications at all levels. It is also aware of the supra-mental experiences through which the Yogi passes in *Samadhi*.

This is due to the fact that it is eternal, beyond time and space, and contains within itself everything that can ever manifest in the realms of time and space.

The Disappearance of Mind's Awareness of Itself

When Meditation passes into *Samadhi*, the mind's awareness of itself disappears. Patanjali calls this disappearance as "*Svarupa sunyamiva*," which means "disappearance of mind's own-form," as it were. (*Yoga Sutras*, 3.3). What is *svarupa*? Everything has two forms: An external form expressing its superficial and non-essential nature, which is called *rupa,* and an internal form constituting its true nature that is called *svarupa*. In the state of Meditation, the mind's *rupa* is the object of Meditation, through which the mind finds expression. The *svarupa* is the mind's awareness of its role. The awareness of its role steadily becomes weaker as Meditation deepens, and it disappears completely when Meditation passes into *Samadhi*. This means dissolution of the subject-object relationship and their fusion in consciousness. The perceiver, the object of perception and the process of Meditation become fused in one state.

Different Cognitions of the Same Object

Each object is a unique combination of the three *gunas* (*See* 1.9 Three Gunas, *above*), and has thus a definite identity of its own. Why then does it appear different to different minds? It is a common experience that no two minds see the same thing alike. One may find 'X' as a good person, another person may find the same 'X' as a bad person. The reason for this difference in cognition is the difference in the conditions of the minds which cognize the thing (*Yoga Sutras*, 4.15). As the minds are in different conditions, they naturally get different impressions from the same object. The mental body that comes in contact with the object of perception is not a passive or static thing. It is vibrating in all sorts of ways, and so the impression received by it is modified by its own state of vibration. It is, therefore, not possible to obtain a true impression of the object as long as the mind is not free from its modifications (*vrttis*).

Is there any possibility of getting a true impression of an object? Yes. When the mind is freed from its modifications, it gets an exact impression of the object without its own modifying influence. So this is possible only in *Samadhi* (*See* 4.18 *Samadhi: Meaning and Kinds, below*). When all the mental modifications have been controlled, then it is possible to know the object as it really is.

Even in our everyday life, we find: the more the mind is influenced by biases, prejudices and other disturbances, the greater is the distortion produced in the impressions that are made upon it by human beings and things. A calm and dispassionate mind alone can see things correctly as far as possible under the limitations of ordinary life.

Analysis of Suffering

Yoga Psychology has made a deep analysis of human suffering. Suffering is intimately connected to our negative emotional states. The Yogic analysis of suffering shows that we create our own suffering through ignorance, ego, attachment, aversion and fear of death. Yoga serves as an effective means of removing our suffering. (*See* 2.8 Suffering, and 2.9 Freedom from Suffering, *below*).

Freedom From Stress

Meditation is an effective means of overcoming stress. When the mind becomes concentrated on one point, the body becomes deeply relaxed. So when one regularly practices Yogic Meditation, there is a gradual change in the physiology of the body reflecting a permanent reduction of stress – slower pulse rate, lower blood pressure, etc. These have a positive effect on physical and mental health. There is no brooding upon anxieties and worries, and therefore the meditator becomes fearless and less anxious psychologically. Consequently the instructions from the cortex to the hypothalamus do not activate either the fight-flight response or the possum response. Moreover as one practices Meditation, there is, as research indicates, an increase in self-confidence and self-acceptance. The meditator's life becomes more relaxed and stable and more under his conscious control. (*See* 4.14 Meditation and Health, *below*).

Habits

Repeated desires, emotions and behavior lead to the formation of habits. A human being is a creature of habits. What we call the personality is nothing but a patterned configuration of habits. Habits may be mental, physiological or behavioral. They give shape to our dependencies. We depend upon worldly objects for satisfying our sensual desires. Our emotional energy is channeled by our habits.

While Western psychology has made intensive study of habits, it has overlooked the most elementary fact regarding them. Since a habit is an unconscious behavior, what happens when the habit is made conscious? As long as we remain unaware of the habit, it remains in the unconscious mind, controls our behavior and dictates our personality. When we become aware of the habit complex, the habit is amenable to modification or elimination.

Meditation increases our conscious awareness of our internal events in the unconscious level. Then we gain conscious control over the habits, and eliminate unhelpful habits.

Concentration in Yoga

There is a fundamental difference between what Concentration of mind means in popular usage and what it means in Yoga Psychology. According to modern psychology, the mind cannot be made to remain fixed on any object for any considerable time. Concentration is thus a controlled movement of the mind within a limited sphere. But according to Yoga Psychology, though Concentration begins with the controlled movement of the mind, it can reach a state in which all movement or change stops. In this ultimate stage the mind becomes one with the essential nature of the object of Concentration.

Yoga Psychology recognizes the limitations of the ordinary type of concentration. The first limitation is that in the ordinary concentration, the mind can never fully realize the essential nature of the object concentrated upon. The second limitation is that in this type of concentration, consciousness always remains confined within the prison-house of the intellect. It cannot be released to function at deeper levels through the subtler vehicles.

Tejas (Brilliance)

Our mind is a subtle body made up of various subtle vibrations. *Tejas* or brilliance is one of them. The developed minds of Yogis have an effulgent aura that can travel and affect those who are prepared to come under its influence in a beneficial way. That is how a strong mind influences a weak mind. That is how telepathy is established between a Yogi and his disciples. One who has purified his mind becomes a center of force. Weaker minds are unconsciously drawn to purified minds, because they derive peace, power, strength and joy from the greater force coming from that mind. For one who has underdeveloped mind, it is necessary to surrender to a virtuous and purified mind, because unless one surrenders, the higher mind takes some time to influence the lower minds.

Purification of the Heart

The purpose of human life is to attain Divinity that is our true nature. Only through purification of our mind we can experience it. There are various paths to purify our minds. They include the path of devotion (Bhakti Yoga), the path of service (Karma Yoga), the path of knowledge (Jnana Yoga), and the path of Meditation (Raja Yoga).

Bhakti. This means deep intense devotion to God. The devotee establishes a close relationship with the Lord. He adores the Lord, remembers Him constantly, sings His names, speaks of His glories, chants His *mantra*, prays and prostrates. The devotee makes total unconditional self-surrender, obtains God's grace, and eventually is absorbed in Him. In *Bhagavad Gita*, Lord Krishna says:

> "A devotee, who fixes his mind on the manifested Lord, worships Him, ever steadfast and endowed with supreme faith, is well-established in Yoga." (12.2)

Jnana Yoga. A jnani who follows the path of knowledge worships the unmanifested Self or Spirit, which is beyond time, space and causation, infinite, attributeless, eternal and indefinable. He is free from desire and aversion and so never thinks of harming others. He rejoices doing services to other beings. He is one with the Lord Himself.

Both worshipers of manifested God and worshipers of unmanifested Brahman reach the same goal. It is, however, very difficult for the embodied to follow the path of Jnana; for, it is very difficult to fix the restless mind on the formless and attributless Self.

How does a devotee reach his goal? A devotee worships the Lord with one-pointed devotion, surrenders himself to the Lord. He becomes an instrument of the Lord in serving others. He develops Divine qualities of universal love, compassion, selflessness, etc. His mind becomes purified, ego disappears and wisdom dawns. His mind becomes absorbed in God's name. He experiences God's grace, joy and bliss. He becomes one with God. "Blessed are the pure in heart, for they shall see God" says the Bible.

Self-surrender is the highest form of devotion. It brings about the destruction of egoism and the fusion of consciousness. The devotee submits himself completely to the Will of the Lord. His mind is purified and he ultimately realizes God.

Karma Yoga. It means selfless service. It is one of the means for purification of the mind. Desires, attachments and aversion pollute the mind, and also are responsible for our sufferings and bondage. Actions done with a sense of doership and for selfish purposes bring bondage and the consequent rebirths. Hence in the *Bhagavad Gita*, Lord Krishna exhorts us:

> "Without attachment do thou always perform actions which should be done, for, by performing actions without attachment, one reaches the Supreme." (3.19)

Performing actions without attachment or selfless service to others is Karma Yoga. Service to others is service to God, because God as the Supreme Self resides in all beings. When our selfless service is dedicated to God, work becomes worship, our heart is purified and eventually we experience the Self within.

Non-attachment

Concentration leads to one-pointedness, prolonged Concentration leads to Meditation, and through Meditation, the mind expands into the Superconscious state. This development, however, requires pure mind, mind without attachments and worldly desires. One who tries to concentrate while remaining attached to the worldly objects will either fail or his acquired power of Concentration will lead him into great danger, because he will use it for selfish purposes. For example, the modern human being has been able to harness the forces of nature, but his attachment to worldly desires has led him to misuse these forces.

Non-attachment does not imply renunciation of the world. One can achieve it while engaged in worldly activities, if Yogic discipline becomes a part of one's daily life. In the higher stages of non-attachment, the senses are under control, and the mind is free from desires, likes and dislikes.

Non-attachment to external objects is intended to conquer desire. It is a process of not requiring or needing anything. In its effect on awareness, non-attachment can be considered as an additional way to remove the normal restrictions on information input from the external environment. Another function of non-attachment is that one can be a pure mirror for external things, and can observe the world as it is. Non-attachment with perfect dispassion (*vairagya*) ultimately leads to Liberation.

Eternal Truth or Highest Knowledge

Yoga Psychology reveals that the mind itself has a higher state of existence, a Superconscious state. When a person's mind rises to that state, then eternal truth or transcendental knowledge comes to him. Sometimes one without an understanding of its science may stumble upon it, as it were. The Yoga Psychology says that there is a great danger in stumbling upon this state. In good many cases, there is the danger of the brain being deranged. One, who stumbles upon this Superconscious state without understanding it, gropes in the dark and opens oneself to hallucinations and some superstitions. So one must gain the Superconscious state scientifically by regular practice of Yoga. Ancient great Yogis had gained this state. It is possible for every human being to do so. Not only it is possible, but also everyone must eventually reach that state. (Swami Vivekananda, *Raja Yoga*, pp. 79–83).

Transpersonal Self

The Transpersonal Self cannot be experienced through therapy, drugs, study or intellectual discourse. It is already residing within our minds, but it can not be realized except by the practice of Yoga. The Self is pure Consciousness (or Awareness without any object), tranquility and eternal peace and joy. It is accomplished by absolute mastery over our senses and emotions.

The Self-realization is preceded by nonidentification with our body, mind, egoism, thoughts and ideas and attachments.

When the mind goes beyond the plane of self-awareness, it experiences *Samadhi* or Superconsciousness. In this state, Enlightenment dawns. The enlightened Yogi finds answers to the ultimate questions: whether there is an immortal soul? Whether there is a God? Is there any supreme intelligence guiding this universe or not? All these questions are beyond the field of reason. All the basic truths, all ethics, all our morality, all that is good and great in human nature, have come from the Superconscious state of illumination. It is very difficult to describe this state of eternal love and light, peace and joy (*See* 4.18 *Samadhi: Meaning* and *Kinds, below*). Personal experience is the only way to comprehend it.

When consciousness, in the state of *Samadhi*, has penetrated into the deepest level of mind, and then finally transcended even that level, the last veil is removed. It becomes totally free from the limitations of the mind, and it is only then its true nature is realized. In this state the knower, the known and the knowing all merge into one Self-illuminated Reality.

It is apparent that we cannot understand the real nature of the state of Superconsciousness by applying the ordinary methods of modern psychology. What is known as consciousness in terms of modern psychology is only consciousness veiled by many layers of the mind. In modern psychology, consciousness is studied through the physical brain. No amount of dissection of the brain and the nervous systems and study of human behavior can unravel the mystery of consciousness. The modern craze of submitting everything to physical examination may succeed with physical things, but no physical method can ever be successful in revealing the nature of consciousness that is of the nature of Spirit. The only effective means of knowing it is the practice of Yoga and directly experiencing it.

2.3: Yoga-An Internal Research

Research

Research is a search for facts. It is a systematic approach to seeking answers to questions. Man is a thinking being. Thinking is his distinctive nature. He is inquisitive; he is curious to know about everything. He wants to know what, where, when, how and why of things. Research is an important means for this purpose. By means of logical and systematic techniques, research discovers new facts, verifies old facts, analyzes their sequences, interrelationships and causal explanations and develops new tools for studying various phenomena.

The search for facts is made through scientific method. This is a systematic rational approach to seeking answers to questions. It is objective, precise, and it arrives at conclusions on the basis of verifiable evidences. Research is objective and logical. It arrives at conclusions on the basis of observable experiences or empirical evidences. Research has helped us to build up bodies of knowledge about ourselves, our environment and the universe. It is directed toward finding answers to pertinent questions and solutions to problems. The purpose of research is not to arrive at an answer that is personally pleasing to the researcher, but rather at one that will stand the test of verifiability.

Questions

We live in two worlds, one the external and the other the internal. Human progress has been made almost in parallel lines along both these worlds. The search began in the external world, and man at first wanted to get answers to his questions about the outside world.

Through his search in the external world, he has gained enormous knowledge about matter and the universe, the flora and fauna of the earth, the solar system, planets, stars, materials, minerals, energy, electric power, atomic power and so on. He has used his scientific knowledge for inventing not only useful things like locomotives, automotives, airplanes, innumerable gadgets, instruments, machinery, etc. but also destructive weapons including missiles and atomic bombs.

The ancient Indian mind, however, got all that could be had from the external world, but it did not feel satisfied with that. It had to fall back, and the search took a different direction altogether, from the external search to the internal, from matter to mind. The questions to which the Indian mind was seeking answers were so deep and fundamental that are in fact beyond the imagination of the modern people of the West. The Indian mind wanted to know: "Who am I? When one dies, what becomes of him? Is there God? Can we see God?" He sought answers to such astounding abstract questions.

We find in the *Vedas* some of those supreme questions asked by seekers, which were answered later by seers in the *Upanishads*:

> There was no sky, and no heaven beyond the sky. What power was there? Who was that power? Who knows the truth? . . .
> How arose this universe? . . .
> Who knows whence? — *Rig Veda*, X.129

The *Upanishads* of India are spiritual treatises of highest knowledge, supreme wisdom. They deal with great questions of fundamental nature asked by the disciples and answered by the great masters.

> "Who does first drive life to start on its journey? What God does prompt the eyes and the ears?"
>
> — *Kena Upanishad,* (1,1)

Nachiketa, a boy, asked the Lord of Death:

"When a man dies, this doubt arises: Some say ' he is,' others say ' he is not.' O King of Death, what is the truth?" (I.1.20)

"Tell me what you see beyond right and wrong, beyond what is done or not done, beyond past and future?" (I.2.14)

— *Katha Upanishad*

Bharadvaja, Satyakama, Gargya and other disciples who were in search of the Supreme Brahman approached the holy sage Pippalada and asked him:

"Venerable Sir, whence are all these beings born? (1.3) "How many powers support the created world? How many illumine this? And which among them is supreme? (2.1) "Whence is this life born? How does it come into this body? How does it distribute itself and establish itself? How does it leave the body?

How does it support what is external? How does it support what is related to the Self?" (3.1)

— *Prasna Upanishad*

The lovers of Brahman ask:

"Venerable Sir,
What is the source of this universe? What is Brahman? From whom do we come? By what power do we live? Where do we find rest ? Who rules our joys and Sorrows? O Seers of Brahman!"

— *Svetasvatara Upanishad*

Valakhilyas asked Prajapati, the creator of all:

"Since this body is like a chariot without consciousness, what is the Spirit that has the power to make it conscious? Who is the driver of the chariot?" (2.3) — *Maitri Upanishad*

The above questions show the supreme thoughts of the Indian mind in the ancient days. Such questions had prompted the ancient Yogis and saints to dive into their own minds in order to discover and experience the noblest and eternal truths. The giant minds of those sages have presented those universal absolute truths in the *Upanishads*, which is the greatest treasure of wisdom that have ever been made available to humanity.

Internal Research vs. External Research

The internal research is fundamentally different from the research conducted in the external world. Every research has certain requirements:

- the researcher
- the object or phenomenon to be studied
- a method of investigation
- a laboratory or a field where the search is made, and
- a logical technique of deduction or induction for arriving at the conclusion.

The external research, the research of a phenomenon or a subject in the physical external world, is comparatively easy. In the external world, innumerable issues are available for study. It is also easy to collect data for analysis; for, many instruments and techniques have been invented and developed for the purpose. The study may be conducted either in the well-equipped laboratories or the field, depending on the nature of the problem under investigation. For example, an astronomer studies stars in an observatory using a telescope. A social scientist may study a social problem like the problem of bringing up young children by working couples. He can draw a sample of such working couples, conduct a survey using telephone or personal interview or a mailing questionnaire, collect data, analyze the data and arrive at logical conclusions.

But in the internal research, the researcher has to study his own mind. He is the researcher, he himself is the laboratory and his own mind is the object of study. What is the method of investigation that is available for this research? The power of observation or attention is the only method available for this study. The knowledge of our internal nature can never be had, until we have first developed the power of observing what is going on within. This task is enormously difficult. Yet we know that we must observe in order to have a real science. What right has a person to say that he has a soul if he does not feel it or that there is a God within, if he does not see Him? If there is a soul we must perceive it; if there is a God we must see

Him; otherwise it is better not to believe. As Swami Vivekananda says "it is better to be an outspoken atheist than a hypocrite" (*Raja Yoga,* p. 10).

What is the stand of the people of today on this idea? Some of them, particularly the so-called "learned" people consider that religion and metaphysics are superstitious and all searches after a God are futile. On the other hand, some have faith in God half-heartedly, and some have mere blind faith. Their faith in God serves, though not for all, as a motive power for becoming good and moral and for doing good to the world. We cannot blame them for holding such ideas, because they are taught to simply believe in the words of ancestors. But a spiritual seeker or Yogi seeks truth, wants to experience truth for himself. The noble longing for truth of this internal researcher is as real as the longing for truth of a modern scientist. When the Yogi has grasped the truth, realized it, experienced it, then alone, declare the *Vedas*, will all doubts vanish and all darkness will disappear: "Ye children of immortality, there is a way out of all this darkness, and that is perceiving Him, who is beyond all darkness. There is no other way."

The science of Raja Yoga places before us a practical and scientifically worked out method of reaching this truth. It gives us a means of observing the internal states. The instrument is the mind itself. The power of attention, when properly guided and directed toward the internal world, will analyze the mind and illumine facts for us. The powers of the mind are like rays of light dissipated; when they are concentrated they illumine. This is our only means of knowledge. Everyone is using it, both in the external and in the internal world. However, for the internal research, the same minute observation has to be directed to the internal world, and this requires a great deal of practice. Turning the mind inward, and focussing all its powers upon the mind itself in order to analyze itself is very difficult indeed, because from childhood onward we have been taught to pay attention only to things external, and hence most of us have nearly lost the faculty of observing the internal mechanism. Yet that is the only scientific approach to the internal search for the ultimate Reality.

All the knowledge in the world has been gained only by the concentration of the powers of the mind. There is no limit to the power of the mind. The more concentrated it is, the more power is brought to bear on one point. That is the secret.

It is easy to concentrate the mind on external things, as the mind naturally goes outward. But it is not so in the internal research where the subject and the object are one; the mind studies the mind.

There is a power of the mind called **reflection**. We work and think at the same time. When we work, a portion of our mind stands by and sees what we are thinking. What a Raja Yogi has to do?

"The powers of the mind should be concentrated and turned back upon it. Then as the darkest places reveal their secrets before the penetrating rays of the sun, so will the concentrated mind penetrate into its own innermost secrets. Thus we shall come to the basis of belief, to the real religion. We shall perceive for ourselves whether or not we have souls, whether or not life lasts for five minutes or for eternity, whether or not there is a God. All this will be revealed to us." (Swami Vivekananda, *Raja Yoga,* p. 14). This is what Raja Yoga teaches us.

Saints and Seers have experienced the ultimate Reality through their inner search, intense practice of Yoga. What has been possible for them is possible for everyone else.

What is the Use of Such Self-Knowledge

First, knowledge itself is the highest reward of knowledge. Second, Self-Knowledge will remove all our misery. When, by analyzing our own minds, we come face to face with something that is never destroyed, and eternally pure and perfect, we will then have no more fear of death. When we know that we are perfect, we will have no more vain desires. Both these causes (fear of death and desires) being absent, there will be no more misery; there will be perfect bliss, even in this body. (Swami Vivekananda, *Raja Yoga,* p. 13).

2.4: Mind and Its Analysis I

What is our Mind?

Modern physiology has identified the mind with the brain. Psychologically it is called *antakarana* (internal instrument). This word is the same thing as *chitta* in Yogic terminology. The body is gross, and in the body is *sukshma sharira*, the fine body or mind. This is also material, only finer. The Atman or Self within us is the real person. It is the Atman that uses the material mind as its instrument. The mind, by means of senses or the brain centers called the *indriyas*, works the visible organs of the body like the eyes, the nose, the ears, etc. The sum total of all the *indriyas* plus the *manas, buddhi, chitta* and *ahamkara* is what is called the mind.

Four-Fold division of the Mind

From *mahat* or cosmic intelligence comes *ahamkara* or ego. From *sattvic ahamkara* or pure ego comes *manas* or the lower mind. From the *rajasic ahamkara* or active ego come the *indriyas*, the faculties of perception and action. From the *tamasic ahamkara* or inert ego come the *tanmatras* or subtle elements. From subtle elements arise gross elements that form the universe. The mind, as understood by Yoga Psychology, is four-fold: *manas,* the lower mind; *buddhi*, the intellect or faculty of discrimination; *ahamkara*, the ego; *chitta*, the mind-stuff. *Manas,* the lower mind, is the link between the senses of perception and action and the *buddhi* or discriminative faculty. It also transmits the orders of *buddhi* to the active senses. *Buddhi* is the correlate of the cosmic intelligence (*mahat*) on the plane of the individual. It is both the will and the faculty of discrimination combined. *Buddhi* sorts out the sensory input. When it arrives at a decision, *ahamkara* steps in and expresses that decision as a thought such as "I like this color," or "I wonder what has happened to him." All such mental activity takes place in the *chitta* or mind-stuff. It retains the impressions of the mental activity in the bed of memory. The unconscious is, therefore, a part of *chitta.*

Chitta

Chitta may be considered as the image-making faculty of the mind. At the deeper levels, the content of the mind at any time can be anything that occupies the field of consciousness and is called *pratyaya* in Yogic terminology. It need not necessarily be a concrete mental image. Our ordinary thinking is done through mental images. Even when we are engaged in abstract thinking these mental images are always present in the background of our mind and continue to change with the process of thinking. The mental images are formed through direct contact with objects in sense-perception or through the faculties of memory or imagination. *Chitta* may, therefore, be defined as the image-making faculty of the mind.

Manas

This is that aspect of the mind that underlies the succession of mental images. The mental images are always changing. A continuous stream of mental images is passing through the mind. *Manas,* therefore, indicates the dynamic aspect of the mind as compared with the static aspect indicated by *chitta.* Mental associations and desires determine the course that the mind follows in this constant change of mental images. In Yoga the change of mental images is controlled with the ultimate objective of inhibiting the change altogether and thus allowing consciousness to pass from one level of the mind to another, step by step. Then in the last stage of *Samadhi* the consciousness transcends the realm of the mind altogether. Every such step leads to the expansion of consciousness, and the last step leads to Self-realization or full awareness of our Divine nature.

Buddhi

This is the light of consciousness that illuminates the mental images. The mind derives its illuminating power from the consciousness that is present in the background. The power of perception determines what the mind can see. The permeation of the mental images by us is brought about through the *buddhi*.

Ahamkara

This is the egoistic center from which the light of consciousness illuminating the mind is projected. The egoistic center relates and coordinates all mental images passing through our own mind and our experiences into a harmonious and integrated whole. We generally refer to it as the "I," the pivot around which our mental life revolves. It is this "I" that is called *ahamkara*. *Ahamkara* is the seat of the individualized consciousness, the very basis of our life as a separate individual. It is through this center that the universal Spirit or *Paramatman* expresses Itself as an individual Spirit or Atman or *Purusha*.

Although the mind consists of the above four aspects, it is actually one unit. A person may be an executive in a company, a husband to his wife, a father to his children, and so on. But he is the same person. Similarly, mind is one unit with several functions. When it thinks and doubts, it is *manas*; when it wills and discriminates, it is *buddhi*; when it arrogates, it is *ahamkara*; when it stores the thoughts of the past and the present, it is *chitta*.

The Characteristics of the Mind

One wonderful quality of the mind is that when one of its aspects functions, all the others begin to function at the same time. When the *manas* is at work, *buddhi* and *ahamkara* work simultaneously along with the *manas*.

Another characteristic of the mind is that it always attaches itself to something. It cannot stand by itself and function independently. It is always dependent on a thought form, symbol, idea or image.

The Origin of the Mind

The origin of the mind is *Atmashakti* (the capacity of the Self). According to the *Bhagavad Gita*, the mind is one of the *ashtaprakrtis* (eight primary elements), namely, earth, water, fire, air, space, *manas*, intellect and ego.

Earth, water, fire, air, space (*akasa*), *manas*, intellect, and ego, these constitute the eightfold division of My Nature."

— (*Bhagavad Gita*, 7.4)

Our mind rests on the cosmic mind, and the cosmic mind rests on Brahman. Just as electricity is generated in a power house and flows into bulbs, so power from the cosmic mind (*mahat*) flows into the individual minds. The cosmic mind is very subtle, and it is in close contact with other minds. Everyone's mind enters into a conscious relationship with other minds. Numerous minds are linked in this way, and this network forms part of *mahat*, the cosmic mind.

Mind: A Subtle Matter

Mind is not a gross, visible, tangible thing. Its existence is nowhere seen. Its magnitude cannot be measured. It does not require a space for its existence. Mind and matter are the two aspects of the same Brahman. Mind precedes matter. This is Vedantic theory. Matter precedes mind. This is scientific theory. .

Mind is the subtle form of matter and hence the prompter of the body. It is made up of subtle, *sattvic tanmatric* matter. Matter is considered to be without a beginning. It is also without a cause. What is without a cause is eternal. So mind is also eternal.

Mind and senses derive their life from the soul that is self-effulgent. By themselves, they are lifeless.

The Seat of the Mind

Mind has various faculties and centers and operates through the corresponding physical centers in the brain. *Manas*, *buddhi* and *chitta* are in the *linga sarira* (subtle body), but they operate through corresponding centers in the physical brain. The brain is not mind as the Westerners think. Mind has its seat in the physical brain. It gains experiences of the physical universe through the vibrations of the brain.

Though mind is all-pervading throughout the body, it has gotten three places to reside during the three states of deep sleep, dreaming and waking. The seat of mind in deep sleep is heart. In dream the seat of the mind is neck. In waking state the seat of the mind is *ajna chakra*, a psychic center between the two eyebrows in the center of the head. (For details, *See* 4.16 Kundalini Yoga: Philosophical Basis and *Chakras. below*). Just note what you do in deep thinking. You hold your finger in the chin, turn the neck to the right side, turn the gaze toward the space between the two eyebrows and then begin to think seriously on the problem on hand. This goes to show that the seat of the mind is *Ajna Chakra*.

Mind and Atman

In the West the psychologists thing that consciousness is a function and attribute of the mind. This view is not correct. It is Atman only that is pure Consciousness. Mind borrows its light from its source, Atmán, the witness of the mental modifications.

The mind is an object of perception for Atman. Atman directly cognizes all the phenomena of the mind, viz., desire, imagination, doubt, belief, disbelief, shame, intelligence, fear, etc. Atman, like the sun, remains quite unattached and unaffected by the modifications of the mind. The underlying substratum of the mind, the source or basis for mind is Atman or Brahman or Absolute Consciousness. The power of powers that gives power to the mind, the light of lights that sheds light on the mind, the support of supports on which the mind rests in sleep is Brahman.

During dream you see splendid, effulgent light. Where does it come from? From Atman. The light that is present in the dream clearly indicates that Atman is self-luminous.

Three Bodies

There are three bodies that enclose the Atman or Self. The innermost is the *karana sharira* (causal or seed body). It is with this body that a Yogi passes on from one physical body to another, and it is from this body that the other two bodies arise, hence the name "seed" or causal body. The next body is the *sukshma sharia* or subtle body. It consists of eighteen *tatvas* (primary substances), namely, the five senses of perception (the faculties of sight, hearing, taste, smell and touch), the five senses of action (faculties of speech, the capacity to hold and grasp, the ability to move, to procreate and to excrete), the five *tanmatras* (subtle elements), the *manas* (lower mind), the *buddhi* (the discriminative faculty) and ego. The outermost body is *sthula sharira* (gross, physical body), which is linked to the total mind through the *prana* (life force). At death the physical body dies and the *prana* dissipates, while the causal body travels to different realms and is subsequently linked with another physical body. The physical body is subject to death, but the Atman is ever-existent. When, through Meditation, the stage of *Samadhi* or Self-realization is attained, the causal body also drops off, and the Atman merges in the Brahman, just as the drop of water becomes one with the mighty ocean.

The Mental Body

Just as the physical body is composed of solid, liquid and gaseous matter, so also the mind is made up of subtle matter of various grades of density with different rates of vibration. A Raja Yogi penetrates through different layers of mind by intense practice.

The mental body varies much in different people. It is composed of coarse or finer matter, according to the extent of unfoldment of consciousness connected with it. In the educated it is active and well defined; in the underdeveloped, it is cloudy and ill-defined.

There are several zones in the mental body just as there are various compartments in the brain for different types of thought.

Every person has a mental world of his own. Every one differs entirely from another person in mode of thinking, temperament, taste, mentality, attitude and outlook.

2.5: Mind and Its Analysis II

Mind is ever-changing

Mind is nothing but a collection of thoughts, and a bundle of habits. It is a heap of desires arising from contact with different objects. It is also a collection of feelings aroused by worldly botherations. It is a collection of ideas gathered from different sources. Those desires, ideas and feelings constantly change. Some of the old desires and feelings leave the mind as new ones arrive. This constant change does not in any way interfere with the harmony of mental operations. Only some of the old desires, ideas and feelings depart. Those that remain work in healthy cooperation with the new arrivals. This harmony sustains the identity of the mental existence.

Every minute mind changes its colors and shape like a chameleon. It is very wavering and unsteady. It evolves through experience. The world is the best teacher.

According to the state of one's knowledge, one's conscience is built up, and it changes from time to time with the correction of his views, in the light of new knowledge gained subsequently.

Conscience is one's own convictions arrived at either instinctively or by reasoning. The conscience of a child or a savage is entirely different from the conscience of a fully grown civilized person. The conscience of a *sattvic* person differs considerably from that of a *rajas*ic person. The conscience of a *sattvic* person is very clean and pure.

Functions of the Mind

Sensation, thought and volition are the threefold functions of the mind.

Thinking, planning, feeling, knowing are the various activities that are going on in the mind. Sometimes you feel. Sometimes you try to know. Sometimes you think seriously. Sometimes you will (volition). Volition brings all the mental faculties into play.

The conscious mind (*manas*) performs the function of receiving sense-impressions and forwarding them to the *buddhi* (intellect) for evaluation. While a portion of the impressions brought by the senses is studied and worked upon by the intellect, the remaining part passes into the realm of *chitta* (the subconscious mind). The conscious mind is ever-changing. It jumps from one object to another, one thought to another. The conscious mind and the senses of perception, together, constitute the instinctive realm of beings. If no higher function of the mind is revealed, one remains as an instinctive animal, and considers life nothing more than food and sex.

Buddhi(intellect) performs the function of analysis, evaluation and organization of the sense-impressions forwarded by the *manas*. This is a process of rationalization. It signifies a developed state of mind. After evaluating the sense-impressions, *buddhi* assorts, accepts or rejects them. It thus acts like a filtering mechanism, allowing the refined impressions to go deeper into one's being.

Ahamkara (ego or the sense of "I-ness") develops the sense of possession and arrogates all to itself. When ego's interests are involved in a process of evaluation, the intellect presents a quicker evaluation in favor of the demand of the ego. The ego of a person, whose intellect is not well developed, is gross and uncultured. It is unenlightened. Therefore such a person tends towards infatuation, identification with things that do not belong to him, and as a consequence, he suffers untold misery.

The fourth aspect of the mind, namely, *chitta* (the subconscious mind) serves as a store-house of the impressions that are processed by the first three aspects of the mind. The end product of the mental function as well as unprocessed impressions are stored in the subconscious mind. The subconscious serves as a reference library for the other three aspects of the mind. It is responsible for recollection, memorization and mental retention. In the practice of Yoga disciplines, it is the subconscious that plays the greatest role. Because a profound change in one's personality cannot be brought about, until the subconscious is overhauled, and its impressions are oriented.

The four aspects of the mind function in close conjunction with one another. For example, you encounter a shining yellow pebble. The eye-sense has merely conveyed to you the golden brilliance. But your "reason" joining with the subconscious understands and recognizes that it is gold. Soon your ego raises its head and whispers unto you, "Take hold of it;" and you assert "This gold is mine, I have found it. I will do anything to keep it;" and by chance the government comes to know about this finding, it is confiscated, and the impressions of your worry go into your subconscious storage.

The functions of the mind arise as ripples in the lake of the mind-stuff. Therefore, they are called *vrittis* or waves in Yoga Philosophy. If there are no thought-waves in the mind, there will be no perception of the world. All our experiences are sustained by different types of thought-waves. Every thought-wave is the result of the fourfold aspects of the mind.

The inter-relationship of the four aspects of the mind should be well understood. If the subconscious is filled with negative impressions arising out of the functions of the conscious mind, the intellect and the ego, it taints the ego or renders it unhealthy. A diseased ego creates abnormal attachments, craves for infatuated relationships, develops an intense desire for more and more material possessions, and it indulges in ostentation, hypocrisy and selfishness. It vitiates the functions of the intellect. The intellect, instead of evaluating things in their true perspective, serves the interests of the ego, and the function of the mind becomes perverted and may lead to the development of criminal inclinations. Hence the importance of purifying the ego through the practice of Yogic disciplines.

What Does Differentiate a Human being from Animal

An animal is not able to "know itself." It has only physical consciousness. It has no self-consciousness. An animal feels the discomfort and pain. It is not able to analyze its own mental states. A human being not only "knows," but he "knows that he knows." This is either mental consciousness or self-consciousness. The human being not only "feels" or "senses" things, but he also has words to express his feelings. He may think of himself as experiencing them. He can separate himself from the sensation of feelings. He is able to think, "I feel; I hear; I see "

In a public building or a factory, the guard strikes ten at the gate. The sound vibrates and passes into the ears of human beings and animals. The animals also hear the ten strikes. But the human beings count them and know through their intellect: "Now it is ten o'clock." They have gotten this special knowledge, whereas animals have gotten ordinary knowledge. It is the special knowledge that differentiates a human being from an animal. Hunger, sleep, fear and procreation are common to both, but a human being alone possesses intellect – the discriminative faculty to differentiate right from wrong, good from bad. He knows what to do, and what not to do.

Mental Perception

Sutras 14–23 of *Yoga Sutras* deal with the theory of mental perception. The three *gunas* are mutually conflicting in their natures, yet they are united in their modifications of particular objects. However, they are unified in different proportions, so they give rise to numerous objects. For example, earth, water and sun, in spite of being different from each other, through the unity of modifications of the *gunas*, give rise to a specific tree.

Though an object is one, yet different minds hold different attitudes to it. For example, gold is loved by the greedy, renounced by ascetics, and is seen as insignificant by the wise. In the unenlightened state there are many conditioned minds, and each one has become a limiting medium for each individual soul. Because of the soul's identification with the mind, it has become individualized and has entered into the world-process.

The objects are not under the control of a mind. If so, when that mind becomes enlightened, its object must vanish. In practical reality this does not happen, because when one mind withdraws its attention from one object, there are many other minds that continue to perceive the object. Therefore objects exist independent of the perceiving mind in an individual.

When the senses come into contact with an object, they bring the perceptions of the object to the mind, which then becomes modified into the form of the object. The Self reflecting in the mind causes the perception of the object. When the senses are not in contact with an object, the mind cannot assume the form of the object, and therefore, the object is not known.

The changes in the thought waves (*vrittis*) of the mind are perceived by the unchanging Self (*Purusha*). The Self is the witness of the thought waves of the mind. It is always aware of the mind and its modifications by reflecting itself in the mind. But the knowledge of the mind and its functions do not cause any change in the Self.

The mind is not self-luminous. It borrows light from the Self which is self-effulgent. The senses perceive objects by the light borrowed from the mind.

In practical life it is seen that a person is aware of his mental conditions through the experiences of pleasure, pain and the like, while at the same time he is also aware of the objects of the world. This proves that the Self which is distinct from the mind, accomplishes the task of all perceptions.

If one mind is considered as the perceiver of another mind, then this will lead to an unending series, for, the perceiving mind will need another mind to perceive it, and so on. Further, since each mind in this endless series will become the basis of one's impressions, there will be a great confusion in the functioning of the memory. Therefore, it is evident that the mind is perceived by the self-luminous and distinct Self.

Though the Self is free of actions and modifications, yet because of its identification with the mind, it is able to know its own mind.

It is similar to the sun's reflection in a mirror illumining the objects inside a room. The reflection of the mind causes the perception of the mind and its other functions; but the Self in itself is ever unchanging and eternal. In other words, the mind that has reflected the Self brings about the duality of seer and seen.

The mind is, in fact, different from both the objects and the Self. But due to the predominance of *sattva* in the mind, the latter, like a transparent crystal, is able to reflect the Self, giving rise to the illusion that the mind in itself is the Self. The mind also reflects the objects of the world and becomes colored by them, giving rise to the illusion that the mind is inseparably related to the objects.

Sources of Knowledge

Inspiration, revelation, insight, intuition, ecstasy, divine sight and bliss (*paramananda state*) are the seven planes of knowledge. There are four sources of knowledge, namely, instinct, reason, intuition and super-intuition (*Atma-Jnana*).

Instinct. When an ant crawls on your right arm, the left arm automatically moves toward the right arm to drive away the ant. The mind does not reason there. When you see a scorpion in front of your leg, you withdraw your leg automatically. This is instinct. Instinct is found in animals and birds. In them, the ego does not interfere with the free Divine flow and Divine play. Hence the work done by them through instinct is perfect than that done by human beings. Look at the wonderful work done by birds in building their nests.

Reason is higher than instinct. It is found only in human beings. It collects facts, analyses, generalizes, reasons out from cause to effect, from effect to cause, from premises to conclusions, from propositions to proofs. It concludes, decides and comes to judgment.

Intuition. This is a spiritual experience. Knowledge through functioning of subtle body is intuition. Sri Aurobindo[18] calls it supramental consciousness. There is direct perception of truth or immediate knowledge through *Samadhi*. You know things by a flash. In intuition there is no reasoning process. It transcends reason, but does not contradict it. Intellect takes a person to the door of intuition and returns back. Intuition is Divine sight. Spiritual flashes and glimpses of truth come through intuition. Inspiration, revelation, and spiritual insight come through intuition.

Atma-Jnana. This means Knowledge of Self. It is above intuition. It transcends the causal body. It is the highest form of knowledge. It is the only Reality. The goal of Yoga is to attain the Knowledge of Self.

The Power of the Human Mind

The mind possesses various kinds of powers and faculties. They lie dormant. You will have to develop the potential faculties by self-restraint and mastery over the passions. When the mind is so much powerful, what to speak anything of the glory of Atman, which is the storehouse of everything, which is the infinite, inexhaustible central magazine of power, knowledge and bliss from which the little mind borrows its light and power! Go to the source by Meditation and tap it. Rely on the Self within.

The important powers of mind are: power of perception, power of memory, power of imagination, power of judgment, will or volition and power to hold.

Perception. This is a power of cognition and knowing through senses like seeing, hearing, smelling and so on.

Memory. This does three things. It grasps. It holds. It brings to memory whenever a thing is needed. Though the grasping is done by the power of perception, the memory power also participates in the act of grasping.

Suppose you hear the sound of a bell in the temple. The memory power grasps it. Then it retains it. When you hear again the sound of that bell, it at once reminds you, "This is the temple bell."

Imagination. You have not seen the "Light Of Truth Universal Shrine" in the form of Lotus at Yogaville, Virginia. When someone who has actually seen it gives you a description, your mind forms a mental picture at once. This is done by the power of imagination of the mind.

Judgment. Power of comparing and contrasting, drawing inferences and conclusion belong to the power of judgment. This power has gotten two aspects: ascertainment and logical reasoning. A is mortal. B is mortal. C is mortal. All human beings are mortal. Mohan is a human being. Therefore Mohan is mortal. These sorts of drawing conclusions through inductive and deductive logic are done by the power of judgment.

When you see a river in full flood in the morning you infer that there ought to have been a rain in the catchment's area during the previous night. This is inference.

Will. This is the power of Atman, the dynamic aspect of Brahman. In Vedanta, will plays a prominent role. It makes one to think, speak and act. Intellect or the discriminative faculty of the mind discriminates, decides and gives knowledge of things. When a decision has been taken, will-power works out the decision through the senses and the body. The senses and body cannot work by themselves without the will stimulating and goading them consciously or unconsciously. It entirely depends upon an individual to make his will-power strong or weak.

Power to hold. This is really a part of memory. It refers to holding fixed and steady ideas on a specific thing. It is opposite to wavering nature. If we say "Shankara holds on to Vedanta," it means that he sticks to Vedanta alone. Nobody can shake him.

Apperception. It is the mind's perception of itself as a conscious agent.

There are many higher mental faculties latent in a human being. His mind is a magazine of power. The unfoldment of these latent powers occurs as a byproduct of intense Yogic practice. However, their unfoldment is not the real purpose of Yoga. It is dangerous to develop psychic powers without cultivating Divine qualities and gaining complete mastery over the mind and senses. One should not be sidetracked by the side shows. The ultimate goal of a Yogi is to attain Self-Knowledge, eternal peace and joy.

Developing Will-power

If you desire to achieve great things, you need strong will-power. Will is the energy of the intellect by which a thought is converted into action. Without will-power one cannot acquire success in any endeavor. It is the will that integrates the mental energy. What does insure strong will-power? Purity, subtleness, faith and devotion to God and one-pointedness of the mind generate and ensure strong will-power. A saint, a holy person, a person of good character and conduct and a celibate generally possess strong will-power. Such persons are quick in making decisions and implementing them. They enjoy peace. They do not swerve at all from their resolve. They wield great power, speak with conviction, force and authority. They are always truthful, straight-forward, chaste and unselfish.

What weakens Will-power. Will-power is weakened by impure thoughts, selfish and sensual desires, egoism, reckless sexual life, ficklemindedness, delusion and sickness.

How to gain Will-power. The following measures will help you to gain will-power:

1. By self-analysis find out your weaknesses and vices, and think about their consequences. Discriminate good from bad, virtue from vice and real from unreal.
2. Resolve to replace your bad thoughts, emotions and desires by good, noble and elevating thoughts and desires, and be firm in your resolve. As you think, so you become.
3. Replace bad habits by good habits.
4. Develop dispassion for undesirable things and momentary sensual pleasures, and thus purify your mind.
5. Cultivate systematically good habits.
6. Realize the evil effects of selfish thoughts and desires, and develop unselfishness.
7. Affirm to remove deep rooted negative thoughts and habits.
8. Perform your daily duties regularly, punctually and methodically.
9. Read good, inspiring and elevating books and biographies of great men and women.
10. Do not read erotic novels, nor see pictures and movies that appeal to lower senses.
11. Seek the company of good people and God-realized persons and serve them.
12. Avoid the company of the wicked and immoral people.

13. Do not indulge in gossips and useless talks.
14. Talk sparingly, but sweetly and usefully.
15. Practice silence once in a week.
16. Regulate your diet. Never overload your diet. Take simple, non-fat vegetarian diet.
17. Be patient, work hard and never yield to temptations.
18. Be guided by high, noble and elevating maxims, and act upon them with zeal and fervor.
19. Regulate your sex-life.
20. Maintain balance of mind in pain and pleasure, profit and loss, and other pairs of opposites.
21. Practice *mantra-Japa*, Concentration and Meditation regularly in the mornings and evenings.
22. Surrender yourself to God and leave everything to Him and make yourself a worthy instrument of God.
23. Never lose hope. Be full of high hopes and keep high ideals before you.
24. Be confident of your strength.
25. Make positive affirmations: affirm and assert: "I am not the body, I am not the limited mind; I am the Omnipotent Self. I am in all, and all exist in me."
26. Practice constantly self-discipline and self-control.
27. Watch the progress, and maintain steady progress in cultivating will-power.
28. Your future pleasure and pain depend upon your present thoughts, desires and deeds. Therefore, cherish always good, noble desires and thoughts and act righteously.

Purity and steadiness of the mind, strong memory and control over senses, and the gaining of gigantic will-power always go together.

2.6: The Mind and Body

Body—The Mold For Mind's Enjoyment

The physical body is the outward manifestation of the mind. Mind is the subtle form of this physical body. The mind contemplating upon the body becomes the body itself, and then, enmeshed in it and it is afflicted by the body. Without water a garden cannot exist. Without mind, the body cannot exist. It is the mind that transacts all business and performs all actions. The physical body is the mold, as it were, made by the mind for its own enjoyment, for the outpouring of its energy and thereby gaining different experiences of this world through the five organs of perception. The gross body knows nothing and is inert. Even when it is dissolved, the mind will assume fresh body of its liking very quickly.

It is the thoughts that make the body. Every change in thought makes a vibration in the mental body, and this, when transmitted to the physical body, causes activity in the nervous cells of the brain. This activity in the nervous cells causes many electrical and chemical changes in them.

When the mind is tuned to a particular thing and dwells on it, a definite vibration sets in, and when this vibration tends to repeat itself, it becomes a habit or automatic. The body follows the mind and imitates its changes. If you concentrate your thoughts, the eyes become fixed.

Face: An Index of Mind

There is close connection between the mind and the body. When the mind becomes tense, the body also becomes tense, and when the mind is relaxed the body is also relaxed. The states of mind are very conspicuously reflected on the face. Face is thus an index of the mind, just as the tongue is an index of the stomach.

The body follows the mind. If the mind imagines falling from a height, the body immediately prepares itself and shows external signs. Fear, anxiety, grief, cheerfulness, anger, all produce their impressions on the face.

You can read the uppermost thought of a person if you carefully observe the signs in his face, conversation and behavior. It needs some acumen, training, intelligence and experience.

The face reflects what is going on inside the mind. You can hardly hide your thoughts. Thoughts of lust, greed, jealousy, anger, revenge, hatred, etc., at once produce their deep impressions on your face. The face is a sensitive reflector of all the thoughts that are flowing in the mind.

Mutual Influence

The mind acts upon the body, and the body reacts upon the mind. Mind has influence over the body. A pure, healthy mind means a healthy body. Grief in the mind weakens the body. Body also influences the mind in its turn. If the body is strong and healthy, the mind also becomes healthy and strong. If the body is sick, the mind also becomes sick. A pain in the stomach causes depression in the mind.

Thoughts and Disease

The primary cause of diseases that afflict the body is bad thoughts. Whatever you hold in your mind will affect the physical body. Any ill feeling or bitterness toward another person will at once affect the body and cause disease in the body. Intense passion, hatred, bitter jealousy, corroding anxiety, fits of hot temper actually destroy the cells of the body and cause disease of the heart, liver, kidneys, spleen and stomach. Violent fits of hot temper cause serious damage to the brain cells. They produce toxins in the blood and suppress the secretion of digestive juices in the alimentary canal. They drain away your energy, vitality, induce premature old age and shorten life.

When the mind is agitated, then the body also is agitated. Wherever the body goes, the mind follows. When both the body and mind are agitated, the *prana* flows in a wrong direction. Instead of pervading the whole body evenly it will vibrate unevenly. Then the food is not digested properly. Diseases arise. If the primary cause of bad thoughts is removed, then all the bodily diseases will disappear.

Purity of mind means healthy body. Therefore, take care of your thinking. Always entertain noble, sublime and pure thoughts. You will then enjoy harmony, health and happiness.

The Root cause of All Evils

The false imagination that you are the body is the root cause of all evils. Out of ignorance, you identify yourself with the body. You become attached to the body. Then the sense of "I," "my" and "mine" arises. You identify yourself with your spouse, children, house, etc. It is identification or attachment that brings about bondage, misery and pain. You never wept when millions of people died in the war. Why? Because, there was no identification and attachment. But you weep profusely when someone in your family dies, because of attachment. The words "my," "mine" produce wonderful effects in the mind. Note the difference in effects produced in the mind, when you hear the two messages: "Dog is dead;" "Your dog is dead."

Pain is in Mind Only

Pain is felt so long as you connect yourself with the mind. When you sleep, there is no pain. If there is an inflammatory swelling on your thigh with throbbing pain, you do not experience any pain at night when you are asleep. Only when the mind is connected with the diseased part through nerves and thinking, you experience pain. There is no pain when the mind is disconnected from the body through anesthesia. During the moments of great joy, the severe pain entirely ceases, as the mind is taken away from the body, from the seat of the pain. If you can consciously withdraw the mind from the diseased part by concentrating it on God or any other attractive object, you will not experience any pain even when you are wide awake. If you have a powerful will and power of endurance, then also you will not experience any pain. By constant thinking of any trouble or disease, you only augment your pain and suffering. Pain is in mind. Atman or Spirit is blissful.

Homeostasis and the Discipline of the Mind

Nature has endowed the human beings with organic capacity to understand the world as well as themselves. From the stage of the higher mammals up to the human being, Nature has been developing and perfecting the mechanism of a built-in-equilibrium, thermostatic to begin with and homeostatic later, within the organism itself. Dealing with the evolutionary significance of this mechanism, the Bristol neurologist Gray Walter says:

> "The acquisition of internal temperature control, thermostasis, was a supreme event in neural, indeed, in all natural history. It made possible the survival of mammals on a cooling globe. That was its general importance in evolution. Its particular importance was that it completed, in one section of the brain, an automatic system of stabilization for the vital functions of the organism – a condition known as homeostasis. With this arrangement, other parts of the brain are left for functions not immediately related to the vital engine or the senses, for functions surpassing the wonders of homeostasis itself. . . .The upper brain is freed from the mental tasks of the body, the regulating functions being delegated to the lower brain. . . . . For all mammals, homeostasis was survival; for man, emancipation." (*The Living Brain*, pp. 16-18).

Relating this physical homeostasis of organic evolution to the mental and spiritual homeostasis of Yoga, Gray Walter concludes: "And once again, as new horizons open, we become aware of old landmarks. The experience of homeostasis, the perfect mechanical calm which it allows brain, has been known for two or three thousand years under various appellations. It is the physiological aspect of all the perfectionist faiths – *nirvana*, the abstraction of the Yogi, the peace that passeth understanding, the derided 'happiness that lies within;' it is a state of grace in which disorder and disease are mechanical slips and errors." (*The Living Brain*, p. 19).

The struggle to go beyond organic pulls and limitations, and realize the freedom of the Spirit in Self-realization, needs to be supported and sustained by a stable moral life; only when this base is secured, can a human being carry forward the struggle direct into the inner world and fashion relevant disciplines, and forge newer instruments out of his psycho-physical energy system, of which a steady mind and a pure intellect are the most important. "This results in a second homeostasis," says Swami Ranganathananda, a great monk of Sri Ramakrishna Order, "acquired by man with the help of his higher brain. This is called in Vedanta and Yoga, *sama* and *damạ*, discipline of the mind and the sense organs." (*Eternal Values for a Changing Society*, vol. III, 1987, p. 165)

Conquer the Mind

Most of the people have no control over their minds. Their minds are greatly under the control of their bodies. Their minds are underdeveloped; they live on physical plane mostly. Develop intellect and through it control the mind. The intellect is developed by abstract thinking and reasoning, by regular Meditation and study of scriptures. (For details, *See* the next Chapter).

When you have controlled the mind, you have perfect control over the body. The body is only a shadow of the mind. It becomes your slave when you have conquered the mind. (For details *See* 3.11 Pratyahara, *below*)

Health

Health is an essential basis for self-development and the practice of Yoga. It depends upon the conditions of both body and mind. "Sound mind in a sound body." This is a well-known proverb. Health is a psychophysical foundation for the soul to discover its true nature. The physical body is like a house in which the Spirit (Self) lives. So it is important to keep the body free from diseases and the mind free from worries and stress. (*See* 4.14 Meditation and Health, *below*).

The ability to use the instrument of the physical body for the attainment of Self-realization is the basis for real health. Of course, the laws of health or the rules of healthy living have to be followed. But in spite of following the laws of health, the physical body may undergo various diseases and afflictions due to Karmic effects and ageing. Nevertheless, the process of your mental and spiritual advancement should not be interrupted or thwarted because of the conditions of the body. You must learn to transcend the body and strive to develop spiritual strength to go up in the spiritual ladder. Promote healthy development in the body and mind by performing good actions and selfless service, cultivation of virtues, and practice of prayer and meditation. At the same time, maintain steady progress in spiritual development in order to attain eternal peace and freedom from the cycle of births and deaths.

2.7: Purification and Control of Mind

The Need for Purifying the Mind

Mind is compared to a mirror. If the mirror is dirty, it cannot show your face clearly. Similarly, if the mind is dirty and full of impurities, lust, anger, greed, etc., you cannot see the Self or Atman clearly. The impure mind cannot reflect the clear image of Brahman. Clean the mind through spiritual practice, Meditation, selfless service, devotion, etc. Then you will realize God.

The scriptures say, "Brahman can be seen by the mind." Here "mind" means "pure mind." Brahman can be seen by a mind that is free from desires and impurities. The *Mundaka Upanishad* declares:

> "The Atman cannot be seen by the eye, nor even by speech, nor by other sense-organs, nor by austerity, nor by work, but when one's mind is purified by the light of knowledge, then alone one can see the Indivisible by meditation." (3.1.8)
>
> "The subtle Atman is to be known by thought in which the senses in five different forms have centered. The whole of a person's thought is pervaded by the senses. When it is purified, the Atman shines forth." (3.1.9)

Brahman can be seen by a mind that is equipped with the four means of salvation. According to Patanjali, one becomes fit for Self-realization when he gains purity of heart, cheerfulness of mind, one-pointedness, and mastery over the senses. (*Yoga Sutras*, 2.41) These are the results of practicing *Yama* and *Niyama* (*See*, 3.4 *Yama* and 3.5 *Niyama*, *below*). Listening to the sacred teachings of a qualified *Guru* and reflection and contemplation on his words also contribute to the purification of the mind. When the pure mind concentrates through an uninterrupted practice of Meditation, then it will attain Enlightenment and experience the Brahman.

Restlessness of the Mind

Endless desires and thoughts make the mind restless, weak and polluted. They make it to forget the real nature of the Self. This out-going tendency of the mind, this restlessness must be stopped and all the desires and thoughts must be checked and controlled, if one wants to gain the real knowledge of the Self and real peace and bliss. Only when the water's surface is clear, calm and undisturbed, can one clearly see one's true reflection in it; but when it is ruffled or the water is muddy, one fails to catch one's clear reflection. Likewise until and unless one's mind is made pure, one-pointed and calm, one cannot get a glimpse of one's true Self.

Even the possession of fabulous wealth cannot make a person happy, if he remains a mere puppet in the hands of his mind and senses. On the contrary, one, who exercises control over his mind and senses, can remain peaceful and happy even without possessing a single penny.

As we think, so we become. We are what our thoughts have made us. The world is nothing but a projection of our own mind. Our weal or woe, pleasure or pain and everything else depend upon our mind.

The Impure Mind

The enemy of Atman is the impure mind that is replete with delusion and a host of thoughts. The mischievous and powerful lower mind is the generator of all pains and fears and the destroyer of all noble spiritual wealth. This impure mind is full of delusion, lust, greed and anger and other impurities. It will spoil you in diverse ways through the "enjoyment" of the sensual pleasures in this world. Destroy the lower impure mind through the higher pure mind. Destroy your instinctive mind through discrimination and the help of your higher *sattvic* mind. Then and then alone will you get eternal, infinite peace and bliss of Atman. Then alone will you become liberated while alive.

Sattvic mind and *Rajasic* mind move in diametrically opposite directions. *Sattvic* mind unifies. *Rajasic* mind separates and divides. Voice from the instinctive mind will mislead you. Purify the mind and hear the voice of conscience. Develop the *sattvic* part of the mind by annihilating the lower impure mind. Slay the lower mind through self-inquiry and Meditation on OM, and rest in you own nature, *Sat-chid-ananda* state.

How to Purify the Mind

Purify the mind by selfless service, *Japa*, *Pranayama* and other spiritual practices. As one iron shapes another iron, the pure mind can correct the impure lower mind. True, virtuous and pure actions, association with the wise (*satsanga*), speaking the truth, practice of compassion and study of scriptures are very great purifiers of mind. Pilgrimage to sacred places is also purifying. Pure devotion, lofty aspirations and all-embarrassing tendencies, all go a long way in developing the higher mind.

Charity, sacrifice, austerity, *Yama, Niyama*, contemplation, service to saints, all tend to purify the mind.

Mantra is a great purifier of mind. It should not be mechanically repeated parrot-like. It should be repeated with feeling and devotion. Then it produces wonderful effects.

Study of philosophical and spiritual books, right thinking, good and positive emotions of love, compassion and joy, noble endeavors and regular and intensive Meditation are means to cultivate the mind. These will bring about rapid transformation of the mind.

Just as a goldsmith purifies gold by burning it several times in the crucible, so also you will have to purify your sensual mind, in the fire of austerity, observance of silence, fasting, repetition of the name of the Lord, etc. Practice Concentration and reflection on the words of spiritual masters and the Upanishadic messages.

As a result of purification of the mind, it becomes more sensitive; it gets easily disturbed by a sound or shock. The greater the sensitiveness, the more difficult to tolerate noises or pressures.

You must do your best to get over this oversensitiveness through self-surrender to God. You must be sensitive and yet have the body and nerves completely under your control.

When the mind is controlled and purified, it will, like a pure and clean mirror, reflect clearly the purity, light and knowledge of the Atman within.

Control of *Indriyas* (Senses).

As the mind functions through senses, control of mind means control of senses. Senses are objectified desires. When the desires arise, senses are put into action. When the desire is fulfilled, the senses shrink through satisfaction.

Mind is fed by senses and it cannot exist without senses. If you have controlled the senses, you have already controlled the mind. But if you fail to restrain your sensual desires and allow your mind to be influenced by senses, you will lose your discriminative power and intuitive vision. In the *Bhagavad Gita*, Lord Krishna warns us:

> "Like a ship is tossed helplessly by a gale, a mind subject to the wandering senses loses its intuitive vision." (2.67)

Senses are mind's manifestations. The desire in the mind to eat has manifested as tongue, teeth and stomach. The desire in the mind to walk has manifested itself as legs and feet. If you control the mind, you can control the senses.

Eyes can only see. Ears can only hear. Tongue can only taste. Skin can only touch. Nose can only smell. But the mind can see, hear, touch and smell. It is the common sensory instrument. It is the power behind the senses. Mind is the substratum of the experience of all other organs. Senses cannot do anything, if the mind is not connected with them. When you are wholly absorbed in the study of an interesting book, you do not hear, when your friend loudly calls you; you are not aware that the clock has struck five. The mind was away at that time. It was not connected with the sense of hearing. The eyes may be wide open during sleep, but they do not see anything because the mind is not there.

Sister Senses

Nose and anus are sister senses. They are born of the same earth element, nose from the *sattvic* portion, anus from the *rajas*ic portion. These two senses are the least mischievous. They can be controlled very easily.

Tongue and genitals are born of water element, the former from the *sattvic* portion and the latter from the *rajas*ic portion. They are sister senses. Eating strengthens the reproductive senses.

Eye and feet are of fire element, eye from *sattvic* aspect, feet from *rajas*ic aspect (*amsa*). They are sister senses. Eyes like to see "sights." Her sisters, feet say, "OK, we are ready to take you to Yellow National Park, be ready."

Skin and hands are sister senses. They are born of air element, skin from the *sattvic* aspect and hands from the *rajas*ic aspect. When skin wants to enjoy smooth articles like silk, the hand says "I can feel through my tactile corpuscles. I shall get fine soft silk for you, my dear sister."

Speech and ear are born of the *akasa* element, ear from the *sattvic* portion and speech from the *rajas*ic portion. They help each other.

Our body, like a bungalow, has two gates, one for entrance and another for exit. Eyes and ears are entrance gates for the reception of forms and sounds. Genital and anus are exit gates. They throw out urine and feces.

Mastering the Mind

Scaling the Mount Everest, skiing on the Alps or exploration in the thick rain forests of Amazon is a big challenge, but these are nothing when compared to the challenge of trying to master our own minds. In the *Bhagavad Gita* Lord Krishna says,

> "Undoubtedly, O mighty-armed Arjuna, the mind is difficult to control and restless; but by practice and by dispassion it may be restrained." (6.35)

In the beginning stage, Meditation may not seem so hard. But when we get into the deeper realms of consciousness, we meet with the greatest challenge. The unconscious mind is like a treacherous jungle, where wild animals like anger, and fear roam at will. To bring the light of consciousness into these vast dark contents, and learn to traverse them safely requires enormous endurance and dedication and capacity to keep our attention constantly on our goal. But when we have succeeded in becoming conscious even in the depths of the unconscious, then we can exercise wisdom everywhere. The sincere spiritual practices transform all our negative thoughts. As Saint Teresa of Avila[19] puts it, it means living in the light that knows no night. Those who can do this are loved and welcomed everywhere. As Jesus put it, they are truly the children of God, bringing peace wherever they go.

We need a challenge that is worthy of our capacities. Making money is not a challenge, neither becoming famous nor achieving power. But becoming rich in loving all, and learning to return love for hatred are the most difficult achievements on the face of the earth. Every one of us can reach these heights through regular intensive practice of Meditation.

Guidelines for the Control of the Mind

Mind is so framed as to run to extremes. Through spiritual practice, it should be brought to a balanced state. It is one-sided by its very nature. It is through mental training that balanced development can be achieved.

Make a vigorous and earnest search within. Be alert and vigilant. Do not trust the mind and the senses.

Mind exercises its authority over yourself through the forces of desire, attachment, craving, past impressions, and habits. It does various tricks. When you learn to know its ways, it lurks like a thief. It will no longer trouble you.

To control the mind, you have to do the following:

1. Get rid of all desires and *vasanas* (subconscious desires). The *Bhagavad Gita* says,
   "A Yogi should renounce all desires that are born of egoistic

will, and should restrain the senses completely by the mind from all sides." (6.24)

"With his intellect held firm, a Yogi should attain quietude by turning the mind away from the objects of the world in gradual stages, by directing it to the Self." (6.25)

2. Control your emotions so as to avoid anger or impatience.
3. Control the thoughts. Always think of noble thoughts. "Whatever you ponder, let your aim be lofty still" says Thiruvalluvar in *Thirukkural,* a great ancient work in Tamil on the philosophy of life.
4. Control the mind itself so that desires, emotions and thoughts may be as little irritable as possible.
5. Give up egoism. It strengthens the mind. When you have given up 'I feeling,' how can criticisms, insults and censure affect you?
6. Give up all attachments to worldly objects by clinging to the lotus feet of the Lord.
7. Give up all expectations and prejudices.
8. Avoid the company of evil persons.
9. Seek the company of good persons.
10. Reduce your wants. Lead a simple life.
11. Do not argue. Arguing creates sense of hostility. It is a sheer waste of energy.
12. Do not compare yourself with others. You are unique in yourself.
13. Give up the idea of name and fame.
14. Surrender yourself to God and consider yourself as an instrument of God.

According to Patanjali friendliness toward happy, compassion for the unhappy, goodwill to the virtuous, benevolent indifference toward the wicked will bring about peace of mind. (*Yoga Sutras*, 1.33)

Your real Self, the Atman, is eternally pure, enlightened, free and unchanging bliss. Therefore you can never know your real

Self as long as your ego-sense identifies itself with the thought-waves. This false identification is the cause of all misery, anxiety, attachment, aversion, etc. In order to become enlightened, you must bring the thought-waves under control. When the lake of the mind becomes clear and still, you know yourself as you really are. You know that you are the Atman. You then abide in your own Self or real nature (*Yoga Sutras*, 1.3).

2.8: Suffering

Introduction

The Philosophy of Yoga is based on the hard realities of life. Those who are not aware of these realities can hardly appreciate the goal and the technique of Yoga. The Philosophy of Yoga is not an armchair academic philosophy that is purely speculative. Academic philosophy does not provide practical solutions to the problems of human life. No wonder the common person treats it with indifference.

In contrast the Yoga Philosophy deals with real and deeper problems of human life, and provides effective means for their solution. The ancient sages and seers who expounded this philosophy were guided by the spirit of scientific inquiry and inspired by religious devotion. They observed the phenomena of life and discovered answers to such basic questions as "Who am I?" "What is the ultimate cause of human misery and suffering?" "How can these afflictions be destroyed permanently?" They discovered permanent solution to the fundamental problems of life.

The philosophy of human suffering or affliction (*klesas*) constitutes the foundation of the Philosophy of Yoga, whose aim is to alleviate our sufferings. The system of Yoga outlined by Patanjali in the*Yoga Sutras* portrays the philosophy of *klesas*. The word "*klesas*" refers to the causes of human pain, affliction or misery. The philosophy of *klesas* is thus an analysis of the underlying or fundamental cause of human misery and suffering, and of the way in which this cause can be removed effectively.

In the the *Yoga Sutras*, Patanjali deals with the whole subject in a systematic and scholarly manner. The *sutras* in which this subject is dealt with are:

Questions	*Numbers of Sutras in Section II*
1. What are *klesas*?	3 to 9
2. How are *klesas* destroyed?	10 and 11
3. Why should they be destroyed?	12 to 15
4. Can the future miseries be destroyed?	16
5. What is the root cause of the miseries?	17
6. How can the root cause be eliminated?	26 to 28

The Causes of Human Suffering

Most of us are so caught up in whirlpool of miseries that we are unable to recognize them. The causes of our miseries are:

(a) ignorance (*avidya*)
(b) egoism (*asmita*)
(c) attachment (*raga*)
(d) aversion (*dvesa*)
(e) the strong desire for life or fear of death (*abhinivesa*) (*Yoga Sutras*, 2.3)

When these causes become active, they strengthen the sway of the *gunas*. (*See* 1.9 Three *Gunas*, *above*). Actually these *klesas* are not separate; one leads to the next. Ignorance is the root cause of the other four causes.

The different States of the Afflictions (*Klesas*)

The causes may exist in the dormant or latent (*prasupta*), feeble or attenuated (*tanu*), overpowered or interrupted (*vichhinna*) or expanded (*Udara*) state.

Dormant State. The dormant state is that in which the *klesa* is present in a latent form. It does not find expression for want of proper condition. For example, in children the *klesas* are not operative, and they exist in a latent state. They are awakened from their unconscious minds as they grow.

Feeble State. In this state, the *klesa* exists in an attenuated or thinned-out condition due to the practice of detachment. When an aspirant practices Yoga and makes some progress in purifying his mind, then the active state of *klesas* is controlled, and thus the *klesas* become thinned-out.

Interrupted State. In this state, a positive mode overpowers the negative without destroying the latter or vice versa. A *klesa* may occasionally be suppressed, being overpowered by its opposite, but it may come back again. For example, a person who has all the love and affection toward another, later turns out to hate him bitterly. When the mood of love dominates the mind, one sees nothing but all that is good and positive in one's friend; but when the mood of hate dominates the mind, one sees nothing but all that is bad and ugly in him.

In human relations, most people do not possess a deeper experience and study of minds. People who appear to be most loving and gentle may hide in their subconscious feelings of hatred and animosity; and those who appear to be hard and dry at the very outset may possess cooling springs of love and affection in their depths. Without a deeper study of human beings, one's life is constantly agitated by the storms of disillusion. Love and hate may alternate; pride and humility may alternate; and so on.

Expanded State. In this state, a *klesa* is fully operative and its operation is as apparent as the waves on the surface of the sea in a storm. In the expanded state, the *klesas* are manifest in their true colors without any distortion or restriction. Most people have their lives dominated by love, hatred, pride and vanity. They seem to be so lost in the external values of life that they continue to live a life of identification, of illusion, of ignorance. They do not feel the need for finding out the ultimate reality, and do not discriminate the real from the unreal, the eternal from the transient.

Burnt-up State. There is also an implied fifth state. When a Yogi continues to advance, and finally succeeds in acquiring intuitive discriminative knowledge that tears the veil of ignorance, all the seeds of the *klesas* are burnt up in the fire of knowledge; so they cannot sprout or become active even when appropriate occasions arise. It is in such a Yogi the *klesas*, like the roasted seeds, reach the burnt-up (*dagdha*) state. (*Yoga Sutras*, 2.4).

Ignorance

Ignorance in this context is not a mere lack of knowledge. It means unawareness of the Reality, and taking the non-eternal as eternal, impurity as purity, evil as good and non-atman as Atman. Most of us are not aware of our real nature. We are not the body, nor the mind and senses. We are the eternal, pure and blissful Atman. But out of ignorance we identify ourselves with our bodies, minds and senses. This illusion is the root cause of miseries.

Pure, eternal joy and peace are the nature of Atman. Our ignorance debars us from this awareness, but the dim, confused longing for happiness remains. So we are driven to seek it in the external world. We accept wretched substitutes. Instead of eternity, we cling to what is changing and impermanent. Instead of purity, we value what is relatively pure. Instead of true happiness, we cling to fleeting pleasure. But alas, our satisfaction is short-lived. Ignorance betrays us. Yet, as we turn sadly away, our eyes fall upon some new object of sensual pleasure. So the cycle of hopeless search, momentary pleasure, pain, disappointment and anxiety goes on.

In the *Bhagavad Gita*, Lord Krishna points out how the brooding on sense-objects leads to self-destruction:

> "By constant brooding on sense objects, attachment to them arises; from attachment arises desire; from desire anger is born." (2.62)
> "From anger arises delusion; from delusion loss of memory; from loss of memory reasoning is ruined, and from loss of reason, one is lost." (2.63)

Everything begins with the mind. When it broods over sensual pleasure, a series of chain reactions sets in. It ultimately ends in self-destruction.

Ignorance is the source from which all afflictions flow, and corresponding latent impressions set in the unconscious mind. It is a wrong perception. It is the opposite of discriminative knowledge. It is a veil that covers the Reality of the Self, and shows the ego as the all important entity in life.

Egoism (*Asmita*)

The ego is the sense of "I and mine." Out of ignorance, we take the body and the mind to be our Self, and consider the activities of the body and mind as our own. Speaking in terms of it, we say, "I am hungry," "I am black," "I am white," "I am sick," "I am happy" and so on.

Egoism takes many forms. They are ambition, pride, desire for name and fame, possessiveness, craving for money, wealth, position and power. All these lead to endless desires, restless activities, expectations, anxieties, disappointment, discontentment, stress and strain and consequent diseases. All these meaningless dramas are the outcome of our wrong identification with the mind and body. We indulge in ceaseless selfish activities in order to satisfy our egoistic desires and bind ourselves to worldly life and bondage and go through the cycle of births and deaths.

The physical body becomes a center around which are associated a number of objects that become part of the "I-ness." Those objects include house and other possessions and life partner, children, kiths and kins. Because of this sense of "I," "my" and "mine," each individual thinks only of himself. He feels different from other people and objects around him. Everything outside himself becomes subservient to him, to be used to bring happiness, comfort, etc. to him. In this way attachment and aversion arise.

Attachment (*Raga*) and Aversion (*Dvesa*)

Things or persons, that make a person feel happy, good or pleasant, and that inflate his ego, attract him. He develops a sense of attachment towards them. (*Yoga Sutras*, 2.7). Such attraction and the consequent attachment are the outcome of the latent impressions of pleasure enjoyed earlier.

Having lost the direct sources of bliss (*ananda*) within, one seeks it in the external world and is attracted to persons or things from that one derives some pleasure or happiness. Such attractions give rise to addictions and attachments. The fear of losing or actual loss of things to which one is attached gives rise to disappointment, anxiety and sorrow.

One may dislike persons, things and circumstances that make him unhappy or uncomfortable or threaten one's security and happiness. (*Yoga Sutras*, 2.8). Aversion also arises out of the misery experienced earlier. A sustained attitude of repulsion casts into the unconscious a subtle stream of impressions of aversion. Of course some objects or people might bring about feelings of likes or dislikes at different times, some might appear to be neutral; given the right conditions, however, these neutral things can easily turn into the objects of liking or disliking.

The likes and dislikes are similar to the two sides of the same coin. They bind us to innumerable persons and things, and condition our life to an unbelievable extent. Our thoughts, feelings and actions are prejudiced by these biases, and there is hardly any freedom left for us. The likes and dislikes are really the breeders of lower desires. They naturally keep us tied down to worldly life. The likes and dislikes are, in fact, responsible for much of our misery and suffering, and they disturb our peace of mind.

The two currents of attachment and aversion are caused by egoism. One's attitudes of love and hatred are based upon one's egoistic interest. When the intellect is impure, the ego, instead of expressing itself in humility, in surrender to God, and in compassion and self-dedication, arrogates to itself, and tends to identification and infatuation. Then one loses the glimpse of one's essential universality. One's identification with one's ego-center leads to the karmic bondage, and the consequent subjection to the cycle of births and deaths.

Clinging to Life (*Abhinivesa*)

Everyone, in fact, every living being, wants continue to live. Even one, who has lived for over ninety years and has nothing more to gain from life, has attachment to life. Even the wise is no exception to this tendency. (*Yoga Sutras*, 2.9). From one's attachments to objects and people and one's feeling of egoism come the deep attachment to life and aversion to death. This strong attachment to life is universal, and it is sustained by some force inherent in life. What is this all powerful force that seems to underlie the current of life?

How does the fear of death come to one's mind? One can only fear death, if he has died before. When the shells of a duck's egg are broken, the duckling makes for water and starts to swim. We may say that the duckling knows how to swim "by instinct." We fear death by instinct. What does instinct mean? According to Yoga science, instinct is a trace of an old repeated experience that has sunk down in the subconscious mind. All experiences are stored in the mind, and when proper opportunity arises, they come to the surface again. We have died hundreds and thousands of times earlier. We know well the pangs of death. Hence our fear of death. This fear demonstrates the experience of previous births and deaths. From the moment we get into a body, we love it so much, that we are afraid to leave it.

In any case, and whatever be its origin, the desire to avoid death and clinging to life is certainly one of the greatest obstacles to enlightenment. This is another *klesa* based on ignorance of our true nature. What is that dies? It is the body that dies, but not the Self or Atman residing in the body. Although the Self is verily immortal and eternal, the fear of death arises out of ignorance, i.e., the wrong identification of the Self with the mortal body.

The different *klesas* are closely connected with one another. They form a series beginning with ignorance and ending with the fear of death. Until the initial cause disappears, the subsequent effects will continue to operate in an unending flow.

2.9: Freedom from Suffering

In the previous chapter we have studied the five-fold causes of human suffering (*klesas*). In this chapter we discuss the methods of removing them.

How are Afflictions (*Klesas*) Destroyed

In Sutras 10 and 11 of Section II of the *Yoga Sutras*, Patanjali gives the general approach to destroying the *klesas*. The *klesas* can exist in two states: active and potential. In their active state they can be recognized easily by their outer expressions. For example, when a person is angry, it is easy to see that aversion is in full operation. When the same person acquires the capacity to keep himself absolutely calm through self-discipline, this *klesa* is reduced to a potential condition, but its seed is still there, and given very favorable conditions, it can become active again.

As stated earlier, the five *klesas* are not independent of each other, but form a series beginning with ignorance and ending with clinging to life. The process of the development of ignorance into its final expression "clinging to life" is a causal process of one stage naturally leading to the next one. To remove the final stage of this fivefold series, we must, therefore, reverse the process. That is, *abhinivesa* must be traced back to *raga-dvesa, raga-dvesa* to *asmita, asmita* to *avidya* and *avidya* to enlightenment. In this reverse process, each effect is re-absorbed in the immediate cause, and the whole series finally disappears.

Stages. There are three stages in the process of destruction of *klesas*. First, they are *attenuated* or *thinned* by the practice of Kriya Yoga. Kriya Yoga is a preparatory practice to Yoga. It consists of austerity (*tapas*), study of scriptures (or self-study) and self-surrender to God. (*Yoga Sutras*, 2.1). The mind of an ordinary person is full of impurities arising out of desires for worldly objects and sensual pleasures, attachments to them, and impressions of past experiences. So the practice of self-purification method of Kriya Yoga is necessary for the purification of the mind. Calmness of the body and senses is attained through austerity; predisposition to realization through the study of scriptures, and tranquility of mind through surrender to God. When Kriya Yoga is properly practiced, it purifies the mind and makes it fit for Yogic *Samadhi* (Absorption in Superconsciousness), and also attenuates the *klesas*. (*Yoga Sutras*, 2.2). When *klesas* become thin, they become ready for extinction.

The mere attenuation of the *klesas* alone is not enough. So long as they remain in "seed" form, the practitioner is not free from danger. Because when favorable conditions arise, the *klesas* can become active again. It is the unscorched "seeds" of *klesas* that account for the sudden fall of Yogis after they have reached great heights of illumination. Therefore the seeds have to be scorched and the potentiality of the *klesas* has to be destroyed. Then only the Yogi could be free from the *klesas*.

Second, the *klesas* are, therefore, *reduced to an unproductive state,* the state of roasted seeds through the practice of Meditation on self-discernment.(*Yoga Sutras*, 2.11). Discriminative knowledge attained through Meditation reduces the *klesas* to the state of scorched seeds. The *klesas* burnt up by the fire of knowledge lose the power of sprouting.

Last, the scorched *klesas* are totally destroyed by the dissolution of the mind. When the mind, through supreme dispassion (*para-vairagya*), merges in its constituent cause, it is dissolved, and along with it the *klesas* also disappear without any chance of re-emergence. (*Yoga Sutras*, 2.10).

How can Ignorance be eliminated

As explained in the previous chapter (2.8 *Suffering*), the root cause for the *klesas* is ignorance. How can this be eliminated? The practitioner has to regularly and effectively practice Yoga in order to attain Enlightenment. This Enlightenment or Awareness of the Reality destroys ignorance. When the sun rises, the darkness disappears. So also when the light of discriminative knowledge dawns, the darkness of ignorance disappears. (*Yoga Sutras*, 2.26).

Knowledge of Atman

There are seven aspects in the lofty experience of the Yogi who is established in the perfect Knowledge of Atman or Enlightenment. (*Yoga Sutras*, 2.27). They are:

1. The Yogi has known all that was to be known. "Knowing the One by knowing which we know everything" so declare the *Upanishads*. The Yogi realizes that source of all spiritual wisdom inside himself, the Kingdom of God within himself.Swami Vivekananda says: "After long searches here and there, in temples and in churches, in earths and in heavens, at last you come back, completing the circle from where you started, to your own soul and find that He, for whom you have been weeping and praying in churches and temples, on whom you were looking as the mystery of all mysteries, shrouded in the clouds, is nearest of the near, is your own Self, the Reality of your life, body and soul." The Yogi has known his Self. For the Realized Yogi, the world of the "knowable" has shrunk to nothingness. It is *Prakrti* that expresses itself in the world of the knowable objects, but when the purpose of *Prakrti* is fulfilled, nothing remains to be known.

2. Pain that is to be abandoned no longer exists for a Yogi. Pain, as we have seen, is caused by our attachments or aversions to external things. As the mind turns away from the objects of the world, when it is established in the Self, the attachments and aversions no longer exist.

3. The experience of the Self is the highest thing to be attained. Having attained this highest thing, the Yogi has attained all that was to be attained.

4. Having done the highest act of maintaining the unobstructed flow of mind in the Self, the Yogi has nothing more to do. This does not mean that he will do nothing at all. On the contrary he

will be very active, but without the sense of doership. He experiences inaction in action. He becomes *akarta*, the non-doer. His actions are not motivated by any attachment or selfish desire. He is freed from the fetters of actions.

He above four refers to the subjective aspects of Self-realization, while the following three refer to the objective aspects of Self-realization or knowledge of the Self.

5. The impressions stored in the unconscious (*chitta*) disappear, and the Yogi's mind has fulfilled its purpose of giving both experience and release to the soul. Therefore it is no longer needed to the Yogi.

6. The *gunas* have gone away to merge in their source, *Prakrti*.

7. The Self remains resting in Its own real nature. "Beholding the Self by the Self, one is satisfied in the Self," says *Bhagavad Gita* (3.17). That is, the Yogi has reached the final state of Eternal Existence. In the words of Swami Vivekananda, "The Yogi becomes peaceful and calm, never to feel any more pain, never to be again deluded, never to be touched by misery. He will know that he is ever-blessed, ever-perfect Almighty." He becomes the Liberated One. There is no more birth and death to him.

Why Should *Klesas* Be Destroyed

Klesas are the underlying cause of the *karmas* that we generate by our thoughts, desires and actions (*Yoga Sutras*, 2.12). Every thought, desire or action produces its corresponding result. Each human soul goes through a continuous series of births and deaths reaping the fruits of thoughts, desires and actions done in the past. During the process of reaping them, new causes are generated and they will bear their fruit in this or future lives.

Law of Karma. Everything that is experienced through our sense organs is recorded in the subconscious. Such impressions are called *samskaras*. These impressions will mold our present and future lives. It is the *klesas* that are responsible for the continuous generation of *karmas*. As long as the *klesas* are operating in the life of an individual, new *samskaras* are being added and there is no possibility of the cycle of births and deaths coming to an end.

The *samskaras* will continue to ripen and yield result in one life after another with its inevitable misery and suffering. The nature of experiences gone through by human beings in theirs varied lives is determined by the nature of the *karmas* performed by them. Virtuous *karmas*, which include thoughts, feelings and actions, give rise to pleasant or joyful experiences, and bad *karmas* give rise to unpleasant experiences. (*Yoga Sutras* 2.14). This is called the Law of Karma or the Law of Causation. This moral law is universal and governs worldly life. For every action, there is a corresponding reaction. If you cause a physical pain to somebody, you will get a corresponding physical pain sooner or later. The Law of Karma works with mathematical precision.

Contentment, forgiveness, self-restraint, non-covetousness, purity, discipline of the senses, wisdom, discriminative learning, truth and non-anger are regarded as virtuous actions. Amity, kindness, benevolence and charity are also virtuous actions. Anger, greed, violence, untruth and incontinence are sinful actions.

If virtue and vice beget respectively pleasurable and painful experiences, the question may arise: "Why not lead a virtuous life so as to ensure a happy life without any painful experiences?" This idea is based on a delusion about the very nature of the so called "happiness."

All Experiences are Painful

Nobody who has developed *viveka* or spiritual discrimination can possibly consider the so called happiness of ordinary life as real happiness. To him all experiences are either actively or potentially full of misery, because pains arise out of certain conditions as change, anxiety, habituation and mutual oppositions of the modifications produced by the *gunas*, which are inherent in life. (*Yoga Sutras*, 2.15).

Everything in the world is in a state of flux, though the change may be so slow that we may not be aware of it. People are afraid of death, but they do not realize that death is merely an incident in the continuous series of changes in and around us. Every cell in the body continuously undergoes change. The whole universe is a swirling flux like water running under a bridge. When the realization of this continuous change in everything dawns upon an individual, then he begins to realize what illusion means. What is permanent? Brahman or Consciousness alone is permanent. Everything else – beauty, power, position, name, fame, pleasure, happiness or achievement – is an illusion.

All worldly pleasures, indulgence and happiness are associated with anxiety, disappointment and fear. For, dependence for our happiness on uncertain and passing things in the external world means fear of losing them. If you have wealth, you always have the fear of losing it. If you love people, then there is the fear of their separation or death.

We acquire habits of various kinds and are used to particular mode of living. But our environment is subject to the law of change and we are placed in new surroundings, situations and people. No sooner do we settle down in a new environment than we are forced out of it. This continuous need for adjustment in life is a source of constant discomfort and pain to every individual. This is a major affliction of life from which everyone would like to be free.

Also as a result of the mutual opposition of the modifications of the *gunas*, everything is sorrowful to a discriminating person. *Sattva*, *rajas* and *tamas*, reacting on one another, give rise to tranquil, intense or inert experience. (*See* 1.9 Three *Gunas*, *above*). Every experience has the aspects of all the three *gunas*. So it is impossible to get uninterrupted pleasure only.

The five kinds of afflictions (*klesas*) are inherent in human life, and produce such conditions that no wise person can consider the so called happiness of ordinary life as real happiness. Of course, to the common human being immersed in worldly life, life may appear to be a mixture of pleasure and pains, joy and sorrow, but to the spiritually awakened wise person, the whole worldly life is a pain and its illusory happiness is a mere sugar-coated pill of misery.

Is It Possible To Avoid This Misery

Is it possible to avoid this misery inherent in human life? People, in general, may say that life is like that, and that one has to take life as it is, and to make best out of it. The ordinary pious person lives in the hope that tomorrow will be better. He resigns to the fate and bears the pains with stoic indifference. The orthodox religions say: "Lead a good life to ensure happiness after death, put your faith in God and hope for the best."

The stand of Yogic Philosophy is totally different from these ideas. According to it, death no more solves your spiritual problem then night solves one's poverty. If one is economically poor he cannot expect to get rich overnight. Similarly if you are poor spiritually, and bound by illusions and ignorance, then you cannot expect to become enlightened in your next life. You have to practice Yoga. It is possible to rise above the illusions and miseries of life, and to gain eternal peace and bliss through Enlightenment *here and now,* while we are still living in the physical body. If we do not attain the Enlightenment, the Knowledge of Atman, while we are still alive, we will have to come back again and again into this world until we have attained this goal. So it is not a question of choosing the path of Yoga or rejecting it. It is only a question of choosing it now or in some future life, a question of gaining Enlightenment as soon as possible so as to avoid the future suffering or postponing the effort and going through further suffering which is otherwise avoidable.

What Is the Permanent Remedy

The goal is not a temporary remedy, but a permanent solution. To root out a disease, we must go to its roots. What is the root cause of misery to be avoided? The root cause of misery is the union of the *Purusha* with the *Prakrti*, the entanglement of the soul with matter (*Yoga Sutras*, 2.17). This is the cause of bondage of the *Purusha* or the soul.

The *Prakrti* (the phenomenal world) is made up of the three *gunas* (*See* 1.9 *Three Gunas, above*). The perception of the phenomenal world is the result of the interactions of the elements (*bhutas*) and the sense organs (*indriyas*). The purpose of the phenomenal world is to provide experience and liberation to the *Purusha*. The *Purusha* is pure Consciousness. It is the ultimate

Reality behind the phenomenal world. Though it is pure, it appears to see through the mind. (*Yoga Sutras*, 2.20). When the pure light of the electric bulb in a cinematography falls on the screen, it assumes the form of the picture being projected. Similarly the pure Consciousness assumes, as it were, the form of the content of the mind. As a result of this mix up, the thinking function of the mind appears to be performed by the *Purusha*.

The wrong identification of the *Purusha* (the soul) with the body and mind is due to ignorance or lack of awareness of its Real nature. (*Yoga Sutras*, 2.24). When the Yogi reaches the final stage of the practice of Yoga, he transcends not only the body but also even the mind, and gets Enlightenment, then his ignorance disappears and he is released from bondage and suffering. Of course, this final stage of Liberation and freedom from suffering is reached by practicing the eightfold Raja Yoga regularly and intensively for a long time. (*See* 3.1 *Raja Yoga, below*).

2.10: References for Section II

1. Arya, Pandit Usharbudh, *Yoga Sutras of Patanjali*, Honesdale: The Himalayan International Institute of Yoga Science and Philosophy, 1986
2. Boss, Medard, *A Psychiatrist Discovers India*, London: Oswald Wolff, 1965
3. Brown, David P., and Engler, Jack, "The Stages of Mindfulness Meditation: A Validation Study."*Journal of Transpersonal Psychology*, 12 (1980), 143–92
4. Ferguson, P and Gowan, J., "Transcendental Meditation: Some Preliminary Findings, *Journal of Humanistic Psychology*, 16 (1976) 51–60
5. Funderburk, James, *Science Studies Yoga,* Honesdale: The Himalayan International Institute of Yoga Science and Philosophy, 1977
6. Garfield, C., "Consciousness Alteration and Fear of Death," *Journal of Transpersonal Psychology*, 7 (1974), 147–75
7. Geraldine Coster, *Yoga and Western Psychology,* New York: Harper Colophon Books, 1972
8. Goleman, Daniel, *The Meditative Mind*, Los Angeles: Jeremy P. Tarcher, Inc., 1988
9. Holmes, Ernest, *The Science of Mind,* New York: Dodd, Mead and Company, 1938
10. James, William, *The Varieties of Religious Experiences*, New York: The Modern Library, 1994
11. Jung, C.G., "Psychology and Religion: West and East," in *Collected Works*, vol. 11, Princeton: Princeton University Press, 1958
12. King, Serge, *Mastering Your Hidden Self*, Wheaten, Ill: The Theosophical Publishing House, 1985
13. Laurie, Sanders G., and Tucker, Melvin J., *Centering: A Guide*

to Inner Growth, Rochester: Destiny Books, 1978

14. Mascaro, Juan, *Upanishads*, London: Penguin Books, 1965
15. Naranjo, Claudio and Ornestein, Robert, E., *On the Psychology of Meditation,* New York The Viking Press, 1972
16. Nuernberger, Phil, *Freedom from Stress – A Holistic Approach*, Honesdale:The Himalayan International Institute of Yoga Science and Philosophy of the USA, 1983
17. Orme, Johnson, D.W., "Autonomic Stability and Transcendental Meditation," *Psychosomatic Medicine*, 35, 4 (1973) 341–49
18. Pelletier, K., "Influence of Transcendental Meditation upon Autokinetic Perception,"*Perceptual and Motor Skills*, 30 (1974), 1031-1034
19. Seeman, W., and others, "A Study of the Influence of Transcendental Meditation on a Measure of Self-actualization," *Journal of Counseling Psychology,* 19, (1972), 184–87
20. Swami Chidananda, *The Philosophy, Psychology and Practice of Yoga,* Shivanandanagar: The Divine Life Society, 1984
21. Swami Gnaneswarananda, *Yoga for Beginners*, Chicago: Vivekananda Vedanta Society, 1975
22. Swami Hariharananda Aranya, *Yoga Philosophy of Patanjali*, Albany: State University of New York Press, 1983
23. Swami Jyotirmayananda, *Raja Yoga: Study of Mind*, Miami: Swami Lalitananda, 1970
24. Swami Krishnananda, *Yoga as a Universal Science*, Shivanandanagar: Divine Life Society, 1983
25. Swami Narayanananda, *The Secrets of Mind-control*, Rishikesh Narayanananda Universal Yoga Trust, 1970
26. Swami Prabhavananda and Christopher Isherwood, *How to Know God: The Yoga Aphorisms of Patanjali*, Hollywood: Vedanta Press, 1981
27. Swami Rama, *Lectures on Yoga*, Honesdale: The Himalayan International Institute of Yoga Science and Philosophy, 1983
28. Swami Rama, *Path of Fire and Light — Advanced Practices of Yoga,* Honesdale: The Himalayan Inter-national Institute of Yoga Science and Philosophy of the U.S.A.,1990
29. Swami Rama, and others, *Yoga and Psychotherapy —The Evolution of Consciousness,* Honesdale: The Himalayan International Institute of Yoga Science and Philosophy of the USA
30. Swami Ranganathananda, *Eternal Values for a Changing*

Society, Vol. III, Bombay Bhartiya Vidya Bhavan, 1987

31. Swami *Satchidananda, The Yoga Sutras of Patanjali,* Yogaville: Integral Yoga Publications, 1990
32. Swami Sivananda, *Mind–Its Mysteries and Control*, Shivanandanagar: Divine Life Society, 1983
33. Swami Vivekananda, *Raja Yoga*, Ramakrisha—Vivekananda Center, 1982
34. Taimni, I. K., *The Science of Yoga*, Wheaton, Ill: The Theosophical Publishing House, 1975
35. Van Nuys, D., "A Novel Technique for Studying Attention During Meditation," *Journal of Transpersonal Psychology,* 3, 3 (1971), 125–34
36. Tart, Charles, ed., *Transpersonal Psychologies*, New York: Harper and Row, 1976
37. Wood, Ernest, *Yoga*, Penguin Books, 1973

SECTION III

3.1: Raja Yoga

Meaning

The system of Yoga described by Patanjali in the *Yoga Sutras* is *Raja Yoga,* the royal path. Raja Yoga is one of the major kinds of Yoga. It is as important as the other kinds of Yoga, such as *Bhakti Yoga, Karma Yoga, Jnana Yoga* and *Japa* Yoga. Raja Yoga encompasses the teachings from all the different paths. It includes various methods. It is the most systematic method of attaining Superconscious state through Meditation.

Raja Yoga is a Yoga of Meditation and also includes all ethical and moral observances, *Asanas* and *Pranayama* as its prerequisites. It is a comprehensive scientific discipline. It can be practiced by people of different faiths, backgrounds and temperaments. It is best suited to those who have a more experimental mystical nature. It envisages all aspects of human life: physical, mental and spiritual. The prescribed practices of Raja Yoga can be scientifically verified by anyone who accepts its methods. It is ideally suited to modern times whose hallmark is verifiability or testability for accepting any hypothesis.

Eightfold Path

Patanjali divides the path of Raja Yoga into eight stages. (*Yoga Sutras*, 2.29). Therefore it is also called *Astanga Yoga* (eightfold path). The eight stages or steps constitute a systematic path of regulation and control in a logical and natural sequence from the gross physical body to the subtler senses, and to the subtlest levels of consciousness. The eight stages or steps are:

Preparatory Practices (*Bahiranga Yoga*)

1. *Yama* (Self-restraints)
2. *Niyama* (Observances)
3. *Asanas* (Postures)
4. *Pranayama* (Vital Energy Control), and
5. *Pratyahara* (Withdrawal of Senses)

   Higher Stages (*Antaranga Yoga*)

6. *Dharana* (Concentration)
7. *Dhyana* (Meditation)
8. *Samadhi* (Absorption or Superconscious State)

> The three-fold higher process of Concentration, Meditation and *Samadhi*, by which the true nature of an object is known is called *Samyama*. (*Yoga Sutras*, 3.4).

The above eight-steps will be described briefly here, and in succeeding Chapters they will be discussed separately in detail.

The first five stages, though not directly connected with Meditation, are of the utmost importance, for they prepare an aspirant's mind and body for the higher stages. Without some practice of the first five stages, most people may not be successful in Meditation. The first five stages constitute the means for overcoming the obstacles to Meditation. They will mold a person's character in the way necessary for spiritual progress. Of course some people will be able to meditate without even knowing the existence of those stages, but they are the few lucky people who have no mental or physical obstacles, and who from birth have been inclined to looking inward and toward the Meditational way of life.

It becomes easier to practice the higher three stages when the preliminary steps have been practiced to a reasonable degree of perfection. The reason for this is that most of us are totally unable to concentrate and meditate because of the continuous wandering of the mind. Only a person with a tranquil mind can be able to meditate.

The types of *disturbances* that prevent Concentration and Meditation are:

(a) *Emotional disturbances* arising out of mental conflicts and imperfections. These are eliminated or at least reduced by practicing the *Yamas* and *Niyamas* (stages 1 and 2).

(b) *Physical discomforts,* such as pain, illness and uncomfortable Posture. These are removed by practicing *Asanas* (stage 3).

(c) *Irregularities in the pranic flow* in the body, which cause disturbances. The technique of *Pranayama* (stage 4) corrects such irregularities.

(d) *Outside distractions,* such as sound, which cause mental disturbance. How is it possible to perform the inner techniques when our mind is absorbed and continually distracted by the outside environment? *Pratyahara* (stage 5) eliminates this source of disturbance by disconnecting the association of the sense organs, eyes, ears, etc. with external happenings. The outer occurrences are still there, of course, but the sense organs no longer send messages to the mind or the mind does not become aware of them.

One can now realize how important the first five stages are in order to practice successfully the higher stages. Without cultivating them, the practitioner will be unable to reach the higher stages.

Yama and *Niyama*

These first two steps consist of ten commitments of Yoga. The *five Yamas* (Restraints) are non-violence, truthfulness, non-stealing, continence, and non-possessiveness. Their practice leads to behavioral modifications and replacement of imperfections by virtues. The five *Niyamas* (Observances) are cleanliness or purity, contentment, austerity (*tapas*), self-study and surrender to God. The *Yamas* and *Niyamas* involve moral training without which no practice of Yoga will be successful.

The beginner should not be discouraged by the immensity of these first two steps of Raja Yoga. He is not expected to perfect the practice of *Yama*s and *Niyama*s before proceeding further, but he should try to practice them as conscientiously as he can. With persistent effort he will eventually be able to perfect them. In the West in Yoga centers, in general, *Asanas* and Breathing Exercises only are taught. The *Yama*s and *Niyama*s are usually neglected, because of the difficulties they entail and the changes of life style that are necessary to practice them. It is true that *Asanas* and Breathing Exercises ensure physical health, but their full benefits can be realized only when the mind is purified and becomes steady and tranquil by practicing the *Yama*s and *Niyama*s.

Asanas

The third step in Raja Yoga is *Asanas* or Postures. There are two types: Meditative Postures and *Asanas* for physical well-being. A steady Meditative Posture leads gradually to a stable mind. A Posture suitable for Meditation should be comfortable and stable, ensuring that the head, neck and chest be erect and in a straight line.

The second kind of Postures is practiced to perfect the body, making it supple and free from disease. These Postures control specific muscles and nerves and hence have therapeutic benefits.

Pranayama

This is the fourth step of Raja Yoga. It means control of *prana*, the vital energy that sustains the body and mind. The grossest manifestation of *prana* is the breath, so *Pranayama* is also called the science of breathing. Regulation of breath leads to regulation of the mind. It also purifies and strengthens the nervous system.

Pratyahara

It means withdrawal and control of the senses. The mind contacts the objects of the world through the five senses of sight, hearing, touch, taste and smell. These sensual experiences set the mind to wandering. The aspirant should therefore acquire the ability to voluntarily draw the senses inward and thus isolate himself from the distractions of the world outside.

Dharana

Dharana or Concentration is the sixth step in Raja Yoga. In Concentration the dissipated powers of the mind are gathered together and directed towards the object of Concentration through continued voluntary attention. Through Concentration the diffused mind is focused and hence made more powerful and penetrative.

Dhyana

Prolonged, unbroken Concentration leads to *Dhyana* or state of Meditation that is the seventh step in Raja Yoga. Concentration makes the mind one-pointed and steady. Meditation expands the focused mind to the Superconscious state by piercing through its conscious and subconscious levels. All methods of Yoga prepare one to reach the stage of Meditation, for only through Meditation can one reach the level of the Superconscious mind and hence attain perfection. Meditation alone can take one to this blissful state of mind. It is possible to attain that state only through persistent and intensive practice. Modern education is superficial, one-sided. It does not help one to know, develop and control one's internal states. Meditation alone can help us to do this. We then become aware of our latent powers and become more creative and dynamic.

Samadhi

Prolonged and deep Meditation leads to the last stage of Raja Yoga, the state of *Samadhi* or Superconscious state. In this state one becomes One with the Divine Self (*Paramatman*) and transcends all imperfections and limitations.

The physical sciences are based on sense perceptions that are interpreted by the rational faculty. Sense perceptions and rationality, however, are limited by time, space and causation. They do not give us a complete understanding of the various forces shaping us and the universe. Yoga science is the soul of all sciences. It solves the basic problems of modern people. It is definite and systematic and it leads one to the highest source of knowledge, intuitive knowledge that reveals the true nature of us.

The teachings of Yoga have been handed down to us from the ancient Yogis of India. A sincere aspirant who follows these teachings can reach the ultimate state and experience the infinite consciousness. He can discover for himself his true nature, the Atman or Brahman within.

3.2: Guru or Teacher

Who is a Guru

The practice of Yoga, like a craft, requires the guidance of a *Guru* or teacher. The word *Guru* is made up of two syllables: "*gu*" and "*ru*." *Gu* means the darkness of ignorance; *ru* means one who dispels. So *Guru* means "one who dispels your ignorance." He is one who helps you in realizing your own Spirit or Atman by removing the ignorance that veils it.

The Need for a Guru

Right from birth we learn through the help of somebody. For a baby the mother is the first *Guru*. It is through her the baby knows its father. The Hindu scriptures say that everyone has four *Gurus: mata* (mother), *pita* (father), *Guru* (spiritual guide) and *Deva* (God). First, the mother shows you the father; then, the father takes you to the *Guru*; and finally the *Guru* takes you to God.

Even for acquiring worldly knowledge, we take the help of many teachers. The need for a *Guru* is much more in the spiritual life, because the spiritual life is much more subtle and deeper.

One may read a lot of books on Yoga and spiritual life, but books can never take the place of a *Guru*. If we could know every thing through books, there would be only publishing houses and no universities and ashrams. Books have information, and you can read them, but they cannot teach you. When you read a book, you may understand or misunderstand what you read. This depends upon your background, level of knowledge and comprehension. But a *Guru* will not allow you to misunderstand. The moment he finds that you have not understood something correctly, he will correct you and also clarify your doubts. A book cannot do that. That is why you need a person who has gone through the path and realized the goal to guide you in treading the spiritual path. Therefore a spiritual teacher is essential. Yoga is not a theory but a practical system. You can learn its subtle aspects only through a spiritual guide.

The ultimate Truth can be revealed only by somebody who has experienced it. No candle can light itself; another lit candle must come and touch it. That is the way Truth passes from the *Guru* to the disciple. The *Guru* shows the path and also the pitfalls on the path, and shows how to overcome them.

A *Guru* is absolutely necessary for every aspirant in the spiritual path. It is only the *Guru* who finds out your defects. The nature of egoism is such that you will not be able to find out your own defects. Just as a person cannot see his back, so also he cannot see his own errors. He must live with a *Guru* for the eradication of his evil qualities and defects.

An aspirant who is under the guidance of a *Guru* is safe from being led astray. The association with *Guru* is an armor and fortress to guard him against all temptations and unfavorable forces of the material world.

Cases of those who had attained perfection without studying under any *Guru* should not be cited as an authority against the necessity for a *Guru*; for , such great people are anomalies of spiritual life and not the common normality. They came into the world after reaching greater heights in their Yogic practices in their earlier births.

Spiritual development needs an impulse to action. The quickening impulse must come from another soul, the *Guru*. The soul from which it comes must possess the power of transmitting it to another; and the disciple to whom it is transmitted must be fit to receive it. Then alone, the spiritual growth will come.

How to Recognize the Guru

In these days there are many Yogis who claim to be perfect masters, and it is not easy to identify a true *Guru* from the many impostors.

In the *Kularnava Tantra,* Lord Shiva says,

> "Many are the *gurus* who are like lamps in homes, But rare is the *Guru* who illumines all like the sun. Many are the *gurus* who are learned in the *Vedas* and the scriptures, But rare is the *Guru* who has attained the Supreme Truth."

If one looks for a medical doctor, lawyer, psychiatrist or any other professional, then he can scan through the yellow pages in a telephone directory. But an aspirant cannot do so to identify a true *Guru*. He should prepare himself by developing mental capacities. When he starts discriminating between right and wrong, and between real and unreal, he will be able to know the true teacher. The *Upanishads*, the ancient Yogic scriptures, state that when the disciple is ready, the *Guru* appears. This means that when an aspirant has longing for Divine wisdom, he will receive Divine help sooner or later.

Mysterious Divine Help

For a sincere aspirant help comes in a mysterious manner. Eknath (sixteenth century) heard a voice from the sky. It said, "See Janardan Pant at Deva Giri. He will put you in the proper path and guide you." He acted accordingly and found his *Guru*. Tukaram (seventeenth century) received his *mantra* "Rama Krishna Hari" in his dream. He repeated this *mantra* and had the *darsana* (vision) of Lord Krishna. Lord Krishna directed Namadev (thirteenth century) to get higher initiation from a Sannyasin at Mallikarjuna. Queen Chudalai assumed the form of Kumbha Muni, appeared before her spouse Sikhidvaja in the forest, and initiated him into the mysteries of *Kaivalya* (Liberation). Madhura Kavi saw a light in the firmament for three days consecutively. It guided him and took him to his *Guru* Nammalvar who was sitting in his *Samadhi* underneath a tamarind tree near Tirunelveli in South India. Tulasidas (sixteenth century) received instruction from an invisible being to see Hanuman and, through Hanuman, to get the Vision of Sri Rama.

The sun requires no torch to make it visible; we do not light a candle to see the sun; when the sun rises we instinctively become aware of its rising. Similarly when a *Guru* comes to help us, the soul instinctively knows that it has found the truth. In the words of Swami Vivekananda, "Truth stands on its evidence; it does not require any other testimony to attest it; it is self-effulgent." Such are the very great teachers; we can get help from the lesser teachers also. How are we to know such a person? We must see what he is and not what he appears. How are we to know what he is?

The Qualities of a True Guru

Who is a true *Guru*? What are his qualities? How can you recognize him? In fact in the *Bhagavad Gita*, Arjuna (the disciple) asks Lord Krishna (the *Guru*) the very same questions, though using a slightly different word instead of "*Guru*;" he asks,

> "O Krishna, what are the characteristics of the sage of steady wisdom who is established in the superconscious state? How does he sit, How does he speak? How does he walk?" (2.54)

A *Guru* is a sage of steady wisdom (*stithapragnyam*), one who has attained Self-realization. He is an enlightened person. How would you recognize him? It is indeed very difficult to recognize a *Guru*, because in outward appearance, he looks like any other person. So by looking at his physical body, you cannot recognize him. Look at his qualities.

Lord Krishna describes his qualities in the verses: 2.55 to 2.57 of *Bhagavad Gita*. The Self-realized sage of steady wisdom is one who has renounced all the desires and is satisfied in the truth of Self. He is not perturbed by adversity. He does not crave for pleasure. He is free from attachment, fear and anger. He is poised in wisdom. He is neither delighted at receiving good nor hates pain. He is, like the ocean, totally contented. He has no wants. As he realized that the ever-changing external world is unreal and that the eternal Atman alone is real, the objects of the world have no value to him. The sage has withdrawn his senses from sense-objects. The *Guru Gita* says that a fully enlightened being is *brahmanandam*, the bliss of the Absolute; *paramasukhandam,* the giver of happiness at all times; and *kevalam jnamurtim,* the embodiment of knowledge, the embodiment of the Truth.

How does the sage of steady wisdom conducts himself? What is his behavior? The self-controlled sage, though moving among the sense-objects, is free from attraction and repulsion. His mind remains calm and balanced. He has no sorrow and anxiety. His peaceful mind is full of bliss. As his senses are under control, his wisdom is steady. What is real to the worldly minded is illusion to the sage. He lives in the Self, unaware of the world. (*Gita,* 2.64 - 65; 2.68-69).

The ocean never wants anything. It never sends invitations to the rivers. The ocean is just there. The rivers fall in love with the ocean and run headlong toward it and enter into it from all sides. But the ocean does not swell up. In the same way, the steady minded sage remains unmoved even when every thing comes to him. (*Bhagavad Gita*, 2.70).

How does a sage of steady wisdom look at things? He looks with equal vision at a brahmin endowed with knowledge and humility, a cow, an elephant, a dog and an outcast. (*Gita*, 5.18). That is, he is totally impartial. He does not make distinctions like ordinary people who differentiate others in terms of language, skin, color, caste, and country. But like Nature or God, a steady-minded sage has equal vision (*samadarshinam*). He has a balanced mind toward well-wishers, friends, enemies, the indifferent, the impartial, the hateful, relatives, saints as well as sinners. (*Gita,* 6.9). To him a clod of earth, a stone and a piece of gold are the same (*Gita*, 6.8).

A realized sage hates none, is friendly and compassionate to all, free from the feeling of "I" and "mine," and is balanced in pairs of opposites: pleasure and pain, cold and heat, honor and dishonor (*Gita*, 6.7, 12.13 and 12.18). He is ever-contented and self-controlled. He is free from joy, envy, fear and anxiety. He neither becomes excited nor depressed. (*Gita,* 12.15).

He is *Satchidananda* (Existence-Knowledge-Bliss) at all times. Nothing will shake him. He neither rejoices, nor hates, nor desires, as he has renounced both good and evil. (*Gita*, 12.17). A realized *Guru* possesses all the above qualities.

A true teacher is pure or sinless. A teacher of secular subjects like physical sciences may be of any character; what he needs is simply intellectual power. But for teaching spiritual sciences, the teacher should be pure. "Blessed are the pure in heart, for they shall see God." A vision of God, a glimpse of the eternal Reality, never comes until the soul is pure. Therefore, in the *Guru* we must look for purity.

The Qualifications of a Guru

The traditional qualifications of a *Guru* have been laid down in the *Mundaka* and *Brahadaranyaka Upanishads*. A summary of them has been made by Shankaracharya in his *Viveka Sudamani* (Crest-Jewel of Discrimination):

1. The *Guru* must be versed in the scriptures. But he need not be a scholar. He must know the spirit of the scriptures. Sri Ramakrisha used to tell a story. A few men once went into a mango orchard, and most of them soon made themselves busy in counting the leaves, examining the color of the leaves, the size of the twigs, the number of branches, and so forth, and then began to note down everything, and got up a wonderful discussion on each of these. But one of them, more sensible than others, kept himself apart, busy in eating the mangoes all the time. Now, who was the cleverest of them all? So leave this counting of leaves, twigs and branches and this note-taking to others; such work has its value in its proper place, but not here in the spiritual. Human Beings never become spiritual through such work; no one has ever seen a strong spiritual person among these "leaf-counters." Spirituality is the highest aim of us; it does not require "leaf-counting." A spiritual person need not know the entire scriptures word by word; he only requires to feel the spirit of the scriptures. One who deals too much in words, loses the spirit. The various methods of speaking a beautiful language and explaining the diction of the scriptures are

only for the enjoyment of the learned; these do not take one to perfection. No great teacher goes that way.

2. The *Guru* must be established in Brahman, ever living in God. He must have attained Self-realization, for if he has not experienced the Truth, how can he carry us to the shore beyond ignorance? The subject to be taught in the spiritual pursuit is God Himself, the Ultimate Truth. The *Guru* must, therefore, be able to show us how to manifest the Divine Being within.

3. The *Guru* should be unsmitten by desire, unmotivated by any selfish purpose. He should have no hankering for lust, name, fame and prestige and money. He should be totally unattached.

4. The *Guru* should be stainless and pure. The genuine *Guru* never thinks of himself as a *Guru*. He puts no airs. He should have no sin, no conceit, no deceit, and no deviousness in him.

5. The spiritual *Guru* ought to be a renunciate. If he owns private property somewhere, has financial investment or is worrying about spouse or family, how effective can he be as a spiritual teacher?

6. What is the motive behind the *Guru*? Does he teach with any ulterior motive of name, fame or gain; or does he do it for pure love for his disciples? Spiritual forces can only be conveyed through the medium of love; no other medium can convey them. Any other motive such as name or fame would destroy the conveying medium.

Guru's Attitude Toward his Disciples

What is the *Guru*'s attitude toward his disciples? Does he advertise in yellow pages and invite people to become his disciples? Not at all. No genuine *Guru* is interested in creating disciples. He will not go out preaching; he is not a missionary. In fact no genuine sage will even declare himself a *Guru*. It is the disciples who recognize him as the *Guru*. They make him a *Guru*. They seek his guidance and call him a teacher. Otherwise he is just there. "Ask it shall be given" says the *Bible*. Knowing the fitness of the student and his eagerness to receive, the *Guru* gives to him. Otherwise he remains as he is.

A true *Guru* does not need advertisements. Have you ever

seen a flower sending out a circular to all the bees saying, "I have honey, come to me?" No. When the flower is in bloom, the bees will come. So when a person really becomes tired of the worldly pursuits and looks for eternal peace and joy, he seeks the guidance of a *Guru*.

The Guru Within

One should not take the physical body or the intelligence of a teacher as the *Guru*. The Self is the real *Guru*, because he has realized the Self. His intellect gets a better light from the Self. The scriptures say,

> "*Guru* is Lord, *Guru* is Divine, *Guru* is your relations, *Guru* is your body, *Guru* is your soul, *Guru* is your Self. There is nothing but the *Guru*."

This means ultimately everything is that Self.

The real *Guru* is the Spirit within you, the Awareness. It is your own conscience. It is a part of the Cosmic Consciousness. It is the God within you that is always watching you. It can guide you, tell you whether you are doing right or wrong. It is the *Guru* within you.

But sometimes you may be weak and not listen to that conscience. So you have an outside *Guru* who has realized the inner Truth and who follows his conscience every time. That *Guru* helps you to know what is right and what is wrong. Sometimes you have doubts as to which inner voice to listen to. Your ego says, "Go ahead and do it." The conscience says, "No, that's not the right thing to do." But you do not know which is the ego and which is the conscience. The *Guru* helps you to get that doubt cleared. Even while helping you, he will gradually teach you how to recognize and follow the inner *Guru*. He will never make you dependent on him. A *Guru* is there to liberate you. Spiritual growth means freedom from bondage. No *Guru* will ever ask you to always be in his physical presence. There are many disciples who rarely even see the *Guru* physically, but still understand his teachings.

That is possible when you really look within, meditate, and see him inside. Then you get all the answers from him.

The teaching is the real teacher. The Truth is eternal. It is just transmitted to you through a physical body. The help that can be given through a physical body is limited; on the spiritual level, the *Guru* can help you much more. In your practices, in your Meditation, you should learn to communicate with the spiritual part of the *Guru*. Always try to communicate at that higher level.

Subsidiary *Gurus*

When the mind is purified through moral life, prayer, meditation, etc., it comes in touch with the inner Light of the Supreme Spirit. The purified mind becomes a channel for the flow of Divine Knowledge. It receives spiritual guidance directly from the Teacher of teachers. When the mind thus learns to open itself to the inner Voice, it can receive instructions from many sources. The *Bhagavatam* speaks of a wandering ascetic who learnt from so many natural objects. From mother earth he learnt the secret of patience, from air he learnt detachment(as air remains unaffected by pleasant or bad odors), from the sky he learnt freedom from limitations, and so on.(2.7.9)

Brother Lawrence, the seventeenth-century French Mystic, spent his life in the kitchen of a monastery. The sight of a leafless tree in mid-winter stirred in him the reflection that leaves would be renewed, and flowers would appear on its branches. This revealed to him the presence and power of God lying hidden in all creation. The spiritual awakening that he experienced sustained him throughout his life.

Guru's Role

In the spiritual field, the *Guru*'s role is unique. You are essentially divine by nature. You have forgotten your true divine essence. So instead of realizing that, you get drowned in world-process more and more. Somebody must remind you of your real nature. It is the *Guru* who does this. He awakens you from your age-long sleep and shows you the way to the Divine. He removes your ignorance and enlightens you. He studies your temperament, eagerness, outlook and level of spiritual development, and prescribes appropriate path and methods. He assesses your progress, corrects your imperfections, guides you through the practice. He is a channel for power that flows down the long line of *Gurus*, dating back many thousands of years.

Initiation. Sri Ramakrishna says, "One must have an awakening of the Spirit within in order to see the unchanging imperishable Reality." How is this first awakening brought about? An illumined *Guru* does this for you through a process of spiritual initiation. The *Guru* transmits the word of God called *mantra* to you. The power of God comes through the *mantra* and through the *mantra* comes the awakening of the Spirit. The power of initiation manifests only in a pure soul who intensely yearns for Self-realization. It is not enough to get directions from the *Guru;* you must struggle incessantly; you must purify yourself through cultivation of virtues and devotion to God; and you must yearn with all your heart to know the Truth.

The initiation is the first stage in guidance into the Yogic process. Initiation is said to be of three kinds: *shakti* (power), *sambhavi* (touch or look) and *mantra* (sacred word). In the *Shakti* initiation, by his mere will the teacher wakes up the dormant spiritual knowledge in you, giving you full or partial realization then and there. He does not even have to touch you or be near you. Generally only an *Avatar* (Incarnation) has the power to give this type of initiation. In the life of Sri Ramakrisha this power was seen on various occasions.

Sambhavi. In this initiation, by a touch or look the *Guru* imparts spirituality. This, too, is unusual, and only great saints have this faculty.

Mantra. All other initiation is by *mantra*, in which the *Guru* utters a sacred word into your ear, thus planting in your mind, as it were, the seed that sprouts into spiritual unfoldment. (For further details, *see* 4.9 *Mantra, below*) This is like putting a drop of curd into a pot of milk in order to ferment and convert the milk into curd quickly. Sometimes an aspirant may receive initiation from a great saint in his dream. A truly inspired dream-experience is as sound as a personal initiation.

The advanced stages include initiation into *Pre-sanyasa* (Pre-monkhood stage) and initiation into *Sanyasa* (Monkhood stage). These initiations are given to those who desire to renounce the worldly life and dedicate their entire life for spiritual practice and service.

The *Guru* will also guide you in practicing advanced techniques of *Pranayama* and Meditation that ultimately lead you to the Superconscious experiences. His illustrious life itself serves as a source of illumination, light, inspiration and message. The *Guru* removes the veil of ignorance that is covering your knowledge. He guides you until you begin to follow your conscience that is the inner *Guru*. Be worthy of *Guru*'s blessings and follow his directions sincerely in order to make steady progress in your inward journey. Gradually, through the *Guru*'s blessings, the hidden faculty of intuition will awaken in you , and your purified intuition will act as your *Guru*.

Often the role of the *Guru* is misunderstood, and the disciples think that the teacher would carry them to the goal. If you see a signpost that says, "New York 200 miles," do you prostrate before the signpost, deck it with garlands and pray, "Please take me to New York?" No. The signpost simply points out the direction and indicates the distance to that place. You must do the walking. The *Guru* is like that. He has gone the route. He knows the journey and is able to guide you on the trip. But you have to follow his teachings.

The *Guru* teaches through his personal example. His every-day conduct is a living ideal to you. Observe his living example and imbibe his virtues. The *Guru* gives teaching according to your temperament and evolution. It is meant for you only. Do not try to impose the teaching you have received on others. You can imbibe or draw from the *Guru* in proportion to the degree of your faith and attention.

Three Aids

There are three aids to realize the Truth or the Ultimate reality: the scriptures, the *Guru* and the spiritual practice. The scriptures tell you that sugar is sweet. The *Guru* will show you that sugar. Your practice will give you the taste. The *Guru* will not put the sugar in your mouth and say, "It is sweet." You have to taste it yourself. Even if you open your mouth and he puts the sugar in it, if your tongue is totally coated, you cannot taste it. So you must be fit to experience the bliss of Atman.

Sometimes when the disciple is fit for tasting the spiritual experience, the *Guru* may transmit that spiritual experience to the disciple. Sri Ramakrishna did this to Swami Vivekananda (then called Narendra). Sri Ramakrishna touched his disciple and Narendra went into *Samadhi*. He tasted the experience of the state of Superconsciousness. To get such a little glimpse, the disciple needs a lot of sincerity, purity of heart and devotion. Of course, he has to practice intensively to gain that experience on a regular basis.

Guru's Tests

The *Guru* may test the students in various ways. Sometimes he may even tempt them. Some misunderstand him and lose their faith in him. In ancient days, the tests were very severe. Once Gorakhnath asked some of his students to climb up a tall tree and throw themselves, head downwards, on a very sharp trident (*Trisula*). Many faithless students kept quiet. But one faithful student at once climbed up the tree with lightning speed and hurled himself downwards. He was protected by the invisible hands of Gorakhnath. He had immediate Self-realization.

Avatars as *Guru*

Besides realized sages or enlightened seers, there are the Teachers of all teachers; i.e., God Himself coming in human form as Incarnations (*Avatars*) of God. They are much higher. They can transmit spirituality with a touch, with a wish, which makes even the most degraded sinners – saints in a second. Sri Krishna,

Buddha, Christ, Sri Ramakrishna and other Incarnations are the greatest manifestations of God; we cannot see God except through the Incarnations.

When the *Avatar* touches a person, his whole soul will change; he will be transformed into just what the *Avatar* is; his whole life will be spiritualized; and spiritual power will emanate from every pore of his body. The *Avatar* can alter the destiny of people, and wipe out their karma. No ordinary teacher has such a power of transformation.

Jesus had the power to bring Divine Light to simple fishermen at his touch. He also had the power to transform impure souls whom people call sinners. When he told them, "Thy sins are forgiven; thy faith has made thee whole; go in peace," they at once felt freed from all impurities.

In modern times Sri Ramakrishna was an Avatar. He had the power to raise disciples to great heights of illumination by a mere touch or look or wish.

The great strength of an *Avatar* does not lie in His miracles or His healing; even devils can do that; but it lies in His teachings. So long as the name of God is not forgotten, those words will continue on and on, and never cease to be. So in worshipping an *Avatar*, in praying to Him, we must always remember what we are seeking. "Not those foolish things of miracle-display," says Swami Vivekananda, "but the wonderful powers of the Spirit, which make man free, give him control over the whole of nature, take off from him the badge of slavery, and reveal God unto him." (*Religion of Love*, 1970, p. 47).

The Eternal Teacher

Real initiation takes place when God awakens your spiritual consciousness. The real *Guru* is the indwelling Supreme Spirit which is "the Goal, the Controller, the Lord, the Witness, the Abode, the Refuge, the Friend, the Origin and Dissolution of the Universe, its Substratum, the Repository of all Knowledge and the Eternal Seed." (*Gita,* 9.18).

The sincere disciples look upon the *Guru* as a visible

manifestation of the Supreme Spirit, the Teacher of teachers, as a channel for the flow of Divine Grace. It is in this spirit that they serve him, obey him and worship him. The great sage Sankaracharya in his *Daksinamurthi Stotrum,* says,

> "I bow to the Divine Guru who, by the application of the Collyrium of Knowledge, opens the eyes of one blinded by the disease of ignorance. I bow to the Divine Guru who imparts to the disciple the fire of Self-knowledge and burns his bonds of karma accumulated through many births.
>
> "I offer my salutations to the beneficent Being who is incarnate in the Guru, the Light of whose absolute Existence shines forth in the world of appearance, who instructs the disciple with the holy text, 'That thou art,' realizing whom the soul never returns to the ocean of birth and death." (3)

3.3: Discipleship

A disciple (Yogic student) is one who seeks spiritual guidance from a *Guru*. He is a seeker of Enlightenment. Discipleship is very difficult to achieve, because it needs wholehearted faith, devotion and intelligent discrimination. The poet Bholenath (19th century)[26] sings,

> "Anyone can easily become a *Guru.* But what is very hard is to become a disciple... No one is ready to receive the teachings; but everyone feels clever enough to give teachings."

So it is rare to find a true disciple. It is easy to become a *Guru*, but it is so difficult to become a disciple. Nature is constantly giving the teachings, yet no one goes to Nature to receive them.

Three Categories of Disciples

In the ancient Tamil writings we come across a wonderful description of the different kinds of disciples. The *top level* disciples are those who behave either like a swan or a cow. What is one great quality that we see in the swan? If you mix water and milk and place it in front of the swan, the swan will put its beak into it, stir the whole thing and be able to extract the milk and leave the water behind.

The cow has a different quality, but it is as good as that of the swan. She will go and graze in one place, eating as much as she can with full Concentration. Then she will come back to the stable, lie down and regurgitate everything she swallowed. She will keep it in the mouth and chew it well. Anything that is raw and not digestible, not good for the system, she will spit out. Finally, she will swallow the good part, digest and assimilate it.

A top level student will have these qualities. He will receive everything, but will have the capacity to separate what is conducive for his growth and what is not. What is useful, he will put to use. He will assimilate it. That kind of discriminating faculty is found in the top grade disciple.

The *middle grade* disciple will be like a parrot or the earth. A parrot repeats whatever it hears. It does not expound on it or develop it; it simply repeats. What is the quality of the earth? Whatever you sow, it gives back. It does not give anything else. If you sow a mango seed, you get a mango tree. If you sow an apple seed, you get an apple tree. Similarly, a middle level student simply repeats whatever he learns; he does not develop it.

For the *low level* disciple there are four examples. First is a pot with holes. Whatever you pour in it, it immediately flows out. It does not retain anything. The next example is a buffalo. If you take a buffalo to a beautiful clear pool of water, it will not stay out of the water to drink. Instead, it will walk in, lie down, stir up the whole thing. It turns the clear water into muddy water, and then just lies there and sleeps. This type of student will make a mess of whatever he hears.

The third example is the goat. The goat never stays in one place to eat. It will go and bite a leaf here, run and bite a leaf somewhere else, run again and bite something else. There are students like that. They will stay in a spiritual center for one week, then go to another center, then do something else. They constantly move around, wanting something quick; they do not stay in one place long enough to learn anything.

Finally, there is the strainer. You pour the tea, and the strainer keeps all the unwanted dusts, and lets the nice tea run through. All the good things are missed, and all the undesirable things are held tight.

Qualifications of a Disciple

Who can find a *Guru*? One who is fit to receive spiritual guidance and is ready for it will find a *Guru*. What are the qualifications of a fitting disciple? He should have sincerity and acknowledge that he knows nothing (in the spiritual sense). He should be an "empty" cup. He should not say, "I do know something; can you add a little more?" When Arjuna was standing on his chariot in the midst of the battlefield, he was overwhelmed and deluded by emotions. He did not want to do his duty and fight, but argued with Lord Krishna with all kinds of philosophical arguments to support his position. But ultimately he realized his foolishness and said,

> "I am overwhelmed by emotions. My mind is confused as to my duty. I entreat you to say decisively what is good for me. I am your disciple.
> I have taken refuge in you. Please instruct me." (*Gita,* 2.7)

That is what you call total surrender. You accept your ignorance. Then you are totally free from egoism. You come with an empty vessel. As long as your ego is in the vessel, whatever the *Guru* puts in would be contaminated.

There is a wonderful Zen story of a proud young aspirant who went to a Master for the first time. Upon seeing the student, the Master, without saying anything, invited him for a cup of tea. The lad happily started talking about his accomplishments to the Master, and as they were talking, the Master began to pour tea into the lad's cup. But instead of filling it and stopping, he kept on pouring even when the cup was flowing over.

The aspirant stared in amazement as the tea was brimming over the top. Finally unable to contain himself, he blurted out, "Master, it's already full and the tea is flowing out on the ground; you cannot put any more." The Master stopped and looked up, and said, "Well, it is the same with you, my son. You are filled to the brim with your own ideas and self-importance. Whatever I say is going to overflow and can't go in, until you empty yourself first."

Unless we overcome the ego and the attachment to pride, we cannot fully understand what the *Guru* teaches, and more importantly the spirit of his teaching. So cutting through pride and self-importance is a major step in our attitude toward our *Guru*. Early in our association, the *Guru* may impart many ideas and precepts to us, but only after many hearings and subsequent meetings we begin to sniff at the scent of Truth. Often times the *Guru* relates many different thoughts. But beneath all those ideas remains constant what he is really saying. What he is saying is not translatable into words; rather it is an inner message, an inner communication that is perceived when we empty ourselves and humble ourselves before him; otherwise we will never hear what the *Guru* is saying.

A seeker of Enlightenment should feel and say, "I'm just empty, hollow. You are holy. Please pour that holiness into this hollowness. I am a "holey" reed, please play your music through me." A flute is just a reed full of holes. It does not have anything inside and therefore whatever the flutist wants to play, he can. A student should be like that.

The Conditions for Fitness. Who is fit to receive the guidance of the *Guru* ? One who satisfies the following three conditions:

The *first* condition is purity. No impure soul can be religious. Purity in thought, word and action is absolutely necessary.

The *second* condition is a real thirst for spiritual knowledge. One, who wants, gets. Wanting spiritual knowledge is a very difficult thing, not so easy as we generally think. Spiritual knowledge does not consist in hearing talks or reading books; rather it is a continuous struggle, a grappling with our own nature, a continuous fight, till the victory is achieved.

The *third* condition is perseverance. The struggle for overcoming ego and purifying the mind is not a question of one or two days, of years, or of lives, but it may be even hundreds of life-times, and the disciple must be ready for that. The disciple, who sets out with such a spirit and determination and practices Yoga with perseverance, finds success.

Qualities to be Developed

A student of Yoga should endeavor to develop the following qualities in order to succeed in Yoga:

(a) Discrimination (*viveka*): increasing understanding of what is true and what is essential.
(b) Dispassion (*vairagya*): increasing strength of will to detach oneself from what is false and erroneous.
(c) Six-fold Virtues (*Shat-sampat*): 1. Serenity of the mind (*Shama*), 2. Control of the senses (*Dama*), 3. Discarding of selfishness (*Uparati*), 4. Endurance and patience (*Titiksha*), 5. Faith and firm conviction (*Shraddha*), and 6. Balance of the mind (*Samadhana*).
(d) Intense aspiration for Self-realization (*Mumukshuttwa*).

He should not complain against his circumstances. He should rather convert every-day activities into a process of self-purification. There is no use of waiting for favorable circumstances. Can one wait for the waves to become still in order to enter into the ocean? He has to make use of all circumstances as means for Yogic practice.

The Attitude of the Disciple toward his Master

What should be the attitude of a disciple toward his *Guru*? Swami Vivekananda, the greatest among the disciples of Sri Ramakrishna, on the basis of his own personal experience, exhorts us:

> "Find the teacher, serve him as a child, open your heart to his influence; see in him God manifested. Our attention should be fixed on the teacher as the highest manifestation of God, and as the power of attention concentrates there, the picture of the teacher as man will melt away, the frame will vanish, and the real God will be left there."

So with a spirit of veneration and devotion we should approach the *Guru*. We should not make the mistake of treating the *Guru* as equal. One of the prime attitude that we should have toward our Master is humility. However, in America where there is the theoretical ideal that all are equal, we find it repugnant to place anyone above ourselves. Americans may see a *Guru* as a mere another person. It is shocking to many of them to see disciples bowing their heads to the feet of a *Guru*. A true disciple sees the *Guru* as the true Spirit personified. He realizes that if he is to understand the teachings of the *Guru*, he must "stand under" him, and humble himself. He must not try to block the *Guru*'s Spirit by his own coloration, nor by his own ego attachments. He should be a receptive vehicle for the *Guru*'s teaching. He should realize that unless he empties himself, he cannot receive that teaching.

Lord Krishna describes the proper attitude of a disciple:

> "Seek this (knowledge) by prostrating, questioning and serving. The wise
> Seers of the Truth will instruct you in that knowledge." (*Gita*, 4.34).

This sloka points out the attitude of a student toward his *Guru*. *First*, he should *prostrate* at the feet of the *Guru*. This is not to glorify him. It does not matter to him whether you fall at his feet or jump on his shoulders. By prostrating, the student annihilates his ego and manifests his humbleness. A good student goes to a Master to receive, to learn, not to exchange his ideas, nor to test the Master's knowledge. He should feel and tell the *Guru*, "I don't know anything. I have taken refuge in you. Please instruct me." It is only then the real *Guru*-disciple relationship begins.

Second, the student should put his *questions* with sincerity to the *Guru* in order to learn from him. "Ask, it shall be given," says the *Bible*. Through questions only, he can get his doubts clarified. It is the duty of the teacher to convince the student.

Third, he should *serve* the teacher. He should not get anything without giving everything he can. By serving the *Guru* he expresses his love and humbleness toward his *Guru*.

Besides, the student must have faith in the *Guru*, and have devotion to him. It is the faith and devotion that connect him with the *Guru*.

Here is a story. Once on a day of religious festival, many devotees had gathered around Kabir (1440–1518).[27] He just kept weaving and weaving. Finally one of the persons in the gathering stood up and asked, "Who is a true disciple?" Kabir gave no answer. He kept on weaving. Again the person got up and asked, "Who is a true disciple?" Kabir did not answer. He kept weaving. The person asked a third time.

At that point, Kabir called his disciple and said, "Kamal come here." Kamal went to him and Kabir said, "Go and get some *prasad* for these people. And when you bring the sweet prasad, add salt to it."

Kamal went and brought the sweet *prasad,* and added salt to it, and distributed it to everyone. Everyone took the *prasad,* but it stayed on their palms!

After a while the same person stood up once again. "Kabir, Who is a true disciple?" He really wanted to know.

Then Kabir said, "Kamal, come here." Kamal went to him. Kabir said, "I have lost my shuttle. Get a lantern and look for it." It was noon time, so there was good light. Kamal brought the lantern; he found the shuttle and gave it to Kabir.

The same person got up and said, "Kabirji, for the last time I am asking. Please tell me who is a true disciple?"

Kabir said, "You still didn't get it? Kamal is a true disciple. He knows that salt is not added to sweet. Yet because I have asked him to do it, he did it. He also knows that he could just pick up the shuttle in the day light without a lantern. But he brought a lantern, because I told him to bring it. That is a true disciple: one who has such humility and obedience. In discipleship there is total annihilation of one's individuality.

Devotion and Faith

A *Guru* will not force anything into the disciple. He will wait until the disciple asks for it, until he becomes ready. This is where the devotion (*Bhakti*) comes in. Unless the disciple has faith, he cannot receive what the *Guru* has to give him. Devotion means that he puts his entire faith in the *Guru*. That faith becomes the connecting link between the *Guru* and the disciple. Once that link and communion is established, even if the *Guru* refuses to teach him, he will learn from the *Guru*, because of the power of faith. By his own faith the disciple will be able to understand what the *Guru* has in his mind; he need not even tell him.

But the devotion to the *Guru* is very difficult. The student constantly has to prove himself to be a true disciple. Many incidents may occur and disturb his faith. But with all that, if he feels, "He is my Master. I have full trust and implicit faith in him. I am not here to question or judge him; I am here to be trained by him." That is deep faith.

If anyone has that faith, he is really fortunate. He is fit to get all because of his faith. He can learn more from the *Guru* than even the *Guru* knows, because his faith itself acts as his *Guru* then. Faith is God. That is why the *Bible* says that if one has faith of the size of a mustard seed, one can move mountains. But if that is shaken, even if a disciple's *Guru* is God Himself, he will not receive anything because there is no communion. Faith is the greatest virtue.

The real teaching or imparting of the true knowledge is not normally done with words. Words have their limitations, but by speaking through silence, in feeling, the disciple receives much more. The *Guru* knows what the disciple needs, and the disciple knows what the *Guru* wants to communicate – all without words.

The real learning, thus, comes more from feelings and observation than from words. How does a child understand the mother? She loves the child so much and the child reciprocates. Even if the mother is far away, she can easily feel when her baby is hungry. In the same way true devotion connects the student's heart with that of the *Guru*, and thus communion takes place between them even without words

Guru Worship

In many Yogic paths, disciples use the *Guru* as an object of worship, as a deity. This practice is frequently misinterpreted as acts of investing the power of God in a human being. Certainly there are some disciples who only worship the body, "the person" of the *Guru*; however, the true intent of the *Guru* worship is the disciple's devotion to the *Guru*'s indwelling Spirit. It is that Spirit that the true disciple perceives in his worship of the *Guru*. In short, the *Guru* worship is just a supplication to the *Guru*'s spiritual essence.

Guru Service

Guru service is an important aspect of the disciple's practice. It is one part of Karma Yoga, the selfless service. The disciple tries to become a perfect channel, an instrument for the Lord's work. Then he can feel the supreme power working through him.

Surrender to *Guru*

It is not enough for the disciple to simply present himself to the *Guru*; he must surrender to the *Guru*. If the *Guru* is to do any real work on him, he must give himself wholeheartedly. In India and other Eastern countries, it is not uncommon for the disciple upon meeting the teacher to kneel down and put his head at the *Guru*'s feet. This symbolizes his humility. Another esoteric meaning for such worship is receiving the *Guru*'s energy; for head is thought of as the North Pole and the feet the South Pole.

As a rule, humility and obedience are the hallmarks of a good disciple. When he surrenders, he is allowing himself to be worked on by the *Guru* or the Divine force around him.

The disciple's self-surrender to the *Guru* and the *Guru*'s grace are interrelated. The surrender draws down the *Guru*'s grace, and the *Guru*'s grace makes the surrender complete. The *Guru*'s grace works through the disciple's practice (*sadhana*). If the disciple sticks to the path tenaciously, it is the grace of the *Guru*. If he resists when temptation assails, it is the *Guru*'s grace. If people receive him with love and reverence, it is the *Guru*'s grace. If he gets all bodily wants, it is the *Guru*'s grace. If he gets encouragement and strength when he is in despair and despondency, it is the *Guru*'s grace If he gets over the body-consciousness and rests in his own Atman and blissful nature, it is the grace of the *Guru*. Let the disciple feel the grace of the *Guru* at every step, and be sincere and truthful to him.

Introspection (Self-analysis)

An aspirant should cultivate introspection or self-analysis in preparation for spiritual training. He should analyze his motives and actions in order to learn about himself. Self-analysis helps him to identify his imperfections and to take appropriate steps to correct them. It helps him to develop an indrawn attitude; it starts the process of detaching his mind from the objects of the world and placing it more securely on the Self. He should dedicate himself to the task. The first little taste of peace that he experiences becomes the impetus for further spiritual efforts. How have some achieved great things in science, exploration, arts, sports, etc.? It is all by determination and dedication. Therefore, self-surrender, introspection, sincere desire and dedication are necessary for a disciple in preparing for receiving the *Guru*'s grace and guidance.

3.4: *Yama*

What is *Yama*

Yama and *Niyama* are the first two stages or steps of Raja Yoga. *Yama* consists of five self- restraints that regulate one's relationship with others. They are: non-hurting (*ahimsa*), truthfulness (*sathya*), non-stealing (*asteya*), celibacy (*brahmacharya*) and non-possessiveness (*aparigraha*). (*Yoga Sutras*, 2.30). The *Niyama*s are five observances to be followed. (*See* next Chapter). These ten commitments constitute the moral code of Raja Yoga. They are similar to the Ten Commandments of the Christian and Jewish faiths, and the ten virtues of Buddhism. In fact, there is no religion without these moral codes. All spiritual life is based on these codes.

The *Yama*s and *Niyama*s are closely connected with higher Yoga. They are meant for purifying the mind. There is direct interaction between the mind and the body. Physical health is dependent on mental health. Scientific findings indicate that most diseases are caused by mental and emotional disturbances. It is therefore necessary to cultivate attitudes and values that ensure a steady and peaceful mind. Mental peace and sound physical health are pre-requirements for practicing Yoga. The *Yama*s and *Niyama*s seek to remove all mental and emotional disturbances and thus to make the mind peaceful and serene. That is why the *Yama*s and *Niyama*s have been prescribed as the first two steps of Raja Yoga.

Let us now discuss briefly the significance of the five self-restraints prescribed under *Yama*.

Ahimsa

Ahimsa means non-hurting any living creature in thoughts, words and deeds as well. On the positive side, *ahimsa* leads to a spontaneous love toward all creatures. The Atman in all beings is one and the same. The cultivation of the attitude of *ahimsa* should start with the cultivation of positive thoughts and tender compassion toward all beings. Feelings of love and compassion purify the mind.

Sathya

Sathya means truthfulness in thought, word and deed. One lie inevitably leads to more lies. Lying is one of the easiest means of getting out of an undesirable situation. In avoiding one difficulty by lying, one creates many other serious difficult situations. Any effort to cover up falsehoods and deceptions creates guilty feelings and inner conflicts in the mind. Therefore truthfulness has to be practiced for keeping the mind free from such disturbances. On the positive side, this practice is absolutely necessary for developing the faculty of intuition and unfoldment of consciousness. Only a pure mind can reflect the ultimate Reality whose essential nature is love and truth.

Asteya

Asteya means not only non-stealing but also refraining from misappropriation, accepting bribes, taking credit for things one has not done or privileges that do not properly belong to him. The desire for what belongs to another is based on underlying feelings of inadequacy and jealousy. A student of Yoga should eliminate such attitudes by cultivating *asteya* and a sense of contentment and completeness.

Brahmacharya

Brahmacharya literally means "to walk in Brahman," that is, being in awareness of Brahman alone. Such a state is possible, only if the mind is free from all sensual desires. Of all sensual desires, the sexual urge is the most powerful and the most destructive. *Brahmacharya* is therefore translated as celibacy or complete abstinence from sex. Many Western writers have a liberal view. They take it to mean moderate indulgence within lawful wedlock.

However, the real Yogic life cannot be combined with the self-indulgence, for sexual indulgence leads to the dissipation of vital energy that needs to be conserved for developing mental faculties essential for spiritual development. A married person, of course, may not be able to give up sex life all at once, but he has to give it up completely when he starts the practice of higher Yoga. Is anyone who is a slave of his passions really fit to embark on this Divine adventure?

Brahmacharya should not, however, be interpreted as suppression of sexual urges, for repression leads only to frustration and emotional upset. It means control of, and freedom from, all sexual cravings. The peace and bliss that accompanies Self-realization are far greater than any transient sexual pleasure. A Yogi whose goal is Self-realization would therefore overcome the obstacles of sexual cravings without any kind of suppression.

It must be clearly understood that the practice of higher Yoga requires complete abstinence from sexual indulgence, not only physical indulgence but even thoughts and emotions connected with sexual pleasures. No compromise on this point is possible.

The human energy that is expressed through sexual action and sexual thought, when checked and controlled, easily transformed into *ojas*, a subtle spiritual energy. It is only a chaste person who can create *ojas* and store it in the brain; that is why chastity has always been considered the highest virtue. An unchaste person loses mental vigor and moral stamina. No wonder all the religious orders that have produced spiritual giants insist upon absolute chastity. There must be perfect chastity in thought, word and deed. Without it the practice of Raja Yoga is futile.

Besides, *Brahmacharya,* in its wider sense, stands not only for abstinence from sexual indulgence but freedom from craving for all kinds of sensual enjoyments, such as disturbing movies, novels, non-sattvic food, and mixing-up with persons of opposite sex. The use of scents and other cosmetics, indulgence in the pleasures of the palate, wearing furs, and similar pleasures of the senses are very common in modern life. It is considered natural and blameless for anybody to indulge in the enjoyments even where they involve terrible suffering to countless living creatures. It is all taken as a matter of course, and very few ever give even a passing thought to these things. For people who are leading the ordinary worldly life, moderate enjoyments that do not involve any suffering to other creatures do not really matter. They are a part of the normal life at their stage of evolution. But for a Yogic aspirant, these enjoyments are harmful not because there is anything "sinful" about them, but because they carry with them the potentiality for constant mental and emotional disturbances. No one who is attracted by the objects of senses can hope to be free from the worries and anxieties that characterize the worldly life.

However, this does not mean that a student of Yoga should not use any kind of objects. To keep himself alive, he has to necessarily use harmless necessaries of life. What is meant is that he has to guard against the cravings for sensual pleasures and attachments to the objects of senses. The Yogi may move among all kinds of objects as anybody else, but his mind should neither be attached to objects that give pleasure, nor be repelled from objects that give pain. He should remain unaffected by the presence or absence of such objects. But the attainment of this state of non-attachment and indifference toward objects requires prolonged and severe self-discipline, and control of senses. This freedom from attachment brings supreme peace of mind and inner strength to the Yogi.

Family life and Celibacy

In the family life, moderation is required with the goal of complete abstention in the future. Of course, what is moderate for one couple may not be for another. To practice strict moderation at the onset of the marriage may produce devastating results, if one partner is more engaged in spiritual practice than the other. If Yoga is to be incorporated into the family structure, then the whole family must participate in the practice, even if only in a small way. If the level is made too high, then some of the members of the family will not desire to take part, and the joint spiritual feeling between the members will be lost. Any way the degree of moderation depends upon the couple's level of dedication to the practice of Yoga.

Limiting sexuality does, however, establish the relationship on a higher spiritual basis.

It is easy to understand why divorces occur, if the marriages are based solely on sexual attraction. If the relationship is based on physical appearance and sex, then the interest will wear off quickly. But if the relationship is based on spirit, there is no depth too deep for it to reach. Unfortunately, many young men and women are excessively body conscious, and they are no better than butchers looking for a good side of beef. This attitude that has trapped people into body-identification permeates all levels of society. The institution of marriage and family has been seriously damaged by it.

Aparigraha

Aparigraha means "non-possessiveness." The tendency to accumulate wealth and worldly goods is very strong in human beings. Of course, as long as we live in the physical world we have to have a few things that are essential for the maintenance of the body. But we are not satisfied with the necessaries of life. We desire to have comforts and luxuries. We do not, however, stop even with all possible comforts and luxuries. We continue to amass wealth and possessions. There is no limit to our desires for material possessions. Apart from the far-reaching imbalances that this human instinct causes in the social and economic fields, its effect on the life of the individual is terrible indeed. Consider the time and energy one spends in the accumulation of possessions and in maintaining and guarding the accumulated things. The worries and anxieties increase more than proportionately with increase in the accumulations. Then consider the constant fear of losing some of them every now and then, and the regret of leaving them behind when one ultimately bids good-bye to this world. What a colossal waste of time, energy and mental force all this involves! Is the precious human life meant for such wastage? No one who is aware of the real purpose of life can afford to waste his limited resources of time and energy in this manner. So the Yogic aspirant does not waste his life in accumulating and maintaining possessions.

He is satisfied with what comes to him in the natural course of life.

It is really what matters is not the quantity of our possessions, but our attitude toward them. A beggar, for instance, could be more attached to his begging bowl than a king to all his treasures. The danger lies not in having material possessions, but in becoming attached to them or in craving more.

A student of Yoga may sometimes be in doubt whether it is feasible or advisable to practice strictly the above five vows or exceptions can be made under special situations. Patanjali sets at rest all such doubts by making it clear that no exceptions can be allowed in practicing them. (*Yoga Sutras*, 2.31).

Morality and Yogic Life

What is the place of morality in Yogic life? There are two kinds of Yoga: lower and higher. The lower Yoga is practiced for attaining certain psychic powers. There is a large number of Yogis scattered throughout India, Tibet and other countries, who possess supernormal powers, but in moral standards they are not different from the ordinary people. Some of them are good people. Others are not innocent and can cause injury to those who cross their path. There is a third class of Yogis who are dangerous and misuse their powers for selfish purposes. The lower Yoga is nothing but misapplication of Yogic practices for self-aggrandizement or satisfaction of conceit and egoism.

The higher Yoga expounded in the *Yoga Sutras* is the genuine Yoga that is used for attaining Enlightenment, and freedom from the illusions and limitations of the lower life.

For the path of higher Yoga, morality of a high order is essential. It is far above the morality of the conventional type. It is superior morality, meant for gaining true and lasting peace and joy. The importance of this morality of high order is not clearly understood by many students of Yoga. Yogic morality appears to be harsh or forbidding. Many aspirants resort to compromises in practicing *Yama*s and *Niyama*s. For example, some take Brahmacharya as compatible with moderate sexual indulgences. Such compromises may seem quite reasonable from the worldly standpoint, but the true purpose of Yoga is not to keep a hold on this world, but to cross the ocean of worldly life. It is not that it is not possible to practice Yoga without giving up worldly enjoyments, but the progress of the practitioner is bound to stop at one stage or another, if he tries to make these compromises.

Another important point is that the virtues of *Yama* and *Niyama* have a much wider scope and deeper significance then their ordinary meaning. Each virtue is more comprehensive and deeper in its meaning than what it is generally considered to be. For example *ahimsa* means not mere non-violence, but it stands for the highest degree of harmlessness, not inflicting any injury, suffering or pain on any living being by thought, word or deed. To what degree of perfection the virtues of *Yama* and *Niyama* can be cultivated is shown in the eleven Sutras: 2.35-45 of *Yoga Sutras*.

Thus the code of morality envisaged in *Yama* and *Niyama* is designed to serve as a very strong foundation for the higher Yogic life. It goes to the very bedrock of human nature. The main object of this supreme ethical code is to eliminate completely all mental and emotional disturbances that characterize the life of an ordinary human being. Hatred, jealousy, dishonesty, deception, greediness, sensuality and possessiveness are some of the common vices of the human beings. As long as a human being is subject to these vices, he will have no freedom from mental and emotional disturbances. As long as these disturbances continue to affect the mind, it is not possible to undertake advanced practice of Yoga.

3.5: *Niyama*

What is *Niyama*

The *Niyamas* are five observances to be followed. They are: *saucha* (purity), *santosha* (contentment), *tapas* (austerity), *swadhyaya* (self-study) and *Ishwara-praniddhana* (surrender to God). (*Yoga Sutras*, 2.32)

How does *Niyamas* differ from *Yamas*? Though both *Yamas* and *Niyamas* seem to have a common purpose, namely, the transmutation of the lower nature, there is a subtle difference between them. The *Yamas* are, in general, moral and prohibitive, while *Niyamas* are disciplinal and constructive. In the observances of the five vows of *Yama* the practitioner is required to react to the incidents and events in his life in a well-defined manner, but the number of occasions that will arise for putting the restraints to test will depend upon his circumstances. For example, if a Yogi lives alone in a jungle as an ascetic, there will hardly arise any occasion for testing any restraint. But *Niyamas* involve regular practices irrespective of the circumstances in which the practitioner is placed.

Saucha (Purity)

Saucha means "purity in both body and mind." What is purity? According to the Yoga Philosophy, the whole universe is a manifestation of the Divine Spirit. To the Enlightened Saint who has attained Divinity, everything is pure and sacred. So the word purity in relation to our life is used in a relative sense.

It is easy to purify the physical body, but it is not so in the case of the mind. The purification of the body is achieved by refining it with *sattvic* diet, pure and non-fat vegetarian diet. Meat, alcohol and smoking make the body unhealthy and utterly useless for the Yogic life. The purification of the mind can be brought about by replacing all undesirable thoughts and emotions by pure and positive thoughts and emotions. It is also necessary to cultivate discrimination. The Yogic aspirant should learn to discriminate between pure and impure thoughts on the basis of whether they lead to greater freedom or to bondage and ignorance. The use of *mantra* and prayer is also a great purifier of the mind. They wash out all the impurities from the mind. Sincerity and perseverance are essential in cultivating mental and physical purity.

Santosha **(Contentment)**

Santosha or contentment is necessary for the Yogic aspirant for keeping his mind in a state of equilibrium. This state of mind does not depend upon one's material status. A beggar can be as content as a monarch. Our desires are insatiable and there is no end to desires. One desire leads to so many other desires. The mind is, therefore, in a constant state of agitation. It is constantly subject to anxieties, worries and disappointments. Besides, we are subject to all kinds of situations and encounters, and we react to them according to our nature. These reactions involve in most cases disturbances of the mind. This state of mind is not conducive to Concentration. So the Yogic aspirant has to transform this state of disturbance into a state of equilibrium and tranquility by a deliberate exercise of the will-power, Meditation and a conscious effort to accept whatever happens to him. He should develop the ability to withstand daily problems without being deeply affected by them, and to remain balanced in both pleasure and pain. This state of equanimity is the surest means for maintaining perfect mental peace.

Tapas **(Asceticism)**

Tapas means "to burn or heat." Anything burnt out is purified. How are mental impurities burnt out? By accepting all the pain that comes to us. Such acceptance makes the mind serene, steady and strong.

Tapas also implies self-discipline. The mind is like a wild horse tied to a chariot. Imagine the body is the chariot, the intellect is the charioteer, the mind is the reins; and the horses are the senses. The Self or true you is the passenger. If the horses are allowed to gallop without reins and charioteer, the journey will not be safe. Although control of the senses often seems to bring pain in the beginning, it eventually ends in happiness. If *tapas* is understood in this sense, we will welcome pain; we will even thank people who cause it, since they are helping us to burn out our impurities.

A simple life free from sensual indulgence, regulated fasting, observance of silence for a day every week, chanting the name of the Lord, and selfless service to fellow men and other beings – all these constitute *tapas*. *Tapas* helps to discipline the mind and to develop the willpower.

In the name of *tapas*, some people practice all sorts of self-torture such as lying on a bed of nails. Lord Krishna, in *Bhagavad Gita*, says that people who torture their bodies are demons because they disturb the pure Self that dwells within their bodies. (17.6). He also states that Yoga is not for him who indulges the flesh nor for him who tortures it. (17.5)

Self-discipline is absolutely necessary for spiritual progress. Some, who are not eager to practice self-discipline, may say, "I shall leave that to my old age or next life. Youth is the time to enjoy life." What do they bring to God in such a case? A worn-out body and a worn-out mind! Do we take worm-eaten fruits or wilted flowers to altar? No. We make fresh and perfect offerings only. In the same way, we should give the Lord the best of ourselves. In fact youth is the favorable stage for spiritual practice. Sri Ramakrishna once said to a young college student: "When a man makes a brick, he puts his trade mark on it while it is still soft. Then, when the brick is dried in the sun and baked in the kiln, the mark becomes permanent. Even so, if you can put the imprint of God on your mind while it is soft, that imprint can never be effaced, but will remain for ever." Self-discipline will not obstruct one's normal life. Rather it will make one's life meaningful and peaceful.

Svadhyaya (Self-Study)

This means study leading to Knowledge of the Self. Scriptures like *Upanishads*, *Bhagavad Gita*, *Thirumantiram*, *Thirukkural*, *Atma bodha*, *Yoga Sutras*, *Bible* and others that will elevate our mind and remind us of our true Self should be studied and understood deeply. The more often we read them, the more we understand. We should contemplate, understand, assimilate and absorb the deeper and deeper thoughts. A deeper knowledge of the scriptures elevates our mind and expands our consciousness. But a mere theoretical knowledge is not enough. How can one that is beyond the mind can really be understood by mere theoretical knowledge? We should transcend the mind and experience the Self. Then only we can really know what the Self is. God can be really understood, only when we become God.

Self-study also means self-analysis or looking at ourselves with greater objectivity, analyzing how different things affect us in our everyday life. By observing and studying ourselves, we can correct the false impressions we have built up and come to see things as they are. This process helps us to uncover many revealing truths about the way we function. For many people, self-inquiry is scary. They feel, "If I start looking into myself, I will come across so many things that I should not know. Ignorance is blissful." Self-inquiry can cause sadness. Nevertheless, if we keep probing deeper, we become aware of our inner conflicts and disturbances, which we should correct in order to attain peace and harmony. This process may lead us to become aware of our Self.

Ishwara-Pranidhana (Surrender to God)

This means surrender to the Supreme Being. This is possible only with infinite faith and dedication. We should dedicate everything, our study, our practices, our actions, our life, to the Lord. We should pray "I am Thine, All is Thine, Thy will be done." "Mine" binds; "Thine" liberates. If we have "mines" all over, they will "undermine" our life. But if we change all "mines" to "Thine," we will always be free and safe. True Yoga means "dedication, giving, loving, Selfless service," which will bring us permanent peace and joy and free our mind from its modifications.

Complete surrender to the Lord is one of the means for removing the veil of egoism. It transforms our "I" feeling into Cosmic Consciousness. In surrender and devotion we reestablish our intimate relation with Cosmic Consciousness. Of course, this is a gradual process and we have to consciously and sincerely practice self-surrender and devotion for a long time to attain success in it. Strong will to surrender is required.

Kriya Yoga

The last three virtues of *Niyama*, namely *Tapas*, Self-study and Surrender to the Supreme Lord constitute Kriya Yoga, says Patanjali, in the first *sutra* of the second section of *Yoga Sutras*.

The word "*kriya*" means preliminary or purifying practice. The term "*Kriya Yoga*" is not understood correctly. In the West many students of Yoga think that *Kriya Yoga* is a separate path of Yoga. Actually *Kriya Yoga* is a preparation for Meditation. There are various *kriyas* or techniques of purification in addition to those given by Patanjali, but the above three constitute the first step on the path, and provide the foundation for all other practices. They will enable us to overcome obstacles and attain *Samadhi* (*Yoga Sutras*, 2.2).

Conclusion

The task of applying the *Yama*s and *Niyama*s to our daily life is difficult indeed, for they are strict codes of conduct. But the students of Yoga need not feel pessimistic and skeptic. They must have faith in themselves. Nothing is impossible if we have faith. Where there is a will, there is a way. If we have the determination, we can accomplish even extraordinary tasks. The initial step may seem difficult, but once we start practicing, we will gain confidence. We may fail now and then. Every failure is a stepping stone to success. We are not expected to attain perfection right away. We should regard the *Yama*s and *Niyama*s as ideals toward which we work with sincerity. We should make sincere efforts to observe them to the fullest extent possible. Even a small degree of success will reduce the intensity of emotional imbalances and mental disturbances. We can achieve greater and greater success by persistent practice and self-evaluation. Finally we can attain perfection and become fit for practicing higher Yoga.

Accomplishments of *Yama-Niyama*

What are the accomplishments of practicing the ten virtues of *Yama-Niyama*? When the practitioner reaches the state of perfection in practicing *Yama-Niyama*, he will encounter the most fascinating manifestations. Patanjali points out these developments in *Sutras* 2.35 to 2.45 of *Yoga Sutras*.

A Yogi who has cultivated *Ahimsa* carries about him an invisible aura surcharged with love and compassion. He is inwardly attuned to all living creatures and automatically inspires confidence and love in them.

A Yogi who has acquired perfection in *Sathya* becomes a mirror of Truth and whatever he says will come true.

On being firmly established in *Asteya*, the Yogi becomes aware of all kinds of treasures in his vicinity.

On being firmly established in *Brahmacharya*, the conserved energy can be transformed into subtle energy for bringing about mental, moral and spiritual regeneration.

When perfection in *Aparigraha* is attained, the Yogi acquires the capacity to have knowledge of his previous births.

From the physical *Saucha* (purity), disgust for one's own body and disinclination to have physical contact with others are developed.

From mental *Saucha* arise pure *sattva*, cheerfulness, one-pointedness, control of senses and fitness for the vision of Self.

From *Santosha* (contentment) arises supreme happiness, the Divine bliss.

When impurities are destroyed by *Tapas*, sense organs and body become perfect, and the Yogi can use them for Yoga without any hindrance from them.

By *Svadhyaya* communion with the personal God is attained.

Ishwara-pranidhana (Surrender to God) can lead ultimately to Samadhi. This implies that surrender to God is practically an alternate and independent path of achieving the goal of Raja Yoga, namely Enlightenment or Self-realization. Surrender to God develops *para vairagya* (supreme dispassion), breaks the bonds of the heart, removes personal desires and thus naturally and inevitably reduces the mind to a state of non-modifications, which is nothing but Samadhi.

3.6: Asanas

Introduction

Patanjali has not described *Asanas* in detail. They were developed later by the exponents of Hatha Yoga. In the manuals on Hatha Yoga, such as *Hatha Yoga Pradipika, Gheranda Samhita* and *Siva Samhita, Asanas* are described in detail.

Asana means Posture. Patanjali has defined Posture as holding the body in a steady and relaxed position. Many of the *Asanas* tend to bring about very marked changes in the body and if practiced correctly and for a sufficiently long time, promote health. A student of Yoga has to practice and perfect *Asanas*, for, an unhealthy body is an obstacle for scaling the higher rungs of the Yoga ladder. Hatha Yoga is therefore necessary to ensure physical health and harmony that are prerequisites for Concentration and Meditation. It is an essential part of *Raja Yoga*.

Hatha Yoga

Hatha Yoga aims at mastery over the body with a view to securing corresponding mastery over the mind. The word "*hatha*" is derived from the roots *ha* (sun), and *tha* (moon). It means equalization and stabilization of the sun breath (the breath that flows through the right nostril) and the moon breath (the breath that flows through the left nostril). Through the regulation of the physiological process, Hatha Yoga releases the dormant energies of human personality.

The principal steps of *Hatha Yoga* are *Asanas* and *Pranayama*. *Asanas* consist of certain bodily Postures such as sun worship, headstand, shoulderstand, etc. They are designed to stimulate the glands, vitalize the body and purify and strengthen the nervous system. *Pranayama* means regulation of the vital forces through breathing exercises.

Kinds of *Asanas*

Asanas are of two kinds: *Asanas* for Meditation, and *Asanas* for physical well-being. The *Asanas* suitable for *Pranayama*, Concentration and Meditation are *padmasana, siddhasana* and *sukhasana* and a few others. They are described later.

Asanas for physical well-being are many. They control specific muscles and nerves in the body and have specific therapeutic effects. They belong to Hatha Yoga. It is necessary to consult a manual on Hatha Yoga and to get personal instruction from a competent teacher.

The Need for *Asanas*

In Raja Yoga the method adopted for unfoldment of consciousness is based essentially on the control of the mind and the stoppage of mental modifications. The technique of Raja Yoga is, therefore, directed toward the elimination of all sources of disturbances to the mind, external and internal. One of the important sources of disturbance to the mind is the physical body. There is close connection between the mind and the body. They always act and react on each other. A student of Yoga must eliminate completely the disturbances arising from the physical body before tackling the internal disturbances. This is achieved through the practice of *Asanas*. When the body is fixed and kept in a particular Posture for a long time, it ceases to be a source of disturbance to the mind. The Yogi has to choose any one of the *Asanas* suitable for the practice of *Pranayama* and Meditation such as *padmasana* or *siddhasana* and then remain in that Posture until he can maintain it without making any movement. Sitting in any Posture becomes uncomfortable after a few minutes. If however that *Asana* is correctly chosen and practiced in the right way, steady and persistent practice will gradually eliminate all these minor discomforts that cause constant distraction to the mind.

Essential Features of *Asanas*

Patanjali has condensed all the essential features of *Asanas* in three *sutras* (2.46-48). The essential features of *Asanas* are:

1. Posture should be steady and comfortable (*Yoga Sutras*, 2.46). These two, steadiness and comfortability, are essential requirements in the practice of *Asanas*. Steadiness means fixing the body in one position without any movement, but there should be no rigidity, because rigidity makes the body tense. What should be aimed at is an ideal combination of immovability and relaxation. It is only then that it is possible to forget the body altogether.

2. In order to achieve steadiness, two approaches have been recommended by Patanjali (*Yoga Sutras*, 2.47). The *first* is the gradual slackening of effort. The keeping of the physical body in an immovable position for a long period of time requires great effort of the will and focus of the mind on the body. But this state of the mind is the opposite of what is aimed at. The mind has to be freed from the awareness of the body, not tied down to it in the effort to keep it in a particular Posture. So the practitioner is advised to relax the effort gradually and transfer the control of the body from the conscious to the sub-conscious mind.

The **second** approach for securing steadiness is Meditation on *Ananta* (endless), the great Serpent that, according to Hindu mythology upholds the earth.*Ananta* is the symbolic repre-sentation of the force that maintains the equilibrium of the earth and keeps it in its orbit around the sun. This force is similar to one that works in a gyroscope used for maintaining an object in a position of equilibrium. Meditation or deep contemplation over that force tends to bring down that force in our life.

3. The most important result of attaining perfection in the practice of *Asanas* is freedom from the disturbing reaction of the pairs of opposites such as heat and cold, humidity and dryness (*Yoga Sutras*, 2.48). They distract the mind and therefore the practitioner has to acquire the capacity of rising above them.

There are also other important benefits of practicing *Asanas*. They are:

4. The body becomes perfectly healthy and resistant to fatigue

and strain.

5. The practitioner acquires fitness for the practice of *Pranayama* with ease.

6. Willpower is developed. It is an outward manifestation of spiritual power.

Meditative Postures

Meditation requires a Posture that is comfortable and steady, one in which the head, neck and trunk are erect and in line. This means that the weight of the body should be distributed around its axis. If the spinal column is not erect, the aspirant's body begins to tremble after a few minutes and thus disturbs his mind; the trunk begins to form a curve, restricting the flow of vital energy through the spinal cord. As a result the gland centers are not energized by the circulation of blood, and the restricted blood circulation upsets the respiratory system. So in order to avoid these problems, the ancient Yogis have formulated four main Postures for practicing *Pranayama* and Meditation. They are *Padmasana* (lotus pose), *Siddasana* (accomplished pose), *Swastikasana* (auspicious Posture) and *Sukhasana* (the easy Posture). All these Postures involve sitting in an upright position with the spine straight.

The Yogis say that there is a subtle energy (*shakti*) at the lower end of the spinal column.(For details *See* 4.16 *Kundalini Yoga, below*). When one is spiritually uplifted this energy rises up in a channel within the spinal column. By keeping the spinal column erect the flow of this energy is not obstructed. The spine may be kept straight by lying flat or standing up, but it creates certain disturbances like sleepiness or restlessness. Therefore the sitting Posture is prescribed for Meditation.

In the beginning stage, you can first sit in *Sukhasana,* but you should slowly try to proceed to the classical Meditational *Asanas* such as *Padmasana* and *Siddhasana*. Persons with very stiff legs or who are infirm from any debilitating disease can practice Meditation on a straight backed chair or lying on a hard bed, if absolutely necessary.

When you sit in a Posture, imagine yourself as firm as a rock.

The more steady you are in your *Asana*, the better is your Concentration.

After a regular practice for several months you will surely be able to sit for two or three hours at a time.

You can sit for twenty or thirty minutes in the beginning. You should progressively prolong the duration of sitting by one or two minutes daily. The ability to sit in *Padmasana* depends not only on the flexibility of the body, but also on the state of the mind. If you believe in your own mind you will eventually be able to sit in *Padmasana*, the mind itself will help to prepare the body.

Do not on any account use undue force or strain to sit in an *Asana*. If you find severe pain in the legs after some time in a Meditational *Asana,* slowly unlock the legs and massage them for a few minutes and then resume the Posture.

Padmasana (Lotus Posture)

This is the most popular Posture for Meditation. Its technique is:

- Sit on the floor on a rug or folded blanket or Meditation pillow.
- Fold one leg and place its foot on the top of the opposite thigh. The sole of the foot must be upward and the heel should touch pelvic bone.
- Fold your other leg and place its foot on the top of the other thigh.

Padmasana can be practiced with either *Jnana Mudra* or *Chin Mudra*. (For details, *See* next Chapter). The spine must be steady and upright. Many practitioners find it comfortable to place a low cushion under their buttocks before assuming the Posture.

The benefits of *Padmasana* are:

- It allows the practitioner to hold his body steady for long periods of time. Steadiness of the body brings steadiness of the mind.
- It directs the proper flow of *prana* from the *Mooladhara*

Chakra to *Sahasrara Chakra*.
- It helps to clear up many physical, nervous and emotional problems.

Siddhasana

This means Accomplished Posture. Its technique is:

- Sit with your legs extended forward.
- Fold your right leg and place its foot sole flat against your left thigh with the heel pressing the perineum, the area between the genitals and the anus.
- Fold your left leg and place its foot on the top of your right calf.
- Press your pelvic bone with your left heel directly above the genitals.
- Put your toes and the other edge of this foot into the space between your right calf and thigh muscles. It may be necessary to move and replace your right leg for this purpose.
- Grasp your right toes, either from above or below your left calf and move them up into the space between your left thigh and calf.
- Your legs should now be locked with the knees on the ground and the left heel directly above the right heel.
- Make your spine steady, straight and erect.

Siddhasana can be practiced with *Jnana Mudra* or *Chin Mudra*.

Its benefits are:

- It facilitates maintaining the spinal steadiness for a longer period.
- It gives control over the sexual function for the maintenance of *brahmacharya* and the redirection of sexual energy upward for spiritual purposes.
- It gives a calming effect on the nervous system.

Swastikasana

This means "Auspicious Posture." It is a comfortable one, and is especially recommended for women. It is similar to the accomplished Posture except that the heels and ankle bones are not aligned.

Its technique is:

- Sit with legs stretched in front of the body.
- Fold the left leg and place the foot near the right thigh muscles.
- Similarly bend the right leg and push it in the space between the left thigh and calf muscles.
- The toes of both feet should lie between the thighs and calves of the two legs.
- The hands can be placed on the knees in *Jnana* or in *Chin Mudra* or they can be placed on the lap.

Sukhasana

This is the simple Cross-legged Posture. It is the ideal Posture for beginners who have difficulty in sitting in any of the classical meditative Postures. Once the practitioner can comfortably do any of the other Postures, *Sukhasana* should be disregarded.

The technique of *Sukhasana* is:

- Sit with legs stretched in front of the body.
- Fold the right foot under the left thigh.
- Fold the left foot under the right thigh.
- Place the hands on the knees
- Keep the head, neck and back straight.

Ardha Padmasana

This Half-lotus Posture can be practiced by those who can nearly do *Padmasana*, but have difficulty in attaining the final phase. This Posture is preferable to *Sukhasana*.

Its technique is:

- Sit with the feet stretched in front of the body.
- Fold the left leg and place the left foot beside the right thigh.
- Fold the right leg and place the right foot on top of the left thigh.
- Keep the back, neck and head straight.

Vajrasana

This is the prayer and meditative Posture of Muslims and Japanese Buddhists.

Its technique is:

- Stand on your knees with your feet stretched backward and your big toes crossed.
- Your knees should be together and your heels should be apart.
- Lower your buttocks on to the insides of your feet. Your heels will be at the side of your hips.
- Place your hands on your knees with the palms downwards.

The benefits of *Vajrasana* are:

- It alters the flow of blood and nervous impulses in the pelvic and visceral regions.
- It is the only Meditational pose for people with sciatica or sacral infections.

The *Asanas* for physical well-being are explained in detail in the manuals on *Hatha Yoga*. *Asanas* should be performed on a carpet or folded blanket in a clean, quiet, well-ventilated-room or in the open air. They may be performed either in the morning or in the evening. Warm bath before the *Asanas* is helpful, as it promotes circulation and reduces stiffness of the joints. The bladder and bowels must be emptied before practicing *Asanas*. At least four hours should have elapsed from the last normal meal. It is beneficial to begin the practice with a chant or prayer. This will center our mind, and the vibrations will calm down the mind.

All Postures should be treated as Meditation in movement. All movement should be slow and controlled. *Asanas* should be performed only to the extent possible; over-straining should be avoided. After each Posture, one should lie on the back in *Savasana* (the Corpse Posture), and relax the body for one or two minutes.

The *Asanas* tone up the nervous, endocrine, circulatory, digestive, urinary and respiratory systems that are significant to physical well-being. Patience, perseverance and regularity ensure success.

The most common *Asanas* are:

- *Nethra Vyayanam* (Eye movements)
- *Surya namaskaram* (Sun worship)
- *Bhujangasana* (the Cobra Posture)
- *Ardha Salabasana* (Half locust Posture)
- *Salabasana* (Locust Posture)
- *Dhanurasana* (Bow Posture)
- *Janusirshasana* (Head to knew Posture)
- *Paschimothanasana* (Forward bending pose)
- *Sarvangasana* (Shoulder stand)
- *Matysasana* (Fish Posture)
- *Ardha Matsyendrasana* (Half-spinal twist)
- *Pavanamuktasana* (Wind-eliminating pose)
- *Shirashasana* (Head stand)
- *Mayurasana* (Peacock Posture)
- *Yoga Mudra* (Yogic seal)
- *Savasana* (Corpse Posture)
- *Yoga Nidra* (Deep relaxation)

The *Asanas* are performed in a specific sequence. First, Eye exercises are performed. Then, three rounds of Sun worship are done. This *Asana* prepares the body for the other *Asanas*. It involves upright position, backward bending and stretching and forward bending and stretching. It tones up the entire body.

Then a series of backward bending and stretching *Asanas*–*Bhujangasana, Shalabhasana* and *Dhanurasana*–are performed. They give the spine backward bend and stretch the abdominal muscles. These promote blood circulation to the back muscles, the spine and spinal nerves and abdominal organs.

Next, the forward bending *Pachimothanasana* is performed. The front abdominal muscles are contracted, the pelvic and lumbosacral nerves are benefited, the spine is rendered supple and the heart is massaged.

Then, upright *Shirashasana* (the head stand) and *Sarvangasana* are performed. *Shirashasana pr*ovides a rich supply of arterial blood to the brain and the cranial nerves, the pituitary gland and the pineal gland. It promotes the general well-being of the practitioner. *Sarvangasana* stimulates thyroid glands and parathyroid glands and maintains them in a healthy condition. It rejuvenates the whole body and combats the effects of old age. *Sarvangasana* is followed by *Matysana*, which is complementary to it. This also stimulates the thyroid and parathyroid glands. It eliminates stiffness in the neck and back, and increases blood circulation to the face and neck.

Next *Mayurasana* is performed. It is a horizontal Posture. It strengthens the forearms, wrists and elbows and gives a liberal blood supply to the digestive organs.

Then *Ardha Matsyendrasana* is done. It gives a sideway twist to the spine in both directions. It has a beneficial effect on the whole nervous system and tones up abdominal organs.

Finally, *Yoga Mudra* is done. It relieves abdominal disorders, tones the nervous system and relieves constipation.

oga Mudra is followed by deep relaxation. Lying in *Savasana* Posture, all the limbs of the body–legs, arms, buttocks, abdomen, chest, shoulders, neck and face–are tensed and relaxed and practitioner falls into Yoga *nidra* or conscious sleep.

The second part of Hatha Yoga is *Pranayama*. It means

regulation of the vital energy through breathing exercises. It aims at the mastery over the vital forces flowing in the body. Through the control of the breath and mobilization of vital forces, it endeavors to secure the release and free flow of the basic psycho-physical energy called *Kundalini* latent in the human system. (For details, *See* Topics 3.8, 3.9 and 3.10 on *Pranayama* and 4.16 on *Kundalini Yoga, below*)

One who acquires success in Haṭha Yoga enjoys vibrant health, youthfulness and longevity. He attains spiritual liberation and supreme bliss through the practice of Raja Yoga.

Hatha Yoga serves as a means for developing the body as a fit and strong instrument for higher spiritual practice.

Hatha Yoga *Asanas* differ from other systems of physical culture. While other systems aim at merely developing a muscular body, Hatha Yoga aims at promoting the physical well-being and the health of the internal organs as well. Thus, complete physical harmony is achieved. It prepares the physical system for *Pranayama* and Meditation.

The chief defect of Hatha Yoga lies in its over-emphasis upon the body. The need for the development of the consciousness is not sufficiently recognized. Therefore it is absolutely necessary to integrate Hatha Yoga with the major kinds of Yoga, namely, the Yoga of Devotion, the Yoga of Meditation (*Raja Yoga*), the Yoga of Action and the Yoga of Knowledge.

3.7: *Mudras* and *Bandhas*

MUDRAS

The word "*Mudra*" means "seal," and the *Mudras* are concerned with the mind. They consist of physical and mental attitudes that have a very important role in the practice of Yoga, bringing about controlled psychic states. There are many types of practices ranging from positions of the hands to subtle methods of Concentration of the mind. *Mudras* form the basis of many of the important Meditational techniques. Only very simple *Mudras* are discussed in this Chapter.

Most of the *Mudras* are very powerful practices. They should, therefore, be learnt very gradually and carefully so that they are not able to harm the body or mind of the practitioner. If any difficulty is experienced while attempting to practice the *Mudras* or if any minor physical imbalance is noticed after practice has been initiated, then you should stop the practice and seek expert guidance.

Chin Mudra

This is a symbol of wisdom. Its technique is:

- Sit in a meditative Posture.
- Place the hands on the corresponding knees.
- Touch the tip of the thumb with the tip of the index finger.
- Point the remaining three fingers.

This *Mudra* can be practiced only when the hands are not being used.

The benefits: Chin Mudra helps in reminding the practitioner of the purpose of life during Meditation. It is called a Symbol of Wisdom, because all the fingers of the hand represent something. The thumb represents the higher or the universal Self. The index finger represents the individual self; the middle finger, the ego; the third or ring finger, the illusion of the mind; and the fourth, the worldly actions and their reactions. During the *Chin Mudra*, the individual self renounces all worldliness and rises up toward the higher Self. While watching the efforts of the individual self, the higher Self gracefully bends down to meet it. So the union of the universal and individual selves is symbolized by this *Mudra*, the Symbol of Wisdom.

Jnana Mudra

Its technique is:

- Sit in a Meditative Posture.
- Fold the index fingers of both hands so that they touch the inside roots of their respective thumbs.
- Spread the other three fingers of each hand so that they are slightly apart.
- Place the hands on your knees with the palms downwards and your three unbent fingers and thumb of each hand pointing toward the floor in front of your knees.

Some people prefer to practice *Jnana Mudra* with the tips of the thumb and index fingers touching. This is also correct.

The benefits of *Jnana Mudra* are the same as those of the *Chin Mudra*. In both cases, Psycho-neural finger locks make the Meditative *Asana* complete and more powerful by redirecting the nervous impulses from the hand upward to the body.

Vishnu Mudra (The Seal of Vishnu)

Its technique is:

- Close the fingers and look at the right palm.

- Hold down the index and middle fingers with the root of the thumb.
- Raise the other two fingers.

Vishnu Mudra is used during *Pranayama*, when the nostrils are changed or closed, as in *Nadi Suddhi*. In this case, thumb is used to close the right nostril and the last two fingers are used to close the left nostril.

Benefits. This *Mudra* makes the changing of the right and left nostrils, and closing them easy during *Pranayama*.

Shanmukhi Mudra (the Six-way Seal)

This *Mudra* is also known as *Yoni Mudra* that literally means the "source attitude." It is used in the practice of Kundalini Yoga. Its technique is:

- Sit in *Padmasana* or *Siddhasana.*
- Raise the elbows sideways to shoulder level.
- Close ears with thumbs, the eyes with index fingers, and place the ring and small fingers above and below the lips to seal the mouth.
- Adjust the middle fingers on either side of the nostrils, ready to close them.
- Then take a slow deep inhalation. Hold the breath and close the nostrils with the middle fingers.
- Retain the breath inside as long as you easily can, while concentrating on the *Bindu Chakra.*
- Release the nostrils and exhale slowly.
- Reseal the nostrils and continue in this way

Caution. Great care should be taken during the entire process to make sure that the eyelids are not pressed too hard. As this is a very advanced practice, one should not attempt it before mastering the standard Yoga Postures and *Nadi Suddhi Pranayama.*

Benefit. Shanmukhi Mudra is a great aid toward the practice of *Pratyahara* or sense control. It helps the mind to turn inward.

Nasagra Mudra

It means "the attitude of the nose." It is used during most of the practices of *Pranayama*, and is, thus, very important. It is practiced while sitting in a Meditative Posture. Its purpose is to enable the practitioner to close off one of his nostrils so that he can inhale or exhale through the opposite one, as instructed by the rules of *Pranayama*.

The technique of *Nasagra Mudra* is:

- Sit in a Meditative Posture.
- Hold the right hand in front of the face.
- Place your left hand on your left knee in *Jnana* or *Chin Mudra*.
- Place the tips of both the middle and index fingers of your right hand together on your forehead at the eyebrow center. These two fingers should be straight.
- In this position the thumb should be beside the right nostril and the ring finger beside the left nostril.
- These fingers are used to close off the nostrils.
- The elbow of the right arm should preferably be in front of, and near to the chest. The forearm should be nearly vertical.
- *Nasagra Mudra* can also be practiced with the hands reversed.

Shambhavi Mudra

The words "*Shambhavi Mudra*" literally mean "the attitude of Lord Siva." This *Mudra* is also known as *bhrumadhya drishti* or the eyebrow center gaze.

The technique of *Shambhavi Mudra* is:

- Sit in a Meditative Posture. Keep your back erect and place the hands on the knees in *Chin* or *Jnana Mudra*.
- Look forward at a fixed point.
- Then look upward as high as possible, without moving the

head.
- Concentrate and focus the eyes on the eyebrow center.

The *Shambhavi Mudra* is a powerful technique for awakening the *Ajna Chakra*, the seat of union between the lower and higher consciousness. Physically it strengthens the muscles of the eyes. It also brings about calmness of the mind and removes stress and anger.

Agochari Mudra

The term "*Agochari Mudra*" means "the unknown attitude." This *Mudra* is also known as *nasikagra drishti* or the nose-tip gaze. It is used in many techniques of Meditation.

The technique of *Agochari Mudra* is:

- Sit in any Meditative Posture.
- Hold the spine erect and the head facing forward.
- Focus the two eyeballs on the tip of the nose.
- Do not strain the eyes. Slowly increase the duration over a period of weeks and months.

Benefits. This *Mudra* develops the powers of Concentration. It awakens the *Mooladhara Chakra.* It brings about introversion and takes the practitioner into the psychic and spiritual planes of consciousness.

Maha Mudra (the Great Seal)

The technique of this *Mudra* is:

- Sit on the floor, with the legs stretched forward.
- Bend the left leg, bringing the heel under the anus. Feel the pressure on the anus.
- Bend forward, catching the right toe with the hands.
- Inhale and retain the breath, practicing *Jalandra Bandha*.
- Fix the gaze between the eyebrows.

- Bend forward more, without any strain, to your maximum limit.
- Hold the position as long as you can comfortably do so.
- Release the pose and the breath.
- Repeat the pose, bending the right leg.

Benefits. *Maha Mudra* aids the cure of consumption, hemorrhoids or pile, enlargement of spleen, constipation, indigestion and various abdominal disorders.

Namaskara Mudra (Salutation Seal)

Its technique is:

- Bring the palms together so that they touch each other opposite the middle of the chest, with the fingers pointing upward.

This hand position is the traditional Hindu way of greeting and saluting.

Ashwini Mudra

The name *Ashwini Mudra* means literally "the attitude of the horse."

Its technique is:

Stage 1

- Sit in any Meditative posture.
- Relax the whole body and close the eyes.
- Contract the sphincter muscles of the anus for a few seconds; feel as if you are sucking the entire rectum up, and hold it.
- Then relax the sphincter muscles for a few seconds.
- Repeat the process as many times as possible.

Stage 2

- Sit as in stage 1.
- Inhale while simultaneously contracting the anus.

- Retain the breath while also holding the contraction of the sphincter muscles.
- Exhale and release the contraction of the anus.
- Repeat as long as is comfortable. Do not strain.

Benefits. By practicing this *Mudra* one is able to gain control of the sphincter muscles of the anus in the same way that a horse has control. When this *Mudra* is performed perfectly, it helps to prevent the escape of pranic energy from the body. The pranic energy can, then, be conserved and directed upwards for higher purposes.

Akashi Mudra

Akashi Mudra means "the attitude of inner space." It is a powerful practice, and must be learned slowly and carefully.

Its technique is

- Sit in any Meditative posture.
- Fold the tongue back against the upper palate.
- Practice *Ujjayi Pranayama* and *Shambhavi Mudra*.
- Simultaneously bend the head backward, but not to the fullest extent; the head should not lean on the top of the shoulders behind the head.
- Breath slowly and deeply. At first the *Ujjayi Pranayama* may irritate the throat in this inclined position of the head, but with practice it will become comfortable.

Benefits. This *Mudra* makes the mind go into a trance when it is perfected. This is not a trance in the Western terminology, but in the Yogic sense where the practitioner achieves a state of heightened consciousness. It brings about calmness and tranquility in the mind.

Vajroli Mudra

The word *vajroli* means "the thunderbolt," which is also the name of the nadi at *Swadhisthana Chakra* (*See* 4.16 Kundalini Yoga, *below*) through which the *prana* related to sexual energy travels. It is said that one of the biggest problems for the aspirant following the path of Meditation is that there is a normal tendency for the spiritual energy of a person to leak out through the sexual system; this is the root cause of sexual desires and urges. Through the practice of *Vajroli Mudra* the sexual energy's gate in the body is controlled, allowing the aspirant to control *prana* and to utilize it for the spiritual awakening.

The technique of this *Mudra* is:

- Sit in any comfortable Meditative *Asana*.
- Place the hands on the knees, close the eyes and relax.
- Try to draw the sexual organs upwards by pulling and tensing the lower abdomen and contracting the urinary system. This contraction is similar to that which is made when one has an urge to go for urination, but wishes to retain for some time.
- The testicle in the male and the vagina in the female should move up a little.

Yoga Mudra (the Yogic Seal)

The technique is:

- Sit in any comfortable Meditative *Asana*.
- Bring the hands back of the body and hold the right wrist with the left hand.
- Exhale and slowly bend forward, as if to touch the floor with the chest.
- Touch the floor with the forehead first, then with the *chin*.
- Breath normally while retaining the *Asana*, inhale while coming out.
- Feel the pressure of the heels against the abdomen.

Those who find it difficult to reach the floor should try to bend forward only up to their capacity and maintain the pose comfortably for some time. Gradually they can try to reach the floor.

Time. Repeat this posture 3 to 5 times for ten seconds at a time. Gradually reduce this repetition and try to retain the Posture once for two minutes.

Benefits. Yoga *Mudra* aids the relief of many disorders of the abdominal viscera. It tones up the nervous system, relieves constipation, and helps to overcome seminal weakness.

BANDHAS

The System of *Bandhas* is a group of inner locks designed to hold *prana* or vital energy within certain areas of the body. *Bandha* means "binding" or "lock." Practicing the *Bandhas* bind the *prana* and directs it toward the different nerve centers and glands according to the Concentration.

Bandhas should be learned under the personal guidance of a teacher and practiced with great care.

Jalandhara Bandha

The term *Jalandhara Bandha* means chin lock. It compresses the pranic force in the trunk region of the body, which is useful in stimulating the Kundalini energy.

Its technique is:

- Sit in any Meditative Posture that allows the knees to firmly touch the floor. *Sukhasana* is thus not suitable.
- Place the palms on the top of the knees.
- Relax the whole body and close the eyes.
- Inhale deeply, retain the breath inside, bend the head forward and press the chin tightly against the chest at the sternum. Straighten the arms and lock them in a fixed position. Simultaneously hunch the shoulders upwards and forwards; this will ensure the arms remain locked.
- The arms should remain on the knees. This is the final Posture.
- Stay in the final Posture as long as you can comfortably retain the breath.

- Then relax the shoulders, bend the arms, slowly release the lock and raise the head. Slowly exhale. Repeat when the breath returns to normal.

Precautions. Never inhale or exhale, as the case may be, until the chin lock is released and the head is upright. Persons with high blood pressure or heart ailments should not practice without expert advice.

Benefits. This *Bandha* brings about the relaxation of the whole body and the mind. It also relaxes the heart by slowing down the heartbeat, and brings tranquility to the mind. The thyroid and parathyroid glands are massaged and their functions improved, enhancing the physical efficiency of the body. This is a good practice for reducing stress, anxiety and anger.

Moola Bandha

The words *moola Bandha* means root lock. This *Bandha* locks the psychic energy in the upper part of the psychic body and does not allow it to descend into the lower limbs. It also stimulates the *Mooladhara Chakra* through mental compression, which helps in the awakening of the Kundalini.

This *Bandha* is usually practiced along with *Jalandhara Bandha* with the breath-retention.

Its technique is:

- Sit in any Meditative Posture with the knees firmly on the ground.
- Place the hands on the knees in *Chin* or *Jnana Mudra*.
- Close the eyes and relax the whole body.
- Concentrate on the trigger point of *Mooladhara Chakra.*
- Contract the sphincters located at the rectum. Feel as if you are sucking the entire rectum upward, and hold it as long as is possible.
- Then slowly release it.
- Relax for a few seconds, and then repeat the practice.

Precaution. This *Bandha* must be perfected gradually and with great care. Do not strain while attempting it.

Benefits. Moola Bandha directs the sex energy upward from its normal downward course. It helps to keep in check nocturnal emissions and aids in maintaining celibacy. It increases the benefit of *Pranayama* during retention.

Uddiyana Bandha (Stomach Lift)

The word *uddhiyana* means "to fly upwards." In this lock the diaphragm and abdomen are made to fly upward, locking the *prana* in the upper body and forcing the vital energy itself to take upward flight.

Technique

- Stand with the feet apart.
- Bend slightly forward, placing the hands on the corresponding knees.
- Empty the lungs by a deep exhalation.
- Contract the front muscles of the abdomen and draw it in, forming a hollow.
- Do not inhale while this lift is being maintained.
- Before the breath can force its way back, release the abdomen and inhale slowly. This makes one round of *Uddhiyana.*
- Repeat the process from three to seven times.

Caution. Uddhiyana should not be held beyond one's capacity. The moment you find that you cannot hold the breath comfortably, release the muscles slowly to bring the abdomen back to the normal position. *Uddhiyana* is to be avoided in cases of circulatory disturbances and serious abdominal troubles.

Time. Repeat this posture from three to seven times, retaining the lift from five to thirty seconds each time.

Benefits. It tones up the nerves of the solar plexus. It relieves constipation, indigestion, and liver troubles; reduces abdominal fat; strengthens flabby stomach. It bestows youth and vitality.

Bandha Traya (The Triple Lock)

Bandha Traya is a combination of *Jalandhra Bandha, Moola Badha* and *Uddhiyana Bandha* and it is practiced during Pranayama.

Its technique is:

- When inhaling and retaining the breath, practice *Moola Bandha.*
- When retaining the breath, practice *Jalandhra Bandha,* along with *Moola Bandha.*
- During exhalation, practice *Uddhiyana.*

Caution. As *Bandha Traya* is a powerful and strenuous practice, it should be learned properly with the help of an adept, and only after the practitioner has perfected *Nadi suddhi* and other *Pranayamas*. Great care must be taken so that there is no undue exertion.

Benefits. *Bandha Traya* charges the whole body with *prana.* It helps in unifying the *prana* and *apana* (the upward and downward movements of the vital energy). It also acts as an aid in awakening the psychic force, *Kundalini.*

Maha Bandha (Great Lock)

Maha Bandha means the great lock. It is a combination of *Moola Bandha, Jalandhra Bandha, Uddhiyana Bandha* and *Bahir Kumbhaka* (external breath retention) as they are practiced in the techniques of *Pranayama.*

Its technique is:

- Sit in *Padmasana, Siddhasana* or *Siddha yoni asana* with your hands on your knees.
- Exhale slowly, completely. Perform *Jalandhara Bandha.*
- Perform *Uddhiyana Bandha.*
- Then perform *Moola Bandha.*
- Maintain this attitude as long as is comfortably possible.
- Alternately center your awareness on the three *Bandhas*

as you retain them.

- Then release first *Moola Bandha.*
- Second, release *Uddhiyana Bandha.*
- Lastly release *Jalandhara Bandha* and make your head upright.
- Exhale and then slowly inhale.
- Exhale and inhale one or more times, and repeat the practice.

Precautions. Maha Bandha is a powerful combined practice. It should not be attempted until one has mastered the three other *Bandhas* and the *Nadi Suddhi Pranayama.*

Benefits. This *Bandha* is used for stimulating the flow of psychic and spiritual energy, and for making the mind introvert in preparation for the practice of Meditation.

3.8: *Pranayama Prana*—The Vital Force

What is *Pranayama*

Pranayama is the fourth step in the eight-step Raja Yoga. It is not, as commonly understood, regulation of breathing. The word *Pranayama* is composed of two words: *prana* and *ayama*. *Prana* means "vital energy," and *ayama* means "control" or "restraint." Therefore *Pranayama* means the control of vital energy. *Prana* is the subtlest aspect in human beings and the universe.

Akasa

According to the Indian philosophy, the universe is composed of two entities: *Akasa* and *Prana*. *Akasa* is the all-penetrating existence. Everything that has form is evolved out of *akasa*. It is *akasa* that has become the air, the liquids, the solids, the sun, the earth, the moon, the stars, the comets, the human body, the animal body, the plants and everything that exists. *Akasa* is so subtle that it cannot be perceived. It can only be seen when it has taken a form.

Prana

By the power of *prana* the universe is evolved out of *akasa*. Just as *akasa* is the omnipresent material of this universe, so is *prana* the omnipresent manifesting power of this universe. At the end of a cycle, all tangible objects resolve back into *akasa*, and all the forces in the universe resolve back into *prana*. In the next cycle, out of *prana* is evolved every energy—motion, gravitation and magnetism. From thought down to physical force, everything is evolved out of *prana*.

Thought is the finest and highest manifestation of the *prana*. Conscious thought is not the whole of thought. There is also what is called instinct or unconscious thought, the lowest plane of thought. If a mosquito bites me, my hand will strike it instinctively. All reflex actions of the body belong to this plane of thought. There is also another plane of thought, conscious thinking, reasoning and judging. Reason is limited. It can go only to a certain length, beyond that it cannot reach. Yogis find that the mind can function on a still higher plane, the Superconsciousness. "When the mind has attained that state, which is called *Samadhi*, it goes beyond the limits of reason and comes face to face with facts which no instinct or reason can ever know. All manipulations of the subtle forces of the body, different manifestations of *prana*, give a push to the mind, help it to go up higher and become Superconscious, from where it acts." (Swami Vivekananda, *Raja Yoga,* p. 38).

Prana – the Vital Force

The vital force in everything is *prana*. It sustains life. Whatever moves or works or has life is but a manifestation of *prana*. It is the power that supports the body and all its moving life forces. The *nadis* are channels for *prana*. When *prana* is in motion and flows through the *nadis,* consciousness arises.

Prana enters the body through the food we eat and the air we breathe. But *prana* is not the food nor the air we breathe. They are merely vehicles.

It is the *prana* that moves the lungs. The motion of the lungs draws in air. So *Pranayama* is not breathing, but controlling that muscular power that moves the lungs. That muscular power, which is transmitted through the nerves to the muscles and from them to the lungs, making them expanding and contracting, is the *prana* that we have to control through the practice of *Pranayama*. When this *prana* has become controlled, then all other actions of *prana* in the body, even muscles and nerves of the body, will slowly come under control. This the Yogi does through *Pranayama*.

Prana causes the senses of perception and organs of action to perform their respective functions. It is the force that holds together the elements of the body. It ignites the internal fire that maintains warmth and metabolism.

Prana is lost from the body in exhalation, excessive exercise, elimination of waste, the emission of semen, the process of childbirth and in times of great emotion. If *prana* is not regulated, the system does not receive an adequate supply of oxygen. The absence of appetite may also indicate an imbalance in *prana*.

If *prana* recedes from any part of the body, whatever be the causes, that part loses its power of action. Death is caused by the outgoing of *prana*. At death, the *prana* exits through the eyes, ears, nose, navel, rectum, urethra or fontanel, leaving an impression at the site of its exit. Its tendency is to leave the body from the site where the mind dwells instinctively or where the inner most feelings reside.

Classification of *Prana*

Ancient Yogis have classified *prana* on the basis of its functions. On entering the body, *prana* divides itself into ten *vayus* that are responsible for directing and administering our mental and physical activities. Of them, five are important. They are: *prana, apana, udana, samana* and *vyana*. Of these, *prana* and *apana* perform the most significant functions.

Prana Vayu rules the region between the larynx and the base of the heart, it governs the verbal mechanism and vocal apparatus, the respiratory system and the muscles engaged in it. Its energy has an upward motion. The processes of inhalation, swallowing and opening mouth are the result of the power of *prana vayu*.

The *prana vayu* within the body gathers at the navel and from there it is distributed throughout the whole body. The energy of *prana* is utilized in the assimilation of food during digestion, and in the action of the vital organs especially the heart.

Apana governs the functions of the kidneys, colon, rectum, bladder, and genitals. It circulates from the navel to the toes. When apana is not functioning properly there is poor elimination of all wastes. When apana is not regulated, one lacks motivation or inclination. He feels lazy, sluggish, heavy and dull.

Samana governs the region between the heart and the navel, and regulates all the metabolic activity involved in digestion. Its function is to digest the food, and separate the nutrients from waste. When *samana* is in disorder the nutritive and waste elements in food are not properly separated and the body may retain toxins. Then the breath becomes short and one may develop gastric disorder.

On the mental level, *samana* gives one the power of discrimination. When it is imbalanced, one may become delirious or delusive.

Udana is the opposite of *prana* in its functions. It forces air out of lungs and body. It rules the body above the larynx. It regulates speech and sound. When *udana* is unregulated, one cannot speak properly, and may have desire to vomit, and breath becomes irregular.

Vyana pervades the entire body. It is a coordinating force in the body. It governs the cutaneous system (skin), senses, body movements, and muscular system, both voluntary and involuntary. It coordinates balance, cerebrospinal system and our interaction with our environment.

When *vyana* is imbalanced, coordination and balance in the body are affected, the thought process becomes inconsistent and sense perceptions are disrupted.

There are other supplementary *vayus*. *Naga vayu* deals with belching and clarity of mind. *Kurma* governs expansion and contraction and sensory nerves. *Krikala* induces hunger and thirst, and causes sneezing. *Devadatta* pervades the whole body. *Dhananjaya* governs the ability to hiccough. These five *vayus* operate on a physical plane only. *Pranayama* is the means of controlling the *vayus*.

Prana and Nervous System

In order to understand the science of *prana* and the door to unlimited power it opens, it is necessary to know the nervous system that coordinates the functions of all other systems in the body. It may be subdivided into the central nervous system and the autonomic nervous system.

The central nervous system consists of the brain, cranial nerves, the spinal cord and spinal nerves. The cranial nerves from the brain and the spinal nerves from the spinal cord are spread throughout the body, forming a network of nerve fibers that carry nerve impulses from and to brain and spinal cord.

The autonomic nervous system regulates involuntary processes such as the secretions of the digestive organs, the beating of the heart and the movement of the lungs. The autonomic system consists of sympathetic and parasympathetic nervous systems which work in opposition to each other and maintain balance. For example, the parasympathetic system operates to slow down the action of the heart and thus regulates the heart beat. The main part of the parasympathetic system is the vagus nerve which supplies and controls all the important vital organs through the different plexuses of the sympathetic system.

Pranayama is intimately connected with the functions of the autonomic nervous system. Through the control of the *prana* the functions of this nervous system, normally considered involuntary, can be brought under conscious control. This can be done by regulating the breath and through the breath, controlling the motion of the lungs, the most vital step in controlling the heart rhythm and the vagus nerve. These, in turn, bring the autonomic nervous system under perfect control. This opens the way for experiencing the higher and subtler levels of mind and power.

Healing and Control of Sickness

Through *Pranayama*, every part of the body can be filled with *prana*, the vital force through our thought, the agent that directs the *prana*. "Control of thought forms is Yoga" says Patanjali. When one is able to do that, he can control the whole body. All the sickness and misery felt in the body can be controlled. He will also be able to cure another person's sickness. But he must not to use this power just for the sake of exhibitions. Such egoistic involvement will certainly cause his downfall from the path of Self-realization.

What is disease? Sometimes in our body, the supply of *prana* gravitates more or less at one part; then the balance is disturbed.

Then disease is caused. Through *Pranayama*, this imbalance in the supply of *prana* can be corrected and thus the disease can be cured. Raja Yoga teaches the control and direction of *prana* through *Pranayama*, and Meditation and other ways.

Health can be transmitted consciously or unconsciously. A very strong person, living with a weak person, will make the latter feel a little stronger, whether he knows it or not. When consciously done, this action becomes quicker and better. If one person has a little more control over his *prana* and can rouse his *prana* to a certain state of vibration, he can transmit it to another person. In fact *prana* can be transmitted to a very great distance, for, there is a continuous mass of matter and there is no distance that admits of gaps.

There are mind-healers, faith-healers, spiritualists and so on. If we examine these different sects, we shall find at the back of their methods the control of *prana*, whether they know it or not. The faith-healers think that faith directly heals a person. It is the *prana* that really does the curing.

One with pure soul, who has controlled his *prana* has the power to bring it into a certain state of vibration that can be transmitted to others, arousing in them similar vibration. This is seen in our everyday actions. For example, the day when a teacher is more enthusiastic, the students enjoy the lecture more.

The great prophets of the world had the most wonderful control of their *prana*, which gave them tremendous will-power; they had brought their *prana* to the highest state of vibration; and this is what gave them power to sway the world. All manifestations of power arise from the control of *prana*. *Prana* flows through *nadis*. Nerves are gross manifestations of the *nadis*.

Breath

Breath is an external manifestation of the force of *prana*. Just as the control of flywheel of an engine controls all other mechanisms in it, so the control of the external breath leads to the control of the gross, subtle, physical and mental aspects of our life. If the motion of the lungs stops, all other manifestations of the force of *prana* in the body will immediately stop. But there are persons who can train themselves in such a manner that the body will live on, even when that motion is stopped. There are some persons who can bury themselves for days and yet live without breathing.

Relationship Between *Prana* and Other Aspects of the Body

In the human body, the breath plays a very vital role, for it establishes relationships between the mind and the body. After working for a certain period of time, it finally ceases. Then the senses and the body become unable to function. So when the breath stops, the link between the body and mind is broken, but the soul, intellect and unconscious mind are not affected. They find another body and begin their work afresh.

So the wise person, who knows that even after death, the soul, intellect and mind remain in tact, does not grieve. One who knows this truth is a true Yogi.

3.9: *Pranayama*: Aims and Benefits

Introduction

Pranayama is one of the most important practices of Yoga science. It is concerned with the control of *prana*, the vital force in the body. This control is exercised through the regulation of the motion of the lungs. Though *prana* is different from breath, still there is a close connection between them. This connection enables us to manipulate the currents of *prana* by manipulating breath. *Pranayama* involves regulation of the three processes of breath: exhalation (*rechaka*), inhalation (*puraka*), and retention (*kumbhaka*), and thus it establishes control over *prana*.

The retention stimulates nerves, equalizes inhalation and exhalation, reduces the weight of the body and decreases the speed of thoughts. The Yogi who is capable of regulating the length of the exhalation and inhalation enjoys health and acquires spiritual power.

Just as the impurities of a metal are burnt away by fire, so the impurities of the mind and senses are burnt away by the control of *prana*, and thus *Pranayama* purifies the mind; it uncovers wisdom that is latent within each person. It is said that through *Pranayama*, the power of levitation is acquired, diseases are cured, spiritual energy is awakened, mental peace and joy, and mental powers are obtained.

The practice of *Pranayama* can be taken up safely, only as a part of full Yogic discipline with practice of *Yama-Niyama*s and *Asanas* under the guidance of a competent teacher.

Aims of *Pranayama*

The aims of *Pranayama* are:

1. To control the flow of *prana* so that the disturbing forces arising from within are eliminated and the mind becomes focused and one-pointed. The entire involuntary is made voluntary, and the voluntary control leads the aspirant to a state of *Samadhi*.
2. To oxygenate the blood and to prevent dissipation of the energy resulting from deoxygenation.
3. To burn up as much waste material as one can. Therefore one should inhale more air and retain the breath.
4. To introduce pressure into the system, maintaining a proper balance between the outside and inside pressures. When this balance is not maintained, then the nerves, mind and muscles are affected. The body trembles and the mind fails to function normally. When the body is full of pressure, one manifests determination, enthusiasm and will-power.
5. To control the thoughts. In the final stage, the breath of life is made perfectly serene, followed by its passage through *Sushumna nadi* to the crown of the head, where the Knowledge of Self (Superconsciousness) is attained.

Benefits

Pranayama enables the practitioner to gain control over the nervous system. The gradual control of the nervous system then enables him to control the mind and *prana*. It helps him to remain unaffected by disturbing thoughts and to keep the body and mind in perfect health. After perfecting *Pranayama*, if one practices control over the mind by means of Concentration and Meditation, then only a student of Yoga can advance in the path of Yoga.

Some people have a capacity to stop the breathing for a short or long period of time and remain like an inert substance. This is not Yoga. Yoga primarily means control over the mind, and not mere control over the body. When the mind is controlled, the body is certainly brought under control.

Pranayama balances the vital principles, brings the mind under volitional control, and directs the vital force through certain nadis in the body.

The perfection of *Pranayama* leads to a decrease in sleep and in the waste products of the body. The practitioner finds his body as light as air. He never perspires, his semen dries up, and the seminal force ascends to come back as nectar. He becomes free from disease and sorrow, and there is neither an increase nor a decrease of the vital principles.

Through *Pranayama* one attains the power to live without air, food or drink, one's mind becomes calm and blissful and spiritual energy is awakened.

Through the practice of *Pranayama*, the psychic centers are activated, and it becomes possible to be aware of the subtler levels of consciousness and the luminosity associated with them. (*Yoga Sutras*, 2.52).

When *Pranayama* is practiced effectively, the Karma which shuts out the discriminative knowledge dwindles away. The practice of *Pranayama* weakens and gradually attenuates the practitioner's Karma that veils revelation and brings about the cycle of births. Thus it has been said: "There is no *Tapas* superior to *Pranayama*; it removes impurities and makes the light of knowledge shine." It is the veil of Karma based on misconception that envelops Enlightenment. Therefore the attenuation of Karma attenuates misconception.

The *sadhaka* gets the capacity to form vivid and sharp mental images and to be able to see them clearly. This is necessary for practicing Concentration effectively. (*Yoga Sutras*, 2.53). From the practice of *Pranayama* the mind acquires fitness for Concentration. During the practice of *Pranayama* the mind is focused on the breath. This improves the mind's ability to concentrate on a desired object.

The light within is covered by a veil of mental darkness. *Pranayama* removes this veil, and the mind becomes clear and fit for Concentration.

Pranayama improves physical health and well-being. This is a secondary benefit. Its main benefit is the control of the waves of the mind through regulation of the *prana*.

During *Pranayama*, the blood is supercharged with extra oxygen. When the breath is retained, more oxygen is injected into the bloodstream. Oxygen is life and so blood is enriched with a lot of life. Moreover along with the air more *prana* goes into the system. Every cell of the body vibrates with new life. The body becomes virus-resistant.

Pranayama purifies the nervous system and eliminates toxins from the body and blood. It produces alertness of mind, good appetite, proper digestion and sound sleep.

Pranayama helps in curing asthma and other respiratory disorders. It eliminates excess mucous that causes hay fever and sinus discomfort. It balances the body temperature.

Pranayama regenerates the body. It charges the body with extra energy and builds stamina and endurance. It expands the chest and lung capacity.

Pranayama reduces food consumption, because you get the required nourishment from the *prana* itself. It reduces the craving for nicotine and revitalizes the lungs and body. It purifies the nadis and nerve centers and channels energy to optimal output.

Pranic Healing and Visualization

Yogis have observed that the breath reflects the condition of the mind. When it is agitated, for example, a person's breathing will be very shallow and quick. By changing the breathing patterns, the mind's condition can be changed.

You can direct your *prana* with your thoughts. The breath and the mind are so interconnected that wherever one goes, the other follows. By sending your thoughts to an affected area, you send your *prana*. This is the secret behind self-healing.

When you do deep breathing, feel that you are inhaling a lot of *prana*, a lot of vital energy. Hold your breath for a few seconds, while thinking that the *prana* is going directly to the affected area and is building it up by removing the dead or diseased cells and tension. Then when you exhale, feel that you are throwing out all of the illness. You can feel that with the inhalation fresh energy comes in, and with the exhalation the collected toxins are thrown out. By doing such visualization, you can cure many of the aches and pains in the body as well as chronic illnesses. *Prana* has that power.

You can achieve tremendous things through visualization. When you practice *Pranayama*, you can visualize light or energy. It can be energy from the sun, the stars, the moon, the ocean, the *Guru* or from God. The energy can be in the form of light or air or water. Feel that you are inhaling energy or light, and feel that is flooding into your system. Feel the healing vibrations, healing energy flowing into the body as you breath deeply.

You can visualize energy in the form of water flowing in and cleansing every part of the system. As you inhale feel that *prana* is being infused and your entire system built up. Then as you exhale, imagine that all the unwanted things are being flushed out.

You can choose any visualization that is most appealing to you and utilize that in your regular practice of *Pranayama*. Align yourself with the Cosmic Energy, the *Prana*, the Cosmic Consciousness and allow yourself to be filled and revitalized as you breathe in.

You can also combine your breathing with the silent repetition of your *mantra* or any holy name. As you inhale, you can repeat the entire *mantra* and repeat it as you exhale. Or you can divide the *mantra* between the inhalation and exhalation. For example, you can repeat "OM" as you inhale and "Shanthi" as you exhale. Imagine that the sound vibrations of the *mantra* are cleansing the body and mind. You also repeat the affirmation: "These holy vibrations are flowing through me and are transforming me."

"*Pranayama* can be a master key in unlocking the gateway to the subtle realm of self-healing, mastering the mind, and spiritual unfoldment." (Swami Satchidananda, *The Breath of Life: Integral Yoga Pranayama* 1993, p. 13).

Conserve *prana* by saving and storing it by regulating your life. Do not waste *prana* by talking too much without any purpose, by overeating and by overdoing or over-indulging in anything. Be moderate in everything.

Preparation for *Pranayama*

An aspirant who wants to practice *Pranayama* exercises has to prepare himself for the practice on the following lines:

1. He must examine his life style and mental outlook and train the body and mind cooperate.
2. It is preferable to lead a quiet life in a place where spiritual seekers and realized persons live. The aspirant should carefully watch his use of energy so that he does not drain himself. He should not mix excessively with others, for such contact leads to attraction and repulsion, and arouses various sorts of unsettling emotions that will disturb his mind. However, the company of sincere and devoted Yogis can be supportive and helpful.
3. The aspirant should regulate his food, activities, sex, sleep and self-preservation so that he does not deviate from his path. Each of these urges has a powerful impact on the human body and mind. There should be a balance in regulating these urges. He should strive for balance and moderation in eating, working and sleeping. Lord Krishna, in the *Bhagavad Gita*, says,
   "If one is regulated in food and entertainment, harmonized in performing actions and balanced in sleeping and waking, then he can perfect Yoga which leads to the cessation of pain." (6.17)
4. A student of Yoga should take care of his diet in order to maintain his body and the nervous system well tuned with the pursuit of higher consciousness. A balanced vegetarian diet, based on grains with legumes (*dahl*), fresh vegetables and low-fat milk and fruits, is the most suitable diet for Yoga students and for others as well, for research findings and experiences of healthy persons show that disease-free health can be maintained by low-fat vegetarian diet alone.

Such care of the diet and periodical fasting are necessary for gaining a control over the *prana*. That is why the ancient epic *Mahabharata* says, "The Yogi acquires power (i.e., proficiency) by eating grains of rice, husks of sesame and barley gruel without fat and avoiding food containing fat. Drinking water mixed with milk, for a fortnight, month, season, or year or observing complete fast for a month, the Yogi acquires power." Foods to be avoided are: meat, processed and fermented foods, harsh spices, raw onions or garlic and white sugar.

5. If the aspirant is a bachelor, he should adopt strict celibacy and conserve his vitality. A married person should be very moderate in sexual involvement.
6. He should strengthen his self-discipline. He should try to control senses, mind, talk and action. Studying and reflecting on inspiring teachings will reinforce self-discipline. The aspirant should conquer anxieties, grief, pain and disappointment through contemplation and devotion. He should avoid negative thoughts. The negative and evil thoughts poison the mind and lead to evil deeds. Therefore he should cherish noble and enlightening thoughts. He should not allow his mind to be dissipated. Excessive talking wastes *prana* and depletes his energy.

The aspirant needs solitude. A quiet place free from external distractions is required. It may be a quiet room in his home, a retreat in the woods or a Meditation room in an Ashram. The room should be airy, and neither too cold nor too hot. Good quality air is essential for Yoga practice. The suitable season for starting the practice of *Pranayama* is fall or spring when the climate is moderate, and air is pure. Dry, pure, cool weather renders the body more active, vigorous and strong, because it strengthens the fibers and leads to better motion of the body fluids.

3.10: *Pranayama* Exercise

Introduction

It might surprise you to know that most of the time, the right and left nostrils do not work equally well. One of the nostrils is always more blocked than the other even when the nasal passages are clear and unobstructed by mucus, and this blockage alternates between the right and left nostrils throughout the day and night. According to Yoga science, this phenomenon is a consequence of the alternation of the flow of subtle energy in the *ida* and *pingala*, main nadis that pass through the *merudanda* (spinal column) on its left and right sides respectfully. Besides, hot and spicy food has a tendency to increase the temperature of the body and cause an increased flow in the right nostril, and exposing oneself to sudden changes of temperature also changes the breath flow.

For Meditation, it is desirable to have equal activation of both the nostrils. There are many techniques for achieving this. Some of the methods for changing the flow of breath from the active to the passive nostril are:

1. Keep the active nostril closed for some time with the fingers. The passive nostril will soon become active.
2. Inhale through the active nostril, close it and exhale through the passive. This process may be repeated several times and then reversed.
3. Inhale deeply, close both nostrils with the fingers, hold the breath as long as is comfortable, and then release it. Repeat this a few times.
4. Make a fist, insert it into the armpit opposite the blocked

nostril and apply pressure with the arm. In a few seconds the blocked nostril will open.

Changing the flow of breath can cure headaches, depression and other disorders. When the right nostril is predominant one tends to be more active and restless. Right nostril's predominance is also conducive to more assertive or aggressive activities. It is helpful to digestion.

When the left nostril is open, one is in a more passive and receptive mood. When both nostrils flow evenly, one has a devotional attitude and feels a sense of harmony and joy. Having both nostrils open is ideal for Meditation.

Let us now consider the simpler exercises of *Pranayama*. The higher stages of *Pranayama* will not, however, be discussed because they involve the techniques of *Bandhas* or locks. The higher techniques must be practiced only under the guidance of a competent teacher.

General Instructions for *Pranayama*

1. Sit upright in any one of the meditative Postures: *Padmasana, Siddhasana, Swastikasana* or *Sukhasana* (*See* 3.6 *Asanas, above*).
2. The Posture should be steady and comfortable with the spine erect and chest well spread out, and hands on the knees. The back, neck and head must be held in a straight line, but relaxed. If the body is crooked, it is harmful to do *Pranayama*, because while inhaling, the chest is forced to expand; but the crooked Posture restricts it, causing strain to the system.
3. The body should be fully relaxed. Tension means wastage of *prana* and distraction of the mind to the area of tension, because wherever the *prana* goes, the mind follows.
4. Beginners may start with simple deep breathing, then *Kapalabhati*, and then *Nadi Suddhi*. The exercises may be practiced in this order:

(a) Deep Breathing
(b) *Kapalabhati*
(c) *Nadi Suddhi*
(d) *Bastrika*
(e) *Sukha Purvaka*
(f) *Brahmari*

5. Always begin the *Pranayamas* with exhalation.
6. If there is any feeling of strain, stop the exercise and relax for a minute or two and then resume.
7. To start with, practice the exercises for ten or fifteen minutes and gradually increase the period of time.
8. The awareness must be on the breath, and keep its flow smooth and even.
9. The benefit of *Pranayama* lies in the controlled exhalation (*rechaka*). Therefore, the exhalation should be very slow, smooth, and controlled. If retention (*kumbaka*) is done beyond one's normal capacity, the *rechaka* cannot be an easy one.
10. The counting of the duration of inhalation, retention (or suspension) and exhalation has to be done by the repetition of a *mantra* like OM, OM. If the mind is fixed on the flow of a sound, then the conception of the passage of time becomes distinct. In order to remember the number of OM repeated, repetition has to be practiced in bunches like "OM-OM, OM-OM, OM-OM-OM." Thus in one bunch seven repetitions of OM are made. Repeating as many such bunches as desired, it is easy to keep the count of repetition.
11. Retention (*kumbaka*) should not be done except in the Intermediate level.
12. *Kumbaka* should always be done at the throat, not at the nose, even if the nose is blocked.
13. During *kumbaka*, there is no particular place for Concentration. The Concentration should just be inward, to observe what is happening. On the inhalation and the exhalation, it would be on the flow of the breath. But during

the retention, just look within and see what is happening.

14. After *Pranayama* is over, just watch the breath. Do not breathe with effort.
15. *Pranayama* practice means working with the very subtle vital energy. Any haste or mistake in *kumbaka* or other intricate techniques might lead to undesirable consequences.
16. Regulate the exhalation and do it more slowly. The slower the exhalation, the shorter the distance the breath travels from the body, and the less *prana* is wasted.
17. Do not strain or go beyond your capacity.
18. As your practice develops, you can reduce the amount of time, spent in *Nadi Sudhi* and *Kapalabhati* and spend more time in *Sukha Purvaka* and *Bastrika.*

Warning. Pranayama should never be done in a hurry, nor should you try to advance too quickly, because you are dealing with vital energy and delicate organs like the lungs and nerve centers.

pecial Note to Women. Women should not do rapid breathing practices (*Kapalabati* and *Bastrika*) during their menstrual period and two or three days thereafter.

Pregnant women, who are regular practitioners, may continue practice for about the first three months, but leave out *Kapalabati* and *Bastrika* thereafter. After childbirth, women may restart *Kapalabati* and *Bastrika* after the fourth or fifth month.

Age. At all age and in all conditions of the body you can start practicing *Pranayama.* However, if you have high blood pressure or coronary disease, you should not practice *Kapalabati* or *Bastrika* without consulting your physician.

***Pranayama* Exercises**

The following simple exercises may be practiced by everyone without any danger. Through them the capacity of lungs will be increased, and this, in turn, will increase one's power of resistance to the modern ills of air pollution and the like.

Simple Deep Breathing: A. Standing Posture

1. After morning ablutions, stand firmly in a calm, quiet and airy place.
2. Exhale through your nostrils, keeping the head, neck and trunk erect.
3. Try to keep the body as motionless as possible except for the stomach muscles and chest that are involved in deep breathing.
4. Exhale through the nostrils, smoothly, without any exertion and without any sound.
5. Having exhaled completely, inhale deeply through the nostrils.
6. Repeat this about ten times every morning.

Benefits. Though the deep breathing exercise does not affect the pranic currents in the body, its practice promotes health and increases the intake of oxygen. Deep rhythmic breathing, with inhalations and exhalations of equal duration is beneficial for low blood pressure, insomnia and heart attack. It strengthens the nervous system and leads to voluntary regulation of the respiratory system. This is the secret of a healthy body and a sound mind.

Simple Deep Breathing: B. Lying Down Posture

1. Lie on the back with the feet apart and the arms along the sides of the body, palms up.
2. Gently close the eyes and place the hands on the upper abdomen, between the rib cage and the navel, in order to feel the movement of the muscles.
3. Inhale and exhale through the nostrils slowly, smoothly and deeply. There should be no noise, jerks or pauses in the breath.
4. Consciously pull in the abdominal muscles while exhaling. If you find difficulty practicing this diaphragmatic movement, you may use your hands to gently push in the abdominal muscles when exhaling.
5. When inhaling, be aware of the abdominal wall pushing out.

There should be a slight movement of the chest.

Practice this method of deep breathing three to five minutes every day. Alternatively the following

three-part deep breathing exercise may be practiced. This is preferable to simple deep breathing.

Three-part Deep Breathing

1. Inhale and fill the stomach and then gradually expand the lower chest and the upper chest until the collar bones rise.
2. Exhale from the upper chest, then contract the lower chest and lastly deflate the stomach, drawing it in, to empty the lungs completely Repeat this about ten times.

If you have difficulty in learning the above exercise, you can lie on your back, placing your hands on your stomach, to feel how it inflates and deflates. Deep breathing can be practiced anytime during the day. As you progress in your practice, you can reduce the time spent on this exercise, as deep breathing is incorporated in the alternate breathing techniques.

Benefits. This method of three-part deep breathing fills the lungs to capacity and empties them thoroughly, enabling you to supercharge the system with seven times as much oxygen and *prana* as in a normal breath.

***Kapalabhati* (The Skull Shining)**

Kapalabhati means "skull shine." It consists of a vigorous forceful expulsion of the breath, using diaphragm and abdominal muscles. The chest remains still. The expulsion of the breath is followed by a relaxation of abdominal muscles resulting in a spontaneous inhalation.

Technique

1. This practice needs a firm and steady Posture because of the contraction of the abdomen during the expulsions. So

sit in a stable Posture with the head, neck and trunk erect and in one line.

2. Exhale forcefully pulling in the abdomen, followed by automatic inhalation as the diaphragm and abdominal muscles relax. This constitutes one cycle.
3. Repeat several cycles in quick succession from seven to twenty-one cycles, depending on your capacity. This constitutes one round.
4. Practice three rounds in the morning and another three rounds in the evening.
5. When *Kapalabhati* is properly learnt, along with the usual method, it can also be done with alternation of nostrils, 2 or 3 times each nostril. That will clear the nostrils and make the breath flow equally through both of them. If one nostril is more blocked, an additional number of expulsions can be done through that nostril to get it opened.

Benefits. Kapalabhati cleanses the nadis in the skull and burns out the excess mucous that causes sinus problems and allergies. It also stimulates the abdominal muscles and digestive organs.

Nadi Suddhi

This means "nerve purification." This exercise involves deep breathing with alternating the nostrils.

Technique

1. Sit in a calm, quiet, airy place in an easy and steady Posture.
2. Keep the head, neck and trunk straight and the body still.
3. Bring the right hand up to the nose. Form *Vishnu Mudra*. That is, fold the index and middle fingers so that the right thumb can be used to close the right nostril and the last two fingers can be used to close the left nostril.
4. Close the right nostril with the right thumb. Exhale slowly and deeply through the left nostril, without any exertion and jerks. And then inhale deeply through the same nostril.
5. Close the left nostril with the last two fingers, open the

right nostril and exhale slowly and completely. Then inhale through the same nostril.

6. Then switch the nostrils and repeat. The pattern is: Exhale, inhale and switch. Exhale, inhale and switch. Remember to make your breathing full and deep, starting each inhalation by releasing the abdomen and allowing it to expand, and continuing while expanding the rib cage, and then the upper chest until the collar bones rise up. Then exhaling slowly, first dropping the collar bones, then contracting the chest, and then the stomach, one part flowing into the other.
7. In the beginning the count and the ratio are not important. The ideal ratio of exhalation to inhalation is 2:1. That is, the exhalation takes twice as long as the inhalation. You can mentally count "OM 1, OM 2, OM 3, etc." Once the 2:1 ratio is accomplished, gradually increase the count until it is 20 (exhalation) to 10 (inhalation).
8. The mind should be fully concentrated on the breath.
9. Repeat the cycle 30 to 50 times.
10. Finally close the exercise when you exhale through the right nostril. Bring back breathing to normal.

Benefits. Nadi Suddhi purifies the nadis or subtle energy channels. It brings health and vitality to every part of the body. It makes the mind calm.

Practice this exercise both in the morning and in the evening.

Brahmari **(Humming Bee)**

Technique

1. Inhale through the nostrils, filling the lungs fully.
2. Exhale, making a humming sound. Try and feel the vibration on the soft palate at the roof of the mouth. Feel and imagine that the vibration is going straight up through the head to the crown of the head and out into the cosmos.
3. Do five rounds at various pitches.

Benefits. *Brahmari Pranayama* tones the vocal chords, creates sound vibrations for Concentration, and enables you to get in touch with the *Pranava* (OM), the primordial hum of the universe.

Bastrika (Bellows Breath)

This is rapid breathing similar to *Kapalabhati*, with the addition of retention of the breath. *Jalandra Bandha* (the chin lock) is used for the retention of breath.

Technique

1. Take a full, deep inhalation.
2. Hold the breath while bending the neck forward, keeping the back and shoulders erect, and bring the chin as close to the chest as possible.
3. Lift the chin, and slowly exhale. Remember that retention is done at the throat, without building pressure in the nose.

In this exercise, the emphasis is on the forceful exhalation by snapping the abdomen inward, as in *Kapalabhati*. You can have a slight effort on the inhalation also. Each round will consist of a series of rapid expulsions and slightly forceful inhalations followed by retention, and finally a slow, deep exhalation.

Do three to five rounds of *Bastrika*.

Benefits. Bastrika exhilarates the blood circulation and stimulates the entire body quickly. It improves digestion, removes phlegm, and helps in curing asthma and other respiratory problems. It builds up and strengthens the entire respiratory system.

Sukha Purvaka (Easy, Comfortable Breathing)

This exercise is an advanced form of *Nadi Suddhi*, the alternate nostril breathing, because it employs retention. When you can comfortably practice *Nadi Suddhi* at a 10 to 20 count (inhalation to exhalation). You can begin *Sukha Purvaka*. It involves exhalation, inhalation and retention. The pattern is: Exhale, inhale, retain, change nostrils; exhale, inhale, retain, change nostrils.

While practicing *Sukha Purvaka*, adopt the following feelings:

(a) As you inhale, feel that you are drawing in energy or *prana*.
(b) While retaining, feel the energy or *prana* being diffused throughout the system and burning up impurities.
(c) While exhaling, feel that all of the impurities are leaving the body and the mind.

Technique

1. Form *Vishnu Mudra* with your right hand as in *Nadi Suddhi.* Close the right nostril with the thumb.
2. Exhale slowly through the left nostril for a count of 20.
3. Then inhale through the same nostril for a count of 10.
4. Close both nostrils and retain the breath for 5 seconds.
5. Release the thumb from the right nostril and exhale slowly and completely through the right nostril for a count of 20.
6. Inhale through the right nostril for a count of 10.
7. Close both nostrils and retain the breath for 5 seconds.
8. Release the left nostril and exhale to a count of 20.
9. Inhale through the left nostril.

Continue breathing with this pattern for 10 to 15 minutes. The retention can be held up to the length of the exhalation.

Benefits. Sukha Purvaka has all the benefits of *Nadi Suddhi*. In addition, it enriches the quality of the blood and ensures optimal physical health. It makes the mind clear and steady. It is an excellent preparation for Meditation.

Closing Remarks

Real *Pranayama* begins when the breath is retained for some time between inhalation and exhalation. The retention of breath is called *Kumbhaka*. It affects the flow of pranic currents in a very marked and fundamental manner and enables you to gain increasing control over these currents. It is dangerous to practice *Kumbhaka* and other advanced *Pranayama* techniques without the guidance of a competent teacher.

In the beginning, Deep Breathing and *Nadi Suddhi* may be practiced. Only after some practice, the *Kapalabhati, Bhastrika* and *Sukha Purvaka* exercises may be attempted.

The advanced stages of *Pranayama* involve locks and retention of the breath. One can harm himself if he attempts retention through locking without guidance and without disciplining his diet, sleep and completely eliminating the desire for sex gratification. Only a competent teacher can advise one to start practicing retention when he is ready for it. Then as the student progresses, the duration of inhalation, retention and exhalation is extended. Finally and only after some mastery has been achieved, retention after exhalation is also attempted.

Pranayama is a complex and highly developed science. The exercises described above are the fundamental ones that can be practiced by all, but there are many more advanced techniques. One should seek the guidance of a competent *Guru* in order to learn the more complex techniques and to achieve perfection in them.

3.11: *Pratyahara*

Introduction

Pratyahara means withdrawal of mind from senses. It is the fifth step of Raja Yoga. Why should mind be withdrawn from the senses? Lack of control over senses leads to a chain reaction that ultimately destroys a person himself. Lord Krishna beautifully presents this fact in the *Bhagavad Gita*:

> "By constantly dwelling upon sense-objects, one develops attachment to them, from attachment arises desire, from desire is born anger." (2.62)
> "From anger arises delusion, from delusion loss of memory, from loss of memory one loses reasoning, and from the loss of reason, one destroys himself." (2.63)

To gain any success in Meditation, the mind has to be withdrawn from the external world and turned inward and focused on the object of Concentration. Besides, the mind has to be purified by cultivating moral and ethical values. All religious and ethical scriptures all over the world teach us moral values: "Be good,""do good," "do not steal," etc. The *Upanishads* contain many ethical injunctions such as: "Speak the truth; follow righteousness," "truth alone prevails, never falsehoods," "do not covet the wealth of others." Telling will not help us. We must know how to control our mind. But the mind is a slave of physical objects; it is restless and wandering; it is a storehouse of memories of past experiences, a stream of thoughts, desires and emotions. So when we sit and start Meditation practice, immediately a stream of thoughts, fantasies, memories and emotions will start flowing; and we will not be able to concentrate the mind on the object of Concentration.

Restlessness of Mind

The problem with our mind is that it is continually receiving data about the outside world through the sense organs: the ears, the eyes, the nose, the tongue and the skin. Innumerable vibrations from all kinds of objects are constantly bombarding the sense organs. Those sense impressions reach the mind through the brain centers. When the sense organs, brain centers and the mind join together, we perceive the objects. The mind is attracted by some of them and desires arise in the mind. Besides, thoughts go on arising from the memories of past experiences stored in the mind. From one thought a series of associated thoughts arise. For example, when a thought of forthcoming vacation arises in the mind, we start thinking about the various choices of spending the vacation, their pros and cons, the arrangements for travel and stay to be made, etc. We are also concerned about the current problems and the future. Thus a constant stream of desires, thoughts, anxieties and imaginations goes on flowing. (See Chapter 2.7 Purification and Control of the Mind, above)

Curtailing Sense Impressions

Thus the main source of desires that go on arising in the mind is sense impressions produced by the objects of the external world. Can this source be curtailed? Actually we do this often. When we are absorbed in an interesting book we automatically lose the awareness of the surroundings. We forget the ticking sound of the clock or voice of the people in another room. How does this happen? This happens because of mind's disconnection with sense organs. This gives us a clue to get the mind cut off from the awareness of our environment. That is, if the mind's association with sense organs is disconnected or if the mind is under control, then the mind will lose the awareness of our environment. This withdrawal of the mind from the sense organs is called *Pratyahara*. When the mind is so withdrawn, due to lack of contact with their corresponding objects, the senses, as it were, follow the nature of the mind, that is, like the mind that has suspended its functions, the senses also stop their functions. (*Yoga Sutras*, 2.54). Just as bees follow the course of the queen bee and rest when the latter rests, so when the mind stops, the senses also stop their activities. In the *Bhagavad Gita* Sri Krishna says,

> "The turbulent senses, O Arjuna, do violently carry away the mind of (even) a wise person, though he be striving (to control them)." (2.60)

Turbulent senses, like wild horses, will hurl down even an advanced Yogi towards the objects of the senses, preventing him from reaching the goal of final Liberation.

> "The mind which follows the wandering senses, carries away his discrimination as the wind (carries away) a boat on the waters." (2.67)

The mind which moves along with the wandering senses, destroys the discrimination of an aspirant and carries him away from his spiritual path.

> "With the senses, the mind and the intellect (ever) controlled, having liberation as his supreme goal, free from desire, fear and anger the sage is verily liberated for ever." (5.28)

Only when a Yogi frees himself from desire, fear and anger by controlling the senses, the mind and the intellect, he can attain Liberation.

Is *Pratyahara* Possible?

Certainly it is possible. We see it practiced by some groups of people. The faith-healers teach people to deny misery, pain and evil. Their philosophy is roundabout, but it is a part of Yoga upon which they have unknowingly stumbled. Where they succeed in making a person cast off suffering by denying it, they really use a part of *Pratyahara*, for they make the mind of the person strong enough to ignore the senses. Similarly, the hypnotists, by their suggestion, excite in the patient a sort of morbid *Pratyahara* for the time being. Of course the hypnotic suggestion can act only upon a week mind.

The control of the brain centers established for a time in a patient by a faith-healer or a hypnotist leads to the ultimate ruin of the patient. It is not really controlling the brain centers by the power of the patient's own will, but it is, as it were, stunning his mind for a time by sudden blows which another's will gives to it. It is similar to controlling a fierce horse by giving a heavy blow on its head. The patient, whose mind is so stunned often, loses his mind gradually, instead of gaining the power of perfect control over it. Every attempt at control that is not voluntary and not made with the individual's own will, not only is disastrous, but also defeats its very purpose. The goal of each soul is freedom from the slavery of matter and thought, mastery of external and internal nature. Instead of leading toward that goal, every will-current coming from another only rivets one more link to the already existing heavy chain of bondage.

Whosoever asks anyone to believe blindly or drags people behind him by the controlling power of his superior will, causes an injury to humanity. Therefore everyone should use his own will to control the body and mind himself. He who has succeeded in attaching or detaching his mind to or from the brain centers at will has succeeded in *Pratyahara*. For, according to Swami Vivekananda, *Pratyahara* means, "Checking the outgoing powers of the mind, freeing it from the thralldom of the senses." When we can do this, then we shall have taken a long step toward freedom, before that we are mere machines.

But it is not easy to control the mind. It is hard indeed to control it! The mind is compared to a maddened monkey that is restless by its own nature. Someone made it drink wine. It became still more restless. Then a scorpion stung it. The poor monkey found his condition worse than ever. To complete its misery a demon entered into him. Are there words to describe the uncontrollable restlessness of the monkey? The human mind is like that monkey! "Incessantly active by its own nature, it then becomes," says Swami Vivekananda, "drunk with the wine of desire, thus increasing its turbulence. After desire has taken possession, comes the sting of the scorpion of jealousy at the success of others; and last of all the demon of pride enters the mind, making it think itself all important." You can imagine how hard it is to control such a mind!

What is the Possibility

The mind is like a naughty child; it does the opposite of what you want it to do. So if you try to detach it from sense impressions, it clings more intensively to them. Instead, sit for some time every day, and allow the mind to run on. Let the monkey jump as much as he can; you simply wait and watch. Until you know what the mind is doing you do not control it. Give it the rein. Many undesirable thoughts may bubble up. You may even wonder how it was possible for you to harbor such hideous thoughts! But how long can the monkey mind jump? You will find that each day the mind's vagaries are becoming less and less violent, that each day it is becoming calmer. You will find that day after day thoughts will be fewer and fewer, until at last the mind is under perfect control. But you must patiently practice every day. The mind, finding itself, being watched in this way, realizes its stillness and becomes still. When the mind withdraws into itself, the sense organs, like faithful dogs, instinctively imitate their master. They withdraw themselves from the respective objects. (*Yoga Sutras*, 2.54)

The *Katha Upanishad* compares the battle with the senses to a journey by a chariot drawn by five horses. It says:

> He whose chariot is driven by reason, and who controls the reins of his mind, reaches the end of the journey, the supreme abode of the All-pervading." (1.3.9)

If the senses are allowed to turn outward, they grasp the pictures of the outside world and transmit those messages to the mind, making it restless. Turned inward, the senses find stillness by taking the form of the mind itself. The *Katha Upanishad* says:

> "When the five senses and the mind are still, and the intellect does not stir, that is the highest state." (2.3.10)
> This steady control of the senses is Yoga. Then one becomes undistracted, for Yoga comes and goes." (2.3.11)

You should not delude yourself into thinking that you have gained mastery even after a few years of practice of *Pratyahara*. In the *Bhagavad Gita* Lord Krishna warns us that,

> "The turbulent senses do violently carry away the mind of even a wise man, though he is striving to control them." (2.60)

Any minute, there can be a slip. You should be always alert and vigilant. For example, if you observe strict celibacy, you should stay away from persons of opposite sex. You need not dislike them, but you should not freely associate with them, nor even to hug and kiss them. Although your mouth will call them "sisters or brothers," your senses will take the action in a different way.

The Outcome of the Self-control of the Mind

The successful practice of *Pratyahara* gives you complete control over the senses. You are no longer their slaves. You become their master. (*Yoga Sutras*, 2.55). In the *Bhagavad Gita* Sri Krishna says,

> "When, like the tortoise which withdraws on all sides its limbs, a yogi withdraws his senses from the senses-objects, then his wisdom becomes steady." (2.58)

A Yogi who is endowed with this power of withdrawal can enter into *Samadhi* even in a crowed place or a battlefield. If the functions of the senses can be stopped along with the suspension of the activities of the mind, whenever desired, that is the best form of senses-control. That is true freedom, and real victory. If you are free from your own mind and senses, nothing can bind you. Even imperial power cannot bind you. You are not afraid of anything.

It is interesting to note how the first five stages of Yoga eliminate one after another the different sources of disturbance to the mind, and prepare it for the final struggle with its own modifications.

First, by *Yama-Niyamas* are eliminated the emotional disturbances caused by moral defects in one's nature.

Second, by *Asanas* the physical disturbances are eliminated.

Third, one has to deal with the disturbances caused by the irregular or inadequate flow of *prana*, the vital force. These disturbances are removed by the practice of *Pranayama.*

Last, through *Pratyahara* is removed the major source of disturbances coming through the sense organs. Thus is accomplished the external Yoga, and the *sadhaka* now becomes capable of treading the stages of internal Yoga.

3.12: References for Section III

1. Deshpande, P.Y., *Authentic Yoga,* Bombay: B.I. Publications, 1979
2. Hari Prasad Shastri, *Yoga,* London: W & G. Foyle Ltd., 1958
3. Integral Yoga Institute, *Integral Yoga Hatha: Step by Step Instructions for Beginners,* Yogaville: Integral Yoga Publications, 1979
4. Mascaro, Juan, *The Upanishads*, London: Penguin Books, 1965
5. Mishra, Ramamurti S., *Fundamentals of Yoga,* New York: Harmony Books, 1987
6. Radhakrishnan S.,ed., *The Principal Upanishads*, London: George Allen & Unwin, 1969
7. Swami Abhedananda, *How to be a Yogi*, Calcutta: Ramakrishna Vedanta Math, 1971
8. Swami Abhedananda, *Yoga: Its Theory and Practice*, Calcutta: Ramakrishna Vedanta Math, 1967
9. Swami Chidananda, *The Philosophy, Psychology and Practice of Yoga,* Shivanandanagar: The Divine Life Society, 1984
10. Swami Gnaneswarananda, *Yoga for Beginners,* Chicago: Vivekananda Vedanta Society, 1975
11. Swami Hariharananda Aranya, *Yoga Philosophy of Patanjali*, Albany: State University of New York Press, 1983
12. Swami Jyotirmayananda, *Raja Yoga: Study of the Mind,* Miami: Swami Lalitananda,1970
13. Swami Krisnananda, *Yoga as a Universal Science,* Shivanandanagar: The Divine Life Society, 1983
14. Swami Prabhavananda, and Isherwood, Christopher, *How to Know God – The Yoga Aphorisms of Patanjali,* Hollywood: Vedanta Press, 1981
15. Swami Rama, *Lectures on Yoga,* Honesdale: The Himalayan International Institute of Yoga Science and Philosophy, 1983
16. Swami Rama, *Path of Fire and Light,* Honesdale: The Himalayan International Institute of Yoga Science and Philosophy, 1990
17. Swami Satchidananda, *Guru and Disciple,* Yogaville: Integral Yoga

Publications, 1977

18. Swami Satchidananda, *Sutras of Patanjali,* Yogaville: Integral Yoga Publications, 1990
19. Swami Satchidananda, *The Breath of Life: Integral Yoga Pranayama*, Yogaville: Integral Yoga Publications, 1993
20. Swami Satyananda, *Meditations,* Monghyr (India): Bihar School of Yoga, 1977
21. Swami Sivananda, *Guru Tattva,* Shivanandanagar: The Divine Life Society, 1976
22. Swami Vivekananda, *Raja Yoga*, New York: Ramakrishna-Vivekananda Center, 1973
23. Taimmi, I.K., *The Science of Yoga*, Wheaton, Ill: The Theosophical Publishing House, 1975
24. Yogashaki Saraswati, *Yoga Sadhana,* Bombay: Wilco Publishing House, 1972

SECTION IV

4.1: Concentration: Meaning and Methods

Meaning

Concentration (*Dharana*) is the sixth step in Raja Yoga and the first one in the three-fold internal combined Yogic process of *Samyama*–Concentration, Meditation and *Samadhi*. Concentration means bringing the scattered mind to a point of focus. It involves freeing the mind from habitual association with desires and feelings, through exercises that reveal its prejudiced and wandering ways, and then focusing it upon a single object or idea.

In everyday life we concentrate while reading a book, while writing, while doing a job, while inserting a thread through the eye of a needle, while driving a car through a busy street and so on. This Concentration is called external, for it is something in the external world that holds our attention. This is a muscular exercise.

Yogic Concentration (*Dharana*), according to Patanjali, is holding the mind within a center of spiritual consciousness in the body or fixing it on some Divine form. (*Yoga Sutras*, 3.1). It involves focusing and holding the mind's attention on an object or idea. Attention is therefore required for Concentration. It is of two kinds, voluntary and involuntary. Voluntary attention is that which is directed toward an object or idea by an effort of the will-power. It requires willpower, determination and mental training. Involuntary attention is spontaneous, and does not demand any training or willpower. Concentration requires voluntary attention. Continued attention leads to Concentration.

Attention (*avadhana*) plays a very great part in Concentration. It is the basis of will. When it is properly guided and directed toward the internal world for purposes of introspection, it will analyze the mind and illumine the very many astounding facts for you.

The force with which anything strikes the mind is generally in proportion to the degree of attention bestowed upon it. Moreover, the great art of memory is attention. Inattentive people have bad memories. Power of attention declines in old age.

Attention is focusing of awareness. It is one of the signs of trained will. It is a rare faculty. Celibacy (*Brahmacharya*) wonderfully develops this power. Attention can be cultivated and developed by persistent practice. All the great persons of the world have risen up through this faculty. It is through the power of attention that mind carries out all its activities.

There was an artisan who used to make arrows. One day he was very busy at his work. He was so much absorbed in his work that he did not notice even a big party of the monarch with his retinue passing in front of his shop. Such must be the nature of your Concentration when you fix your mind on God.

Concentration is a great instrument not only in spiritual life and meditation but it is also very much desirable in practical worldly life to achieve success. The story of Arjuna, in a contest at archery after completion of his studies, beautifully illustrates this. At the termination of the courses of archery, the *Guru* Kripacharya wanted to test the skill of his hundred and six pupils. The target was the eye of a wooden bird hung from a branch of a tall tree by a thread in the air. One by one, the Kauravas and Pandavas came to hit the mark. At last came Arjuna. He stood on the assigned place, bent his bow and put the arrow to it. The Acharya now asked him what he saw? Arjuna said, "The head of the bird." The Acharya asked , "What is the target?" The reply was, "The eye of the bird." "Look closer, what do you see now?" "Only the eye of the bird." "Shoot." The arrow hit the eye. In the concentration Arjuna saw nothing but the eye. Concentration has to be so exact and minute in archery. So it is to be in all affairs of the world, and more so in meditation.

Mind's Wandering

In the beginning stage, when you sit for Meditation and try to concentrate on the chosen object of Concentration, you will find that the mind drifts away within a few seconds. This is a common problem for everyone in the beginning stage. This is the very nature of the mind, for the mind is nothing but a flow of thoughts. It is generally compared to a drunken mad monkey. It is stung by scorpion of desires, haunted by ghost of senses. No wonder it is constantly restless, and thought after thought goes on arising in it.

Mind is also compared to quick silver because its rays are scattered over various objects. It is compared to a moving air, because it is wavering (*chanchala*). It is compared to a furious rutting elephant, because of its passionate impetuosity. Mind is known as the "Great Bird," because it jumps from one object to another object, just as a bird jumps from one twig to another, from one tree to another.

All along from the childhood, the mind has been trained to look externally, and indulge in endless thoughts of worldly objects, desires, aversions, emotions, memories, beliefs, daydreams and problems of life. So when you sit quietly and start to concentrate, the mind habitually runs to its old grooves. What else can you expect? You need not feel discouraged and helpless. Make determined effort and do regular practice to tame the mind and gently bring it under control.

In the initial stage of practice, subtle extraordinary sense perceptions may occur. They can give you some confidence, and encourage perseverance. (*Yoga Sutras*, 1.35). If you concentrate on the tip of your nose, you will experience an extraordinary smell of perfume. If Concentration is fixed on the tip of the tongue, you will get a nice taste; if on the palate, a supernormal sense of color; if on the middle of the tongue, a supernormal sense of touch; if on the root of the tongue, a supernormal sense of hearing. Such experiences are of no value in themselves, but they will give you confidence, and serve to prove what can be done with the mind.

Objects for Concentration

The object to be chosen for Concentration can be either a sacred name, a mystic *mantra*, the cosmic syllable OM, OM Shanthi, Hari OM, etc. or a form. The form may be that of your personal God such as Sri Krishna, Siva, Vishnu, Jesus or Buddha or your *Guru*. If you concentrate on a physical form, after a time you can create its mental picture. If you do not want a particular human form, then you can choose the visual image of the sun, the moon, a star, flower, flame or any other form you like, because the Lord is present everywhere in every form.

According to Patanjali, there are six main objects on which one can concentrate:

1. Inner Light: The ancient Yogis believed that there was a center of spiritual consciousness, called "the Lotus of the Heart," situated between the abdomen and the thorax, which could be revealed in deep Meditation. They claimed that it had the form of a lotus with an inner light. It was said to be "beyond all sorrow and worry," since those who saw it were filled with an extraordinary sense of peace and joy. From the earliest times, the masters of Yoga emphasized the importance of meditating upon this glowing Lotus. (*Yoga Sutras*, 1.36). The *Kaivalya Upanishad* says:

> "Brahman is higher than heaven, shines in the cave of the heart. . . . (3)
> "In a solitary place, seated oneself in an easy posture, with a pure heart, . . controlling all the senses, bowing with devotion to the Guru, Meditate on the lotus of the heart, pure and devoid of passion, in the center of which is the pure, the sorrowless, the inconceivable, the unmanifested, the blissful (Brahman) . . ." (5, 6)

In the *Chandogya Upanishad* we read:

> "Within the city of Brahman, in our own body, there is the heart and within the heart there is a small shrine in the shape of a lotus. Within it dwells that which is to be sought after and

realized." (8.1.1)

The *Mundaka Upanishad* says:

"Within the Lotus of the Heart, He dwells, where the nerves meet like the spokes of a wheel. Meditate upon Him as OM. May you be successful in crossing over the ocean of darkness." (2.2.6)

Concentrate on this glowing Lotus of the Heart, because it localizes our image of the spiritual consciousness toward which we are struggling.

2. *The Heart of a Great Soul.* You can concentrate on a great soul's heart that is free from passion (*Yoga Sutras*, 1.37). Let your mind dwell on some holy personality, like Lord Krishna, Buddha, Christ or Ramakrishna. Concentrate upon His heart. Try to feel the saint's heart has become your heart. Both Hindus and Christians practice this form of Meditation.

3. *Dream Experience.* Sometimes you may have dreams of Divine beings. If you have such dreams, remember them and let your mind dwell on them. (*Yoga Sutras*, 1.38). In Indian scriptures we find many instances of such holy dreams and even *mantra* initiations are received in dreams. If you have not had any such dream, then imagine the peace of deep sleep, and concentrate upon it.

4. *OM.* Concentration on OM is one of the highest forms of Meditation (*Yoga Sutras*, 1.28). OM is the highest name of God. It stands for the supreme truth. It is infinite consciousness and bliss. The inner meanings can be studied in the *Mandukya Upanishad* and other scriptures. All Meditation and mystic practices should begin and end with OM.

5. *Chakras.* Fix the mind upon any one of the higher centers of spiritual consciousness called *Chakras* (*See* 4.16 *Kundalini Yoga, below*). Scriptures speak of seven centers of consciousness: lotuses at the navel, the organ of reproduction, the organ of evacuation, heart, throat, forehead and the crown of the head. When the mind

is fixed on any one of the first three lower centers, it is attached to worldliness. A Yogi should not concentrate on these centers. He can fix the mind on heart or any other higher centers. (*Yoga Sutras*, 3.1).

6. *Divine Form.* You can also concentrate on your personal God, trying to visualize the form either within a lotus of a *chakra* or outside your own body. (*Yoga Sutras*, 3.1). By meditating on the God's form, you will begin to develop Divine qualities.

7. *Anything That Elevates.* One of the most attractive features of Patanjali's philosophy is its universality. There is no attempt to impose any particular cult upon the spiritual aspirant. Patanjali clearly says "you can mediate on anything that will elevate you." (*Yoga Sutras*, 1.39)

Purpose of Concentration

The experiences of Yogis since ages have shown that one can control one's mind through practice. The mind is like a lake disturbed by the rising waves of thoughts. The practice of Concentration helps to still the waves and when your thoughts are stilled, you can see your reflection in the water of the lake and know your own true nature. According to Yoga Science, we are not restricted to the three states of waking, dreaming and deep sleep. There is a fourth state called *turiya,* the state of Superconsciousness. To attain it, you must regularly try to concentrate and bring your mind to a focus, after which through Meditation you can expand it to the Superconscious state. The purpose of Concentration is to gather together the dissipated energies of your mind, and to lead your concentrated mind to the state of Superconsciousness.

The effort of gathering the mental rays on a point is similar to gathering the rays of the sun through a lens on a sheet of paper. When the rays are sharply focused to a point on the paper, the concentrated solar energy produces ignition and the sheet of paper burns. In the same way, the concentrated mind is powerful and is capable of piercing through the deep layers of the consciousness.

When the mind is controlled and becomes desireless or free from sense-objects, the state of Meditation (*dhyana*) is achieved.

Concentration is therefore the master key that opens the gates of Meditation, because prolonged Concentration results in Meditation. In fact, it is difficult to discern the dividing line between the two.

Without Concentration the energy of the mind is dissipated in vague thoughts, worries and fantasies. A disciplined person expresses himself more clearly through Concentration; a person of ordinary intellect, with highly developed Concentration, is more creative then the highly intellectual person of poor Concentration.

Patanjali has given elaborate treatment to the science of Concentration in *Yoga Sutras*, for, he realized its utility in calming an agitated mind. With steady practice the nervous system and the mind are relaxed, and the mind then becomes calm, steady and one-pointed. You are thus led to the Superconscious state where you experience the Divine bliss.

Methods of Concentration

Concentration may be broadly classified into (a) external and (b) internal, depending upon the object of Concentration. The method chosen should be based on one's temperament, but once the method has been chosen, the aspirant should practice it faithfully for at least three months, only then he will begin to see the results.

In the external method, the eyes are open and focused on an external object such as a point, flower, steady flame of a candle, a picture of personal God or the *Guru*. Or one could use a mirror and gaze at the midspace between the eyebrows in the reflection. The gaze should be steady but there should be no strain on the eyes. The nasal gaze and frontal gaze are also effective methods for developing Concentration. In the nasal gaze the eyes are gently focused on the tip of the nose, whereas in the frontal gaze the space between the eyebrows is the point of Concentration. There should be no violent or forceful effort involved in this practice. The duration of Concentration can be from half a minute to half an hour. In the beginning one may concentrate on an external object.

In the internal method the eyes are closed, and the mind is focused (1) on a word or sound, (2) on breathing, (3) on a mental image, or (4) on a psychic center or *Chakra*.

Concentration on a Mental Image. Concentration of a mental image makes the mind steady. In the beginning the mental image chosen should be that of a concrete, simple object such as a *yantra*, a small illuminated circle or a soothing light. Efforts should be made to hold the mental image for as long as possible. Other suitable images are the written form of OM, the form of personal God or the *Guru*.

Concentration on a Word or Sound. Concentration on the eternal word OM or a *mantra* creates vibrations and forms a mental image. When this subtle form is established in the mind, the mind becomes steady.

When the *mantra* is chosen by the *Guru*, the aspirant may have "psychic" experiences such as hearing celestial sounds, smelling exquisite fragrances or knowing the future. Such experiences inspire confidence, but they are not an end in themselves. The only real goal is ultimate Truth or Self-realization.

Concentration on a Chakra. Either *Ajna Chakra* or *Anahata Chakra* is generally chosen for Concentration. The *Ajna Chakra* is located between the eyebrows. This is also known as "the Divine eye." Imagine there is a lotus full of effulgent light. This is a very important and sensitive center. Concentration on this center makes the mind inwardly directed, one-pointed and steady. Powers of clairvoyance and retrospection also result from this Concentration.

The *Anahata Chakra* is the heart center. Concentration on this *chakra* leads to great joy, for the *Anahata Chakra* is the seat of all emotions and feelings. It is the Yogic heart between the two breasts, not the heart of flesh. Yogis avoid Concentration on the lower centers.

Those who are emotional and sensitive are advised to concentrate on the *Anahata Chakra* while those who are intellectual are advised to concentrate on the *Ajna Chakra*. Prolonged Concentration leads to Meditation.

There are many other methods of Concentration mentioned in the *Upanishads* and in Yoga manuals, but they are not elaborated upon and are revealed only to initiates by competent *Gurus*.

Yogic methods for developing Concentration are scientific and exact, and all of them involve conscious method of Concentration. Then in the second stage of Concentration, involuntary movements of the mind are brought under conscious control.

4.2: Concentration Process

Requirements

Some of the important requirements of Concentration are:

1. Do not disturb your mind. Do not associate with persons whose ideas are disturbing. You know that certain persons, certain places, certain foods, repel you. Avoid them.
2. Have confidence in your own mental ability. Have faith that you can concentrate. Do not think that you cannot concentrate. Go on without thinking of success or failure.
3. Give up all argumentation and other distractions. What is there in the dry, intellectual jargons! They can only throw the mind off its balance and disturb it. The things of the subtler planes have to be realized. Talking cannot do that. So give up all vain talks.
4. Read only spiritual books, scriptures and books written by persons who had spiritual experiences.
5. A strict diet is necessary in order to maintain sound health. A simple, non-fat vegetarian diet with fruits, cereals and vegetables is desirable, for it gives energy and promotes mental peace.
6. Practice regularly the first five disciplines of Raja Yoga – *Yama*, *Niyama*, *Asana, Pratyahara* and *Pranayama* – in order to maintain sound physical and mental health and to purify your mind.
7. Practice each day some mental exercises like gazing, visualizing, focusing on breath, counting breath, and so on in order to improve your capacity to concentrate on a specific

object. (*See* 4.3 *Concentration and Mental Exercises, below*)

8. A mere attempt to practice Concentration for a few minutes at the Meditation time alone is not enough. The whole day should be Meditation in action. (*See* 4.12 *Meditation in Action, below*). You should consciously practice Concentration of attention on whatever you do: walking, Yoga *Asanas*, prayer, eating, working, reading, etc., holding the mind quiet attentively on each activity as it comes along. Such deliberate attention to the activity on hand extends the period of technical training in Concentration to the whole day.

For further requirements, *read* 4.7 Prerequisites of Meditation, *below*.

Preparation for, and the Process of, Concentration

The preparation for, and the process of, practicing Concentration are described below.

1. Select a definite time each day for this purpose; early morning and evening hours are the best time for Yoga practice.
2. Select a suitable place for sitting for Meditation. If you select a room in your living place, it should be quiet, clean and airy. The light should not be very bright, and the temperature should be moderate.
3. Concentration should not be practiced immediately after a heavy meal, as it causes discomfort and drowsiness.
4. Do not try to concentrate when you are physically or mentally tired.
5. Concentration is easy when the mind and body are relaxed and when the nerves have been purified by *Pranayama*. It is therefore desirable to practice some Yoga *Asanas* and deep relaxation first. Deep breathing, with regulation of the breath, stills the mind.
6. Sit in a comfortable Posture. The Postures recommended for Meditation in 3.6 *Asanas* are suitable for Concentration.
7. The mind should be undisturbed and free from worldly worries

and emotional problems. Assume an attitude of detachment. Gently close the eyes, withdraw the mind from sense objects, and say to yourself, "I am not the body, senses, and mind. I am the eternal Atman. How can the emotions and impulses disturb me? I am completely detached." With these positive thoughts calm the mind.

8. Try to be a mere witness to your mental activity. Let the thoughts come and go; do not get involved in them.
9. Assert clearly that for the next few moments that you are concerned only with bringing the mind under the control of the inner Self.
10. Turn the mind to the object chosen for Concentration. (This has been discussed in the previous Chapter 4.1). Focus the mind upon the object.
11. Use your will in a natural way, but do not try to force attention. The natural role of will is quietly erasing all that interferes with a given project, leaving the field clear for the chosen activity. The will works from within on its own power, and it is a very quiet internal human attribute.
12. In the beginning, practice Concentration for about ten minutes. After gaining some experience gradually increase the duration of the time period.
13. When the attention drifts away from the one-pointedness and the mind indulges in distracting thoughts, the flow of breath is interrupted. If the breath is perfectly smooth, Concentration can be held on the chosen object, and the awareness can expand. Therefore, it is desirable to focus your attention on the breath and normalize it, and at the same time, bring back the attention to the object of Concentration. Whenever there is a drift, bring back the attention again and again to the object of Concentration. As a result of such repeated practice, the duration of one-pointedness gradually becomes lengthened, the repetition of *mantra* creates a new groove, and the mind begins to spontaneously flow into the new groove, and thus Concentration is strengthened.

Stages of Concentration

There are five stages in the progressive process of Concentration: analysis, reflection, bliss, pure ego and pure Consciousness. (*Yoga Sutras*, 1.17-18). First, you have to train the mind to focus on something concrete – a spiritually significant object or symbol like the image of a chosen deity, a *yantra* or *mantra*. If you focus the mind on a concrete object, the mind examines or analyses the object and understands it. But you should guard against the tendency to consider the chosen symbol alone is the only absolute form of the ultimate Reality. Such idolatrous attitude leads to dogmatism, fanaticism and parochialism. The greatest need of our present time is to rise above such parochial outlook and develop a cosmic perspective in religion. There is no difference between the symbol representing one religion and the symbol representing another religion. A symbol is just a means to facilitate the training of the mind in focusing its attention.

In the second stage the mind pierces the outer material layer, reflects on its inner subtle essence. As a result of this contemplation, the mind understands the inner secret and the powers of the object, and you gain power over that object. When you progress in Concentration you may find yourself suddenly possessed of psychic powers. The possession of such powers presents a terrible temptation to misuse them for personal selfish motives. You should be aware of this danger. What matters is purity and awareness of the ultimate goal. Patanjali warns us that if we are drawn to these powers, we shall miss the supreme goal.

Third is the stage of *ananda* or bliss, when you concentrate upon the mind itself. In this subtle stage, there is only joy and no reasoning or reflection.

In the fourth stage, you concentrate upon the pure "I-ness." You are just aware of your individuality, nothing else. This is a process of going inward, not evolution, but involution. The unmanifested appears as manifest and then returns to the unmanifested. As you are in the concrete world with the three *gunas* of *sattva*, *rajas* and *tamas*, you have to work from what you see now, from the known you work back toward the unknown, the unmanifested consciousness. Such Concentration is certainly difficult, but it is still within the *Prakriti*. Therefore it has its temptations and dangers. The past impressions (*samskaras*) are still buried in the mind in their seed form.

The buried seeds of *samskaras* can still come into conscious mind when proper opportunity arises, and pull you back into worldly experiences. That is why all these four stages should be passed and you should get into the fifth stage of the supreme feat – Concentration upon Consciousness itself. This is the state of perfect Yoga, in which you pass beyond the *Prakriti,* beyond all objective knowledge, into union with the Atman, the unmanifested universal Consciousness. This stage can only be reached when the thought waves have been stilled and the mind has been cleared of all its *samskaras*, both the evil and the good. In that state, even the ego feeling is not there and the seeds of past impressions are rendered harmless. Only the Consciousness is there and nothing else. Once that is achieved and you are completely liberated and no more rebirth for you, for it is the *samskaras* that drive us from birth to birth. Although you still live in the world, you are not then involved in it. The world is just a shadow from which you are completely free. You become a *Jivanmukta* – one who lives but at the same time is liberated. (For details, *See* 4. 21 *Jivanmukta, below*). The *Jivanmukta*'s thoughts, words and actions are "burnt seeds," and so they cannot bring forth any more *samskaras*, and cannot create any new bondage. When the *Jivanmukta*'s present life ends, he will be united with the Atman forever.

Benefits of Concentration

Concentration will bring several benefits. The main benefit is that it makes ourselves an instrument or channel through which the power of Divinity can flow and accomplish its great goal. Patanjali declares that a human being could come to his own true state only by the successful practice of complete control of mind. Control of the mind is the best means of freedom from envy, jealousy, resentment, discontent, delusion, self-deception, pride, anger and fear. Without it, character building cannot take place, and with it, it cannot fail. Any study is effective in proportion to the mental Concentration brought to bear upon it; and the practice largely increases the reproductive powers of memory.

Besides, Concentration will give power. It implies great self-control. It will calm down nervous excitement, bring peace, enable us to see things more clearly. The temperament will be better and the health will improve. Sound health will be one of the first signs. Defects in the voice will go away. Those who practice hard will get many other signs such as sounds of bells, specks of light. When these things appear, know that you are progressing fast.

The work that takes six hours can be done more efficiently in two hours. You will find that your ideas are becoming clearer and more systematic. You will be able to understand many things of life that, prior to the practice of Concentration, were beyond your mental reach. You will feel peaceful and balanced. You will be quick to decide. You will be able to perform your work more effectively.

The benefits of Concentration are beyond ordinary descriptions. One must experience for oneself. Begin the practice of Concentration from this very moment and enjoy the abundance of energy that God had endowed in your mind.

4.3: Concentration and Mental Exercises

Introduction

Concentration is the focusing of all mental energies upon one object or one idea. In order to improve the faculty of Concentration, various mental exercises can be practiced. You can set aside some time each day for this purpose. It is desirable to practice the exercises at a set time, preferably in the early morning.

It is advisable to practice the mental exercises under the most favorable circumstances. You should be alone, and you should know that you will not be disturbed for some time. There should be no draft in the room; the light should not be too bright; the temperature should be agreeable. The room should preferably be sparsely furnished. Sit facing a bare wall.

First, practice Yoga *Asanas* before you commence the mental techniques. If not, practice some physical relaxation, a few deep breathing and stretching exercises. It is not good to perform mental exercises while physically or mentally tired.

Next, sit in a comfortable and steady meditative Posture and practice *Pranayama*. Regulation of breath quiets the mind. Then practice the exercises with great diligence. Intensity of effort is more important than duration of practice. In the beginning the sessions may last about ten minutes. The whole time may be sent on the practice of one exercise, or you can do several exercises during one session. Once a particular exercise has been mastered to a degree, you may commence the next.

Gazing (*Trataka*)

This is a popular exercise. It brings about stillness of the mind.

Without blinking look at a point or a small object for one or two minutes, as long as possible without straining the eyes. It is desirable to close the eyes and rest them when there is discomfort, and then repeat the exercise. With practice, the duration of each uninterrupted gazing period can be lengthened considerably.

You may also look steadily at the point of the nose, the point midway between the eyebrows, or the steady flame of a candle.

Nasal Gaze

Fix the gaze on the light visualized at the bridge between the two nostrils with the eyebrows raised slightly. Let the mind concentrate on the energy of life in the heart. Be aware of the flow of the breath in and out of the nostrils. Initially nasal gazing should be practiced for brief periods of time, and the period of time can be increased gradually. Those with weak nerves should not undertake this practice without the personal supervision of an expert.

Visualization

Visualization is the calling up of an image with such Concentration and imagination that the picture seen with the mind's eye is as vivid as the actual object would be. If you evoke the image of a rose, you will see the magnificent flower clearly projected on the screen of the mind, and admire its gracious form and its beautiful color. Similarly you can visualize the image of a candle light in the mind's eye.

Various exercises of Concentration on light are suggested in the Yoga manuals. Concentration on light between the eyebrows is called subtle Concentration. You may also concentrate on an ocean of light in your heart, or on the image of a flame in the region of the navel.

If Concentration is done consistently on these lights whenever they appear, you will develop a powerful intentional force or resolve, and a time will come when you will be able to recall these lights at will.

Cultivating the Shadow Person

To do this exercise, stand in the sun when the sky is perfectly clear so that your shadow appears clearly and distinctly in front of you, approximately five to ten feet in length. Focus your attention on your shadow at a point at the base of its neck. Hold this view with the eyes steady, the lids slightly opened, for as long as you can. When the eyes become tired and begin to tear, close and open them once or twice, and then raise the head to look into the clear sky. There you will see a figure, a full shadow. Hold this figure in your Concentration as long as you possibly can. By practicing this exercise regularly, the shadow will become transparent, and then you will see two shadows. The first, an outer shell, will appear gradually more transparent, and eventually you will see features on the shadow. Finally these features will turn to face you and you will realize you are looking at yourself.

Listening to Ticking of a Clock

In a quiet room in which there is a softly ticking clock, try to hear the ticking sound at some distance away. Direct your full attention to listening. Once you can discern it, you may make the exercise more difficult by sitting further away.

Observation

You may concentrate on any given object such as an apple, placed at eye level, at such a distance that continuous observation of it does not strain the eyes. After settling down, begin to look at it with special interest. Observe all its peculiarities in detail. Study its shape, size, etc. Attention should be focused on the object until its every feature is firmly imprinted on the mind, so that one can see it just as clearly with the eyes closed as with the eyes open.

Observation and Recall

After closely observing an object, close your eyes and attempt to reconstruct it in the mind, giving meticulous attention to even the most minute detail. You may use any object.

With the practice of this exercise, the powers of observation and memory are increased. In everyday life you will discover many interesting facts about common objects.

Thought Observations

Allow the thoughts to come and go as they please. You just observe them as an objective spectator. Dissociate yourself from the thoughts, give your mind free rein, and attentively observe the ensuing mental activity. Watch the incessant parade of thoughts passing through your mind in quick succession. If hideous thoughts happen to come into the field of consciousness, do not be appalled, but remain a dispassionate observer. Sitting calmly, you should realize that repulsive ideas are but manifestations of the lower nature, which you are striving to overcome.

At first the mind, freed from all controls, will race on, but gradually its activity will diminish.

At the end of the exercise, you may reflect back on your various thoughts, recognizing each for what it was. You may also try to discover a pattern in their coming and going, and try to see how the different thoughts were associated.

Concentration on the Breath

Breathing calmly, focus the entire attention of the mind on the flow of air that comes in and goes out through the nostrils. This practice has a profound stabilizing effect on the mind. This exercise will be of great use in times of tension. It is also useful to people who suffer from insomnia.

Counting Breaths

A simple exercise for developing Concentration of mind is the counting of breaths. While sitting quietly and breathing calmly, mentally count every inhalation. Continue to breathe evenly and rhythmically, oblivious to the outside world, and undisturbed by thoughts that may try to intrude into your mind. Count to one hundred using rosary or your fingers for counting every hundred.

If you become distracted and the count is broken, make a mental note of the number at which you lost count. With patience you will be able to reach a higher total without being disturbed.

Pranic Breath

Prana, vital energy, is the basic force that animates all matter. While you breath in, you should feel that you are deeply inhaling an abundance of *Prana*. Hold the breath as long as is comfortable, and during retention, visualize that the vital force is moving throughout the body, revitalizing every part. Should a particular organ need special attention, single it out and mentally give it an extra help of the cosmic energy. If you desire to increase your power of thought, you can send an ample flow of *Prana* to the brain.

Solar Plexus Charging

In the upper part of the abdomen, on either side of the spinal column, lies the solar plexus, a compact bundle of nerves connected with the sympathetic nervous system. It is a large and important nerve center, situated, as it is, in a dominant position in the middle of the body, from which it governs the vital organs. The solar plexus has been identified with the Yogic *Manipura Chakra*, a subtle center within the spinal column at the level of the navel, and it is seen as a storehouse for Pranic energy.

Prana is all around you in the atmosphere. While breathing in slowly and evenly, visualize a golden stream of *Prana* entering the head at the crown. Consciously direct the stream of that vital energy to the solar plexus. While breathing out, circulate the *Prana* in and around the solar plexus, increasing the speed of the circulation with every new exhalation.

The Positive Breath

You choose a positive quality you would like to possess. It may be health or mental peace or any other mental quality. If it is health that you have decided upon, you breathe in deeply through the nose, and feel that you inhale abundant health. If you have decided upon a moral or mental quality, you likewise feel it flowing into you as you inhale deeply. The quality chosen can be will-power, detachment, selflessness or any other virtue important from the Yogic point of view.

Expelling Undesirable Characteristics

If there is any undesirable characteristic that is an obstacle to progress in your program for self-development and Yoga, then select that fault to be eliminated, isolate it from yourself, and use it in expelling practice.

While you breathe out through the nose, feel that you are expelling the unwanted quality through the nostrils.

Reflection at the End of the Day

This is a mental exercise to be practiced before retiring. You can think back on the day just passed, asking yourself honestly whether you acted throughout as a good Yoga student should. If you had gone wrong in some situation during the day, you should reflect on it and ask yourself why you erred. You should examine the reasons for this failure, and finally you should mentally relieve the whole scene. At the conclusion of the exercise, you should resolve to overcome any weakness or faults you have shown.

4.4: Meditation

Introduction

Concentration culminates in Meditation (*Dhyana*). Meditation is the primary technique of Yoga. The word "Meditation" (*Dhyana*) is not properly understood in the Western world. In the Encyclopedia Britannica, for instance, the word "Meditation" has been explained as Concentration, but the word Concentration has not been explained. Modern dictionaries define Meditation variously as follows:

1. Sustained reflection; the turning or revolving of any subject in the mind; close or continued thought.
2. A private devotional act consisting of deliberate reflection upon some spiritual truth or mystery accompanied by mental prayer and resolutions as to future conduct.
3. A private religious or devotional exercise consisting of a continuous application of the mind to the consideration of some religious or moral truth or the like, in order to promote holiness or love of God.

None of the above definitions explains the word "Meditation" accurately.

Misconceptions

There are also several misconceptions about Meditation. For example, those who have turned to Meditation from drug experimentation expect from Meditation something similar to being "high." Meditation is not similar to drug experience. It has a superior goal of experiencing the highest state of Consciousness.

Some think of Meditation as contemplation. Contemplation is sitting quietly and thinking through all the aspects of a problem in order to find a solution to it. Yoga Meditation is not a problem-solving contemplation. It is far more subtle than contemplation. It is bringing one's mind to a centered inward state and fixing it on a *mantra* or any other object of Concentration prescribed by a spiritual teacher.

Though various religions are using Meditation, Meditation is not a religion. Everyone can meditate, irrespective of his religious faith.

Meditation has no intrinsic link with any particular culture. Meditation practice is found in all areas of the world. Eastern methods of Meditation have been fully and systematically developed than others and thus they serve as models for the process. Just as the use of American technology in any particular country does not turn the user into an American, so also the use of Meditation does not turn a person into a Hindu or a Zen monk.

Meditation is not a form of hypnosis. In hypnosis, you surrender your own control to the hypnotist's suggestion. But in Meditation you expand conscious self-control and awareness. While changes resulting from hypnosis are not lasting, those who practice Meditation over a period of time experience significant physiological and psychological benefits. (*See* 4.13 Benefits of Meditation and 4.14 Meditation and Health, *below*).

Meditation is not a specific way of life. It is useful to people of all walks of life: professionals, technical workers, homemakers and students. Everyone can practice it and benefit from it.

Meaning

Meditation is an uninterrupted focus of the mind on the object of Concentration, leading one to the highest level of consciousness and unto the goal of Self-realization. It is a means for liberating the mind from all disturbing thoughts. It is an inward journey from the gross, to the subtle, to the most subtle aspect of one's being, the Spirit or Atman. It is the final rung on the ladder of Yoga to attain illumination or *Samadhi*. In the *Bhagavad Gita* Lord Krishna says,

> "With the mind not moving towards any other thing, made steadfast by the practice of habitual meditation, one goes to the transcendental Supreme Being." (8.8)

The Yogi who meditates constantly without allowing the mind to wander to sensual objects reaches the Supreme Being.

> "When thy intellect . . . shall stand immovable and steady in the Self, then thou shall attain Self-realization." (2.53)

When the Yogi's intellect becomes steady without distraction and doubt and firmly established in the Self, then he attains Self-realization.

Meditation and *Nididhyasana*

Two Sanskrit words, *Dhyana* and *nididhyasana,* are related to Meditation. Sometimes both of them are translated as Meditation. However, there is a difference between these two words. The more appropriate meaning of *nididhyasana* is "reflection" and "contemplation," and it is used in the monastic tradition of the Vedantists[28]. In this method a senior monk assigns a new student a certain truth to reflect upon. The truth may be a great utterance from *Vedas* such as "Thou art That," or "I am Brahman." Starting with analysis and discursive thinking, the student continues to reflect upon the truth, until he transcends the intellect and realizes the inner, intuitive aspect of the truth.

On the other hand, *Dhyana* or Meditation is a different process. In it, the conscious mind is stilled. Through the withdrawal of the mind from senses, and through Concentration, one-pointedness of mind is achieved, and then Concentration flows into Meditation. This uninterrupted flow of Meditation leads to the Knowledge of the Self.

Meditation is an inward journey in which you study your own Self. Its aim is Self-realization, a direct vision of Truth. It is a way of going from the known to the unknown. It helps you to discover the ultimate unifying principle of the universe. When you realize the importance of life and its purpose, then you turn to the science of Meditation and finds the solution to the deeper problems of life.

Theology says that God exists and that we should believe in Him. Philosophy says that we should know the relationship between the individual, the universe, and the creator. Meditation gives a direct vision of God in the temple of the body. A meditator does not have to search, roam or wander in pursuit of God; he finds Him within. He realizes his Divine nature.

Types of Meditation

Meditation is of various types according to the object chosen for Concentration. It can be concrete or abstract or symbolic. Meditation on a physical form such as a candle flame or a deity is concrete. Meditation on an idea or sound is abstract. Meditation on a physical form, which symbolizes a spiritual idea is a symbolic Meditation, e.g., meditating upon a Divine form with the feeling that you are lifting yourself to the heights of infinity or meditating upon a sound symbol like OM with a profound understanding of the nature of Divinity symbolized by it.

Japa

Japa is the repetition of a *mantra* or Divine Name during the practice of Meditation. The Sanskrit root *pa* stands for that which removes or destroys all impurities and obstructions, and the root *ja* stands for that which puts an end to the cycle of births and deaths. Therefore, *Japa* is an indirect means for Liberation. By destroying obstructions to Knowledge, *Japa* paves the way for Liberation.

In listless thinking, as in deliberate thinking, we do not know what our next thought will be. But in *Japa*, we definitely know what is coming next. If something else comes, we are off the track, and we bring back the chosen thought. In the process we learn how to dismiss unwanted thoughts and retain the one we have chosen. This is an important result of *Japa* as a technique. The repetition becomes a technique for keeping our mind directed for a length of time, and also for helping the mind to gain a certain depth. Between two successive repetitions, there is an interval with no form or shape. This is what we call peace or silence.

The mind–a Dancer. In a Sanskrit text *Pancadasi*, the mind is likened to a dancer on a lighted stage. The dancer portrays a variety of aesthetic sentiments – love, helplessness, anger, cruelty, fright and so on. The light on the stage lights up the dancer in all of her moods and forms, and when she makes her exit, it lights up the empty stage. Whether the dancer performs various dance forms or leaves the stage, the light remains uninvolved. It merely illumines.

The light itself is not a "doer," much less an "enjoyer" of the dance. It also does not light up the stage as one of its jobs. The nature of light is to illumine and it illumines. Therefore, the light has no doership. Similarly, when we have a thought and it goes away, what remains is silence, which is likened to the empty stage without a dancer.

In *Japa*, being aware of the interval is as important as the repetition, because it is the interval that reveals our true nature – silence, awareness.

Automatic Japa. Once we are committed to mentally repeating a given *mantra*, our mind automatically goes to *Japa* whenever it is free. Just as water draining from the mountains creates new ravines, a new track is created towards which the mind repeatedly goes. In this way, *Japa* becomes a way of keeping the mind meaningfully occupied.

Effects of Japa. Japa enables us to replace distracting thoughts with the chosen *mantra*. It eliminates the chain of thinking and is helpful in gaining mastery over our mind. Lord Krishna, in the *Bhagavad Gita* says,

> "Among the various forms of rituals and many means through which I am invoked, among them I am *Japa*." (10.25)

This shows the greatness of *Japa* as a technique of Meditation. God-realization is possible, only when the mind is controlled and purified. Constant *Japa* arrests the restless nature of the mind. It conserves all the physical and mental energies for removing the veil from the indwelling Truth. The *mantra* or the Divine Name is an unfailing key that unlocks the gates of the heart, permitting an outflow of immortal love, wisdom and power.

"God's all-powerful Name," says Swami Ramdas,[29] "takes the aspiring soul to the highest summit of Truth. What is required first is an absolute faith in the greatness and potency of the Name, which comes only by the Grace of the Lord. When the Name becomes the sole mainstay and refuge of the aspirant who thirsts for the highest goal of life – God-realization – he or she marches towards the goal not only in rapid strides but also with a heart filled with courage and cheerfulness."[30]

When we do *Japa,* we must be aware that we are repeating the Name of One who is within us. Without it, the repetition becomes merely mechanical and does not help us in any way. When we tune ourselves with the Name, we tune ourselves with God. We must keep this central fact in our mind when doing *Japa.* Then the practice will gradually make us aware of Divine existence within us. This idea grows into an experience when we actually feel His presence. As we become aware of Him within us, we become aware of Him also without us. We feel His presence everywhere. Of all the disciplines for controlling the restless mind, none is so easy and effective as *Japa.* But some are not able to repeat the Name continuously although they desire to do so. It is because of their greater love for the perishable objects of the world.

As we think so we become. So if our mind is fixed with an intense love for the Divine Name, this love will automatically enable us to repeat the Name constantly. When thus the mind is absorbed with the love of God and filled with the music of His Name, we will experience the Divine ecstasy. When we are in this Joy, Swami Ramdas says, the vision of God will flash out. Thus *Japa* is the easiest and best method by which you can purify yourself preparatory to God-experience. Swami Ramdas affirms that no other spiritual practice could so easily grant you purity – absolute freedom from lust, greed and wrath.

Japa is an all-inclusive and all-sufficient practice by which you can be ever in tune with God and finally merge yourself in Him.

Japa is thinking of God constantly to the exclusion of everything else. God-thought keeps away every other thought. This thought also ultimately disappears, affirms Swami Ramdas, and you realize your identity with God.

Laya Meditation

Laya Meditation involves Concentration of the mind on sound. The normal awareness of external things is altered by focusing on hearing an internal mystic sound, which is called *Anahata*. The mind will become steady and absorbed in the sound on which it focuses. In space, sound is produced by the movement of sound waves in the air. In the body also there are currents that flow and produce sound when Yoga is practiced.

To do this practice, sit in *Siddhasana* and focus the attention on the spot between the eyebrows. Turn the eyes upward and let the lids remain closed. The eyes, ears, nose, and mouth should be closed. With a calm and controlled mind listen for a sound in the right ear, and eventually you will hear a clear sound. In the beginning the sound will be very loud and varied, but with continued practice it will become increasingly subtle. Finally, after further practice, the sound will resemble tinkling noise, the sound of a flute or the hum of bees. This sound is produced within and cannot be heard by anyone else.

When your mind is intently engaged in listening to this *Anahata* sound you become captivated by it and overcome distractions. Practice listening to the *Anahata* sound in the heart with a calm and concentrated mind. When the mind focuses on the sound, it becomes steady. Mental activity is suspended when the mind is absorbed in the sound. Then you forget all external objects and loose awareness of yourself, and the mind is absorbed in eternal bliss. Finally, you may interpenetrate the *Anahata* sound and attain the state of *Samadhi*.

The *Anahata* sound comes from the heart-center (*Anahata Chakra*). It cannot be heard by you until the heart is free from all impurities. Thus, the practice of Concentration and absorption with sound is only possible after considerable preparation.

Meditation in Monism (Vedanta)

Monism is the original form of the Vedanta, based on the intuitive experiences of the sages of the *Upanishads*. (For details, *See* 1.6 The Philosophical Basis of Yoga: A. Vedanta or Advaita Philosophy, *above*). In Monism the ultimate Reality is One only and it is called Brahman. In Monism the practical procedure consists in denying the absolute existence of body, mind and ego, as well as the universe, which are only relatively real, and arriving at the One Absolute Reality, Brahman. The Self of all beings is identical with Brahman.

Monistic Meditation is the Meditation on the Absolute. As the Absolute is beyond form and beyond attributes, this type of Meditation is the most difficult of all. It is not thinking of the mere formlessness such as a vacant space, the blue sky or the shoreless ocean. It is only thinking of the universal Space (*Mahakasa*). A higher and subtler form of infinity is the mental infinity called *Chittakasa* or the space of the mind from which infinite thought-forms arise as in the dream state. But the true Absolute Infinity of Monism, is the Infinity of the Spirit, called *Chidakasa*, the Void beyond all forms and attributes. This is the negation of everything conceivable or expressible and it is described in the *Upanishadic* words, "not this," "not that." This is inconceivably higher than the infinity of the universe and the mind, because both the universe and the mind are limited; but the Infinity of the Spirit, the Atman or Brahman is the true Infinity, the true Absolute of Monism.

From the above it must be clear that Monistic Meditation is bound to be difficult even in the case of those who have arrived at an intellectual conviction of the identity of the Atman or the Self in a human being with Brahman.

Four Forms of Disciplines. Vedanta, therefore, prescribes four forms of preliminary disciplines for Monistic aspirants, without undergoing which Monistic seekers cannot successfully attempt their Meditation.

1. The *first* is the constant *discrimination* between the Real and the unreal. The aspirant is to discriminate constantly between the Absolute Reality and the relative reality of the universe and its phenomena. Vedanta boldly asserts that the universe with its myriad

forms and the body-mind-ego complex of human beings as well are ephemeral. This assertion is based on the experience of the Seers.

Even this discrimination between the Real and the unreal is insufficient to help the seeker in Monistic Meditation, because we live in this world and so we encounter obstacles from all sorts of worldly objects. Therefore, with a view to protecting our minds from those obstacles to the practice of discrimination, three other forms of disciplines are enjoined.

2. The second discipline prescribed is the practice of the following six virtues:

(a) Checking the mind from the pursuit of all objects except hearing the *Upanishads* and other teachings of Vedanta,
(b) Checking the senses of perception and action from all objects except hearing the *Upanishads* and other teachings of Vedanta,
(c) Keeping the senses so restrained from drifting along their old course to senses objects,
(d) Remaining unruffled by pleasure and pain, profit and loss, prosperity and adversity, honor and dishonor and other pairs of opposites,
(e) Constantly concentrating the mind on hearing the *Upanishads* and other teachings of Vedanta, and practicing such virtues as modesty, humility, devotion, purity and selfless service, and
(f) Faith in God, faith in the *Upanishads* and other teachings of the Vedanta; faith in the *Guru* and faith in one's own capacity to realize the Truth.

3. The third discipline is the relinquishment of the desire for the fruits of action in this world or in the heaven (*svarga*).

4. Finally the seeker is exhorted to create in himself a Divine discontent and a thirst for Liberation from the bondage of worldliness by attaining Illumination.

These disciplines prepare the mind for steadiness in daily

Meditation on the Atman, the Pure Consciousness in us, and on its identity with the Transcendental Consciousness.

In order to help us in Monistic Meditation, Vedanta gives an unchallengeable definition of the Absolute Reality. It is That which remains unaffected throughout all time – past, present and future.

With a view to ascertaining the nature of the Reality, the Seers of India first studied the objective phenomena. They noted that objects change with lapse of time. The universe also changes. Thus what we see is not a permanent reality. They further found that not only the objective universe but also the observer changes from time to time. His body and mind change constantly.

The Seers also investigated the three States of Consciousness– waking, dream and dreamless sleep. In the waking state the universe appears as real, tangible, perceptible to the senses. In the dream state the universe becomes thin and attenuated. In the sleep we do not see anything; the universe has entirely disappeared, and we are not even aware that we are sleeping; but when we wake up in the morning, we remember to have slept well or ill, as the case may be. Now every act of remembrance is an act of re-cognition. This means that the cognition took place even in sleep without our knowledge. Who could this cognizer be? The *Upanishads* declare that the cognizer in sleep is Consciousness itself. It directly registers sleep without the help of the mind and ego, for these do not function in sleep.

Consciousness is present in our waking and dream states, but it takes the help of the mind and the ego to perceive and know. In sleep state there is neither the ego of sleep nor that of waking; yet we all feel and know intuitively the identity of our personality in waking, dream and sleep states.

This notion of the identity and continuity of our personality can arise only when something exists as a background of the States of consciousness. This is Pure Consciousness. It is behind the three states of waking, dream and dreamless sleep. It is also behind all stages of life such as infancy, youth, middle age and old age. It has been existing eternally throughout our past lives and will exist throughout the future. It is immutable, beginningless and endless.

It is *eternal Consciousness.* The moment a seeker will realize It, he will realize Its identity with the Supreme Spirit, Brahman. Our goal is to be the Atman. The Atman is shining in Its own glory undimmed by its adjuncts. (*See*: Swami Nikhilananda, tr., *Vedantasara*, Calcutta: Advaita Ashrama, 1968).

Meditation on the Four Great Utterances

The essence of the *Vedas*, and that of the highest mystic experiences have been expressed in the following four great utterances, called *Maha Vakyas:*

1. *Prajnanam Brahma* – Brahman is pure Consciousness
2. *Tat Twam Asi* – Thou art That
3. *Aham Brahma Asm* – I am Brahman
4. *Ayam Atma Brahma* – This very Self is Brahman

1. *Prajnanam Brahma.* This is a *Maha Vakya* of *Rig Veda.* Brahman is the cause, source, sustenance and support of the universe. Brahman is the supreme Divinity. He is the source of all powers. He is Existence, Knowledge and Bliss.

Meditate on Pure Consciousness as the basis of all that exists. Negate the names and forms that are expressions of mental consciousness. The world is superimposed on consciousness. It is a product of *Maya* or Divine illusion. When ignorance is eliminated by knowledge, when intuitive vision dawns on us, everything is perceived as Brahman, the Self or pure Consciousness.

Thus you should meditate on:

> "All is Brahman. Nothing exists, nothing belongs to me. Pleasure and pain, gain and loss, success and failure – all conditions of life are expressions of Brahman. Here lies the end of sorrow, the termination of fear, the cessation of misery. All is pure Consciousness. *Prajnanam* Brahman OM."

2. *Tat Twam Asi.* This a *Maha Vakya* of *Sama Veda*. It means "Thou are That." You are That. "That Consciousness is your very

Self," thus instructs the *Guru* to his disciple. You are not this passing personality. You are not this body, nor senses, nor mind, not the intellect and not even this ego that asserts and arrogates. You are much beyond all finite media that you consider, in ignorance, to be your very Self.

Think deeply. Reflect calmly, Meditate on:

"That which shines in the sun, sheds luster through the moon.
That which surges in the ocean and races through the wind.
That which is the Beauty of the beautiful, Joy of the joyous, the Essence of all . . . is your very Self."

Therefore meditate:

"I am not this limited being. I am That which is Brahman.
I am not subject to birth and death. I am That, immortal Absolute.
I am not limited by time and space. I am That unlimited Divinity.
I am not this finite personality. I am That, the Supreme Self."

3. *Aham Brahma Asmi.* This is a *Maha Vakya* of *Yajur Veda*. This means "I am the Absolute." Here 'I' refers to the pure 'I'. That which is beyond all limitations, That which is beyond *Maya* or illusion is Brahman. That which is the basis of the world, is the basis of the life in me. I am Brahman. Thus meditate on:

"I am the Imperishable Self.
I am the Absolute beyond death.
I am That I am.
I am the Self-effulgent Consciousness.
I am verily Brahman."

Enquire "Who am I?" Rise above the body, mind and senses. Here you will realize "I am Brahman, the goal of my life. I am That Brahman."

4. *Ayam Atma Brahma.* This is a *Maha Vakya* of *Atharva Veda*. Brahman is not far away. Brahman is the very Self. Your

Self is not a limited personality. It is not subject to birth and death; it is not subject to *karmas* and afflictions.

Thus you should meditate on:

> "I am full, I am perfect.
> There is no desire in me.
> Because there is nothing apart from me.
> I am the Self in all."

Meditation on OM

The *Upanishads*, the basic texts of the Vedanta Philosophy, assert the practice of Meditation on OM as a dynamic means for attaining Self-realization. The *Mundaka Upanishad* says:

> "Pranava (OM) is the bow. The individual soul is the arrow, Brahman or the Absolute is the target, O Aspirant, hit the target with persistent vigilance; and just as the arrow becomes one with the target, so you become merged in Brahman (the Absolute)." (2.2.4)

Patanjali Maharishi in his *Yoga Sutras* enjoins,

> "Pranava or OM expresses God (*Ishwara*); It must be repeated with Meditation upon its meaning. Hence comes the Knowledge of the Atman and destruction of the obstacles to that Knowledge." (1.27, 28, 29).

Lord Krishna proclaims in the *Bhagavad Gita*:

> "I am Pranava (OM) in the *Vedas*." (7.8)

While meditating upon OM (AUM), you should understand the implications of 'A' and meditate: "I am all this physical universe, as far as 'A' extends."

Then you must negate the idea of the physicality of things, and enter into the plane of the mind and assert your Meditation on the

'U' aspect of OM: "I am the Cosmic Mind, and all minds are waves in the ocean of the Cosmic Mind."

You must transcend the mind as well, and meditate upon the unmanifested *Maya* (the causal plane of the universe) by asserting the 'M' aspect of OM: "I am the Cosmic Self, the ruler and sustainer of *Maya*; I am the Spirit, the prompter of the operations of *Prakriti* (Nature), I am the source, sustenance, and the termination of the world-process."

Further you must go beyond the three planes, physical, astral and causal, and attain the revelation of the attributeless Self or Brahman denoted by the sound OM.

Meditation Upon the Self or Atman

The ultimate goal of Meditation is to experience the Self or Atman. The Self is pure Consciousness, and the experience of Self is a state of absolute knowledge and bliss. It is variously called *Samadhi, Nirvana,* Cosmic Consciousness and so on. When the mind is completely centered for an extended period of time without any distractions, you become aware of the essence of your being the Atman.

Atman in us is covered by three bodies. The outermost is the physical body, composed of gross matter. Beneath this is the subtle body, composed of subtler counterparts of gross matter. The innermost body is the causal body that has been formed out of our actions as per the Law of Karma. In normal waking consciousness all the three bodies exist between you and Atman, but during the dream state the physical body is removed, and in the state of dreamless sleep only the causal body shrouds Atman. You are therefore closest to Atman in the state of dreamless sleep, but no memory of the experience remains when you wake up, for this body is difficult to penetrate. That is why you cannot attain realization of Atman merely through dreamless sleep. One of the methods of Meditation brings back into the waking state the experience of the state of dreamless sleep, and it involves dwelling upon, and trying to strengthen, the sense of peace that lingers into the waking state after experiencing the dreamless sleep.

In the *Upanishads*, it is stated that the Atman dwells within the lotus of the heart, but here heart does not refer to the heart of flesh, but to the *Anahata Chakra*. In the *Katha Upanishad* the Atman is described as a smokeless, pure, illumined flame the size of the thumb in the shrine of the heart. (2.1.13). In their deeper states of Meditation Yogis experience the lotus of the heart where, bathed in its inner light, they experience Divine bliss.

One of the most advanced methods of Meditation is Meditation upon the lotus of the heart after you have made your mind steady through Concentration. Then, withdrawing from the objects of the senses, you enter the shrine of Atman and, meditating on it, transcend the body and experience a higher Knowledge. Finally you attain *Samadhi*, in which you achieve Oneness with the Atman.

Meditation in Raja Yoga

According to the different levels of his mental unfoldment, a Yogi may meditate upon a gross object, or a sound (*mantra*) or a subtle mode of mind as he advances on the ascending rungs of Yoga. Meditation leads to *Samadhi* wherein the Yogi rises to a mystic expansion transcending the subject-object relationship involved in the process of Meditation. He then experiences his true nature, the eternal Self.

Meditation in Bhakti Yoga

A devotee focuses his mind on *Ishta Devata,* chosen personal God (Lord Rama, Lord Krishna, Shiva, Lord Buddha or Jesus Christ) invoking the Divine presence in his heart. This is called *upasana*. It is done during *Japa* or repetition of Divine Name or *Mantra* of the Deity. It involves thought of God to the exclusion of all others. (*Narada Bhakti Sutras,* 9). The mind is to allow only one thought on God, and exclude all others. All words and actions are also dedicated to the Lord. Great pain results when the mind forgets the Lord. (*N.B.S.*, 19). Should the mind stray a bit, it is brought back to God-thought. True Bhakti is unceasing remembrance of God. (*N.B.S.*, 36). At all times with heart and soul, God alone is to be remembered. (*N.B.S.*, 79). So Bhakti Yoga is exclusive meditation on God only. When it becomes more intensive the devotee gets the vision of God. (*See* the subheading *Japa* this Chapter, *above*)

Meditation in Jnana Yoga

An aspirant listens to the exposition of Vedanta Philosophy by the *Guru*; he reflects upon the teachings until his intellect is able to grasp the implication.

When he understands the nature of the Self as the Reality beyond the body, mind and sense, ego and the sense of individuality, he commences the Meditation on "I am Brahman" (*Aham Brahma Asmi*). This is called *Nididhysana.* He withdraws the mind from the objects of the world and purifies his mind. He, then, begins to experience the Self in varying degrees of expansion, when he goes beyond the mind, his "I consciousness" dissolves in the experience of the Universal Reality.

Just as a Bhakta has to constantly remember God, a Jnani has to directly to dwell on the Atman itself, i.e., on Self-awareness. *Gita* says, "Keep the mind on the Self itself and on nothing else." (6. 25). *Brahma Sutras*, the ancient scripture on Vedanta, also states, "For one who sets his mind on Self, freedom (*Moksha*) is the result." (1.1.27). His mind has to join the Self." (1.1.19). "By the meditation on *Brahman* (Attributeless Self), the hidden glory of the Self reveals itself." (2.2.5). "The *Niddhyasana* has to be continued (till the Self-experience dawns)." (4.1.1). But "Meditation shall not be on any symbol, for Self is not that." (4.1.4). Thus there are two stages in Jnana Yoga. First, an aspirant attains intellectual conviction on the existence of the Eternal Self through reflection upon the teachings on Vedanta, discrimination of the Real from the unreal, and dispassion. Second, he constantly meditates on the Self till experience of the Self dawns.

A Jnana Yogi may also meditate upon *Soham*, a Vedantic *mantra* for Meditation. It means "That am I."

He focuses the mind on *Ajna Chakra* between the eyebrows, associating the sound "*So*" with the incoming breath and "*Ham*" with outgoing breath. He should feel that the incoming breath creates the sound "*So*" automatically, and the outgoing breath creates "*Ham.*" Along with the mental visualization of the sound associated with breathing, he should try to assert the meaning of these two words.

A Jnana Yogi may also meditate on the Self by adopting a symbol of space in the region of his heart. Within the space he visualizes the abstract presence of the infinite Self. He may meditate upon the nature of the Self, reflecting upon the teachings, "I am not this body, I am not this mind, nor the senses . . . I am immortal Self."

Meditation in Kundalini Yoga

In Kundalini Yoga Meditation is practiced on various psychic centers or *Chakra*s and the pranic energy is led in *Shusmna nadi* to unfold the centers. (*See* 4.16 Kundalini Yoga: Philosophical Basis and *Chakras*; 4.17 Awakening Kundalini, *below*).

Indispensability of Meditation for God-Realization

Atman is the storehouse of all powers. Mind is only an instrument of Atman. It should be properly disciplined. Just as you develop the physical body through physical exercises or *Asanas*, you will have to train the mind through Meditation. Then only the gross mind will become subtle. To keep the mind charged with the power of supreme wisdom, you must keep it always in touch with the light of Knowledge of Self through constant and intense Meditation. You must keep up an unceasing flow of the Cosmic Consciousness.

Leading a virtuous life is not by itself sufficient for God-realization. Concentration of mind is absolutely necessary. A good, virtuous life only prepares the mind as a fit instrument for Concentration and Meditation. It is Concentration and Meditation that eventually lead to Self-realization.

God is within you. He is seated in the Lotus of your heart. You will have to seek Him through Meditation with a pure mind. All the visible things are *Maya*. *Maya* causes havoc through the mind. Meditation is the only way to conquer *Maya*. Buddha, Dattatreya, all had conquered *Maya* and mind through deep Meditation only. Solitude and Meditation are two important requisites for Self-Realization.

4.5: Prerequisites of Meditation

The Yoga of Meditation requires disciplined life and cultivation of ethical and moral values. Meditation cannot be achieved without integrating and perfecting one's life in every detail. The practice of Meditation without the cultivation of ethical safeguards may lead to self-deception and hallucination. Therefore, an aspirant has to examine his way of life, his mental outlook and behavioral pattern in terms of the requirements of Meditation. It calls for several prerequisites.

Physical Health

The body must be healthy and fit for the practice of Yoga. Sound health is essential for maintaining sound mind. Health can be maintained by disciplined and regulated life-style, sattvic food and Hatha Yoga *Asanas* and *Pranayama*. Hatha Yoga promotes health. *Pranayama* makes the body light, and balances the breath and the mind.

Diet

The food that you eat can be an aid or a hindrance to your spiritual progress. Foods that stimulate the system and create mental and physical unrest are *rajasic*. They include coffee and tea, canned foods and those grown with chemicals, meat, spices, onion, garlic, hot pepper, alcohol, tobacco and intoxicating drugs. They cause over-stimulation, discomfort and lead to various diseases. These *rajasic* foods should be avoided.

Foods that lead to lethargy are *tamasic*, and they also should be avoided. They include foods that consume a large amount of energy in digestion such as meat, stale and rotten foods and highly refined foods such as white sugar, white flour, polished rice, pickled foods, leftovers and preservative-added foods. *Tamas*ic foods cause tiredness, inertia and restlessness as well.

Foods that give energy and calmness of mind are *sattvic* foods. They are the most desirable foods for human beings. The most ideal foods in this category are fruits, nuts and seeds that are eaten in their natural state. They are, however, difficult to digest, and should not be taken in too large a quantity. Other *sattvic* foods are vegetables, soy beans, roots, pure milk and grains. By experimenting with foods, you may find certain foods make you tired while others make you restless. Then you can avoid such foods. A sudden change in diet is not advisable; it causes physiological and mental conflicts. Substitute healthy foods when you give up harmful foods.

Moderation

Moderation in diet, work, rest and sleep is essential for Yogic life. Buddha after passing through severe austerities, adopted and taught a moderate path. Lord Krishna says in the *Bhagavad Gita*:

> "Yoga is not for one who eats too much, nor by one who does not eat at all, nor for one who sleeps too much, nor for one who does not sleep at all." (6.16)
>
> "Yoga becomes destroyer of pain for one who is moderate in eating and recreation, who is moderate in sleep and wakefulness." (6.17)

Peaceful Living

Success in Meditation is closely related to peaceful living. A prayerful attitude to work is most helpful; whatever activity we may be engaged in, we must be aware of the Divine Presence in every situation. This helps us to prevent distracting thoughts and useless desires entering into our mind, and thus make the mind tuned to the meditative mood; if we then sit for the practice of Meditation at the selected time, mind will easily become stilled and concentrated.

Constant watch over our thought-waves is essential for attaining concentrated Meditation on God. Lord Krishna says in the *Bhagavad Gita*,

> "Thus always keeping the mind balanced, the Yogi, with the mind controlled, attains to the peace abiding in Me, which culminates in liberation." (6.15)

Right Outlook

Just as a farmer prepares his land before sowing seeds for raising a crop, you have to develop right outlook, genuine love and devotion to God and towards all beings. You have to develop a universal love, which will keep the "field" of your mind fit and ready to receive the spiritual seed. Do not neglect this virtue. A peevish, complaining and unsociable being can never become a Yogi. You have to be all-loving, and become a living channel for carrying the message of love and friendship to all beings. It is only by wholehearted devotion and sincere love, says Mira Bai, an Indian mystic saint of sixteenth century, that perfection is attained.

Attitude toward People

You have to cultivate positive and benevolent attitudes, and avoid negative attitudes in order to maintain mental peace. When you come across different types of persons in your everyday life, whether you will be able to retain your mental peace undisturbed? This depends upon your attitude toward them.

You may encounter four types of persons: happy persons, unhappy ones, virtuous persons and wicked people. If you meet someone who is happy, you should not tend to envy him and be jealous of his success. You must rather learn to feel happy and express friendliness toward him. If someone is unhappy, you should feel sorry and compassionate to him instead of despising him. If possible, you should lend a helping hand.

If you happen to come across a virtuous person, you should not take his virtue as a reflection upon your shortcomings and thus become irritated. On the contrary you should feel delighted and try to emulate his great qualities.

Sometimes you may come across wicked people. What should be your attitude toward them? You should not try to advise such persons, because wicked people seldom take advice. So you should just be indifferent to them, with prayer for their refinement. Thus by adopting these attitudes—friendliness toward the happy, compassion for the unhappy, delight in the virtuous, and benevolent indifference toward the wicked – you can maintain your mental peace undisturbed. (*Yoga Sutras*, 1.33)

Good Associations (*Sat sangha*)

Living with like minded people is conducive to Meditation. On the other hand the company of those who are agitated, distracted and immersed in worldly concerns is harmful to the practice of Meditation.

In the beginning of spiritual practice, it is necessary for an aspirant to fence himself by keeping good associations. The young aspirant, like the newly planted seedling, can easily be destroyed by outside forces, unless protected by a fence of good associations or associations with virtuous people. As said by Shankaracharya, "One of the immediate benefits of keeping good company is that you find that you are not in a bad company." Bad company makes it difficult to do spiritual practice.

Austerity (*Tapas*)

Austerity is one of the purifying practices that prepare you for Meditation. It means giving up your dependence on external comforts, luxuries and addictions, freeing the mind from the demands of the senses and endless desires. But it does not mean self-torture. It just involves simple living with moderation in eating, sleeping and activities. It also involves mental purity by avoiding unnecessary talking, meaningless discussion, impure thoughts and reading bad literature. Without regulating physical and mental habits, the mind cannot become a useful tool for Meditation.

Awareness of purpose

A clear understanding of the basic purpose of Yogic Meditation is essential. Its purpose is to go beyond the limits of mundane thinking, beyond the mind and enlarge the field of awareness to realize the ultimate Reality. It is for this reason you are given a *mantra* on which you can focus. The *mantra* permits you to turn your attention to something that is outside the circle of mundane thoughts.

Self-analysis

Self-analysis is another purifying process. It involves looking at yourself with greater objectivity, analyzing how various things affect you in your daily life. Through introspection you must identify your imperfections, and correct them so as to achieve progress in your spiritual development.

Surrender and Devotion

Your ego, the sense of "I and mine" makes you to wrongly identify yourself with your body and mind and get entangled in the various dramas of worldly life. The cultivation of surrender and devotion to the Supreme Consciousness (God) helps to overcome your ego and false identification, and to realize your true nature. (*See* 4.6 Obstacles to Meditation, *above*)

Prayer

Prayer is one of the most wonderful tools available for transforming your personality. It should not involve asking for some boon or help. True prayer involves self-surrender and dedication of yourself to the Lord. It is a means for cultivating Divine qualities and humbleness and for making you an humble instrument in the hands of God.

Silence

Silence is golden. You should observe silence at least for a day every week. It will enable you to save energy, avoid misunderstandings with others, and to turn inward and develop your consciousness.

Solitary Place and Seclusion

A solitary sattvic place with spiritual vibratory conditions and temperate climate is a requisite for Concentration and Meditation because the brain gets hot during Meditation. The places like the banks of a pure river, mountains, lovely gardens, sacred temples elevate the mind in Meditation. Of course the ideal conditions cannot always be attained. We must select the best that is possible, and put up with some inconveniences. We should be able to abstract ourselves from the distracting causes.

For intense practice of Yoga of Meditation, seclusion for a period of time is indispensable. Lord Krishna says in the *Bhagavad Gita*: "Let a Yogi try constantly to keep his mind steady, remaining in solitude, keeping his body and mind under control, and free from hope and greed. " (6.10)

Mental Training

For Meditation a properly trained mind is needed. You must have a calm, clear, pure, subtle, sharp, steady and one-pointed intellect to understand the concept of Brahman or Atman. Brahman is pure and subtle and you need a pure and subtle mind to approach Brahman.

You should learn to train your attention faculty to concentrate. Only then you can practice Meditation. Typically human mind is restless and distracted, and attention jumps from one thought to another. But Meditation requires quiet and steady mind. Therefore training in attention and Concentration is a prerequisite for Meditation. (*See* 4.2 Concentration Process and 4.3 Concentration and Mental Exercises, *above*).

Only a trained mind can control the body and meditate regularly without losing sight of its goal. All attachments should be ruthlessly cut asunder completely. Lord Krishna in the *Bhagavad Gita* says: "Renouncing all desires that are born of egoistic will and completely restraining all senses by the mind from all sides, let the Yogi attain to quietude gradually by fixing the mind on the Self without thinking of anything else." (6.24, 25)

> "If one is without attachment on meeting with good or bad, and neither rejoices nor hates, his wisdom is established." (2.57)

Mastering the Mind

At times desires, expectations, disappointments, anxieties, worries, memories of past enjoyments, reactions to current situations, lose of things to which you are attached and so forth make your mind restless. Such states need not discourage you. They are common to most of us. Do not let your mind mislead you. Make a firm resolution to practice Meditation regularly, and right earnestly start practicing it. Sometimes in Meditation the mind behaves wonderfully; it becomes calm and concentrated easily, and you are encouraged. But if at other times the mind behaves badly, refuses to quiet down and is restless, then you are discouraged. You may be tempted to feel that you could not succeed in Meditation. Do not allow such depressing states of mind discourage you and make you to discontinue. Keep trying. A voracious horse kicks, rears and attempts to throw away the rider, but if the rider manages to stay firmly in the saddle, then the horse quiets down, knowing it has found its master. The mind behaves in the same way. It will try to dislodge you, but upon finding that you cannot be shaken off, it will become your slave. (*See* 2.7 Purification and Control of Mind, *above*).

Dispassion and Discrimination

Dispassion or non-attachment plays an important part in self-discipline. It means absence of attraction and aversion to worldly objects. In the earlier stages of spiritual unfoldment the lower desires for worldly objects and pleasures have to be replaced by the higher desire for seeking the Reality or God. Later even that desire should be given up.

Real dispassion lies in the correct attitude of one's mind. You may live in this world, but the world should not live in your mind. A boat may float on water, but water should never get into the boat. Love one and all, serve all, but never become attached to anyone or anything.

Dispassion and discrimination always go together. They are the two aspects of the same process of mental transformation. Discriminate the real from the unreal, the Self from the non-self.

Feeling of Eternity

Approach Meditation with the feeling of eternity. Feel absolutely unrelated to worldly things. Eternity is beyond time, space and all phenomena. It is a condition in which none of the relative things exists. When seeking to think of the eternal Lord, make an effort for the time being to go beyond all relationships. Feel: "You have no body, no mind; the whole universe has vanished. God alone is." Then only the mind will feel God's gracious presence. Thus, before you enter the place of Meditation, you must leave everything relative outside.

4.6: Meditative Traditions

Introduction

Over centuries Meditation seems to have assumed different forms such as Yoga Meditation, Zen Meditation, Superconscious Meditation, Jewish Meditation, Christian Meditation, Transcendental Meditation, etc.. The sitting Postures, the method of Concentration and other procedures may vary from form to form. But these differences are superficial, and at the deepest level, all Meditation involves the process of fixing the mind on a particular idea or object and all Meditation forms have come from the same ancient traditional process.

Meditation is practiced in some form or other in each of the great religious traditions of the world. However, the practice of Meditation is generally confined to more serious and advanced followers of a particular faith interested in spiritual advancement.

Even though Meditation has been associated with various spiritual traditions, its practice does not necessarily involve following the dogma of a particular religion. Meditation is a universal experimental discipline for the development of one's consciousness; it should not be identified with the religion itself. While it can enhance one's understanding of one's faith, it can also be practiced without any involvement in any religion.

Without sufficient understanding of how and why Meditation is practiced, the meditative process cannot lead to the highest state of Consciousness, but if the process is properly understood, there will be inner peace and bliss. In trying to achieve this meditative experience, however, the aspirant is restricted by the traditional boundaries of his accepted metaphysical and religious beliefs.

Every theological system requires its followers to believe in a definite way, with definite notions of God, soul, heaven, hell, sin and virtue. But any pre-determined notions that one carries to the deeper states of Meditation binds the meditator and prevents him from crossing the boundaries of the conditioned mind. One can get higher experiences from this kind of Meditation, but they are limited. Consequently, when one is restricted by a dogma, one cannot realize the universal truth that the Self within is the Self of all. In a Meditation bounded by a dogma, this truth is not realized by the meditator.

Superconscious Meditation

In the system of Superconscious Meditation practiced by ancient sages and saints of India, one does not move from some unconscious principle toward a higher state of experience, for the higher state of experience is not a separate state and it actually encompasses all degrees of consciousness. In fact the prefix 'super' is used only for linguistic convenience. All that is of life and consciousness is of Superconscious principle. Life, Consciousness, soul (*jiva*), *chit,* energy and *shakti* are all one and the same. This Oneness, this Unity is Superconsciousness. It is the name of all names. All beings, objects and experiences arise from it, have their existence in it and they finally subside into it.

The ancient sages and saints have lived in the experience of Superconsciousness as their primary mode of being. Superconsciousness should not be viewed as one state among many, but as the total mode of existence. Being is consciousness and consciousness is being; *sat* is *chit,* and *chit* is *sat.*

Are bubbles, waves and tides different from the ocean? The ocean with all the tides, waves and bubbles is one. What a bubble is to the ocean, the entire universe with all its atoms, galaxies and vast space is to the Superconsciousness. We are not speaking of the awareness of that bubble, universe or an individual human being has of itself in relation to the ocean, the Superconsciousness, but of the awareness that the ocean has of the bubble and of itself, the Superconscious Being has of Itself and of the universe. This awareness is Superconscious Meditation.

Superconscious Meditation, thus, is not a transcendental experience. It is not an altered state of Consciousness. Since there is nothing below or above it, nothing before or beyond it, there is nothing to transcend. All things and all thoughts are its emanations. All other states of Consciousness are its derivations.

All that we experience in wakefulness, dreams or deep sleep are simply modes, modifications and waves arising from the Superconsciousness. The waves of time, space and causation arise from it. It is all inclusive. In such an oceanic Consciousness of a realized Yogi or a *siddha,* there is no "going into" Meditation.

For those who have not merged their awareness into that ocean, there have to be processes and techniques. What is the source of this teaching? The process of emanation of the manifest from the unmanifest is the process of teaching. Various individual minds are the eddies and whirls in the ocean called the Golden Womb of the universe, *Hiranya Garbha*. All the energies that manifest in these eddies and whirls are the energies of the Golden Womb.

The minds of great rishis, saints and masters are those powerful tides in the Golden Womb, that carry along huge and little waves as they move. Little minds are linked to great minds, which, in turn, dwell as one in the Golden Womb. Only those who understand this link and the process of linkage can teach Meditation.

So in Superconscious Meditation there is no going in from outside, but the individual is being pulled within.

This amazing wonder is celebrated in *Saundaryalahari* (Song of the Waves of Beauty), one of the two major texts of Superconscious Meditation, composed by the great sage Shankaracharya. The other text of this system is *Mandukya Karika*, the expository verses of the sage Gaudapada on the *Mandukya Upanishad.*

The *Mandukya Upanishad* is one of the shortest *Upanishads*, expounding the mysteries of the word OM in twelve sentences. Gaudapada wrote 234 verses of exposition on this Upanishad. Shankaracharya, who was the disciple of Govindapada who was Gaudapada's disciple, wrote a detailed commentary on this work. Like *Saundaryalahari*, the *Karika* also can be understood fully only by one who dwells in Superconsciousness. We can speak only as bubble would, not as one with the oceanic Consciousness.

Superconsciousness is described in the seventh verse of the *Mandukya Upanishad* in these words:

> "The Superconsciousness (*Turiya*) is neither external, nor consciousness, neither semi-consciousness, nor, neither consciousness, nor unconsciousness. (It is) unseen, nonempirical, indefinable, inconceivable, indescribable, the essence of knowledge of the One-self and of evolution, and non-dual, peaceful and benign. It is Atman, the Self, the fourth. It is to be known."

This description is given only after defining the other three states of consciousness. All states of consciousness are internally self-evident. No extensive evidence can be found to prove or disprove the accuracy of the experience of any state of consciousness. Superconsciousness is the Universal Spirit, the indivisible Brahman.

The *Mundaka Upanishad* describes in Chapter 2:

> "It is Self luminous and more subtle than the smallest; but in It rest all the worlds and their beings. It is the eternal Brahman, and It is life, speech and mind. It is true, it is immortal." (2.2.2)
> "It is the radiant Light of all lights. There the sun shines not, nor the moon, nor the stars, lightning shines not and much less earthly fire. From Its Light all these give light, and Its radiance illumines all this world." (2.2.10–11)
> "Spreading before and behind, right and left, and above and below, is Brahman, the Eternal. Verily Brahman is all. It is the greatest." (2.2.12)

The *Katha Upanishad* narrates that when the boy Nachiketa was offered by the Lord of Death the entire earth as an empire and the choice of fair maidens with chariots and musical instruments, he said, "All these pleasures pass away. O Lord, give me the gift that upon arriving where one does not return, one does not reincarnate." *Yama* taught Nachiketa the supreme wisdom. Then Nachiketa reached Brahman, the Spirit Supreme and became immortal and pure.

The *Maitri Upanishad* describes:

> "In the beginning all was Brahman, the infinite One. It is immeasurable,inapprehensible, beyond conception, never born, beyond reasoning, beyond thought. Its self is space. At the dissolution, into It the universe returns. It is that luminous form that gives heat in the sun, light on the fire, and fire in the stomach that digests food. He who is in all is.One. He who knows this becomes one with the One." (6.17)

When the soul rises to the heights of purity, one's choice is very clear. Shvetaketu's father said to him: "Son, these rivers flow from east to west, from north to south, and they all flow to the sea. While they are bound to the two banks, each one says, 'I am the Ganges, I am this river, I am another river.' The water at that time seems to become that river, but when all the rivers have flown to the one common repository of all waters, to the ocean, then they no longer know themselves to be the Ganges or various other streams and rivers; they know themselves to be one oceanic water. And all drops of water then belong to that one ocean, so while you are in the bondage of ignorance, you do not know that you are not of this body, you are not of that body. But that one drop that is within you, though it is at the present moment bound to the banks of your body, you will soon transcend. For the pure Consciousness is your essential Self. That is your only Self. You flow into One oceanic Consciousness. You are then the Cosmic Reality that alone is Truth. You are That. (*Chandogya Upanishad,* Chapter VI, Section 10)

He continued, "As you place a lump of salt in water, it dissolves in the water and cannot be separated, cannot be seen as separate in the water. But my son, you taste that water! Whether you taste it from this corner of the vessel, or from another corner of the vessel, whether you taste it from the top or from the bottom, it is one saline water. For the salt has permeated every particle of that water. You look for Self, you do not find Self. But like the salt permeated in the water, you, the Self have permeated all the three bodies, all the five sheaths, all the seven *Chakras*, the centers of Consciousness. You have permeated your urges and your emotions. Know thyself. You are that Essence. You are that Reality. *Tat tvam Asi*. Svetaketu, Thou art That." (*Chandogya Upanishad*, Chapter VI, Section 13).

So down the lines of sages, this teaching of the Superconscious Meditation has descended. The return of the individual soul to the great oceanic Superconsciousness takes place through a long journey in the Meditation path.

The Buddhist Meditation

The classical Buddhist *Abhidahamma* is a detailed traditional psychology of state of Consciousness. In the fifth century AD, the monk Buddhaghosa summarized the portion of *Abhidahamma* about Meditation into the *Visuddhimagga*, the path of purification. *Visuddhimagga* describes the preparation for Meditation, and the process of Meditation and experiences of *Nibbana* (Nirvana).

A meditator starts his practice under the guidance of a teacher. Practice begins with *sila,* virtue or moral purity. The purification consists of prohibitions and observances regarding daily monastic life. This discipline aims at purification of thought, word and deed. It involves control of senses and non-attachment. The goal of purification is to make the mind calm and ripe for Meditation.

The meditator selects a single object and fixes the mind on it. The *Visuddhimagga* gives a list of forty Meditation objects suited to different types of temperaments, and specifies the appropriate physical surroundings for each type. For example, to the lustful meditator is assigned a cramped, windowless hut in an ugly location.

At the outset, the meditator's focus wanders between the object of Meditation and distracting thoughts. He brings back his focus to the object again and again. The Concentration gradually increases. By continually focusing on the object of Meditation, the meditator experien ces *Jhana*, full absorption. In this state, the mind sinks into the object and fixed in it for a moment. With continued practice, the *Jhana* state can be held for longer intervals.

To go deeper still, the meditator has to abandon all forms of mental pleasure and attain "formless" *Jhana*. Finally he reaches the state of *Nirvana* (Liberation). The number of times the meditator enters the *Nirvanic* state determines his level of mastery. In *Nirvana*, desire, attachment and selfishness are burned out. The awakened person is called *Arahant* or Saint. Having no feelings of 'self,' his acts are purely functional for maintenance of his body and for the good of others.

Meditation in Jainism

The word 'Jainism' comes from the word jina that means "one who has conquered one's inner enemies." Mahavira was the last prophet in the line of twenty-four Tirthankaras of Jainism. A Tirthankara is a great sage who builds bridges among people. Mahavira was a contemporary to Buddha. Those who are eager to follow the path of conquering their inner enemies are known as Jain. Jaina is not a religion but a way of living. Any person who follows non-violence, who has relativity in thinking, and who knows the invisible vibrations of the karmas is a Jain.

The whole emphasis is on inside transformation. Meditation requires long practice. Silence plays a great role in it. Jainism is a path of finding yourself in being.

Meditation starts with this idea: turn off for a while your outer activity in order to enter the receptive mood of your soul. First, you sit for a while. Take an asana. It is called *kayotsarga*. "*Kaya*" means "the body," and "*utsarga*" means "to drop." Forget the body tension, and allow it to relax. For as long as there is tension in the body, you would not be able to experience the flow of life. When you have done *kayotsarga*, you can turn to the mind and the breath. Breathe deeply and take in fresh oxygen. Use the *mantra* "*virum*." It means "brave." Be brave enough to accept the real nature of yourself. When you breathe in, you use *vi*, and when you breathe out, you use *rum*. To enjoy your blissfulness in a relaxed mood, you need bravery, because the mind is loaded with worry, anxiety, fear and other negatives. The mind is not ready to enjoy *Sat-chit-ananda,* the Immortal-consciousness-bliss. By reciting the *mantra* and focusing on breath, you engage your mind. The *mantra* is a banana to the monkey mind. Soul does not need *mantra*, because soul itself is *Sat-chit-ananda.*

When you use the *mantra* "*virum,*" you are going inside. You feel calm. There are three stages as you go inward. In the first stage, your mind is reciting *mantra*, but at the same time it is bringing many distractions.

Then you use the word *Kohum* that means "Who am I?" You ask yourself this question: "Who am I?" Meditation starts with this first step. Without knowing yourself, you will not reach your Self. Recite "*Kohum*." Then the answer comes: "I am form. I am body. I am so and so . . ." Your name comes, your emotions come. Passion comes. You say "*Naham*," not me. My name was given after I was born. Somebody has given me this name. "What was I before then?" There comes the body. Before the body, you were there. You entered the body. But who was it that entered the body? You are going deeper now. Go on removing the layers. Go deeper and deeper. Get the right knowledge through a right teacher. The teaching goes inside and permeates your consciousness. When you become calm, the teaching goes deeper and deeper, and then a process of churning takes place. That is introspection. Erase your past. Live in the present. This is mental Meditation. Purify yourself through austerity. When the time comes you will see the light.

The third word in Meditation is "*sohum,*" which means "I am I." Realizing *sohum,* you reach the state of bliss. In this way you use Meditation in order to reach your higher Self.

Zen (Ch'an) Meditation

The word "*Zen*" or "*Ch'an*" is a cognate of the Pali word *jhana* that was derived from the Sanskrit word *Dhyana* (Meditation). The *Visuddhimagga* tradition of Buddhism reached Japan from India during the fifth century through China where the people used words of one syllable only.

Under the influence of Buddhism, two important Schools of

Meditation (*Ch'an*) developed in China. One is the Northern Gradual School of Shen-hsiu. The other is the Southern Abrupt School of Hui-neng.

According to the Northern School, Meditation is a gradual process of Self-unfoldment; Meditation gradually leads to Enlightenment. Sustained intellectual effort, moral discipline, spiritual practice, ethical action, and others are important requisites for the attainment of Enlightenment. This approach appeals particularly to the intellectual and ethical types of people. The method of Meditation conceived here is that of the "dust-wiping" type. So long as our mind, which is like a mirror, is full of the dust of impure desires and impulses, it does not fully and faithfully reflect the light of the Truth. Meditation consists in gradually wiping out the dust of the mental mirror through Concentration upon spiritual truths, and regulation of the affairs of life in accordance with the spiritual ideal. The sun of spiritual illumination shines out when the clouds of ignorance and the mist of desires are cleared away from the mental firmament. Thus Meditation is a gradual process of transition, through self-discipline, from ignorance to knowledge, from bondage to freedom, from mental cognition to spiritual realization.

The Southern Abrupt School of Hui-neng is the latest form of development of Zen Buddhism. It maintains that the difference between ignorance and knowledge is a radical and fundamental difference. Spiritual insight (*Satori*) is a qualitatively different dimension of experience. There are no degrees of spiritual insight. Either a person has it, or he does not have it. Until he has atained it, there is only the process of groping in the dark. Intuition flares up, like a flash of lightning, abruptly and mysteriously, when the mind is absolutely relaxed and free from all effort and preoccupation. This sudden awakening of spiritual intuition may arise through living contact with an illuminated *Guru* or spontaneous spiritual blooming.

The Southern School believes in the "self-seeing" type of Meditation as distinguished from the dust-wiping type. Meditation is not a strenuous striving for a determinate psychical condition. It is rather an art of allowing things to develop.

In spiritual wisdom, being appears not as separate from seeing, but as inseparably identical with seeing and experiencing. This seeing is also acting. It is the flux of life itself, the creative advance of the spirit. The equation "seeing = being = acting" expresses the essence of the self-seeing type of Meditation. It is free and spontaneous living in harmony with the Unconscious, like the shining of the sun or blooming of a flower. (*Refer* D.T. Suzuki, *Zen Buddhism*, New York: Doubleday Anchor Books, 1956).

Zen Meditation begins with a firm grounding in Concentration; a wide variety of Concentration techniques are employed. *Samadhi* in Zen terminology is the "great fixation" or "a state of Oneness" in which the differences between things dissolve so that they appear to the meditator as same. This is an intermediate stage on the path toward Zen's final Realization. The wisdom of insight follows and flows from *Samadhi*.

Among Zen techniques are some unique methods for achieving *Samadhi*. One of them is called the *koan* or question. Assigned a *koan* such as "What was your face before you were born?" Or "What is *Mu*?," the aspirant keeps the *koan* constantly in mind. As he discovers that his rational mind is unable to solve the insoluble, he reaches a feverish pitch of Concentration from which arises a supreme frustration. As this happens, what once was a fully stated *koan* is reduced to an emblematic fragment, simply "*Mu*." When his discursive faculty finally exhausts itself, the moment of "Realization" comes to the meditator. His thought ceases and he enters the state of *Daigi* or "Fixation." His *koan* "yields up all its secrets," as he attains *Samadhi*. The meditator must come out of that state, be awakened from it. That moment of coming out of *Samadhi* and seeing it for what it is, is *Satori*. Zen teachers stress the need to ripen an initial *Satori* through further Meditation until it finally permeates the meditator's whole life. In the final stage of "no mind," the spontaneous clarity of *Satori* manifests in his all acts. Here means and ends coalesce. Having experienced the impermanence of all things, that "life is pain, that all forms are *ku*, empty or void," he ceases clinging to the phenomenal world, yet continues to act.

Jewish Meditation

In Judaism, the hidden teachings, which bear the light that illumines rituals, scriptures and services, are called *Kabbalah*, which means "to receive." These teachings, it is said, originated with the angels, who were instructed by God. *Kabbalah*, which stretches back to antiquity, reached its heyday in the Middle Ages.

In order to purify the body, the mystic goes to what is called a *mikvab*. That is a special ritual bath. Thus the body is prepared for the study of *kabbalah*, which means "to receive" that which is implied in the *Torah*, the Hebrew Bible.

Next the mind is prepared. The mind is symbolic of lights. So two candles are lighted. They are symbolic of the two inclinations in each one of us, good and bad, virtue and evil. To concentrate on the light until you no longer know which is which; two have become one.

Kabbalah seeks to train the aspirant to enter into a state of higher consciousness, the Paradise within. When the aspirant contacts a *Maggid* or teacher, his training begins in earnest. The prerequisite for his spiritual development is training of his will, his capacity for unwavering attention. For this, the *kabbalist* turns to Meditation. The *maggid* gives instructions for self-purification and Meditation.

In general, Meditation in *kabbalah* is an offshoot of the normal prayers of the devout Jew. Meditative Concentration allows the kabbalist to delve into the depths of a particular subject, a word in a prayer, and to remain one-pointed on the subject.

There are two worlds, the upper and the lower worlds. They are connected by seven balls called the seven rungs of Meditation.

The Hebrew word for Meditation is *Kavanah*. Each letter stands for a concept, and therefore it gives you the method of how to meditate. The first letter "k" stands for *kitov,* which means "all is well." The second letter "a" stands for *ahavah*, meaning "love," to express love every moment in our lives. The next letter "v" stands for *vi-dui*vi-dui, to confess our short comings, to become mature enough to say, "I have made a mistake." The next letter "n" stands for *ne-oth*, meaning "to let go." That is, let God take over after I have done everything humanly possible. The next letter "a" stands for *amunah,* faith. The seventh letter "h" stands for *hithahavoth,* the ecstasy.

Every Jew meditates sitting on the floor, having a candle in front of him. The aim is to reach God. The *kabbalistic* name for God is *Ein Sof,* which means the "circle," the One who has no beginning and no end.

The meditator concentrates on each word of regular prayer with his full attention, to the point at which his mind transcends the simple meaning of the words; thought expands and ascends to its origin.

The writings of Abraham Abulafia contain a detailed description of *kabbalist* Meditation. It combines various letters of the Hebrew alphabet for Meditation on the holy names of God. This method is distinctive from prayer; the aspirant meditates in seclusion at given hours under the guidance of his *Maggid.* As he repeats the name, he directs his attention upward from *yesod*, the limited ordinary mind into *tiferet*, an awareness beyond ego. That is, he directs his thought away from all forms of this world, focusing on the name. If his effort meets with God's grace, the self will suddenly rise up beyond *Tiferet* to an ecstatic state called *Daat* or Knowledge. Here his sense of separation from God dissolves. He is filled with a great joy. When he emerges from this state, he will again become aware of the inner repetition.

The end of the *kabbalist*'s path is *Devekut*, in which the seeker's soul cleaves to God. When he stabilizes his consciousness at this level, he becomes a *zaddik*, a saint. The Holy Spirit dwells in him. (Goleman, Daniel, 1988, pp. 48–52).

Meditation in Christianity

In the early Christianity Meditation was practiced in all the monasteries, and the cross, a symbol for physical suffering, mortification and earthly struggle, was also a symbol for spiritual victory.

References to Meditation pervade both the old Testament and the *Gospels*. In the *Psalms* one reads:

> Let the words of my mouth and the Meditation of my heart be acceptable in Thy sight. O Lord, my rock and my redeemer. (*Psalm* 19.14)
> Be still and know that I am God. (*Psalm* 46.10)
> Let me hear what God the Lord will speak . . . to those who turn to Him in their hearts. (*Psalm* 85.8)
> I commune with my heart in the night. I meditate and search my Spirit. (*Psalm* 77.6)
> May my Meditation be pleasing to Him, for I rejoice in the Lord. (*Psalm* 104.34)
> On the glorious splendor of Thy majesty, and on Thy wondrous works, I will meditate. (*Psalm* 145.5)

Further references to Meditation are found in the New Testament. It often shows Jesus retiring from the crowds to be alone in Meditation.

Meditation is the means for gaining the Self-Knowledge. This has been reaffirmed by the mystics of Christianity. For example,

> Our Meditation in the present life should be in the praise of God; for the external exultation of our life here or after will be the praise of God; and none can become fit for the future life who hath not practiced himself for it now.(St. Augustine) No one can be saved without Self-Knowledge. (St. Bernard)

The first Christian monks were hermits who lived during the fourth century AD in the most remote parts of the barren Egyptian desert. The Meditation practices and modes of living of these earliest Christian monks bear strong similarity to those of the Hindu and Buddhist monks of the East. While Jesus and His teachings were their inspiration, the meditative techniques adopted by them for finding their God seem to have borrowed from the East.

The Desert Fathers meditated with verbal or silent repetition of a single phrase from the Scriptures, a Christian equivalent of *mantra*. The most popular was *Kyrie*, "Lord Jesus Christ, Son of God, have mercy on me, a sinner."

These Fathers emphasized purity. Purification was used to aid Concentration. They practiced prayer for this purpose. The goal of the Desert Fathers was "nowhereness and no mindness," a condition known as *quies*, which means "rest." One who attains a state of effortless constant prayer becomes the abode of the Holy Spirit.

St. Anthony, one of the Desert Fathers established a School of Meditation in AD 310 on a mountain called St. Anthony, sixty-five miles south of Cairo. There he guided thousands of monks on the path of Meditation. Similar guidance was given in another monastery of Tabenna in upper Egypt founded by Paul in AD 300.

In all, there were about five thousand monks practicing Meditation and austerity in the Desert of Nitra in Egypt around that time.

It is mentioned in various scriptures that two monks from India accompanied Alexander the Great to the Middle East and established a School of Meditation in the region where Anthony and Paul had founded their monasteries. The early Eastern Christianity had a long line of sages and their ascetic and Meditation practices were same as those practiced by Indian monks and sages. This was also the time when Patanjali's Yoga of Meditation was influencing the various sects and religions of the Far, and middle East.

It is also interesting to note that Yogic breathing was practiced in the fifth century AD by the Hesychast monks. In addition, the spiritual writings of the Hesychastic period teach that the human body has certain focal points that correspond to the *Chakra*s of Yoga, the navel, the heart, the throat and the mid-brow. The monks, like the Yogis, would concentrate upon these points along with rhythmic breathing and prayerful words.

Later, during the Middle Ages, the confluence of Hesychastic prayer and Meditation continued to prevail in Christian monasteries. The great Byzantine mystic St. Simeon (949-1022) practiced and taught these methods of Meditation.

Besides, the orders of Rosicrucians and the Freemasons used the symbol for the mother sound, OM. (See *Lectures on Masonic*

Symbolism by Albert Pike).

Somewhere, however, the thread between early and modern Christianity was broken, especially regarding the tradition of Meditation, and that is the reason why the modern Christians do not receive initiation in Meditation. As the western culture has now become more secular, Meditational practices have disappeared from Christian religion, although there are still many Christian monks who continue in the meditative tradition.

Meditation in Sufism

Sufism is a mystic order of Islam. The most typical Sufi is the dervish (*dar-veesh*). This is a rare type of human being whom you hardly ever come across these days. The dervish is someone whose mind has been blown (that is, whose heart has been broken). The *dervish* is madly in love with God, the One you love. As Ibn Arabi, one of the greatest Sufis says, "He is the One whom every lover loves in every beloved." The heart of the *dervish* becomes so sensitive that he is able to be aware of the suffering of humanity. As a result, he develops a tremendous intuition.

The Sufi, through Meditation, is looking for that which the *rishi* is seeking beyond life. There is a very deep emotion behind the Meditation of the Sufi. He seeks to annihilate himself so that he may come closer to the beloved. This is an extreme form of love. This is the first step.

The next step in Meditation is contemplation. In this, Sufi experiences himself as the Self of all beings. This is exactly what is found in the *Isa Upanishad:* "He who sees all beings in his own Self, and his own Self in all beings, . . . then what delusion and what sorrow can be to him who has seen the oneness?" It is a wonderful feeling of being freed from the tyranny of the ego.

The next stage in the Meditation of the Sufis is to see the attributes, which are the first layer behind the appearance of things. In other words, his consciousness is geared to the attributes rather than to the physical expression. So behind all things he sees their meaningfulness. He feels that all creation is a means whereby the One he loves is able to manifest Himself. The Hindus call this step

Panmatra, the subtle Reality.

Then the Sufi passes through a crisis where he feels that he is imposing a limitation on the Consciousness of God, which is passing through him. He feels "I am the eyes through which God sees." Then at a certain stage, he centers himself in Cosmic Consciousness and watches his personal consciousness from that vantage point. This is the stage of "I am God." Al Hallaj, a great Sufi master says that as long as you are conscious of your individual self, you can only think of yourself as an instrument of the God, but once you are annihilated, you are the God. This echoes the *Upanishadic* statement: "Thou are That." The same thing is experienced through Yoga. In *turiya*, the final stage, Atman takes over. The fundamental practice of the Sufis is "there is no God but God." It means that there is only One being. So in Sufism Meditation is a process of Self-discovery.

Transcendental Meditation

TM is a Meditation technique developed by Maharishi Mahesh Yogi. It is a classic Hindu *mantra* Meditation in a modern Western package. The theory behind TM, "Science of Creative Intelligence," is an updated restatement of the basic teachings of Sankaracharya's eighth century Advaita School of Vedantic thought. Sankaracharya's highly successful religious crusade against Buddhism revived Hinduism in India, offering a final state of non-duality rather than Nirvana to the seeker. The goal of Advaita is union of the seeker's mind with the formless Brahman or infinite Consciousness through *Samadhi*. This is also the goal in TM.

Like all Advaita Yogis, Maharishi sees that "duality is the fundamental cause of suffering." His technique for transcending duality begins with a repetition of a *mantra*. A proper *mantra* is selected for each individual.

In TM, the meditator learns to avoid effortful Concentration. He is told to bring his mind gently back to the *mantra* as it wanders. In effect, this process is one of becoming one-pointed, though Concentration is passive, rather than forced.

According to Maharishi, TM entails " . . . turning the attention inward toward the subtler levels of a thought until the mind transcends the experience of the subtlest state of the thought and arrives at the source of thought . . ."

The goal of *mantra* is what Maharishi calls "Transcendental Consciousness," when mind "arrives at the direct experience of bliss, it loses all contact with the outside and is centered in the state of Transcendental bliss, Consciousness."

The next phase in Maharishi's program is the infusion of Transcendental Consciousness into the waking, dreaming and sleeping states by alternating normal activity with periods of Meditation. The state thereby achieved, he calls, "Cosmic Consciousness" in which "no activity, however rigorous, can take one out of Being."

Maharishi denies the need to impose renunciation on oneself. He sees purification as a part of Cosmic Consciousness. It is an effect of transcendence, not a prerequisite. According to him "proficiency in the virtues can only be gained by repeated experience of *Samadhi*." Perhaps this is a watering down approach to sell his technique to westerners who generally find it difficult to practice *Yama*, *Niyama*s and vegetarian diet.

Maharishi elaborates the transition from Transcendental to Cosmic Consciousness: "From this state of pure Being, the mind comes back again to experience the thought in the relative world . . With more and more practice, the ability of the mind to maintain its essential nature increases. When this happens the mind and its essential nature of the state of Transcendental Being become one, and the mind is then capable of retaining its essential nature - Being - while engaged in thought, speech or action."

The meditator in Cosmic Consciousness finds this inner peace persisting in all circumstances as a "pure awareness" along with activity. Although the effects of transcendence during Meditation can wear off after Meditation is over, once mastered, Cosmic Consciousness is permanent. During waking, he remains relatively detached from sense perception, although he is more sensitive to both his own thought processes, and external events.

As Cosmic Consciousness deepens, the meditator finds the bliss of Transcendental Consciousness persisting now in other states.

As this bliss pervades other areas of his life, he finds that by comparison sensual pleasures are not so enchanting as before. While he still has desires, his actions are no longer driven by them. His state is one of equanimity. Life in Cosmic Consciousness is tensionless. "The Enlightened man lives a life of fulfillment."

The next step in the progression is God Consciousness. This state is the result of devotion while in Cosmic Consciousness. In this state the meditator surrenders his individuality. This is "the most purified state." He now dwells in perfect harmony with nature and the Divine.

4.7: How to Meditate?

Preparation for Meditation

Meditation should not be undertaken in a haphazard way. It requires adequate preparation. Meditation is a continuation of Concentration. Preparation for it is described in 4.2. Concentration Practice, *above*. Preparation is as important as the process of Meditation. It consists of bringing the mind to perfect calmness. Never attempt to practice Meditation when you are under emotional stress or when the breath is disturbed.

Prayer. As Yoga is a spiritual discipline, it is desirable to begin your practice with a chant or prayer. This will elevate your mind. Sit in a comfortable cross-legged position.

Invoke the presence of the Lord. Dedicate yourself to Him, pray for the removal of obstacles and fix your mind on Him.

Recite with deep devotion:

OM OM OM
Hari OM, Hari OM
Hari Hari Hari OM
OM Namah Shivaya Gurave
Satchidananda Moortaye
Nish Prapanjaya Shantaya
Niralambaya Tejase

OM! Salutations to the *Guru* who is auspicious,
The embodiment of Truth-Knowledge-Bliss,
Who is free from world awareness, and peaceful
Who needs no support, who is Self-effulgent like the sun.

OM Tryambakam Yajaamahe
Sugandim Pushti Vardhanam
Urvaarukamiva Bandhanaan
Mrityor Mujisheeya Ma Amritat
OM! We worship the Omniscient One
Who brings fragrance and nourishes all beings
May He liberate us from the fear of death and
Let us realize our Immortality.

Send a vibration of holy thought to all creation. Mentally repeat: "Let all beings be happy; let all beings be peaceful. Let all beings be blissful."

OM Shanthi Shanthi Shanthi. Om peace peace peace.

Place. All places are not beneficial for a beginner. Though a secluded place near a lake or ocean or on a mountain is a favorable place for the practice of Meditation, there may be practical constraints in choosing such a place for regular practice. Select a clean, quiet and secluded room for practicing Meditation. Do not use that room for sleeping; keep it holy like a place of worship. Place pictures that are pleasing and flowers in that room. Burn incense in the morning and evening. Have no quarrel or anger or unholy thought in that room. Allow only like-minded persons to enter it. Then an atmosphere of holiness will gradually emerge in the room with a powerful vibration of spiritual forces, so that when you are miserable or when your mind is disturbed, if you then enter the room you will feel inner peace. This is the real idea behind the temple and the church.

Cleansing. Keep the stomach, bowels and bladder empty; clean the body to make feel fresh for Meditation; wear loose and comfortable clothing.

Spot. It should be such that you can sit facing the East; as the earth rotates in that direction, it is natural to face that direction. If you cannot face East, then face the North, for a magnetic current is always flowing toward the North Pole. Facing South during Meditation will create a negative effect on your mental functioning, but facing East or North will create a positive effect.

Timing. Select a suitable time. There are certain vibrations that control the whole of nature during certain periods of the day. Nature is composed of three *gunas*: *sattva*, *rajas* and *tamas* (*See* 1.9 Three *Gunas*. above). The external world is made up of these *gunas*. The influence of *sattva* is predominant at certain periods of the day. They are sunrise, midday, sunset and midnight. They are called junctures (*sandhyas*). The period of deepest tranquility lasts for forty-five minutes during each of these four periods. Between four A.M. and six A.M. the ozone is more abundant. Hence it is a wonderful time to practice *Pranayama* and Meditation. Since Meditation is a spiritual exercise requiring peace and poise, the above four junctures are considered to be the most favorable times for its practice. You can achieve better results by practicing during those timings than at other times. Those favorable times also have power because of the collective thought vibrations of Yogis who perform their practices at these times.

Many may not find it possible to practice Meditation four times every day. It is desirable to practice at least twice a day at sunrise and sunset. Make it a rule not to eat until you have practiced. Regularity is more important.

Preliminary Steps

Every time you meditate, you should go through the six preliminary steps of Yoga in order to reach a meditative state.

1. The first step is to establish the right state of mind. You should be mindful of the *Yama*s and *Niyama*s: the ten principles of living graciously in the world help you in composing your mind and establishing harmony within yourself. For details *See* 3.4 *Yama* and 3.5 *Niyama*, above)
2. The next step is to practice *Asanas* in order to relax the body and nerves. Physical relaxation leads to calmness of the mind. (*See* 3.6 *Asanas, above*)
3. Sit in a comfortable meditative Posture with the head, neck and trunk erect and in one straight line. A comfortable and

convenient Posture of the body rests the mind and enables you to go within yourself. .

4. Practice a few rounds of *Pranayama* exercises, deep breathing, *kapalabhati*, and *Nadi Shuddhi* (*See* 3. 10 *Pranayama Exercises, above*). These exercises purify the body and nervous system, make the mind alert and prepare it for withdrawal from senses, and for Concentration.
5. Withdraw your mind from the senses of perception, keep off the mind from your anxieties, botherations and the past. Just experience the present moment; be "here and now."
6. Make a determination (*sankalpa*), by mentally reaffirming, "I am not the body, I am not the senses, I am not the mind. They are my instruments only. I am the eternal Atman."
7. Make a determination that you are not going to move any part of your body until you finish the Meditation. The moment your body hears this determination, it will obey you. But that determination will have to be very strong.
   "Whatever people think, they will obtain it as they think, if they remain steadfast in their will." says the sage Tiruvalluvar in *Tirukural*, the masterpiece of classical Tamil literature of India.
8. Think that your body is firm, strong and healthy; for it is the best instrument you have. Think of it as being so strong that with the help of this body you will cross the ocean of life. Freedom will never be reached by the weak; throw away all weakness. Tell your body that it is strong. Tell your mind that it is strong. Have unbounded faith and hope in yourself.
9. Concentrate your mind on the chosen object of Concentration (*See* 4.1 Concentration: Meaning and Methods, *above*).

When you try to focus your mind on the object, whether form, idea or *mantra*, you will find the mind running here and there. Whenever you become aware of it, bring the mind gently back to the point. In a few minutes it might run to another idea; bring it back. This constant effort of bringing the mind back again and again to the point is what you call Concentration (*Dharana*). You have not yet fixed the mind; you are trying to fix it. When the fixing of the mind stays a little longer, you are approaching Meditation. But do not think you are wasting your time if your mind is not fully controlled. No one has ever achieved Meditation right away.

When you repeat a *mantra*, repeat it mentally. Try to feel the inner vibration by your mental repetition. To do that, you have to draw your mind completely inward and then you will be able to hear the sound within. The sound is not only produced after you say it audibly, there is an inaudible sound within you that you can hear, the inner voice. One should be very careful in trying to watch for that sound.

Concentration makes the mind one-pointed and prolonged. Concentration enables you to go deeper, piercing the conscious and unconscious levels of the mind. Practice regularly with perseverance and devotion, you will eventually reach the state of Superconsciousness. Of course, you need the guidance and grace of the *Guru* and the Grace of the Lord.

Meditation Process

Meditation is a practice of focusing the mind upon the object of Concentration, consciously identifying with it. In Meditation there are three factors: the meditator, the process of Meditation, and the object or focus of the Meditation. First, the awareness of the process is gradually eliminated. With each repetition of the *mantra*, it becomes increasingly automatic, and awareness of the process decreases until finally one ceases to be aware of it at all. An ever-increasing ease develops, until at last the repetition is done quite automatically and quite unconsciously.

Next, the meditator is no longer aware of himself, because the mind identifies itself with the object of Meditation and dwells in its sphere.

Finally, the object itself disappears and the awareness of one's separateness is lost. The knower, the known and the knowledge become one. Then there is no play of the mind, nor is there a state of forgetfulness, but rather a state of Absolute Consciousness.

When the mind is in a deep meditative state, objective consciousness ceases and abstract reasoning cannot take place.

How to Meditate

Swami Sivananda, the great sage and founder of Divine Life Society at Rishikesh, Himalayas, gives the following instructions:

- Free yourself from all passions, emotions and impulses. Subjugate the senses. Withdraw the mind from worldly objects. Now the mind will be calm, pure, subtle and one-pointed.
- Fix your trained, disciplined mind on the Infinite Self. Do not think of anything else. Do not allow any worldly thought to enter the mind.
- Just as the river Ganges flows continuously towards the sea, thoughts of God should flow continuously toward the Lord. Just as oil, when poured from one vessel to another, flows in an unbroken continuous stream, so also the mind should "flow" toward God in one continuous stream.
- Make the thoughts of Brahman or Divine Presence flow like flood. Renounce the thoughts of worldly objects. There is struggle in the beginning. It is trying indeed. But later on, as you grow stronger and stronger and as you grow in purity, the thought of Brahman becomes steady. You get strength from Atman. Inner strength grows when all the thoughts of worldly objects are thinned out and the mind becomes one-pointed.
- When you start a fire, heaping up some straw and thin pieces of wood, initially the fire becomes extinguished quickly. You blow it again several times through the mouth of the blow-pipe. After some time it becomes a steady conflagration. Then you can hardly extinguish it even with great efforts. Even so, in the beginning of Meditation, you may fall down from Meditation to your old grooves. You will have to lift up your mind again and again and fix it on the goal. When the Meditation becomes deep and steady, you become established in Atman eventually. It becomes habitual. Use the blow-pipe of intense dispassion and intense Meditation to kindle the fire of Meditation.

- During Meditation, note how long you can sustain one-pointedness. Watch the mind very carefully. If it is for twenty minutes, try to increase the period to thirty or forty minutes and so on. Fill the mind with the thoughts of God again and again.
- Allow the one idea of Brahman or Atman to flow gently and continuously. Fasten the mind with a fine silk thread to His lotus feet. Repeat your *mantra* mentally. The idea of infinity, the idea of an ocean of light, the idea of all-knowledge and bliss should accompany the mental repetition of *mantra*.
- When you begin to sweep a room that was kept closed for six months, various kinds of dirt come out from the corners of the room. Similarly, during Meditation, under pressure of Yoga, through the Grace of God, various kinds of impurities float about on the surface of the mind. The old thought impressions revolt when you try to suppress them. Do not be afraid. They lose their strength after some time. You have to tame the mind just as you tame a wild elephant. Make the mind self-introspective. Substitute good, virtuous, sublime thoughts. Feed the mind with ennobling aspirations and ideals. Old vicious impressions will be gradually thinned out and eventually fade away. Now the thoughts of Brahman will stay. Let the thoughts of Brahman to flow steadily like continuous flow of oil. At this state, the whole universe will appear as *Sat-Chid-Ananda* only. This thought also will die. You will then enter *Sahajananda* state of *Samadhi*. (*See* 4. 18 *Samadhi: Meaning and Kinds, below*).

Closing Chant. Close the Meditation with chants.
Asatho Ma Sat Gamaya
Thamaso Ma Jyothir Gamaya
Mirthyor Ma Amrutham Gamaya
Lead us from unreal to Real
Lead us from darkness to Light
Lead us from mortality to Immortality.

Loka Samasta Sukino Bhavanthu.
May the Universe be filled with peace and joy.

OM Shanthi, Shanthi, Shanthi.
OM peace, peace, peace.

The Phases of Meditation

Meditation has four stages. In the first stage, there is still an awareness of the differentiation of concrete things. In the second stage, there is an enjoyment and comprehension of universal oneness. In the third stage, there is a realization of individual Self. The first three stages are "with seed," that is, there is some subject or object in one's awareness. The fourth state, Meditation without seed, is the state beyond the mind, in which the Superconsciousness alone exists. (*See* 4. 18 *Samadhi: Meaning and Kinds, below*).

4.8: *Mantra*

Meaning

Meditation is a process of focusing the mind on a chosen object of Concentration. *Mantra* is the most well-known object of Concentration. It is a set of words or sounds, such as "*OM Shanti,*" "*Hari OM,*" "*OM Namasivaya,*" "*Amen Jesus,*" etc., on which the mind is focused in order to attain a state of one-pointedness. The Sanskrit word "*mantra*" means "that which liberates the mind from bondage and sufferings." By repeating a *mantra* over and over again, we become identified with it and experience what it represents.

Mantra is based on the understanding that sound is the medium of creation, the dynamic force of the Absolute. *Rig Veda* says, "In the beginning was Brahman, with whom was the word; and the word was truly the Supreme Brahman." Echoing this statement, almost exactly, Bible says, "In the Beginning was the word and the word was God." The "word" here means sound.

In the Yogic tradition the sound "OM" or "AUM" is considered to be the vibration from which everything else is created. In the Jewish and Christian religions, it is "*Amen,*" and in the Islamic religion, it is "*Ameen.*"

The *Mandukya Upanishad* expounds the meaning of OM (AUM):

"OM. This eternal Word is all this. What was, what is and what shall be, and what beyond is OM. All this is Brahman. Om is the symbol of Brahman. It stands for the manifested world and the unmanifested Absolute as well." (1 and 2)

The *Mandukya Upanishad* divides OM (AUM) into four stages: A, U, M, and OM. "A" is the root sound, beginning of all sounds. Every language begins with the letter "A" or "ah." It is pronounced by simply opening the mouth, without touching any part of the tongue or palate. "U" rolls from the very root up to the lips. "M" is produced by closing the lips. OM represents the entire process of sound. OM is the origin or seed from which all other sounds and words come. It is the most ancient word for God.

OM, the hum-sound is called *Pranava*, because it is connected with *prana*. *Prana* is the basic vibration that always exists whether it is manifesting or not. It is never-ending. Scientists find that when the manifested objects are reduced to their unmanifested condition, they go back to the atomic vibration. Nobody can stop that vibration. Similarly, even without repeating it, the basic sound is always vibrating in you. It is the seed from which all other sounds manifest. The entire world evolves from that and goes back into that again. So no other name can be more adequate to represent God. OM was not invented by anybody. God Himself manifested as OM.

The Origin of *Mantras*

The *mantras* are not words or sounds formulated by Sanskrit scholars. They are sounds or vibrations experienced by the Himalayan sages in the highest states of Enlightenment. When those sages transcend their own finite individuality and attain Cosmic Consciousness, they experience many things: bliss, Knowledge of Self, sounds, and many other things that cannot be described in words. When they return from these states and relate to us at our state of consciousness, they sometimes bring back those "sounds" or vibrations experienced. The basic sounds of Sanskrit are related to a higher vibratory state of consciousness and therefore most *mantras* are in Sanskrit, although there are *mantras* in other languages as well.

The sound is like an encapsulated form or a seed of vibration experienced. Being a seed, that sound can actually grow into the whole experience itself. This seed is what we call a *mantra*.

Some of the *mantras* received today were experienced many

thousand years ago and personally passed on through a chain of teachers and disciples.

A *mantra* that is read in a book or given to you by someone who is not a spiritual *Guru* will not have the effect of the same *mantra* received from a *Guru*. The *Guru* gives a *mantra* most suitable to your personality and circumstances, like a doctor gives a suitable prescription.

Receiving a *mantra* is an initiation into that spiritual tradition from which knowledge of the *mantra* arose. You are connected to that tradition through the *mantra* initiation.

A *mantra* is not a secret sound. But you may be asked not to reveal your *mantra* to others. This is done to keep the practice of Meditation uncontaminated by the doubts and others' criticisms that would arise, if it were revealed to your acquaintances. Such doubts dilute the effectiveness of the *mantra*.

You should have total faith in your *mantra* and be absorbed in it. You should make "it" completely "yourself" and "you" completely "it." When you and that *mantra* become one, you will also become one with that higher state of Consciousness that the *mantra* represents.

The *mantra* is really as a tiny seed planted within you. If it is used properly with the right attitude, the tiny seed grows and transforms your personality. It has a powerful effect on the unconscious mind. It guides you, giving joy, purpose and direction to your life.

Effects of Meditation with a *Mantra*

The repetition of a *mantra* over and over again helps you to keep the mind on the object it represents and its rhythm has an effect on the body. The repetition of the *mantra* in Meditation counteracts the sleepiness of *tamas* and the excitability of *rajas*, and establishes *sattva*.

We would be able to appreciate the power of the *mantra* only through direct experience. People who have never tried the practice of repeating the name of God are apt to scoff at it; it may seem to them empty and mechanical.

Most of us, in our daily life, do not consecutively think about a particular idea or problem. More usually we are in a state of constant flux or reverie, disconnected sense impressions, irrelevant memories, varying moods, worries, anxieties, meaningless imaginations and so on. If we introduce into this reverie the repetition of the name of God or a *mantra*, we shall find that we can control our moods. "As you think, so you become." If you constantly think that you are strong, you will certainly become strong. Similarly the repetition of a *mantra* will change the condition of your mind. Through constant practice, the repetition becomes automatic; it becomes a habit. Mere repetition of a *mantra* is, of course, insufficient, as Patanjali points out. We must also meditate upon its meaning. (*Yoga Sutras*, 1.28). But if we persevere in our repetition, it will lead us to think of the meaning without forgetting the repetition.

From the repetition of the *mantra* all the obstacles to the Knowledge of Atman disappear and dawns the Knowledge of Atman. (*Yoga Sutras*, 1.29). You are tuned to the Cosmic power. By that tuning you will feel that force within you, you imbibe Divine qualities, get the Cosmic vision, transcend all your limitations and finally become that transcendental Reality. Normally the mind and body limit you, but by holding something Infinite, you slowly raise yourself from the finite objects that bind you and transcend them. Through that you get rid of all the obstacles and your path is made easy.

Witnessing State and *Mantra*

When we sit for Meditation, thoughts of past impressions, memories, unfinished tasks and current problems will come up and distract our attention. Then we should just observe them, maintaining a witnessing state, instead of being caught in the shadow play of our mind. Let the thoughts come and go.

The use of a *mantra* as an object of Concentration can strengthen the witnessing state. It gives us a sense of direction for establishing ourselves in the position of observation. When we repeat the *mantra* mentally, then like any other thing, it goes down into subconscious mind, and whatever goes in has to come out sooner or later. How much the *mantra* goes in depends upon how much attention we give it. The *mantra*, which we have put in, begins to come out after some time along with the *samskaras*. If we quiet the mind and stand back and observe, the *samskaras* along with the *mantra* begin to rise up. Then we begin to be aware of the *mantra* instead of repeating it. Eventually we reach a stage of being with the *mantra*. We are then observing *from* the *mantra*. These are then the steps in using the *mantra*:

First, we repeat the *mantra*;
Second we listen to it;
Third we observe from it.

In this way, the *mantra* becomes a very important guiding technique in the Meditation process.

This process of "internalization" of the *mantra* makes the object, that is, the *mantra*, to become subject. *Mantra*, then, helps us to progress more rapidly in Self-awareness.

Our witnessing self gradually becomes stronger and stronger; its capacity increases, and it can go to a higher level of observance. This gradualness is a beautiful aspect of Meditation.

We should not allow the survival factors of food, sleep, and such others to pre-empt our attention. We should not allow self-preservation to become a pressing issue. Meditation is basically an adventurous exploration of a vast part of ourselves that we did not know about before. Exploration cannot be done out of desperation. It is always done out of curiosity. We should meditate in an adventurous spirit. Then we will progress and reach the goal.

Mantra Japa

Japa means repetition of a *mantra* for centering the mind. By the constant repetition of the *mantra* given by the *Guru*, you are merged in the sound vibration. Starting with mere repetition of the *mantra*, you are led spontaneously to Meditation upon its meaning and then to the realization of the truth it represents. The *mantra* also works on the level of your unconscious mind, controlling your moods and combating and controlling undesirable emotions like anger, greed, lust and so on. It purifies your mind, enabling you to attain a higher degree of Concentration.

Mantra Japa is to be done in full faith, with devotion and sincerity of purpose. *Japa* can be done with Meditation or otherwise. When doing it you should keep the meaning of the *mantra* in the mind. It is to be done with feeling. It should vibrate along with your heart-beats.

The repetition of *mantra* can take three main forms: (1) mental, (2) whispering and (3) loud. Mental recitation is the highest form of *Japa*. *Japa* should not be done in a hurry. *Mantra* should be pronounced very distinctly. Sit erect in a steady Posture. Repeat it wherever you go and whatever work you may do.

Japa with mala (beads) helps one to keep the mind alert and to fix it constantly on the *mantra*. *Japa-mala* (rosary) contains one hundred and eight beads made out of the roots of the tulasi plant or of glass or sandal wood. In counting the beads, slips occur and sometimes two beads are counted together as one. In order to allow a margin for slips, eight extra beads are provided. Thus a counting of the full rosary of one hundred and eight beads really implies only one hundred repetitions.

Where the two ends of the rosary are brought together into a knot there is a bigger bead. This is called *Meru* and considered to be the seat of the *Mantra*-Deity. In counting the beads, one should start clockwise from the first bead from the *Meru*. When one completes the circle and reaches the *Meru* again, turn the *mala* inside out and start clockwise, keep the *mala* on the ring finger, and use the thumb and the middle finger to count and slide.

Mantra can be effective only when the mind is purified. The secret of the correct use of a *mantra* is to coordinate its practice with a life of self-discipline and purity. The *mantra* reveals its potential more and more when it is assimilated into the deeper realms and finally to the higher state. As you go on repeating your *mantra*, the subconscious mind gradually stores it and brings it forth later during times of trial or difficulty to help and guide you.

Japa, truthfulness and personal purity contribute more than anything else to success in Meditation and spiritual life. *Japa* controls the mind and protects it from going astray, and thus is helpful to the practice of truthfulness. It is also essential for achieving personal purity, as it purifies both the conscious and subconscious minds.

When an object is perceived with the help of the senses and mind, there arises in the mind a modification of its substance that is an exact impression of the object perceived. This explains why by *Japa* of *mantra*, worship and Meditation, the mind takes the form of the object of worship and is rendered pure for the time being through the purity and holiness of the God worshipped. By continuous practice the mind thinks only of this object to the exclusion of all else, and becomes steady in its purity. This is the purpose of spiritual discipline.

When you reach a higher level of consciousness, you will experience subtle sound with in. It is called *Anahata* sound. It can faintly be heard if you close your ears with the thumbs and concentrate totally on the sound in the right ear. This requires some practice. The *mantra* is a vehicle to take you to the source of this inner sound in which you merge and experience your true nature. Ultimately it will lead you to the state of *Samadhi*, Self-realization

Ajapa Japa

This is Concentration upon the natural sound of the breath that continually repeats the *mantra* "*Soham.*" "*So*" means "That," the Absolute beyond all relativity of existence, and "*Ham*" means "I am." Therefore, *Soham* means "That Brahman I am."
The technique of *Ajapa Japa* is:

- Sit comfortably in a meditative Posture with spine erect.
- Close your eyes.
- Concentrate on your breath. Breathe slowly and deeply; after a while you will find the breathing slowing down, but continue to follow it.
- You need not repeat *Soham* yourself, just listen. You will be

able to hear that sound.

- After practicing this for some time, you may begin to hear a humming musical note within you.
- Constantly listen to that note. It is part of the Cosmic vibration. By concentrating on this inner vibration, you are in tune with the Cosmic sound.

Let there be a complete void except for this musical note. By remaining in this state, you are sending out powerful peace vibrations into the world. Your mind expands. You will feel very light. You will transcend your body, and will feel One with the Cosmic mind.

After sitting for some time in silence, slowly direct your attention toward your breathing and gently make the breath a little deeper. Continue to deepen the breath for a few minutes, and then close the Meditation with closing chants.

4.9: Obstacles to Meditation

There are several obstacles to Meditation. They may be grouped under physical, psychological or mental and psycho-social problems. They are, however, not mutually exclusive, but are inter-related. The physical problems that obstruct the practice of Meditation include sickness, dietary habits, aches and pains and irregular breathing. Psychological or mental problems that cause hindrance to Meditation are many. They include ignorance, egoism, doubts, self-alienation, emotions, laziness, drowsiness, depression and distraction.

Sickness

The first obstruction to the practice of Meditation is disease or ill-health. If the body is not fit, the practice is not possible. Disease affects the mind. It makes you dull and lazy, also causes aches and pains. The body resists all unaccustomed disciplines and will perhaps try to sabotage them by alarming displays of weakness, fainting spells, violent headaches and so forth. The resistance is subconscious. The symptoms it produces are genuine. It is no good trying to fight them by sheer force. Therefore we have to keep the body in good health; we have to take care of our dietary habits, and practice Hatha Yoga *Asanas* in order to maintain sound health. However health is not an end in itself. It is only a means to an end.

Dietary Habits

Dietary habits influence health. Untimely eating, eating more frequently, over-eating, eating heavy foods like meat cause digestive problems. Emotional upsets and tension also affect the digestion.

If the body is occupied with digestion, it is difficult to do Meditation. Fat-free vegetarian diet is the most appropriate food for maintaining good health. The daily schedule and eating habits should be regulated in such a way that one will be physiologically ready to do Meditation in the selected time in the morning and evening.

Aches and Pains

The next obstacle is physical discomfort arising out of aches and pains. These are very common problems. Any ache or pain will distract the mind. The major technique that has been developed to deal with the problem of aches and pain is Hatha Yoga. The purpose of the Hatha Yoga *Asanas* is to stretch and relax various parts of the body. The *asanas* systematically prepare the body for the meditative Posture.

The next thing is to choose the correct meditative Posture. Even if you are in perfect health, if you sit in an awkward Posture to do Meditation, you will soon feel aches and pains. So you should keep the body in an erect position so as to maintain perfect balance. Success in proper Posture comes with some experimentation. (*See* 3.6 Asanas, *above*).

Irregular Breathing

If our breathing pattern is not correct, it can become an obstacle. Breath may be jerky, irregular and imbalanced. Such defective breath can be very distracting. It disrupts the whole flow of energy or *prana* in the body, and affects the digestive and other systems. By practicing *Pranayama* breath has to be regulated and balanced. When breath is regulated, the mind becomes calm and steady. (*See* 3.9 Pranayama: Aims and Benefits; and 3.10 *Pranayama* Exercises, *above*).

Ignorance

Ignorance is the root cause of all other obstacles. In the worldly sense ignorance refers to the lack of knowledge pertaining to the mode of living, health, diet, work and rest. It leads to ill health and wrong habits.

In the spiritual sense ignorance is lack of awareness of our real nature. It means considering the impermanent as permanent, the impure as pure, the painful as pleasant, and the non-self as the Self. (*Yoga Sutras*, 2.5). The body, senses and mind are impermanent and non-self. Self or Atman is eternal, real, never changing and omniscient.

Pure, eternal joy and peace are our real nature. Our ignorance veils our insight. We fail to perceive our inner eternal peace and joy, and instead seek it in the external world. We cling to impermanent worldly pleasures and fall into the whirlpool of endless desires and consequent sufferings and Karmic bondage. When we attain Enlightenment through the practice of Yoga, then ignorance disappears.

Egoism

Egoism is the feeling of "I, me, mine." This prevents us from realizing our true nature. It is the ego that is the basis of all mental dramas, desires, attachments, aversion, selfishness, Karmic bondage and so on. It creates all kinds of problems, troubles, anxieties and fear. It disturbs our mental peace. Ignorance of our true nature is the cause of egoism. It is very difficult to get rid off the ego. It veils our eyes and we forget our real nature. By self-analysis, scripture-study, deep devotion to God and surrender to God we have to overcome our ego. We must read the life stories of great sages and saints and learn lessons from their lives. We are nothing when compared to those great souls. Let us realize that we are just instruments in the hands of God. It is He who functions through us. Our minds, intellect and bodies and senses all function only because of the Consciousness within. That life force is part of the Cosmic Consciousness, God. We should realize this.

Problem of Self-Alienation

Meditation is a self-integrating process, and hence any form of self-alienation becomes a hindrance to Meditation. Self-alienation is a state of mind in which one takes a falsified personality of oneself for one's true personality. For example, a person glorifying himself in enormous wealth or in a highly powerful position may become "nobody" overnight when he loses his wealth or position. This feeling of "emptiness" arises, because he was living in a money-self or power-self rather than his own real-self. There can be alienation of self from people around oneself, caused by the inability to accept or follow social customs and traditions of society. Then the mind becomes restless due to self-isolation from other people. An improper use of one's position in society is also a cause of self-alienation. In such situations, instead of discovering himself, a self-alienated person often tries to forget himself by indulging in sensual pleasures, drinks and drugs. No meaning can be sought in life by fleeing from oneself; but one should instead turn inward toward the true Self within. This is the art of self-discovery, the way of Meditation.

Doubt

The next obstruction is doubt. We always feel doubtful about things we do not see. We cannot live upon words, however we may try. So doubt comes to us as to whether there is any truth in these things or not; even the best of us will doubt sometimes. With practice, within a few days, a little glimpse will come to give one faith and encouragement.

By listening to spiritual discourses and reflecting over the scriptural messages we can remove doubts in the path of Yoga.

Laziness

Laziness is a *tamas*ic quality. It is a great obstacle to progress. It is a sign of weakness and failure. It is tempting to relax from our duties and take refuge in ill-health. We should never listen to the prompting of laziness. We should overcome it by determination and will-power.

Emotional Problems

Emotional turmoil stirs up one's entire physiology. Digestive system is affected. Emotional problem creates concentration of energy in the heart area. The even-flow of energy in the body is thus totally disrupted. The energy is not only stirred up, it is also expended. With anger, for instance, energy is rapidly dissipated and wasted. Extreme anger is often followed by shakiness, weakness and lethargy.

In order to control the emotional problems, we have to work with the breath. Breath and emotions function in an inter-related way. When the breathing is regulated, then the emotions are calmed down. The regulation of breath is direct and simple. Breath gently and deeply a few times; then breathing will become normal and balanced.

Sensual Desires

Craving for sensual pleasures is a great obstacle in the path of Yoga. The mind that goes after material things and pleasures through sensual desires cannot concentrate on one object. It becomes restless like a mad monkey. There is no end to desires. Hidden desires for fame, name, power, wealth and sex and subtle memories of pleasures enjoyed may cause serious distractions in the mind.

Success in Meditation will not come until we disband the conflicting hosts of desires that perpetually carry on their evil war within us. We must contemplate on the fleeting nature of worldly pleasures, and discipline our mind and senses. Study of scriptures and company of wise people will help us to develop dispassion.

Distracting Thoughts

The thoughts buried in your subconscious mind rise up to conscious awareness during Meditation. Many find this as their major obstacle. When distracting thoughts remain in the unconscious, they lead to disturbances in your functioning, and to irrational behavior. You have no control over those thoughts. But when you allow them to surface, you are no longer a slave to them. They now come under your conscious purview. But do not try to exert an active control over such surfaced thoughts. Just be a passive observer, letting them to come and go. As you do this, you will find that the distracting thoughts will slowly diminish and eventually disappear. You should resist the tendency to get involved in those thoughts, otherwise they may pull you away from your center. For example, when you are concentrating on your *mantra*, a thought of your favorite game arises, you may get lost in a train of associations about it. You should also guard against the alternative tendency of fighting with those distracting thoughts. If you forcefully bring your mind back to your object of Concentration, the distracting thoughts will intrude again and again. The more you force your mind to concentrate on your object, the stronger the intruding thoughts become, until you feel frustrated and give up Meditation entirely.

So do not be involved with the distracting thoughts in any manner, but simply watch them coming into your awareness, and let them go, without giving them any attention. At the same time, do not try to accomplish any particular goal in your Meditation. Simply cultivate a neutral attitude. If you maintain this position you will experience a peaceful state. Gradually as you sustain this neutral state for a longer period of time, the intensity of disturbing thoughts will diminish, and eventually become fully neutralized. Then you will easily experience greater depth in your Meditation.

Drowsiness and Wild Imaginations

When the mind has been withdrawn from objects through dispassion and *Prathyahara,* do not allow it to go into sleep or wild imagination. When you constantly contemplate on the meaning of the *Maha vakya* "*Aham Brahma Asmi*" or "*Tat Tvam Asi,*" all the senses will stop. But owing to the force of *Samskaras* (the impressions of past thoughts and experiences), wild imaginations will continue. Mind builds castles in the air. This is termed *manoratha* in Sanskrit. This is a serious obstacle to Meditation. Sometimes, during the course of Meditation, the mind suddenly slips into its old grooves for sleeping. A mixture of drowsiness and wild imaginations is mistaken by aspirants for deep Meditation and *Samadhi*. This is a wrong notion. Stupefaction arising from fear or wander, and mental restlessness are other disturbing factors in Meditation. Be thoughtful, careful and vigilant. Stand up for a few minutes and dash cold water on the face, if drowsiness comes in. Remove the two obstacles of drowsiness and wild imagination by self-inquiry, *Pranayama* and light *sattvic* diet.

Depression

Very often, depression comes in Meditation in the beginning stage owing to previous *Samskaras*, influence of bad company, cloudy days, indigestion and constipation. It must be removed quickly by cheerful thoughts, a brisk walk, laughing, prayer, *Pranayama*, etc.

Distraction

Scents, soft beds, novel-reading, dramas, cinemas, vulgar music, dancing, company of opposite sex, *rajas*ic diet – all these excite passions and cause disturbances of the mind. Too much talking and too much mixing disturb the mind in Meditation.

Impulses disturb Meditation. Sex impulse and ambition are two real disturbing factors in Meditation. They may attack you again and again. They should be rooted out by great efforts, Self-inquiry, discrimination and devotion to God.

Psychosocial Problems

Some people often complain that they are not able to meditate because of problems arising from others: "My spouse thinks it is ridiculous;" "when you have three kids it is just impossible," "my job takes up all my time," and the like. Most of these problems are really not problems with others; they are problems in us and reflect our inability to regulate ourselves. So we choose someone or our work as a target to blame. Coping with our children can be exhausting or exhilarating depending upon our attitude toward them. Similarly if we have a positive and pleasant attitude toward work, we will not feel exhausted. If we consider work as play, we can enjoy it, and we can feel comfortable to sit for Meditation.

Overcoming Obstacles

Sri Swami Sivananda gives us the following general advice to overcome obstacles:

- Assimilate the Divine ideas. Saturate the mind with thoughts of Brahman, Divine glory and sublime spiritual thoughts in order to become established in the Divine Consciousness.
- Free yourself from the base thoughts of the mind, the useless imaginations. Just as you render the turbid water pure by adding clearing nut, so also make the turbid mind pure by Divine thoughts. Ceaselessly think of Atman. Then only spiritual knowledge will dawn.
- It is the actions of the mind that bind you to *Karmas*. Liberate yourself from the vagaries of the mind. Purge the mind of all its impurities, then it will become very calm.
- Spiritual practice is a life-long process. Every day, every hour, every minute is an onward march. Obstacles are innumerable in this great voyage. But so long as you hold God as your guide, there is nothing to worry about.
- If you conquer one obstacle, another obstacle is ready to manifest. If you control the sense of taste, another sense is simply waiting to assault you. If you remove greed, anger is waiting to hurl you down. Therefore great patience, perseverance, vigilance and undaunted strength are needed.

Other Guidelines

A spiritual practitioner should also follow the following guidelines to guard against the obstacles that he may encounter while practicing Yoga:

- Do not swerve in observing strictly the code of moral conduct.
- Do not lose hope and get dejected by small failures. Every failure is a stepping stone to success.
- Do not be carried away by temporary experiences like Divine vision, light, and sound. They just indicate some progress in your spiritual practice.
- Do not be tempted to extol your spiritual attainments to friends and others, for any praise can make you egoistic and any censure may dishearten you.
- Do not be tempted to display supernatural powers. It is

dangerous to use them for personal benefits and glory. Such powers are not real attainments, but rather serious hindrances to attaining the final goal of Self-realization.

- Beware of any partial rising of the *Kundalini Shakti*. If it is not properly canalized and taken care of, it would cause various disruptions, and when it falls down suddenly to the lowest center, you will feel an abnormal craving for sexual enjoyment, and if you are not strong enough, it will ruin your spiritual endeavor.
- Another danger is facing reaction time that may come at any stage. Do not then get dejected and loose hope. By fasting, prayer, *Japa*, and Meditation, overcome the reaction period.
- Develop infinite patience, perseverance, courage and hope. Carry on your practice in spite of setbacks and failures. Have faith in yourself, faith in God, and faith in your *Guru*. Stop not till you reach the goal.

4.10: Signs of Progress

When you ascend the ladder of Meditation, you experience more and more delight, joy, peace of mind, control over senses and mastery over the lower self. You find the Brahman operating through your life. You become balanced in pain and pleasure, gain and loss. You become a source of inspiration to others. Your life becomes a model to others.

By the practice of Meditation, intellect becomes sharp; thinking becomes clear. Work efficiency increases. You are ever fresh and energetic. You work tirelessly for the benefit of humanity.

Meditation develops in you a better understanding of the purpose of life. You receive strength to remain balanced in the midst of various emotional problems of life. You are not swayed by the attraction of fleeting pleasures of worldly life. When your mind is not fettered by lust and greed, you attain the fearless state.

Meditation endows you with fresh mental and spiritual energy. Every cell of the body is flooded with spiritual energy.

You may experience various mystic visions. The *Svetasvatara Upanishad* declares:

> "Fog, smoke, sun, wind, fire flies, fire, lightning, crystal and moon – these are the preliminary forms which precede the vision of Brahman in Yoga." (2.11)
>
> When the Yogi has full power over his body composed of the elements of earth, water, fire, air and ether, then he obtains a new body of spiritual fire that is beyond illness, old age and death.

The first fruits of the practice of Yoga are: Health, and a clear complexion, lightness of the body, a pleasant scent and a sweet voice and freedom from restless greed. (For details, *See* 4.15 Experiences in Meditation, *below*)

Inward Progress

The gradual inward progress is mostly unseen, like the quiet unfolding of a bud into a flower in the hours of the night. Therefore do not be dejected. Do not depress yourself with the idea that you are not progressing.

Real spiritual progress is known by the peacefulness, serenity, and calmness that you manifest in the waking state. You will be cheerful and contented. You will be dispassionate and discriminative.

You will experience lights, visions, divine smell, divine taste. The idea that all forms are forms of the Lord will get stronger and stronger in you. You will feel everywhere the presence of God. You will experience the nearness of God. You will always develop a burning desire for selfless service.

Watch whether you are stationary in the spiritual path or retrogressing or advancing. If your practice thickens your veil and fattens your egoism, it is not then a spiritual practice. Remember this point well. Watch, introspect. Practice self-analysis and kill ruthlessly this formidable egoism. This is an important step. Egoism will lurk as a thief and assume various forms like a chameleon or a dramatic actor.

Continue Practice

Do not stop practice when you get a few glimpses of realization. Continue practice until you are fully established in the unconditioned Brahman, unmanifest Supreme Consciousness. If you stop practice and are involved in the worldly affairs, you are likely to meet with downfall. The reaction will be tremendous. Numerous persons have been so ruined. A glimpse cannot give you perfect safety.

Do not let failures discourage you, but go on doing your best. Do not brood over your past mistakes and failures, as this will only fill your mind with grief, regret and depression. Do not repeat them in the future. Be cautious. Just identify the causes that led to your failures and try to remove them in the future. Strengthen yourself with new vigor and virtues. Develop your will-power.

Every temptation that is resisted, every evil thought that is curbed, every desire that is subdued, every bitter word that is withheld, every noble aspiration that is encouraged, every sublime thought that is cultivated, adds to the development of will-power, good character and spiritual progress.

Every bit of practice has its own effect. No practice ever goes in vain. Every bit of it is credited immediately toward your evolution. This is the law. Do not think negative thoughts but calmly go on with the practice. Be regular in it. Little by little, the power accumulates and it will grow. Ultimately, the cumulative force of all the continuous earnest practice over a long period of life has its inevitable grand consummation at the supreme moment, when it bears fruit in the form of blissful Realization.

Keep Up the Progress

Every day robs from you one part of your precious life. Therefore, you should be very earnest in plunging yourself into constant practice. Lord Krishna, in the *Bhagavad Gita*, exhorts:

> "Practice Yoga with firmness and with an unwavering mind." (6.23)

March forward with new hope, determination and vigilance. Waver not. Fear not. Doubt not. You have infinite strength within you. Therefore do not lose heart. Obstacles are stepping stones to success. They will develop your will-power. Choose the positive path. You will enjoy the everlasting peace of the Eternal. (Swami Sivananda, *Bliss Divine*, pp. 474–83).

Practice hard. Plunge in and work without thinking of the result. "If you are brave enough," says Swami Vivekananda, "in six months you will be a perfect Yogi. But those who take up just a bit of it and a little of everything else make no progress. It is of no use simply to take course of lessons. To succeed you must have tremendous perseverance, tremendous will. 'I will drink the ocean,' says the persevering soul, 'and at my will mountains will crumble.' Have that sort of energy, that sort of will, work hard and you will reach the goal." (*Raja Yoga,* pp. 73-74).

Causes for Failures in Meditation

Beware of causes for failures in Meditation. Some practice Meditation for a period of 15 years and yet they do not make any real progress. Why? This is due to lack of earnestness, dispassion, of keen longing for liberation and of intense constant practice. There is always a complaint amongst the aspirants. "I am meditating for the last 12 years. I have not made any progress. I have no realization." What is the reason? They have not plunged themselves in deep Meditation into the innermost recesses of their hearts. They have not properly assimilated and saturated the mind with the thoughts of God. They have not done regular systematic practice. They have not disciplined the senses. They have not collected all the outgoing rays of the mind. They have not made the self-determination. They have not given their full mind to God. They have not kept the Divine Consciousness flowing.

Learn lessons from such failures. Be vigilant and careful. Do not allow your dispassion to wane. Be firm and be steady in practice.

Just as one who foolishly runs after two rabbits will not catch any one of them, so also a meditator who runs after two conflicting thoughts – Divine thoughts for ten minutes and then worldly conflicting thoughts for the next ten minutes—will not succeed in anything in attaining the Divine Consciousness.

You must run after one rabbit only with vigor, strength and one-pointedness. You are sure to catch it. You must have only Divine thoughts at all times. Then you are sure to realize God soon.

You must not be too hasty in longing for the fruits at once, when you take to mediation. Haste makes waste. Meditate regularly. Then your mind will, by degrees, be ripened and in the end, the endless Atman will be reached; you will get Self-realization.

You will have to exert in the beginning to get an equilibrium of mind. Later on, you will have habitual balanced state of mind. So is the case with Meditation. After some years of practice, Meditation becomes habitual.

4.11: Experiences in Meditation

Happenings During Meditation

The following things may happen during the practice of Meditation:

1. The practice of Meditation leads to the formation of new grooves in the brain, and the mind moves upwards in the new spiritual grooves. When the mind becomes steady in Meditation, the eye-balls also become steady. A yogi whose mind is calm will have steady eyes; there will be no winking at all. The eyes will be lustrous, red or pure white.
2. When you enter into very deep, silent Meditation, the breathing will become still. There may be occasional slow movement of the lungs and the abdomen. From the nature of the breathing, you can infer the degree of Concentration.
3. After the mind has been purified, an abstract image is formed in the purified mind by listening to spiritual discourses, reading holy scriptures and thoughts of Brahman. This abstract image melts later on into deep Meditation. What is left behind is pure existence (*chinmatra*) alone.
4. In profound and continued Meditation thinking ceases. There is only one idea of "Brahman I am." When this idea also is given up, *Nirvikalpa Samadhi* ensues. Just as salt melts in water, the sattvic mind melts in silence in its substratum, Brahman.

Experiences

The experiences that the meditators may get are varied. Various persons get various spiritual experiences. They depend upon their temperament, mode of practice, object of Concentration and various other factors. Some hear melodious sounds in the ears. Some see lights. Some get spiritual bliss (*ananda*). Some get both brightness and bliss. Some see visions of different lustrous things such as crystal, stars, lamps, etc. These are only hints of advancement in Meditation.

The *Shiva Sutras*, a scripture on Philosophy of Saivism, says, "The stages of Yoga are filled with wonders." Some discover astonishing worlds within them. The outer forms of light – sun, moon, stars, fire, etc. – have their inner counterparts. We go through life unaware of this, until our inner effulgence begins to reveal itself during Meditation. The scriptures say, "What is here is also there; and what is not here is nowhere."

At some point, suddenly you perceive that your entire inner being is filled with radiant energy of light. The poet-saint Kabir once said,

> "Look around inside you, the blue sky opens out further and further, a million suns come forward with light, when I sit firmly in that inner world."

Swami Sivananda narrates the experiences which meditators get during Meditation: The sudden illumination is like a "flash of lightning." You will be spell-bound in ecstasy and awe. You will tremble with awe, just as Arjuna did when he had the *isvarupa-darsana* (Vision of the full Cosmic Form) of Lord Krishna. So bright and glorious is the light environing the Divine that you will be dazzled and bewildered.

The color of lights that you see varies according to the *Tattva* that flows through the nostrils: If there is *agni tattva* (fire), you will see red-colored lights. If *akasa tattva* (space) flows, you will have blue-colored lights. If *apsa tattva* (water) prevails, you will see white-colored lights. If there is *prithvi tattva* (earth), you will have yellow lights. If there is *vayu tattva* (air), you will see black color. You can change the *tattva* by various ways. But the best way is by thought. "As you think, so you become." When the *agni tattva* flows, think intently of *akasa tattva, akasa tattva* will begin to flow soon.

Saint Teresa of Avila (1515–82)[31] writes, "The light that is now revealed is so different from any earthly light . . . . The inner light is a natural light, and all other kinds of lights seem artificial by comparison. It is a light which is never followed by darkness. And nothing can disturb it."

Sound. Another wonder that you encounter as you go deeper in Meditation is *nada,* the Divine sound. The scriptures list at least ten classical forms of sound: the humming of bees, the roar of the ocean, the ringing of the bells, the blowing of the conch, the strumming of the veena, the ringing of the cymbals, the whistling of the flute, the pounding of a drum, an echo and the roar of thunder.

Most of these sounds originate from the heart chakra, which is called *anahata* meaning 'unstuck sound,' a sound that is not produced. "When *megha nada* (thunder) comes," Swami Muktananda (1908–82)[32] says, "you fall into tremendous ecstasy. Just as the rain follows thunder in the atmosphere, so a shower of nectar begins to fall when the thunder sounds in the inner space."

Celestial fragrances and tastes come as strange experiences in Meditation.

Some may experience that they are rising from their seats. Some experience that they fly in the air.

Visions. Meditators often have visions of the sun or the moon in Meditation. There is also a flame which they see. It is the flame of the individual soul, and it is found in the heart. The light of the Supreme Self is in the *Sahasrara*, the crown chakra at the crown of the head. All the lights can be seen in *Sahasrara,* which is called the blazing light of a thousand suns. Another common vision in Meditation is that of fire which is the great purifier.

Rapture. During Meditation, you get rapture or ecstasy. It is of five kinds: The lesser thrill, momentary rapture, flooding rapture, transporting rapture and all-pervading rapture. The lesser thrill is only able to raise the hairs of the body. The momentary rapture is like the productions of lightning, moment by moment. Like waves breaking on the seashore, the flooding rapture descends rapidly on the body and breaks. Transporting rapture is strong and lifts the body up to the extent of launching it into the air. When the all-pervading rapture arises, the whole body is completely surcharged, blown like a full-bladder.

Crossing the Body-Consciousness

Aspirants are eager to get spiritual experiences soon. When they get them, they are afraid. They are awfully alarmed when they go above the body-consciousness. They entertain a passing wonder whether they will come back or not. Why should they be afraid at all? It does not matter much whether they return to body-consciousness or not. All our efforts are mainly directed toward getting over this body-consciousness. We are used to certain limitations. When these limitations suddenly drop away, we feel that there is no definite base left to stand upon. That is the reason why we are afraid when we go above the body-consciousness. That is a novel experience. Courage is needed. *Sruti* says, "This Atman can hardly be attained by weak (timid) persons." All sorts of forces have to be encountered on the way. A dacoit or an anarchist can easily realize God, because he is fearless. A push in the right direction is only necessary for him. How Jagai and Madhai, rogues of the first order, became great saints! They pelted stones at Nityananda, the disciple of Lord Gouranga. Nityananda won them by pure Divine love. Dacoit Ratnakara became Sage Valmiki.

Visions of Spirits

Sometimes bad spirits will trouble you. They may have ugly, fierce faces with long teeth. Drive them with your strong will. Give the word of command: "Get out." They will go away. They are elemental. They will not do any harm to the practitioners. Your courage will be tested here. If you are timid, you cannot march further. Draw power and courage from the Atman within, the inexhaustible source. You will come across very good spirits also. They will help you a lot in your onward march.

There is a kind of vision one occasionally gets during Meditation.

You may see a dazzling light with abrupt motion. You may see a head of marvelous form, of the color of a flame, red as fire and very awful to look at. It has three wings of marvelous length and breadth, white as a dazzling cloud. At times the wings would beat terribly, and again would be still. Now and again there is beating with its extended wings.

Some of the visions that you see during Meditation are your own materialized thoughts, while some others are real, objective visions.

Break Veil After Veil

If you get experiences of the glimpses of Self during intense Meditation, if you see a blazing light and if you get visions of angels, rishis, munis, or any other extraordinary experiences, do not fall back in terror. Do not mistake them for phantoms. Do not give up the practice. Persevere diligently. Break veil after veil.

If there is any error in practice, at once consult the realized souls and remove the mistake. If your general health is sound, if you are cheerful, happy, and strong physically and mentally, if your mind is peaceful and unruffled, if you get bliss in Meditation, and if your will is growing strong, pure and irresistible, think that you are improving in Meditation and everything is going all right.

March on boldly. Do not look back. Cross the intense void and darkness. Pierce the layer of desire. Melt the subtle ego. Real nature will shine by itself. You will experience the *Turiya* state.

Dangers and Remedies

Nervous overstrain can occur from too great intensity, and show itself in digestive problems, headaches, hypertension and the like. It may be relieved by the practice of deep relaxation, learning to work with greater impersonality with less self-interest, less desire to excel and so on.

Do not focus attention upon the psychic centers of the body, for these are easily disturbed and such disturbance is dangerous to health and sanity and also hard to cure. (See *The Chakras* by C.W. Leadbeater: Section on "Danger of Premature Awakening of Kundalini").

It is best not to seek psychic power directly. They arise naturally at a considerable later period. They are then under conscious control.

Stunts of any kind such as special breathing, long hours of practice are certainly to be avoided. They easily lead to nerve strain or self-delusion.

4.12: Practical Hints for Meditation

The following few practical hints will help you in your practice of Meditation.

1. Practice Meditation systematically and regularly. Regularity is of paramount importance.
2. Do not meditate right after a meal. Wait at least for three hours.
3. For early morning Meditations, do a few *asanas*, take a cold or mild hot shower or wash the face with cold water to make the body and mind fully awaken and alert.
4. Place a firm cushion or pillow or a folded blanket under the buttocks to make the sitting more comfortable.
5. Make sure that the clothing is comfortable and sufficiently warm.
6. Use a well ventilated room for Meditation.
7. Sit facing North or East in lotus or cross-legged comfortable Posture.
8. Keep the spine, neck and head erect in a straight line.
9. Best to meditate in the same place and at the same time every day.
10. Prepare well by doing *Pranayama* and chanting.
11. Early morning (4-7 am) and evening sunset time are very good times to meditate.
12. Schedule your practice in a methodical way. Make a firm, clear determination. Don't overstretch at once; be reasonable and realistic. Stick to your schedule.

13. Do not be disheartened if you do not succeed in the beginning. Every failure is a stepping stone to success. With every effort, subconscious mind is cutting a fresh groove. When the worldly grooves have been replaced by the groove of Meditation, the mind will naturally enter into a meditative state without difficulty.
14. Don't be anxious or disturbed over the distracting thoughts that come to the mind during your sitting. Simply try to ignore them. Do not try to force them out, you will create an enemy then. Learn to let them go.
15. Tend to the process of Meditation rather than to the goal. Meditation is a science. If you do it properly, you will get the results.
16. Approach your practice with a sense of adventure.
17. Associate with other spiritual seekers.
18. Read uplifting spiritual works.
19. Laziness is the greatest enemy. Life is short; time is fleeting and the obstacles are many. Conquer them by sincere effort and devotion. Help comes from a higher level to sincere aspirants.
20. Dedicate your practice to the Lord. He works through you.
21. Be consistent in your method of Meditation. Do not change it again and again.
22. While meditating do not strain the eyes and the brain. It is a serious mistake to strain them. Many beginners commit this grave mistake, and get easily tired soon and get headaches.
23. Whenever the mind wanders, gently bring it back to the object of Concentration. By repeated effort, the mind will eventually become one-pointed.
24. If there is much strain in meditating, reduce the duration for a few days. When you have regained the normal tone; increase the duration.
25. Be firm in dispassion and sattvic virtues such as patience, perseverance, mercy, love, forgiveness, purity, etc.
26. Conserve your mental energy by stopping useless thinking. Then you will save abundant reserve energy for Meditation.

27. Remember the triplet: purification, Concentration, absorption. Purify the mind. Get rid of impurities of desire, hatred, etc.; perform selfless service. The mind will be absorbed eventually.
    "OM is the bow, one's Self is the arrow and Brahman is the target to be aimed at. Brahman is to be hit without making a mistake. Thus one becomes united with Brahman, as the arrow becomes one with the target."
    — *Mundaka Upanishad*, (2.2.4)
28. Practice becomes firmly grounded when tended for a long time, without interruption and in all earnestness.

4.13: Meditation in Action

Meaning

Most people have only a short time to practice Meditation each day, as they have many obligations and tasks to do throughout the day, and they are immersed in them. For Meditation to be of real value it should have some carryover and it should provide purpose, direction and a sense of peace and harmony throughout the day. This is accomplished through Meditation in action. It means the application of meditative approach to our daily activities. Then our entire sixteen or eighteen waking hours can be transformed into a meditative practice. Ultimately a time will come when our whole life will be one long Meditation, and yet we will be as active as ever!

Mental Peace

During Meditation and at times during the day we may feel a sense of peace and calmness. It is possible to develop that experience even in the midst of activity. That peace and joy do not depend upon external environment, but on our attitude toward it. We cannot always govern circumstances, but we can govern our *responses* to them. If we just accept things as they are and view them with a balanced state of mind, we can always maintain our inherent peace and joy. When we apply what we learn about controlling the mind in Meditation to everyday life in the world, every action will become part of our meditative experience.

Witnessing Attitude

In our sitting Meditation we withdraw our awareness from the external world and try to center our mind on a single object such as a *mantra* or our breath. Other thoughts hidden in our memory come to our awareness and distract our attention. As we advance in Meditation we learn just to observe them as a silent witness, instead of being involved with them.

We can learn to apply the same technique to our complex worldly situation. In a wheel, the outer most part is spinning rapidly, but its hub is still. In the same way when we are engaged in the activities of the day, if we can have a part of our mind focused on our meditative center within, then we will be able to maintain mental peace and tranquility. When we inspire our daily life with strength drawn from faith in the Divinity within, then we have infinite power to draw upon as well as greater wisdom to act rightly. Let us link the external busy life with the deeper internal life of tranquility and peace, and thus to learn to preserve an unruffled stillness of spirit even amid varied vicissitudes of life.

Being in the Golden Present

One of the techniques learned in Meditation is to remain in the experience of the present moment. As we meditate, memories of past and thoughts of future toss our mind. We learn to watch them coming and going rather than becoming caught up in them. By cultivating the same attitude in the midst of action, we can achieve calmness and serenity in our everyday life.

We spent a lot of time in needless concern about the future, and worry about things instead of working in the present moment to correct whatever is causing the problem. This absorption in worries and expectations takes us away from the joy and happiness existing right now.

The best way of effectively dealing with the future is to center on the present and take care of it in the best possible way. By worrying about the future we merely create more difficulties for ourselves. Such worries affect our ability to handle difficult situations effectively in the present and even create the future difficulties that we were afraid might occur. For example, if a student is not able to solve some of the problems in the examination paper, he begins to anticipate failure in the examination. His worries about the outcome distract him and he becomes unable to solve the other easy problems. Thus he is not able to concentrate his mind to deal effectively with the task on hand. Many of us have similar experiences in other situations. Worrying about the anticipated problems is not the way to avoid them. Our future is created out of our thoughts and actions in the present.

Attitude Toward Work

Many of us have a negative attitude toward our routine tasks. We perform them only because they have to be done. So we find them as drudgery and uninteresting. We look for the time when they will be finished and can then enjoy our leisure. Can we suddenly change that frame of mind after finishing the tasks to enjoy leisure? No. The same dull feeling will be carried forward.

Pain and pleasure do not reside in the external situations but in our attitude of mind. Every activity can be considered as a play. Then we can enjoy it and find it interesting and pleasant, and we can experience peace and joy.

When we rush through activities simply to get them finished, we do not do them effectively and rather complicate things. It is only by paying careful attention to each activity that we can perform it effectively. But careful attention does not imply getting emotionally attached to it. It just means being mindful, sensitive and gentle to each activity. As we train our minds to focus on the task on hand, we will derive joy in doing it and need not run here and there for happiness. Let us shed off our selfish attitude to work. There is no need to renounce our work and flee from the haunts of mundane sphere, but let us renounce our selfish attitude to work and do it in the spirit of serving humanity. This is practical spirituality.

Dedication of Actions

Action itself becomes a form of Meditation when it is performed as an offering unto the Lord. Whatever is our avocation in life, if we perform all actions for the good of humanity and God's creation, our actions become an integral part of our spiritual discipline. The more we perform our actions as a selfless offering to the Divine, the more they become instrumental to our union with the Divine.

Spiritually-oriented action is free, spontaneous, relaxed and non-attached. When we learn to view our actions in relation to the supreme ideal of life, they become increasingly agreeable and pleasant. Steadfast devotion to the ideal of life releases our latent energies. It turns the whole arena of active life into a medium of joyful self-expansion. The spiritual orientation enables us to perform the various duties of life in a relaxed attitude. Even in the midst of a full flood of activity, we can maintain our self-poise and peace of mind, because our central motivation is derived not from any ego drive but from the spirit of dedication to the Divine. We act not for our self-aggrandizement but for the glory of God. We act not for our personal name and fame, but as an instrument of the Divine Will. Every virtuous action, regardless of the outward consequences, contributes to the enrichment of our inner being

Concentration

When we are busily engaged in several activities in a day, our attention is likely to become diverted and the quality of performance suffers. But if we apply the method of Concentration cultivated during the practice of Meditation to our daily activities, then we will be able to perform them more effectively. Perform every activity with attentiveness.

Letting Go

In our daily life we are attached to certain things. For example you may be attached to your car. You may feel that you cannot get on without it. If it breaks down you feel helpless and paralyzed. But your car is a mere instrument for your use. Should you make it a source of unhappiness through your attachment to it? You must learn to let go of your dependency on objects. Through the practice of Meditation, you learn to give up the attitude of clinging to things. You develop an attitude of dispassion. You do not have to give up your car or any other possession. Only the attachment to your possessions has to be given up. Nothing is indispensable.

The external environment in which we are living is a projection of our imaginations, hopes and expectation. If we understand and appreciate that we are creating our own environment, then our attitude toward our situations would be different. Instead of blaming others for our situation, we would cultivate a positive attitude toward them and make our life pleasant.

Creative Ideas

During Meditation we may get most creative solutions to unresolved situations. Then we are not concerned with solving problems, but we can make use of such thoughts in solving problems creatively in the course of our daily life.

Detached Self-observation

During Meditation we develop the method of detached self-observation. We learn to just observe, watch without being reactive or upset over anything. We simply allow all ideas, feelings, desires, impulses, distracting thoughts, etc. to fly freely across the mental horizon. We watch them in a spirit of non-attachment. We let them come and go. This provides an opportunity to know our own nature. We can apply this method of self-observation in the midst of daily activities. Let us cultivate the habit of observing ourselves in the different situations of life, taking note of how we react emotionally in changing circumstances and in dealing with different people. In the light of such observation we can correct our shortcomings, angularities, idiosyncrasy and emotional immaturity, and perfect our reactions and responses to environmental changes. Objective self-awareness and constructive self-evaluation serve as an invaluable aid to gradual self-perfection.

We move from morning till night in the midst of activities and interests. The world confronts us ceaselessly. By detaching ourselves for a few minutes from those activities and putting ourselves into a serene state of reverie, we may obtain higher protection and right guidance for all those activities.

Open Relationship with Others

In modern society we are repeatedly taught to look outside of ourselves to find happiness. As a result, our relationships to people, objects and circumstances are based on our likes and dislikes. We like those from whom we expect to receive benefits or pleasures; we avoid those that we think will be harmful to us. Such likes and dislikes vitiate our perception and plunge us into a sea of emotional disturbances. We do not realize that our very inner nature is peace and joy, and that our happiness and fulfillment do not come from outside. Those who practice Meditation get this enlightenment, and become more open in their relationships with people and things. They experience joy and happiness from within, and express that joy in their relationships.

Controlling Our Thoughts and Emotions

We ordinarily are not aware of our hidden aspects. If I cling to someone else for his sympathy, care or emotional response, it is because he is reflecting those qualities that I do not recognize within. Similarly if I reject another, it is because he reflects qualities that I find as unacceptable to me. The application of meditative experience to daily life helps us to know that the world is our projection, and to recognize our own qualities rather than chasing or running away from them as they are mirrored in the world. By observing our thoughts, desires and moods, we recognize our subtle internal states, and become less dominated by them. Our self-awareness enables us to master our thoughts and impulses.

Objective Observation of the World

In judging others and outside world we project our own qualities. But when self-awareness develops, we learn to view the world more objectively. The meditative process speeds up such awareness and objective observation of the external world. Each step in objective awareness is a step toward freedom, self-mastery and disentanglement from the external world.

Modern human being is egoistic, pleasure-seeking, greedy and power-seeking and faces fear of death, fear of losing possessions and position. Impelled by selfish motives and desires, he commits various evils, undergoes various sufferings and loses his inner peace and happiness. The basic cause for such turmoil is his ignorance of his real nature and wrong identification of himself with his body and mind. Meditation helps him to realize his true nature and the fleeting nature of worldly pleasures.

Enjoying Work

Ordinary persons work for the sake of a reward. They would not work at all if they knew that they were not going to be rewarded. Some people do not like their work. Yet they tolerate it because they are paid for it. Such persons spend most of their time in frustration, complaining that their life is a drudge. The quality of their performance suffers. They lose their peace of mind and undergo stress and strain. Meditation and practice of Karma Yoga enable them to realize that they can really enjoy their work if they work for the sake of work. Lord Krishna, in the *Bhagavad Gita*, says:

> A Yogi attains peace by renouncing the fruits of his action. But a non-Yogi Impelled by desires is bound by his attachment to the fruits." (5.12)

Benefit to Sitting Meditation

Just as Meditation in action is benefited by the sitting Meditation, the latter is also benefited by the former. Most of the disturbances in the mind that come to our awareness when we sit for Meditation is the outcome of unfinished business, discomfort, tensions and disappointments experienced in the daily life. If we lead a disorganized and turbulent life we will carry over our disease into the sitting Meditation. We can avoid this obstacle to Meditation if we practice Meditation in action. Otherwise we will be like Penelope in Homer's Odyssey. She wove a tapestry each day and unraveled it each night. When we meditate each day, we may make some progress in calming our mind, but when we start the day, we become involved in the recurrences of previous dramas and they disturb us when we sit to meditate the next day. Thus each day we make a leap forward toward tranquility, and then we slip back into the whirlpool of distracting thoughts. Many meditators live in this way and they find that they have not made any progress though they have been meditating for years.

But if we practice Meditation in action, we will learn not to identify with the distractions that occur through the day. Instead of becoming lost in dramas of everyday life, we will perform our duties and deal with the situations in a balanced manner. With such balanced mind if we sit for Meditation, our mind will already be relatively calm. Even if there are a few distracting thoughts, they will not disturb us much. We will be able to go even deeper toward a state of expansion of consciousness and inner joy.

Schedule of Meditation in Action

A daily schedule of Meditation in action is suggested below:

- Start your day in a positive, dynamic and spiritual frame of mind. Before plunging into the daily round of activities, practice Meditation at least for ten or fifteen minutes. This is separate from your daily round of Meditation practice. First, offer prayers to the Lord. Next, read a few pages from a book of spiritual wisdom and inspiration. Carefully reflect upon their significance and relevance to your life and human relations. Then sit in an erect Posture and concentrate upon such Divine values as truthfulness, honesty, selflessness, non-attachment, dedicated service, and the like. Reflect upon yourself as an integral part of the Cosmic Spirit. Fix in your mind the idea of being essentially an instrument of the Divine.
- Make a mental survey of all the important activities and contacts that you propose to go through during the day.
- Visualize yourself performing them in the most appropriate way in accordance with the spiritual ideal of life. Carefully select matters of prior importance.
- Embark upon your daily round of duties with the attitude of serving the Divine.

- Whenever you get a little free time, reaffirm in your mind the spiritual ideal of life, and rededicate yourself as an instrument of the Divine.
- Repeat in your mind your *mantra*. It offers you Divine protection and keeps alive your sense of direction in life.
- Finally before retiring at night, practice Meditation for a few minutes. Then make a critical review of all the activities, events, experiences and contacts of the day. Draw lessons from the mistakes made and brush aside all further thoughts and feelings about them.
- Offer thanks to the Lord for having made use of you as His instrument. Whatever ideas and emotions that may pop up, offer them to the Lord with prayer and place yourself in the peaceful embrace of sleep.

4.14: Benefits of Meditation

A regular and systematic practice of Meditation yields a number of specific benefits. Considerable changes take place in the mind, brain and the nervous system by the practice of Meditation. New nerve currents, new vibrations, new avenues, new grooves, new cells, new channels are formed. The whole mind and the nervous system are remodeled. You will develop a new heart, a new mind, new feelings, new outlook and a new view of the universe as God in manifestation.

Meditation acts as a powerful tonic for the body and mind and nerves. The holy vibrations penetrate all the cells of the body, and cure the diseases of the body. The powerful soothing waves that arise during Meditation exercise a benign influence on the mind, nerves, organs and cells of the body.

Stress Reduction

Stress accumulates in all of us. When stress builds up, it has a dangerous effort on health. Meditation offers an effective means of relieving the stress of life. When the mind becomes concentrated on one point, the body becomes deeply relaxed. The physiology of the body undergoes a gradual change, reflecting a permanent reduction of stress – slower pulse rate, a lower and more stable blood pressure, balanced breathing pattern and lower blood lactate levels. The physiological change is a consequence of reduction in mental stress and anxiety, increase in self-confidence and maturity. This growing maturity is reflected in our behavior. Our life becomes more relaxed and stable. (*See* 4.14 Meditation and Health, *below*).

Skill Development

The development of inner Concentration leads to the development of useful skills such as Concentration on the work on hand, and the consequent work effectiveness, perceptual awareness, greater control over thoughts and feelings.

Transformation of Egoism

A gradual transformation of egoism takes place as a result of increase in our inner awareness. Slowly we begin to identify with our real Self.

During the process of establishing our new identity with the Superconscious Self, we slowly disidentify with our body, thoughts and attachments. As we give up our past identities, we become aware of our potential for self-control, freedom from disruptive habits.

Positive Emotions

Meditation develops the most precious capacity of transforming anger into compassion, fear into fearlessness and hatred into love. The practice of Meditation leads to the development of positive emotions of love, joy and peace. This *love* is pure love, an expansion of oneself. It is expressed in selflessness in thought, word and action. It is free from attachment and dependency. It seeks no reward. It removes our self-imposed boundaries and we become universal.

Joy is what we experience when we love. It expresses itself in laughter. It is the light that illumines our path through life. Joy is cultivated by seeking others' happiness.

When we accept everything as it is, instead of wishing that it should be like this or that, we experience the fullness of joy. This is the basis for peace or tranquility.

Peace is a dynamic quality of balance and harmony. "As love is the outward flowing of energy in selflessness, and joy is the experience of accepting the natural Divinity of all life, peace is the experience we have when we know and accept ourselves for what we are."

When, through Meditation, we realize our true spiritual identity, the habits, doubts, fears, and selfish motives fade away, and we experience an inner calm and serenity.

Special Intelligence

Fire is of two kinds: ordinary fire and special fire. Ordinary fire is hidden in all trees and woods. It is of no use for burning purposes. Special fire is formed by rubbing a match or rubbing two pieces of wood. It is useful for cooking and heating purposes. Similarly intelligence is of two kinds: ordinary intelligence and special intelligence. Ordinary intelligence cannot destroy your ignorance. It is only the special intelligence that can destroy the basic ignorance that envelops your Reality, Atman. This special intelligence is developed when you meditate on the Infinite with a pure heart.

Purification

In Meditation, you are in spiritual contact with the unchanging Light. You are cleansed of all impurities. This Light cleanses the soul that touches it. The sun light focused on piece of paper through a lens ignites the paper. Similarly if your mind is devotedly focused on God, your shortcomings are burnt by the fire of Divine Light.

This purifying process leads to a deeper insight into Truth. This is the action of Grace of the Lord upon the soul in Meditation. In this inflowing Grace, arises that Light of the mind into which God is sending a ray of His unclouded splendor. This Light is vastly potent.

Peace and Bliss

Effective Meditation leads to mental peace and bliss. This bliss is a million time superior to sensual pleasure. You will get the full bliss of the Divine glory only when you merge deep into silent Meditation. In the *Bhagavad Gita* Lord Krishna says,

> "Thus, always keeping the mind balanced, the Yogi, with the mind controlled, attains to the peace abiding in Me, which culminates in Liberation." (6.15)

Control Over Mind

All actions, whether internal or external, can be done only when the mind is united with the organs. If you have control over the mind by steady practice, you can regulate your moods and emotions, and you will not do foolish and wrong actions.

Sattva Guna

Meditation results in the development of *sattva* guna denoted by peace, contentment, serenity of the mind, steadiness, inspiration and intuitive perception.

Transformation of Personality

Through Meditation you gain confidence, inspiration, and clarity of mind. Pride, lust, ill-will, doubt, discontentment and fear are driven out. You are cleansed of dullness, sloth and all faults, and you understand the transient nature of things.

The nature of the mind changes, moving gradually into a higher state of consciousness. Gradually you get rid of your attraction for money, fame, power, pride and false vanity and become absorbed in the great Infinity. .

Meditation thus subtly transforms your entire personality and brings to you freedom and harmony. It removes the ignorance that is the source of your suffering. When your awareness fully expands and you directly experience your Superconsciousness, your ignorance disappears.

As you practice Meditation and all the supporting disciplines of *Yama-Niyama*s, *Asanas*, *Pranayama* and Control of Senses, you go on learning to plug the holes that drain off your energy and capacity; you correct harmful breathing habits; you free your mind from worries and anxieties and release your stress and tensions.

Meditation stabilizes your emotions, increases your self-acceptance, intensifies your Concentration powers. All these lead to the development of your mental faculties of will-power, discrimination, dispassion, clear perception and self-confidence.

When, through Meditation, you come to experience directly your true spiritual identity, you experience unfoldment of the subtle potentials of your deeper mind.

Meditation integrates the mental energy to focus itself on subtler and richer planes of existence. It enables you to work from a deeper center, with the vivid vision of the life's mission.

Eradication of Fear

Among the various sources of stress, fear seems to be the greatest one. It is a "will-killer;" it cripples us and prevents us from becoming creative, thus destroying our human potential.

What is the *cause* of fear? "Wherever there is duality, there is fear," declare the *Upanishads*. We are ignorant of our real nature, eternal Self, and because of this ignorance, the vision of non-duality is lost and a world of duality and multiplicity arises.

The ignorance gives rise to egoism and identification with the body that is subject to change, decay and death. Consequently the fear of losing one's life arises. Thus, with ignorance as the root, the tree of fear grows from the unconscious, spreads its branches in the astral body in the form of subtle desires and cravings arising out of egoism, and manifests in the form of various thoughts, desires and longings in the day-to-day life as the fruits and flowers of the tree, leading to involvement in physical objects and sensual pleasures.

Fear of losing the body is the subtle form of fear. There are numerous other fears shaking the mind such as fear of losing the objects of love, fear of becoming poor, fear of public criticism, fear of sickness and disease, fear of an unknown future and so on.

Arising from ignorance, fed by the waters of imagination, fear grows like frost over tender crops. It thwarts the blooms of virtue, and destroys all that is good and auspicious. It weakens will, intensifies attachment, creates disharmony in family, and in the world, upsets the flow of energy in the system.

Fear obscures the faculty of intuition, mars the clarity of reason, and generates negative thoughts, emotions and actions, and ultimately ruins the life.

How can the fear be eradicated? As thoughts mold the mind, practice Meditation on positive ideas. Meditate on God, using sublime attributes of infinity, immortality, profound peace, limitless joy, supreme bliss. Engage yourself in creative activities. Practice Karma Yoga to purify the subconscious.

Develop intense love of God. Dedicate every thing to God. Feel the Divine force behind all that happens. Feel that you are an instrument in the hands of God. He is acting through you.

Elevate your mind by studying scriptures that awaken Divine sentiments. Cultivate positive thoughts and virtues. Enquire "who am I?" With the rising of inquiry, development of intuitive wisdom and dawn of Enlightenment, the darkness of fear is completely dispelled.

Meditate on: "I am the fearless, non-dual Self, I am beyond body, senses, mind, intellect, time and space. I am Existence-Knowledge-Bliss absolute. I am Brahman." Eradicate fear by Self-realization, and rest in absolute Peace and Bliss.

4.15: Meditation and Health

Introduction

The past thirty years have provided consistent clinical and scientific evidence in support of the medical benefits of Meditation. Meditation is found to be an effective means for increasing man's health and happiness. The regular practice of Meditation leads to a healthier and more effective human being. More specifically, the practitioners of Meditation have—

- lower triglyceride levels
- lower and more stable heart rate
- lower blood pressure
- a slower and more stable respiratory rate
- a more stable galvanic skin response
- fewer psychosomatic symptoms (headaches, colds, gastric disturbances)
- lower levels of anxiety and fear
- higher scores on self-actualization inventories
- increased capacity for loving and caring relationships

In fact many substantial benefits are derived from Meditation. When compared with non-practitioners, practitioners are healthier, happier and more effective persons. They enjoy greater peace and harmony. Both personal experiences and research show that Meditation is an important and effective means for promoting personal health and effectiveness.

The Physiological effects of Meditation

Meditation is a powerful method of controlling physiological processes and also of controlling physiological reactions to psychological events. During Meditation the metabolism slows down, for there is a sharp reduction in oxygen consumption and carbondioxide output. There may be about 20% decrease in oxygen consumption because of slower respiration rate.

Meditation has a noticeable influence on blood pressure. Blood pressure drops during and after Meditation. Therefore Meditation is recommended for people suffering from high blood pressure. The heart rate also slows down to a few beats per minute; the blood flow increases, because the activities of the sympathetic nerve system (one of whose functions is to constrict the blood vessels) are reduced and therefore constriction of the blood vessels is automatically decreased, resulting in a greater flow of blood.

This increased blood flow gives such benefits as reduction in the lactate level. Lactate is a substance produced mainly in the muscles when there is no free oxygen. It is profusely produced during periods of intense activity when the muscles perform extensive work. Then the muscles expend more energy than that allowed by the oxygen supply to the muscles. Now lactate is produced to provide for the much required extra energy. During periods of rest, lactate is slowly broken down into other substances. In Meditation the distribution of available oxygen to the muscles increases and the lactate is more quickly and effectively removed. Production of lactate is stimulated by the sympathetic nerve system; but the inhibition of this nerve system during Meditation automatically reduces production of lactate. What is the benefit of reduction in the level of lactate?

Persons suffering from anxiety, neurosis, tension and high blood pressure have a high level of lactate compared to when they are calm and tranquil and have normal blood pressure. Meditation reduces the lactate level and so consequently reduces blood pressure and all types of anxiety symptoms. Anxiety is the cause of many of the physical ailments and mental diseases. Meditation is a superior remedy to these diseases, as it does away with their root cause itself.

The Fight or Flight Defense Mechanism Of the Body

The sympathetic nerve system and the adrenal glands serve as the fight or flight defense system of the body. These two systems compliment each other. During the times of stress, danger or fear, the adrenal glands secrete a hormone called adrenaline, which prepares the body for fight or flight. It makes the body more efficient by increasing the heart rate and the respiration rate, and by improving eyesight, hearing, etc. It also inhibits the digestive functions so that the energy can be more usefully employed to face the threatening situation. This system is for short term dangers. For threats that last a longer period of time, the sympathetic nerve system takes over and keeps the body at a continuous higher level of intensity. Eventually, when the threat has disappeared the body functions return to their usual level of activity.

However, the stressful and competitive modern life-style is such that many people almost continually operate at a high level of preparedness for fight or flight. It may be from the fear of the boss, fear of competition, fear of economic recession, fear of losing job or status, fear of bankruptcy, and so on. Under these conditions, an individual always tenses his muscles, squints his eyes, bites his nails and so on, in reaction to various situations.

These habitual reactions are the forerunners of psychosomatic diseases. When a person is manifesting these tensions, whether he knows it or not, he is really preparing himself for the fight or flight reaction and so the sympathetic nerve system and the adrenal glands continue to be active. This prolonged stimulation of the adrenal glands and the sympathetic nerve system can lead to such ailments as high blood pressure, diabetes, coronary thrombosis, peptic and duodenal ulcers, backache, skin problems, muscular twitches and a host of other ailments.

The only sure method of counteracting, preventing and curing these ailments is to completely relax the whole body and mind every day. Sound sleep, of course, is the usual remedy. But most people are so tense that they do not even relax during sleep, and they are still trying to solve their problems whilst sleeping. Sleep is generally inadequate to relax, balance and eradicate the damaging effects of the over-use of the adrenal and sympathetic nerve systems. It is only during deep relaxation that the body processes can finally recuperate and return to their normal level of activity. Meditation is the means to do this. It is a panacea for modern life. It is the sure means of attaining positive health of both the mind and the body.

We must not only learn to relax but also change our responses to our situations so as to attain harmonization and integration with the environment. The mind-body system must be re-programmed toward this goal.

An important part of the brain is the limbic system. It compares data stored in our memory with the incoming sense data; It analyses it in terms of previous experiences. It intensifies emotional responses to data that does not harmonize or fit in with our previous memory. Thus if something happens to us that is unexpected or different from our previous experiences, the limbic system immediately creates an emotional reaction such as anger, stress, etc. This eventually triggers off the adrenal glands, which release the hormone adrenaline into the blood system. This then makes the whole body tense—the heart beats faster, the respiration rate increases, and so on. It is in this state that many present day people spend much of their life, with all types of diseases.

Yet, at the same time, a part of the limbic system called the septal region acts in the opposite direction. It reduces our emotional responses; It releases tension and creates relaxation of the body and the mind. By Meditation we can make the septal part of the limbic system operate for the predominant part of our life. We can then live a life of relaxation, do our work more efficiently and be free from diseases.

Meditation and Stress Management

Stress is the most debilitating problem in the modern society. It is the outcome of the modern way of life, as explained above. It is caused by non-regulation of functioning of our mind and body.

Stress comes in different forms:

1. Emotional or mental stress arising out of our interaction with our environment
2. Digestive stress coming from poor eating habits
3. Environmental stress caused by smoke, noise and air pollution

Stress is harmful because we are unconsciously creating it and become accustomed to it. It is distinctively different from what we normally call a disease. It has no biological basis such as a germ or virus or bad water. There is no external cause for stress. The source of stress is the *way* we as individuals think, feel and act.

Stress is a dangerous "dis-ease." It leads to an incredible variety of disorders: heart disease, psychosomatic disease, sleeplessness, common cold, headache and emotional disturbance as explained under the previous subheading.

Effect of Stress on Mental Health

Most people live in a "pressure-cooker" environment. They are unable to handle difficult situations adequately with the time pressures and competition. Too much stress inhibits creative thinking and causes mental illness, high blood pressure, headache or ulcers. Richard Rahe's research has shown that major changes in one's living or work conditions such as change of job, relocation, divorce, family problem and the like lead to increased levels of stress. Stress is closely associated with tension, worry, anxiety and nervous disability.

We cannot easily change our work situations or social situations, but we can easily change our internal response to the pressures generated by these situations. That is the key to successful stress management. For example the work of Dr. Abraham Maslow with the Self-actualized people (those who have achieved high degree of psychological maturity) has shown that such people do not create the same degree of stress for themselves as others do. They suffer from fewer illnesses. Yet many of them hold high positions in stress-related jobs. But they usually find joy in their work. They are consistently high achievers. They have greater concern for others' welfare. They have learned how to manage stress.

Stress Management and Holistic Medicine

Traditional medical treatment is focused upon the symptoms, but does little for the underlying cause. In looking for the causes externally, we have not paid attention to the real source of stress, namely, *the way we think, feel and react.* As we are the cause of this psychosomatic malady, we can also be its cure.

The new emerging therapeutic approach called Holistic Health is based on the realization that everyone is responsible for his own health, rather than upon the doctor or the drug. It is an interdisciplinary approach to health that places the responsibility and the tools for increased well-being with the individual. Holistic health provides us with the framework necessary to understand and really conquer stress. Utilizing such tools as bio-feedback and Meditation, it gives us a functional approach to conquering stress that is based on training rather than on therapy, prevention rather than cure. This modern approach has its roots in Yoga science.

Bio-feedback. It is an important tool of holistic medicine, a sophisticated electronic instrument. It gives one immediate information about what is happening inside his body—the psychological and mental patterns which result in a psychosomatic dysfunction. For example, as reported in Meditational Therapy, the patients who had suffered from chronic tension headaches for twenty to thirty years were able to eliminate their headaches within six weeks through a bio-feedback therapy program. After only six weeks of stress reduction training through relaxation, *Pranayama*, Meditation, and biofeedback training, the symptoms were entirely gone. No drugs were used.

Bio-feedback therapy is equally successful in treating many other diseases that are related to stress. For example, Dr. Chandra Patel in England has shown that a combination of bio-feedback, relaxation and *Pranayama* has been used to successfully reduce high blood pressure. This therapy offers us real hope in freeing ourselves from stress through our own efforts without medication.

Meditation: Pathway to Freedom

In the modern technologically advanced society, we encounter many social and economic pressures of everyday life. We live in a stressful complex external environment that creates disturbances in our inner mental world. Can we be able to cope up with the external pressures and tension and yet retain tranquility and peace of mind? Yes, we can retain our balance while functioning in the modern society by practicing Meditation. It is the art of living and being in the world. It is a practical systematic method of knowing ourselves and eliminating and preventing inner conflicts in order to maintain inner peace and joy.

How do we lose our peace and create stress? Our mind habitually identifies itself with the objects and experiences of the world. This is reflected in our thoughts and emotions. It is this—*our reaction to external situations—that causes stress* and creates serious problems for us. If we learn to witness this thinking process as a silent observer instead of identifying with it, we gain access to our unconscious mind that controls our behavior. As we continue to develop a strong sense of observation we are able to break our identification with the deep thoughts and images of unconscious mind. Then we become free from the very source of stress, namely, the sense of identity with the thinking process. Our mind is then in balance. The method for doing this is Meditation. It is the systematic way be which we gain freedom from stress. Through inner Concentration our attention penetrates the unconscious mind. To do this a focal point is needed for our mind. Breath awareness is a good focal point. It not only develops inner Concentration, but also leads to balance the autonomic nervous system. When this happens, we not only have control over stress, we also develop conscious mastery over both our physiological processes and our emotional events.

When we observe breath mentally, the stream of thoughts inside the mind stops, because we cannot have both at the same time. As a result of turning off the thinking faculty, our body becomes more relaxed. This is a natural response of the body to the mind's calmness.

How Does Meditation Work

How does Meditation work? What does happen when we

meditate? The key to answering these questions lies in understanding the relationship between Meditation and the emotions. The physical, mental behavioral benefits that are derived from the practice of Meditation reflect a more balanced and harmonious emotional state. Modern science is confirming the ancient wisdom by recognizing the supremacy of mind as the determinant of health and well-being. The new disciplines of bio-feedback, behavioral medicine and psychoneuroimmunology indicate that the mind is in fact a major determining factor in health and disease.

Yoga science has given us a detailed psychological analysis of the mind, and its various functions. (*See* 2.1–2 *Yoga Psychology;* and 2.4–5 Mind and Its Analysis, *above*). As a result we have a better understanding of the emotions on the individual's health.

From the Yogic viewpoint, we are a unique combination of animal, human and Divine aspects. Our animal nature is our physical structure, the body; our human aspect is our mind with its reflective consciousness; our Divinity is the universal Consciousness (Atman) that pervades mind and body. It is the successful integration of spirit, mind and body that leads to the fulfillment of human potential. Our mundane life is mainly governed by four primitive urges: self-preservation, food, sleep, and procreation. These urges are common to animals and human beings. We, human beings, also have a higher urge for Self-unfoldment. These drives give rise to various needs and desires. Desires are endless.

It is at the level of desires that our emotions respond. Depending on whether we experience an object as pleasurable or painful, the urge is either temporarily satisfied or ignored. With the repeated pleasure, the individual develops an attachment to the object; if the pain is the outcome, he develops an aversion to the object. The *Yoga Sutras* say:

> "Attachment is that which dwells upon pleasure." (2.7)
> "Aversion is that which dwells upon pain." (2.8)

Unfulfilled or blocked desires cause such emotional disturbances as frustration, anger, jealousy, stress and disappointment. The source of emotional disturbance is not the desire or the object, but our reaction—attachment or aversion—to the object. The difficulty in getting the object or its non-availability or the fear of losing it causes disturbance. If the disturbance is intensive or continues long enough, our physical health is affected and we get disease.

All material objects including thoughts, beliefs and people are constantly undergoing change. Thus if we become dependent upon an object or a person, we become insecure. There is an unconscious recognition that the things, upon which we are dependent including our bodies and minds, are going to change. This unconscious recognition is the root cause of our most basic fear, the fear of death.

The above description of the primitive urges, desires, and negative emotions provides the background for the Yogic analysis of suffering (*klesas*), which is intimately connected with our negative emotions. (*See* 2.8 Suffering, *above*). According to this analysis, we create our own suffering through our ignorance, ego and negative emotions. The source of all suffering is the ignorance of our spiritual identity. Instead of realizing that we are eternal and omnipotent Self, we consider ourselves to be the mortal mind-body complex.

Even on the mundane level, it is ignorance that enslaves us to the habit of our mind-body complex. Our habits are unconscious behavior and they form the basis of our attachments and aversion.

What does happen when we become conscious of our habits? As long as the habits remain in the unconscious level, they condition our behavior; but the moment we become aware of the habits, they are amenable to modification or elimination.

The primal fear of death is also due to our ignorance, our wrong identification with the body that is subject to decay and death. Thus it is our ignorance, our lack of awareness that is the cause of our suffering. So by the direct experience of our eternal Self, we eliminate ignorance and along with it we also eradicate our sufferings.

How do we get the experience of our eternal Self? By unfolding and expanding our consciousness through proper and regular practice of deep Meditation. Our progress in it depends upon our capacity for Concentration, for it is Concentration that enables us to penetrate the veil of mind so as to reach the Superconscious state. When our Meditation deepens, we begin to experience spiritual awakening. Then our emotions come under control and we experience inner peace and harmony. Eventually we experience Superconsciousness and achieve the purpose of our life.

Meditational Therapy

Gary Schwartz, a psychologist of Harvard University conducted research into Meditation and found that meditators' anxiety levels were much lower than those of non-meditators, and that meditators had fewer psychological or psychosomatic problems such as cold, headaches and sleeplessness. He presented a paper on "Pros and Cons of Meditation" at American Psychological Association meeting, Montreal, September 1973.

Daniel Goleman's study at Harvard revealed the lower incidence of anxiety and psychosomatic disorders and rapid stress recovery among meditators. ("Meditation as an Intervention in Stress Reactivity," *Journal of Clinical and Consulting Psychology*, 44 (1976): 456–66).

A Harvard Group's study showed that Meditation sharpens attention and alertness. (Davidson, R.J. and others, "Attentional and Affective Concomitants of Meditation: A Cross-sectional Study," *Journal of Abnormal Psychology,* 85, 1976: 235–38).

The mid-1970's saw a flood of research on Meditation's health benefits (*See* Shapiro and Walsh, R., *Meditation: Classical and Contemporary Views*, New York: Aldine, 1984, for the most complete survey). Their findings were: Meditation was helpful in many ways. The regular practice of Meditation lessened the frequency of colds and headaches and reduced the severity of hypertension. It was a stress management tool par excellence, and a quick and easy relaxation technique. It was effective in getting deep relaxation. The neuroendocrine changes brought about by becoming deeply relaxed have turned out to be more profound than was first believed by earlier investigators. More biologically sophisticated investigations have revealed profound effects on immune function as well as a range of other changes with specific clinical applications such as its use by elders to increase the strength of their immune defenses against tumors and viruses, use by students during the stress of examinations to increase the levels of helper cells that defend against infectious disease, its use in fighting heart disease, and decreasing blood pressure.

Dr. Dean Ornish, a devotee of Rev. Swami Satchidanananda, founder of Integral Yoga Institutes in USA and other countries, has found that Meditation along with *Asanas*, *Pranayama* and low-fat vegetarian diet was useful in reversing heart disease without medication. His program has ushered in a Yogic and medical revolution. More and more people are being attracted to Yoga and vegetarianism. Several hospitals are implementing his program. (*See* Dean Ornish, (1) *Stress, Diet and Your Heart,* (2) *Dr. Dean Ornish's Program for Reversing Heart Disease*, (3) *Eat More, Weigh Less*).

Meditation, coupled with Yoga *Asanas* is also found to be useful in treating diabetes, asthmatics, kidney dialysis, cancer chemotherapy, gastrointestinal disorders, insomnia, emphysema and skin disorders, and as an adjunct in psychotherapy as well.

4.16: Kundalini Yoga: Philosophical Basis and *Chakra*

The Kundalini Yoga is the most advanced approach to studying the internal world. The term "*kundalini*" comes from the Sanskrit word "*kundala*" that means "coiled one." Kundalini is the dormant Cosmic energy that resides, coiled like a serpent, at the bottom of the spinal column. It is symbolized as a snake with three and a half coils sleeping at the perineum or *Muladhara Chakra* in the human body. The three coils represent the three *Gunas* of nature: *Sattva*, *Rajas* and *Tamas*. The half coil represents the effects of the *Gunas* known as *vikritis*.

Nadis

According to the Yogic theory, *prana* or the life force circulates in the body through a network of seventy-two thousand nadis, thus activating all organs and senses. Among them *Sushumna, Ida,* and *Pingala* are the most important nadis. *Sushumna* is the principal nadi. It rises from the basal plexus and passes through the center of the spinal cord up to the crown of the head. *Ida* and *Pingala* encircle the *Sushumna* as a figure eight on its left and right sides respectively.

Sushumna is closed at the lower end, situated near what is called the sacral plexus, which, according to modern physiology, is triangular in form. The different plexuses that have their centers in the spinal canal can very well stand for the different "lotuses" of *Chakras* described by the Yoga science. There are several centers, starting with the *Muladhara*, the basic center, and ending with the *Sahasrara*, the thousand-petalled lotus in the brain. So if we take the different plexuses as representing these lotuses, the idea of Yoga science can be understood very easily in the language of modern physiology.

Sushumna, *Ida* and *Pingala* nadis meet at three points—at the base of the spine, at the neck and at the middle of the head. In an average person the passage through the *Sushumna* is entirely blocked. The minimum energy needed for normal life runs through the *Ida* and *Pingala*. The subtle energy that blocks the upward passage of the *Sushumna* is the dormant state of Kundalini. The endeavor of a Yogi is to open the middle channel by practicing *Pranayama* exercises and Meditation. The *Pranayama* exercise prescribed for this purpose is inhalation-retention- exhalation in the ratio of 1:4:2. Some recommend the ratio of 1:2:2.

Aim of Kundalini Yoga

The aim of Kundalini Yoga is to awaken the sleeping or dormant kundalini and to channel it upward through the *Chakras* (psychic centers) of the *Sushumna* nadi. When it reaches the *Sahasrara Chakra* at the crown of the head, the practitioner attains the highest state of Consciousness and Enlightenment. Awakening Kundalini is a highly systematic method of attaining Self-realization. It requires an intensive practice over a long period of time.

Philosophical Basis

Kundalini Yoga is based on the subtle philosophy of Tantra. During sixth or seventh century AD the Tantra system of Philosophy, a distinctive system of mysticism, had been developed. The word *tantra* means "rules to govern." The ultimate reality that is called Brahman by Vedantists is called *Shiva* by the Tantrics. According to the Vedanta, the power of Brahman, by which Brahman manifests the universe, is *Maya*. In the Tantra, it is called *Shakti* or power. The object of the Tantrics is to experience the unity of Shakti and Shiva, the ultimate Reality. Shakti is called the Divine Mother of the universe. The two principles of Shiva and Shakti are eternally and inseparably united, but an illusion of separation is created between them.

Dynamic and Latent Energy

Energy exists in two forms: dynamic and latent. All activities or forces of motion have a static background and when consciousness manifests itself as the creative or dynamic principle, it divides itself into these two aspects.

By means of their observation and experiment the sages of the Tantra system discovered that the potentiality of perfection lies within a human being in the form of a very subtle energy. The ancients used to talk in terms of beautiful similes, metaphors and figures of speech.. Accepting the metaphor of a sleeping serpent they described this energy of potential perfection by the word *kundalini* that means "the coiled-up one," as stated earlier. When a serpent is in a state of inertia, its coils itself up. So the term "*Kundalini Shakti,*" translated as "the serpent power," is only a metaphorical expression. It symbolizes the potential energy or power.

Microcosm and Macrocosm

According to Tantric philosophy, a human being is a miniature universe or a microcosm of the macro-cosmic universe. The principles that govern the universe also govern every individual. Thus, the human microcosm contains all of the constituents of the external world: earth, water, fire, air and space. The system of Tantra emphasizes the subtle connections between the external universe and the human microcosm.

Kundalini—The Highest Energy

Kundalini is the highest manifestation of consciousness in the body. It represents the creative force of the world as manifested in human beings. Kundalini is a creative energy in a static state. It embodies all powers and all forms. It is the center for all manifestations of energy. All forms emanate from this source, traverse the whole body and then return to it, just as electricity runs out of the positive pole of a battery and returns to it by way of the negative pole.

Kundalini is said to be the origin of the three *Gunas*: *Sattva*, *Rajas* and *Tamas*. (*See* 1.9 Three *Gunas*, *above*). It is the fountainhead of energy and knowledge. From the seat of Kundalini arise the *vayus* (the energies within the body), *bindu* (the seed of life), and *nadha* (sound), the very source of speech. Kundalini is not an object of visualization, but a most subtle entity as light. Just as all the powers of this universe exist in God, so do all the powers of the individual exist in Kundalini.

Manifest Energy

This has three aspects: neutral, centripetal (toward center), and centrifugal (away from the center). In the nervous system, centripetal currents are called sensory or afferent currents, and the centrifugal currents are called motor or efferent currents. These currents exist in their neutral state in Kundalini at the *Muladhara Chakra*. Nutrition and oxygen are taken into the body by the centripetal currents; carbon dioxide and other wastes are expelled by the centrifugal currents.

In the system of Tantra the human body is seen as a reservoir with vast quantities of energy that are not used for maintaining human life. It is this untapped energy that is symbolized as the serpent, Kundalini, resting in her abode at the base of the spinal column. This energy is the static support of the entire body and all its pranic energies. It is the Divine force for the body, evolved from the energy of Shakti. Pranic energy is more subtle than electrical energy. (*See* 3.8 *Pranayama: Prana*–The Vital Force, *above*).

The vital force of Shakti in the body is organized around specific centers called *Chakra*s

Chakras

The *Chakra*s are psychic centers located in the various parts of *Sushumna* nadi. In order to understand the spiritual evolution and transformation of the Yoga practitioner, it is important to understand the *Chakra*s fully, since the energy focused in the *Chakra*s determines the personality and level of awareness of the individual. As the practitioner evolves, his personality becomes gradually more refined and purified.

1. *Muladhara Chakra.* This *Chakra* is at the perineum, base of the spinal column, between the genitals and the anus. This is the location of the mouth or opening of *Sushumna.* The *kanda* or root from which all the subtle nadis originate is found here, and *Sushumna* nadi comes out of the kanda. This *Chakra* is *muladhara*, the root support *Chakra. Muladhara* is the earth region and is represented by a square surrounded by four lotus petals at the four corners of the square. These petals symbolize four *vrittis* (manifestations). The *bija* (seed sound vibration) of this *Chakra* is *lam.* The yellow color and the sense of smell are the manifestations of *Muladhara Chakra*. This center is related to the instinct for survival. Until one gains mastery over this *Chakra*, insecurity, fear, and paranoia are the major emotions and attitudes associated with it. The terror of total annihilation disturbs one at this level and colors his view of the world. Anyone whose level of awareness is focused at this center sees the world as a jungle where he needs to fight for his very existence.

2. *Svadhisthana Chakra.* This is situated in the section of the vertebral corresponding to the genital area. This location is about half-way between the navel and sex organ. *Svadhisthana* means "her own abode." This is the center of Kundalini's original abode, before she became intoxicated and fell down to the *Muladhara Chakra*, where she is said to lie in a coiled, dormant state. This *Chakra* has six petals whose color is vermilion. These petals represent the six *vrittis* of indulgence, absence of empathy, destructiveness, delusion, disdain and suspicion. The *bija* of this *Chakra* is *vam.* It is responsible for the sense of taste. One whose energy is manifested from this *Chakra* views the world from the perspective of lust, sexual pleasure and repression. The Tantric texts say that one who achieves mastery over this *Chakra* is free from all enemies and becomes like the sun, removing the darkness of ignorance with his light. His words flow like nectar in expressing the wealth of his wisdom.

3. *Manipura Chakra.* This *Chakra* is located in that part of the vertebral column corresponding to the solar plexus. *Manipura* means "filled with jewels." There are ten lotus petals at *Manipura*

indicating the following *vrittis*: Spiritual ignorance, treachery, jealousy, shame, delusion, disgust, fear, foolishness, discontent, and sadness. At the center of *Manipura* is a triangle with the color of fire. Its root sound is *ram*. The sense of sight arises from this *Chakra*. This center determines the assimilation of food. This is the center of the ego. It brings out one's concern with power, competition, domination, aggression and passivity. Integration at this level leads to assertiveness, cooperation and dynamic energy.

4. *Anahata Chakra*. This is located between the breasts in the region of the heart. *Anahata* means "unstuck sound." By intense Concentration at this *Chakra*, one may hear the sound of bells within. This *Chakra* divides the body into two parts: the upper and the lower. Three centers in the lower part represent the primitive expression of consciousness. They are concerned with sensual desires and negative emotions. But when consciousness rises above the horizon of the diaphragm, one becomes truly human, and higher consciousness dawns.

Anahata is a center of equilibrium. It is symbolized by a twelve-petaled lotus. Its *bija* is *yam*. Its color is smoky gray. It is related to the element air, and the sense of touch. It is the center from which one feels unconditional love toward others, and seeks to offer service. Compassion, selfless love and empathy are the attributes of this *Chakra*.

5. *Vishuddha Chakra*. This *Chakra* is located at the hollow of the throat. *Vishuddha* means "purified." It has sixteen lotus petals. Each contains one of the sixteen vowel sounds of the Sanskrit alphabet. This *Chakra* is connected with the element of *akasa*. Its color is blue and its root sound is *ham*. It controls the sense of hearing. It is the seat of receptivity and creativity. It generates the qualities of devotion, surrender, trust and willingness.

6. *Ajna Chakra*. This is located at the space between the eyebrows at the "third eye" within the *Sushumna*. *Ajna* means "all-knowing." This center is the terminal of *Ida*, *Pingala* and *Sushumna*. The qualities of introspection and discriminative intellect are related to this center. One who has mastered this level has inner vision, and acquires higher intuitive knowledge and wisdom.

This *Chakra*'s *mantra* is OM.

Meditation on *Vishuddha* and *Ajna* awakens spirituality and leads one to obtain the experiences of the inner world.

7. *Sahasrara Chakra.* This is located at the crown of the head, *brahmarandhra.* It is the seat of pure Consciousness. *Sahasrara* means the thousand petaled lotus. This is the abode of Shiva, pure Consciousness. One who has attained this level is in a state of *Samadhi*. Here the individual Self and the Cosmic Self merge.

Chakras and States of Consciousness

The two lowest centers–*Muladhara* and *Svadhishthana Chakra*s–may be grouped together and they represent the most primitive states of consciousness that are most closely tied to the physical world. The *Muladhara* is the base where all our past *samskaras* or experiences rest. If one can gain absolute control over this center, one will be able to remember everything concerning his previous lives. The second center *Svadhisthana* is the home of the lower self. It is the source of all our animal tendencies. Both these two centers are linked to the basic instincts for the survival of the individual and of the species. When energy is focused in these centers, pure Consciousness is obscured and the individual identifies himself with the grossest material plane of existence. These *Chakra*s have the quality of *tamas*.

The third *Chakra*, *Manipura*, marks the climax of all material enjoyment, power, name, fame, prosperity and the like. It thus represents the worldly level of consciousness. There is a focus on egoism. The predominant characteristic is *rajasic guna*. Until a Yogi has transcended the *Manipura*, a natural downward current is trying to press the light of Kundalini to the base again. He is not secure until he is able to rise above this center.

The fourth *Chakra*, *Anahata*, is the middle one. When the Yogi comes to this stage of unfoldment, he becomes spiritual. He manifests selfless love, friendship, forgiveness, peace, and fellowship to all beings.

The fifth *Chakra–Vishuddha* – represents a movement away from worldly relationships to a world of purity. One who is operating at this level exhibits pure goodness, pure truth, creativity, intuition and wisdom. His quality is predominantly *sattvic.*

The *Ajna*, the sixth center, is the stage of manifesting absolute knowledge. The Yogi enjoys absolute freedom, satisfaction and bliss in this state of unfoldment.

The seventh and highest *Chakra*, the *Sahasrara Chakra* is the seat of pure Consciousness, the abode of Shiva. One who operates at this level is a realized Yogi. He becomes One with Brahman, the ultimate Reality.(*See* next Chapter for further details).

4.17: Awakening Kundalini

Introduction

In the previous Chapter we have discussed the philosophical basis of Kundalini Yoga and the *Chakra*s through which Kundalini has to be channeled upward.

Now let us discuss the awakening of Kundalini and its scientific basis. Ordinarily, Shiva and Shakti are separated, with Shiva residing at the crown of the head, and Shakti (Kundalini) residing dormant at the base of the spine. Only a small part of the energy of Shakti functions in the *Chakra*s and nadis in order to maintain the ordinary functions of the ordinary individual. The rest of this energy remains in a potential form. Human beings remain unaware of this vast reservoir of energy. Those who are capable of transforming Kundalini from its latent to its active stage become super beings. This transformation is possible only after awakening the Kundalini by intense practice of Yoga under the guidance of a realized *Guru*.

When the Kundalini awakens the Yogi feels a unique and soothing heat and light at the base of his spine. The awakened Kundalini is then made to travel upwards by means of a highly symbolic form of Meditation (*See* The next sub-heading in this Chapter), which unfolds higher and higher spiritual qualities in the Yogi.

This process of unfolding the higher qualities has been symbolized as the blooming of the lotus flowers. As the light of the Kundalini travels upwards through the *Sushumna* it touches and illumines the different psychic centers or *Chakra*s that are symbolized in the form of lotuses. Before the rise of the light of the Kundalini all these lotuses remain drooping-heads down and wilted. But as soon as the light of the Kundalini touches a lotus, it straightens up and attains full bloom and beauty. Thus, the light of the Kundalini proceeds higher and higher making the lotuses of *Chakras* to bloom, and finally reaches the Superconscious plane. This is symbolized by a thousand-petalled lotus located in the brain center. This is conceived as an Ocean of Infinite Light, Knowledge, Existence and Bliss. The little light of the Kundalini, moving all the way up, becomes merged in that Infinite Ocean of Light in the thousand-petalled lotus. This merger marks the attainment of the highest state of *Samadhi* or Superconscious State.

Physiological Basis

Let us examine the awakening of Kundalini in terms of modern Physiology. Physiology shows that the nerve center, which regulates the breathing system, has a controlling action over the whole system of nerve currents. Now we can see why rhythmical breathing is practiced. In the first place, from it comes a tendency of all the molecules in the body to move in the same direction. When the mind becomes one-pointed and is thus transformed into a strong will, the nerve currents too change into a motion similar to electricity. Therefore when all the motions of the body have become perfectly rhythmical, the body becomes a gigantic battery of will. This tremendous will is exactly what the Yogi wants to acquire. This is the physiological basis of *Pranayama*. It brings a rhythmic action on the body and helps us, through the respiratory center, to control the other centers. The aim of *Pranayama* is to awaken the coiled-up power of Kundalini in the *Muladhara*.

Everything that we see or imagine or dream is perceived in space. This is the ordinary physical space called the *Mahakasa*. When a Yogi reads the thoughts of other persons or perceives supersensuous objects, he sees them in another space called the *Chitakasa,* the mental space. When perception has become objectless and the soul shines in its own nature, it is called the *Chidakasa* or Knowledge space. When the Kundalini is aroused and enters the canal of the *Sushumna*, all the perceptions are in the mental space. When it reaches the other end of the canal, the perception becomes objectless and it is in the Knowledge space.

Just as electric current flows through a wire, so also all the sensations and motions of the body are being sent into the brain, and sent out of it, through the nerve fibers. The columns of the sensory and motor fibers in the spinal cord are the *Ida* and *Pingala* of the Yoga Science. They are the main channels through which the afferent and efferent currents travel. But why should not the mind send news without any nerve? The Yoga Science says that if you can do that you have gotten rid of the bondage of matter. How can you do it? This is done by making the current pass through the *Sushumna* without any nerve fiber to act as wires. Then alone there would be no more bondage of the body and all knowledge would come to us. The *Sushumna* canal is, in ordinary persons, closed up at the lower end. By practicing Kundalini Yoga, it is opened and the energy is made to travel through it.

When a sensation is carried to a brain center, the center reacts. This reaction in an automatic center is followed by motion; in the conscious center it is followed first by perception, and second by motion. All perception is the reaction to action from outside. How then, do perceptions arise in dreams? There is then no action from outside. The sensations must therefore have been coiled up somewhere. For instance, I see a city. The perception of that city is from my reaction to the sensations brought from outside objects comprising that city. Even after a long time I can remember the city. Dreams are exactly the same phenomena, only in a milder form. But whence is the action that brings about the milder form of similar vibrations in the brain? Certainly not from the primary sensations. Therefore the sensations might have been coiled up somewhere and their action brings out the mild reaction that we call dream perception.

The center where all these residual sensations are, as it were, stored up, is *Muladara* and the coiled-up energy is Kundalini. It is very probable that the residual motor energy is also stored up in the same center, since, after deep study or Meditation the part of the body where the *Muladhara* center is located – probably the sacral plexus–becomes heated. Now, if this coiled-up energy is aroused and made active and then consciously made to travel up the *Sushumna* canal, as it acts upon center after center, a tremendous reaction will set in. When a minute portion of the energy travels along a nerve fiber and causes a reaction from the centers, the perception is either dream or imagination. But when by the power of long internal Meditation, the vast mass of stored-up energy travels along the *Sushumna* and strikes the centers, then there is supersensual perception. When it reaches brain, the region of all sensations, the whole brain reacts, and the result is the full blaze of illumination, the perception of the Self.

Thus the awakening of the Kundalini is the only way to the attaining of Divine wisdom, Superconsciousness or Realization of the Self or the Spirit. The awakening may come in various ways: through Meditation, devotion to God or the power of the analytic will. All worship, consciously or unconsciously, leads to this end. The devotee who thinks that he is receiving a response to his prayers does not know that the fulfillment comes from his own Self by waking up a bit of the coiled-up power within himself. Thus what people worship under various names is the Real power coiled-up in every being, the Mother of eternal happiness.

Prerequisites

The practitioners of Yoga are warned not to arouse the Kundalini prematurely. Just as fruits should ripen naturally, Kundalini should awaken naturally. It is the Divine power within you. It seems to be sleeping, but it is waiting to make use of you when you are ready. So instead of trying to handle God's power, let God handle you when you are ready. That should be your approach to Yoga. Refine yourself and when you are ready, the Kundalini energy will awaken by itself. If you try to arouse it prematurely when you are still impure, you will ruin yourself. Self-purification is a pre-requirement. It is imperative to adhere to the rules of *Yama* and *Niyama*, the Yogic "Commandments" and purify the mind. (*See* 3.4 *Yama* and 3.5 *Niyama, above*). Yogic practice to arouse the Kundalini should be practiced only under the guidance of a realized *Guru*. One who has not purified his mind and has not become selfless will bring harm to himself and others if he attempts to misuse this highest spiritual energy for his own material or egoistic goals. A competent *Guru* will not encourage the student to develop psychic powers because they are only side paths. Pursuing powers as goals drakes him off the main path of Enlightenment. Kundalini awakens naturally, when you become pure and thus become ready. Then you will become a wonderful instrument in the hands of God. You will become free from ego and selfishness. You will become a universal person, a friend to everyone. You will see the whole world as your family and as God's manifestation.

Preparation for Awakening Kundalini

The Tantric tradition is highly systematized and organized. It is imperative that the student should systematically follow the basic instructions and master the preliminary practices before the teacher can lead him to more advanced practices. Otherwise the student would only harm himself mentally, physically and emotionally.

First, the student must work with his physical body to achieve sound health and maintain it. He should practice Hatha Yoga and *Pranayama*. Hatha Yoga activates the various glands and purifies the nadis. *Pranayama* makes the mind calm.

He must overcome laziness and develop the ability to regulate his habits so that the body does not become a barrier to his progress. He should avoid extremes in food, sleep and work to keep the body balanced and healthy. Some misguided students have the wrong idea that drugs can lead one to Enlightenment. The use of drugs is dangerous and harmful to health.

Next, the student must cultivate virtues like faith, devotion, humility, purity, dispassion, discrimination, compassion, serenity, self-control, fearlessness, patience, perseverance so that selfishness, pettiness and egoism do not hold him back on the path. He must purify his heart through selfless service and devotion to God.

The student must cultivate faithfulness and determination. Many students begin their practices and soon become impatient. They either abandon their practices, jump from one practice to another, or change their path. Such unsteadiness will not allow them to progress. Some students think that if they do not get extraordinary experiences, their *mantra* must be wrong or that there could be a better teacher or practice. They seek a new *mantra* or a new teacher. Such students will make no progress. Some do not practice regularly; yet they expect extraordinary experiences to be dawn.

Most of the students today expect to have their Kundalini awakened by *Gurus* rather than through their own efforts. Some claim that their Kundalini was raised by a teacher's gaze, touch or grace. Such students mistake the body's shakiness, jerks or other movements that indicate physical or emotional imbalances, for the movements of Kundalini. Emotional reactions and hallucinations are also mistaken for valid experiences.

To genuinely awaken Kundalini one must prepare oneself, and then patiently and with faithfulness and determination do one's practices. Then only one can progress. A number of specific methods have been developed to help the students to awaken the sleeping Kundalini energy. The *Guru* selects the method appropriate for each student according to the student's capacities, inclinations and level of attainment.

Without sustained practice in purifying oneself and strengthening one's capacity to assimilate such a flood of energy, the awakening of this latent power would deeply disturb, disorient, and cause serious damages to him. Therefore one should purify and strengthen oneself. Then only one will be prepared to face the full awakening of all that is latent within him.

Kundalini Awakening

Kundalini can be awakened by various methods. Raja Yogis awaken Kundalini by the practice of Concentration and Meditation, and *Mantra Japa*. Devotees awaken it by devotion; Jnanis or the followers of the path of Wisdom awaken it by intuition brought about by reasoning and inquiry; and Karma Yogis by the selfless service to humanity.

The methods to be practiced have been described in Tantra texts, *Cheranda Samhita* and *Hatha Yoga Pradipika*.

When Kundalini is aroused through intense Yoga practices, it travels up through the Psychic Centers (*Chakra*s) in successive stages and finally reaches the seventh *Chakra* at the crown of the head. As it reaches the higher *Chakra*s, it produces various degrees of enlightenment.

When the mind is attached to worldliness, it dwells in the three lower centers – at the naval, the reproductive organ and the organ of evacuation. These centers have animalistic tendencies that pull you down. The mind then has no higher spiritual ambitions or visions. It is immersed in the cravings of lust and greed. If the Kundalini rises by itself, it will pass through the lower centers and come to the heart center right away.

The fourth center is at the heart. When the mind learns to dwell there, one experiences his first spiritual awakening. Then he has the vision of light all around. Seeing this Divine light, he becomes filled with wonder and says, "Ah, how blissful!" His mind does not then run to the lower centers.

The fifth center is at the throat. One, whose mind has reached this center is freed from ignorance and delusion. He does not enjoy hearing or talking of anything but God.

When the Kundalini reaches the sixth center at the center of the head, there is the direct vision of God, day and night. Even then, there is a little trace of ego left in the aspirant. It is like a light in a lantern; one feels as if one could touch the light, but cannot, because of the obstructing pane of glass.

The seventh center is at the top of the head. When the Kundalini energy reaches it, *Samadhi* is attained. One becomes a knower of Brahman, united with Brahman.

Meditation for Attaining the Superconscious State

The technique of Meditation for this purpose is:

- Sit on your regular Meditation seat, in the correct posture. Practice alternate nostril *Pranayama* exercise. Visualize a luminous channel *Sushumna* running all the way from the base of the spine to the crown of the head.
- Feel that by Divine grace, by means of your breathing exercise and by the power of your thought, the passage to *Sushumna*

at the base of the spine has been opened and a stream of spiritual energy (Kundalini) is flowing upward into it from the U-shaped conduit, formed by the junction of the *Ida* and the *Pingala*. This energy flow takes the form of a small, white soothing light like flame of a candle. This light is slowly traveling upwards through the channel of the *Sushumna*.

- The light touches and illumines the lotus of the first center of the *Muladhara*. Then its drooped lotus bud straightens up and opens its beautiful four petals in brilliant red color.
- Next visualize the light of the Kundalini traveling further up, gently and reaches the next *Chakra Svadhisthana*. The light touches and illumines the lotus bud of this center. The bud blooms, and its six petals open up, in vermilion color.
- The light travels upwards to the *Manipura* center at the navel. It illumines its ten-petalled lotus, scarlet in color.
- The light then proceeds upwards to the *Anahata* center in the heart region. There it touches and illumines the twelve-petalled lotus that is unfolded in brilliant blue, manifesting wonderful spiritual qualities in you.
- Next the light goes to the *Vishuddha* center and touches its lotus, which opens and shows its sixteen petals in gray color, manifesting marvelous spiritual qualities in you.
- Then the light travels up and touches the *Ajna* center at the center of the head. The two-petalled lotus of this center stands up, emanating effulgent light of white color. With the unfoldment of higher state of Consciousness you feel the supreme bliss and experience the Reality, knowing which nothing else is to be known. But still the subject-object awareness remains.
- Finally, the light of the Kundalini travels still higher and leaves the channel of the *Sushumna* and enters *Sahasrara* center at the brain. Its thousand-petalled lotus symbolizes the transcendental state of Absolute Existence-Knowledge-Bliss (*Satchidananda*). Visualize this state as an Ocean of cool light, brilliant and effulgent. The light of Kundalini becomes One with the Ocean of Infinite Light.

When you reach this point in Meditation, you transcend your ego, your body, your mind and all pairs of opposites. Then you are free from the cycle of births and deaths and suffering.

The symbols of lotus centers stand for the different levels of consciousness through which the soul passes on in its journey towards the Infinite Perfection. This is the state of *Nirvikalpa Samadhi*, which cannot be described, but can only be experienced.

4.18: Samadhi: Meaning and Kinds

Meaning

Concentration culminates in Meditation, and Meditation in *Samadhi*. When Meditation reaches its intensity, the mind is completely absorbed in the object of Meditation. It identifies itself with the object. This is *Samadhi*. *Samadhi* means absorption. According to Raja Yoga, when the individual consciousness expands itself to become the universal consciousness, when *jiva* becomes *Purusha*, then the word *Samadhi* is used. It is a state beyond thought, word and action.

In other Schools of Meditation, the word *Samadhi* is not used. In the Meditative School of Buddhism, the word *Nirvana*, which means "nakedness" is used to describe the highest state of consciousness; through negation one experiences a void or "nakedness."

The School of Vedanta or Advaita Philosophy defines something beyond *Nirvana* as *Sakshatkara*, the highest state. This is comparable to the *Samadhi* of Raja Yoga.

Characteristics

Just as the pure crystal assumes the color of the object placed near it, so the mind, when it is cleared of thought waves, achieves identity with the object of its Concentration. This state of knower, knowable and knowledge becoming One is *Samadhi* (*Yoga Sutras*, 1.41). In the state of *Samadhi*, the meditator, the mind and meditated become One. The mind loses its awareness and becomes identical with the object of Meditation.

Samadhi is not a state that can be obtained easily, but if a Yogi achieves it, he experiences the all-pervading Atman or Superconsciousness. In this state the senses, mind and intellect cease to function. In the *Bhagavad Gita,* Lord Krishna says, "When the perfectly controlled mind rests in the Self only, free from longing for the objects of desires, then it is said, 'the Yogi is united' (That is, he has become One with Brahman)." (6.18)

Just as a river, which merges into the sea, does lose its name and form and becomes one with the sea, so does the meditator's soul merge into the Supreme Spirit, and all limitations disappear. In *Samadhi*, there is neither seeing nor hearing, there is neither physical nor mental awareness. There is only spiritual or Superconsciousness. There is only Existence (*Sat*). When the mind melts in Brahman, there is no mind, and no body-consciousness, but Brahman alone exists.

It is complete realization of the Atman. The Atman is experienced as total existence, consciousness and joy. In this experience, all sense of individual separateness and differentiation is lost. In Shankaracharya's *Crest Jewel of Discrimination*, the disciple who has reached *Samadhi* exclaims: "My mind fell like a hailstone into that vast expanse of Brahman's Ocean. Touching one drop of it, I melted away and became one with Brahman. Now, though I return to human consciousness, I abide in the joy of the Atman. Where is this universe? Who took it away? Has it merged into something else? A while ago, I beheld it; now it exists no longer. This is wonderful indeed! Here is the Ocean of Brahman, full of endless joy. How can I accept or reject anything? Is there anything apart or distinct from Brahman? Now, finally and clearly, I know that I am the Atman, whose nature is eternal joy. I see nothing, I know nothing that is separate from me."

When a Yogi comes out of *Samadhi*, he returns to consciousness of the objective universe, but this consciousness differs from that we all experience. To him the external world is a mere appearance. In Shankaracharya's words, "It is and is not." He no longer identifies the external world with the Atman. He sees it only as a reflection of the Atman like an image in a mirror, since it is projected by the Reality.

Samadhi is different from the first three states of consciousness: waking, dreaming and sleeping. It is the fourth state called *Turiya*, where there is no play of mind. It is a state of absolute or pure Consciousness that baffles all attempts at description. It is the final goal of all beings. It is Liberation or Freedom from all Suffering.

Samadhi is not a state of forgetfulness. There is perfect awareness, Awareness of the Atman, the Spirit itself, that is beyond perception, beyond thought, beyond description. It is the end of evolution. It is eternal peace and bliss. The Yogi becomes one with *Satchidananda* (Existence- Knowledge-Bliss).

Samadhi is not a stone-like inert state as many people imagine. A life in the Spirit (Atman) is not annihilation. When the limitations of the empirical existence are transcended, the Cosmic life is intensified and the Yogi has enrichment of Self. He will have a richer inner life, and expanded Cosmic life.

Some people think that any form of quietness of the mind or trance is *Samadhi*, but that has nothing to do with *Samadhi*. Trance is a state of mental inactivity; it is a torpid (*tamasika*) state. Mere cessation of mental activity is, therefore, not *Samadhi*. It would be *Samadhi*, only if mental activity could be stopped at will and the mind could be fixed intently on the object of Concentration. In ordinary trance, the mind is not voluntarily fixed on any of the above. As a result of anesthesia, the mind appears also to have reached a state of inactivity, but it is a state of unconsciousness. Hysteria and other similar mental diseases are of the same nature. These are involuntary and torpid states, while *Samadhi* is a voluntary and conscious state.

Kinds of Samadhi

Samadhi is of two kinds: (a) *Samprajnata* or *Savikalpa* (with form) and (b) *Asamprajnata* or *Nirvikalpa* (without form). (*Yoga Sutras*, 1.14). According to the nature of the object used for Concentration, *Samprajanata Samadhi* is subdivided into four forms: (1) *Savitarka Samadhi*, (2) *Savichara Samadhi*, (3) *Sananda Samadhi*, (4) *Sasmita Samadhi*. As against *Savitarka Samadhi*, there is (5) *Nirvitarka Samadhi*. Similarly, as against

Savichara Samadhi, there is (6) *Nirvichara Samadhi*. All these are Samadhis with seed (*sabiji*). *Asamprajnata Samàdhi* is *Samadhi* without seed or form. Thus the different kinds of *Samadhis* are:

1. *Samprajnata* (or *Sabija*) *Samadhi*
2. *Savitarka Samadhi*
3. *Nirvitarka Samadhi*
4. *Savichara Samadhi*
5. *Nirvichara Samadhi*
6. *Sananda Samadhi*
7. *Sasmita Samadhi*
8. *Asamprajnata* (or *Nirbija*) *Samadhi*

Let us examine the meaning of each of the above kinds of *Samadhis*.

Samprajnata Samadhi. This is attained during Meditation when the mind is cut off completely from the physical world and fixed on the object of Meditation. This is a state of intensive concentration on one thing, gross or subtle. The object of Meditation may be gross (like a flower or the symbol of one's Chosen Deity), or subtle or blissful feeling or pure "I"-sense. Whatever may be the object on which mind is concentrated, the main characteristic of *Samprajnata* Samadhi is that it perpetuates duality in the mind, namely, the meditator apart from the object of Meditation; the mind does not completely merge in the Self.

To attain this *Samadhi* the Kundalini must rise up fully from *Muladhara Chakra* and reach the *Ajna Chakra* at the head-center, and its movement lies between the *Visuddha Chakra* and the *Ajna Chakra*.

In *Samprajnata Samadhi* there is content of the mind (*pratyaya*), the buried seeds of desires and attachments. They can still come into the conscious mind when the proper opportunity arises, and pull the Yogi into worldly experience. Therefore *Samprajnata Samadhi* is also known as *Sabija Samadhi* or *Samadhi* with seed or *Savikalpa Samadhi*. Hence this is not the highest form of Samdhi. From *Ajna Chakra*, the Kundalini must be channeled into *Sahasrara Chakra*. It is only when It reaches *Sahasrara* and reunites with Shiva that *Asamprajnata Samadhi* is attained.

If one takes some finite thing as the object of Concentration and goes into *Samadhi* in his Meditation, it is a lower *Samadhi*; it reveals, says Patanjali, the truth about that object. But it is not a higher form of *Samadhi* and does not reveal the ultimate truth, the Cosmic Consciousness. Professor Yukawa, the Japanese physicist who won the Nobel prize for physics for his prediction of the particle called the meson, said that the new idea came to him when he was alone, late at night and he had passed into a state of Meditation on the problem. Newton, too, passed into Meditation state in which he was totally insensible to the world around him. Many artists speak of such experiences as the source of their inspiration.

But Patanjali makes it clear that Meditation on anything finite will not give release from the illusions and the consequent sufferings of worldly life. The attachment to any worldly success that may come as a result of the lower *Samadhi* strengthens the bonds of ignorance, and then it will become increasingly difficult to throw them off and enter again into *Samadhi*.

Savitarka Samadhi. This is reached by meditating upon a gross object with awareness of its name, form and knowledge. (*Yoga Sutras*, 1.42). This is the lowest kind of *Samprajnata* Samadhi.

All our ordinary awareness is a combination of name, form and knowledge. For example, when we look at a chair, we are aware of (1) the name of the object (chair), (2) its form (size, shape, color, etc.) and (3) our own knowledge of the object. Through intense Concentration we may become identified with the chair. Yet we retain a mixture of name, form and knowledge in the mind.

Nirvitkara Samadhi. This is entered into when one meditates upon a gross object without awareness of its name, form and knowledge. There is awareness of the object only, but nothing is known about it. (*Yoga Sutras*, 143): This is a higher state of Samadhi.

It is the uncontrolled function of memory that leads to mental imagination. Memory links an object with time, space and other associations. By attaining success in *Savitarka Samadhi,* a Yogi is able to enter into meditation on the object without being distracted by its name and associated ideas. At this stage the mind, being pure like a crystal, becomes so colored by the object that it seems to have no existence in itself.

Savichara Samadhi. This is reached when a Yogi enters the subtle state meditating upon a subtle element of space, air, fire, water or earth with awareness of its name, form and knowledge (*Yoga Sutras,* 1.44). Meditative analysis is its special feature.

Nirvichara Samadhi. A Yogi attains this Samadhi by meditating upon a subtle element without awareness of its name, form and knowledge. Then his mind identifies itself without any distortion caused by imagination or memory. (*Yoga Sutras,* 1.44).

Sananda Samadhi. This is a blissful Samadhi. When *Nirvichara Samadhi* becomes intensified, the Yogi's mind ascends from the gross and subtle planes to the subtler plane of ego-principle. Then the thought of I am (*Aham Asmi*) alone shines, and his Samadhi becomes extremely joyous. Through a special kind of Pranayama, the body becomes calm when a feeling of bliss pervades the body. If Concentration is focused on that feeling alone, a feeling of bliss pervades all the sense-organs.

Sasmita Samadhi. With increasing purity of the mind-stuff, a Yogi goes beyond the ego-center and discovers the ego's causal plane. Then the Samadhi is called *Sasmita Samadhi,* i.e., Samadhi pertaining to the source of ego, namely the Cosmic mind or *Mahat.* This is a state of pure I-sense (*Asmita*) or the state of pure *chitta* illumined by the consciousness containing the seed of ego principle. In this state the mind becomes luminous, because the impurities of *rajas* and *tamas* have been removed.

There is no trace of illusion or ignorance at this point.

As a result of success in *Sasmita Samadhi,* the Yogi attains intuitive vision which reveals the Self to be distinct from the *Chitta.* This intuitive vision enables him to develop dispassion even towards the purified state of the *Chitta.* This is known as supreme dispassion (*Para Vairagya*). With the fullness of intuitional knowledge, the

Yogi discovers the nature of the Self. Then the intuitive intellect (*Prajna*) of the Yogi becomes filled with the Truth (*Ritambhara*) (*Yoga Sutras,* 1.48). *Rita* and *Satya* are synonyms, but there is a little difference between the two; *Satya* is the conceptual fact, while *Rita* is the perceptual fact. The term "*Rita*" has been used to indicate the direct realization of Truth.

Intuitional knowledge (*Ritambhara Prajna*) surpasses all knowledge of the world. This wisdom is totally different from the knowledge gained by inference and study of scriptures. (*Yoga Sutras*,1.49). Patanjali makes a distinction between wisdom obtained by direct Superconscious experience and the knowledge gained by study of scriptures. The scriptures can teach us about the existence and glory of God. But we cannot claim to know God. God can be experienced only when we transcend the mind. Mind cannot understand God, because mind is matter, and matter cannot understand something more subtle than itself. We can realize God only when we transcend the mind through non-reflective Samadhi. "Realization", says Swami Vivekananda, "is real religion, all the rest is only preparation – hearing lectures or reading books or reasoning is merely preparing the ground; it is not religion." Religion is, in fact, a severe practical and empirical research. You accept nothing but your own experience.

Sabija Samadhi. The six *Samprajnata Samadhis* are all within the realm of phenomenal world, and they are called *Sabija Samadhis* or Samadhis with a seed, which could bring one back into bondage or mental disturbance (*Yoga Sutras*, 1.46). Those Samadhis are only preparations for the highest state of experience of Brahman. In this connection, Baghavan Sri Ramakrishna used to tell a parable:

A disciple once came to a teacher to learn to meditate on God. The teacher gave him instructions, but the disciple soon returned and said that he could not carry them out; every time he tried to meditate, he found himself thinking about his pet buffalo. "Well then", said the teacher, "you meditate on that buffalo you're so fond of." The disciple shut himself up in a room and began to concentrate on the buffalo. After some days, the teacher knocked at his door, and the disciple answered: "Sir, I am sorry I can't come out to greet you. This door is too small. My horns will be in the way." Then the teacher smiled and said, "Splendid! You have become identified with the object of your Concentration. Now fix the Concentration upon God and you will easily succeed."

If the seeds of desire and attachment still remain within the mind, they are dangerous, for they can germinate at any time so long as you have not completely purified the mind. That is why an aspirant should first purify his mind before he practices deep Meditation.

Even the so called scientific discoveries and inventions are the result of Concentration. The scientists meditated on the gross elements, and discovered many things, created many instruments and machines, and we are enjoying the benefits. They had gone deeper and deeper and ultimately gone into the atom itself. They have discovered the secret of the atom, but what is happening now with that secret? It has become a terrifying force. Is there anything wrong with the atomic energy? Nothing. We cannot blame it. What else has to be blamed? The minds of the people who use that force. If we go into the secrets of the universe and gain control over them, we should have pure minds to make the proper use of them. Otherwise we will bring destruction on the entire humanity. The purification of mind is, therefore, indispensable.

Nirbija or Asamprajnata Samadhi. How is the final stage reached? Patanjali explains this. The sublime impression produced by intuitive intellect (*Ritambhara Prajna*) wipes out all other impressions (*Samskaras*). (*Yoga Sutras,* 1.50). When even this impression is wiped out through the development of supreme dispassion (*Para Vairagya*), all thought-waves or impressions in the mind disappear, then one enters *Nirbija* (seedless) *Samadhi,* which puts an end to the seed of the world-process. (*Yoga Sutras* 1.51). Even with the pure knowledge(*Ritambhara Prajna*) gained through proficiency in *Nirvichara,* the subtle mind exists. Even the feeling "I have realized God" should go. Then only the Yogi is totally free and attains *Nirbija Samadhi.* It leads him to Liberation. This is the highest experience. The Yogi is established in his *svarupa* (real nature), consciousness of the Self (*Purusha*). It may take one life or many lives for reaching this goal, depending upon the advancement of the Yogi.

The States of the Mind and Samadhi

There are **five** states of the mind. The mind is constituted by the three *Gunas*: *sattva*, *rajas* and *tamas*. The different proportions in which these *gunas* are present and operative in the mind determine different states of the mind. These states are: restless (*ksipta*), torpid (*mudha*), distracted (*viksipta*), concentrated (*ekagra*) and restrained (*niruddha*). In each of these, there is some kind of repression of mental modifications. Yoga cannot be attained in the first three states of the mind.

In the first state of restlessness the mind is dominated by *rajas* and *tamas*, and it is attracted by the sense-objects and the means of attaining power. It jumps from one thing to another like a restless monkey. This condition is not at all conducive to Yoga, because it is difficult to focus the restless mind on the selected object of Concentration.

The next state of torpidity is due to the predominance of *tamas*, and so the mind has a tendency towards vice, ignorance, sleep and the like. In the third condition of distracted state, the mind is free from the sway of *tamas* and has only a touch of *rajas* in it. It has the capacity of manifesting virtue, knowledge and so on. This is a stage of temporary Concentration of the mind on an object, followed by distraction. But the mind is not free from ignorance and other afflictions.

In the next state of concentrated mind, the impurity of *rajas* is purged and *sattva* predominates. It marks the beginning of prolonged Concentration of the mind on any object so as to reveal its true nature. When the mind continues to meditate on an object, it assumes the form of the object. This state is called *Samprajnata Samadhi*. Even in this state the mental processes are not altogether arrested.

In the last level of the restrained state, there is cessation of all mental functions and the mind rests in its original state of calmness and tranquility. This state is called *Asamprajnata Samadhi.* In this state the whole world of objects cease to exist for the Yogi, and the Self abides in its own essence as pure Consciousness. It requires a long and arduous practice of Yoga to maintain oneself steadily in this state.

Nirvikalpa Samadhi. Asamprajnata Samadhi is called *Nirvikalpa* in the Vedanta System of Philosophy. "*Nirvikalpa*" means "without alternatives." This *Samadhi* is seedless, because it is nothing but pure, undifferentiated Consciousness; it contains no phenomenal impressions, no seeds of desire and attachment. The Jnani dwells on the Truth that 'Atman is Brahman' or on his own pure Awareness, emptying the mind of all ideas. Brahman is not "an object of Concentration." In Brahman, the knower and the known become One. The Yogi becomes one with Brahman; he attains Liberation, Immortality at once. There is no more birth or death for him. "*Nirvikalpa* is beyond all expression," says Bhagavan Sri Ramakrishna.

Shankaracharya describes this *Samadhi* as follows:

> "There is a continuous consciousness of the unity of Atman and Brahman. There is no longer any identification of the Atman with its coverings. All sense of duality disappears. There is pure, unified Consciousness. One who is well established in this Consciousness is said to be illuminated.
>
> One is said to be free even in this life when he is established in Illumination. His bliss is unending. He almost forgets this world of appearances. Even though his mind is dissolved in Brahman, he is fully awake, free from the ignorance of waking life. He is fully conscious, but free from any craving. Such a person is said to be free even in this life.
>
> For him, the sorrows of this world are over. Though he possesses a finite body, he remains united with the Infinite. His heart knows no anxiety. Such a person is said to be free even in this life."

Only when the Kundalini reaches *Sahasrara,* and unites with Brahman or *Siva,* can *Nirvikalpa Samadhi* be attained. It is a unique experience beyond all expressions. It is experienced by a very few sages. To attain *Nirvikalpa Samadhi* the mind must become pure and holy and be divested of all desires, impurities, attachments and aversions, and even the desire for Liberation must be discarded.

In the state of *Nirvikalpa Samadhi*, there is no consciousness of the body and the outer world, no trace of ego and the senses. The mind merges in the Supreme Consciousness. The ordinary consciousness becomes One with the Ocean of Consciousness. What remains is the Ocean of Consciousness in Itself.

One who attains *Nirvikalpa Samadhi* can no longer retain his physical body. In that state the life-breath lingers for twenty-one days and then passes out. For, when a drop of water once enters the ocean how can it retain its individuality? It is impossible. Likewise an ordinary soul once entering and merging itself in Brahman becomes One with Brahman. But great souls, such as the Incarnations of God, Messiahs, Prophets and other great Saints, who come to this world with a Divine mission, can come down from the state of *Samadhi* and keep the "Purified Ego of Knowledge" so as to work for the suffering humanity. They are called *Jivanmuktas*. (*See* 4.21 *Jivanmukta, below*). They bring the Kundalini back to the region of the sixth center (*Ajna Chakra*) or to that of the fifth center (*Visuddha Chakra*) and impart their Message to the people and show them the Path of Freedom. Such Sages can enter into the *Samadhi* and also come down to the plane of relative consciousness at will.

Sahaja Samadhi. If *Nirvikalpa Samadhi* gets established by constant experience, it becomes *Sahaja Samadhi*. Sri Ramana Maharaj of Tiruvannamalai (South India) was one of the best examples of this Samadhi. A *Jivanmukta* is in *Sahaja Samadhi.*

Sri Ramakrisna's Experience of *Nirvikalpa* Samadhi

Sri Ramakrishna (1836 –1886), the God-man of India, started his spiritual career as a priest of Kali temple at Dakshineswar, a village about four miles north of Calcutta. The worship in the Kali temple intensified Sri Ramakrishna's yearning for a living vision of the

Divine Mother Kali. He plunged deep in spiritual practice – night-long Meditation, singing devotional songs and bitter weeping. He felt the pangs of a child separated from its mother. He was overpowered with a great restlessness and could not bear the separation from the Mother any longer. Life seemed to be not worth living without a vision of the Mother. He resolved to put an end to his life. Suddenly his glance fell on a sword that was dangling in a corner of the temple. When Sri Ramakrishna jumped up and seized it, suddenly the blessed Mother revealed Herself. He saw a limitless, infinite effulgent Ocean of Consciousness.

The first vision of the Divine Mother made Sri Ramakrishna more eager for Her uninterrupted vision. He continued his intense spiritual practice. During this period he had many experiences. His vision became deeper and more intimate. Even while retaining consciousness of the outer world he would see the Divine Mother as tangibly as seeing the temples, the trees and the people around him.

Sri Ramakrishna continued his dualistic worship. He had visions of Rama and Krishna. Later he practiced Islam in 1866 and saw the vision of Mohammed and in 1874 he practiced Christianity and realized Jesus, and thus established the unity of all religions.

Prior to the above experience, in 1864, a wandering monk called Totapuri visited Dakshineswar. He was a realized Advaita Vedantist. He asked Sri Ramakrishna to take up the practice of Jnana Yoga and attain *Nirvikalpa Samadhi*. With the permission of the Divine Mother, Sri Ramakrishna agreed to the proposal.

Totapuri initiated Sri Ramakrishna into the monastic order and began to teach him the great truths of Vedanta, and asked him to withdraw the mind completely from all objects and dive deep into the Atman. But in spite of all his attempts he could not altogether cross the realm of the name and form and bring his mind to the unconditioned state. He had no difficulty in taking the mind from all the objects of the world. But the radiant figure of the Blissful Mother, the Embodiment of the essence of Pure Consciousness, appeared before him as living reality. Her bewitching smile prevented him from passing into the Great Beyond. Again and again he tried, but She stood in his way every time. In despair, he said to Totapuri: "It is hopeless. I cannot raise my mind to the unconditioned state and come face to face with Atman." Totapuri grew excited and sharply said: "What? You can't do it? But you have to." He cast his eyes around. Finding a piece of glass he took it up and pierced Sri Ramakrishna's forehead in-between the eyebrows. "Concentrate the mind on this point !" he thundered. Then with stern determination Sri Ramakrishna again sat to meditate. When the gracious form of the Divine Mother appeared before him, he used his discrimination as a sword and with it clove Her into two. The last barrier fell. His Spirit at once soared beyond the relative plane and He lost himself in *Samadhi*. He sat motionless like a log of wood. Totapuri greatly astonished to see the motionless body of Sri Ramakrishna. "Is it really true?" exclaimed Totapuri, "My God! This young man has attained in a few minutes what it took me forty years of intense practice. This is nothing short of a miracle !"

Sri Ramakrishna remained completely absorbed in *Samadhi* for three days. With the help of Totapuri, Sri Ramakrishna's mind finally came down to the relative plane.

The Divine Mother asked Sri Ramakrishna not to be lost in the featureless Absolute but to remain in *bhavamuka* (exalted state of spiritual experience), on the threshold of relative Consciousness, the border line between the Absolute and the Relative. He was to keep himself at the sixth center (*Ajna Chakra*). He gently oscillated back and forth across the dividing line. Ecstatic devotion to the Divine Mother alternated with serene absorption in the Ocean of Absolute Unity. He thus bridged the gulf between the Personal and the Impersonal, the Immanent and the Transcendent aspects of Reality. This is a unique experience in the recorded spiritual history of the world. (Swami Nikhilananda, *The Gospel of Sri Ramakrishna,* Madras: Sri Ramakrishna Math, 1986, pp. 30–31).

4.19: Samadhi in Different Kinds of Yoga

Introduction

A Raja Yogi gets *Samadhi* by restraining the mental modifications (*chitta-viitti-nirodha*). A Bhakta gets *Samadhi* through deep devotion (*prema*) of the Lord. A Vedanti gets *Samadhi* through discrimination and Concentration on the pure Brahman.

It is only the Raja Yogi who attempts to control the mental modifications. (*Yoga Sutras*, 1.2). A Vedanti has always *Atma-Bhava, Brahma-Bhava* (mood) in the midst of worldly objects. So he does not try to annihilate the mental modifications. There is no *Pratyahara* for him. He rejects name and form and takes everything as Brahman. A Bhakta sees God in all objects. He also does not check mental modifications. He, like the Vedanti, changes his mental attitude. It is the mind that creates all the differences and separateness. The world is all bliss (*ananda*) only. If you change your angle of vision, your mental attitude, you will find heaven on earth.

Through Hatha Yoga

A Hatha Yogi attains *Samadhi* by awakening Kundalini Sakthi and channeling it upwards to *Sahasrara Chakra*. He achieves this through advanced *Pranayama* techniques such as *Bastrika Pranayama* and Yogic process of *Bandhas*. He units *Prana* and *Apana* by *Bandhas* and drives the united *Prana-Apana* into the *Sushumna* Nadi. When Kundalini Sakthi is awakened, it ascends upward toward *Sahasrara Chakra*, and takes along with it the mind and *prana* also. The Yogi is shut out from the awareness of the physical world. Then he enters into *Samadhi* (Superconscious state). It is very difficult to bring him down to objective consciousness by merely shaking his body. Hatha Yogis have remained buried underneath the earth in *Samadhi* for years together.

Through Raja Yoga

As explained in the previous Chapter, deep Meditation leads to *Samadhi* or Oneness with Atman. If you can fix the mind for ten seconds steadily on a particular object, it is Concentration (*Dharana*). Ten such *Dharanas* become Meditation (*Dhyana*). Ten such *Dhyanas* form a *Samadhi*. The mind loses its own consciousness and becomes identified with the object of Meditation. Just as a toy made of salt melts in water, so the mind melts in Brahman in *Nirvikalpa Samadhi*. A sudden stroke of mystic illumination puts an end to all the empirical existence, and the remembrance of this world or the narrow individuality absolutely leaves the Self.

In the case of trained Yogis, you cannot say where *Pratyahara* ends and *Dharana* begins; where *Dharana* ends and *Dhyana* begins; where *Dhyana* ends and *Samadhi* begins. The moment they sit on the seat, all the processes occur simultaneously with lightning speed and they enter into *Samadhi* at their conscious will. In the case of beginners, *Pratyahara* first takes place. Then *Dharana* begins. Then *Dhyana* slowly commences. Constant and intense practice will lead to *Samadhi*.

Yogic Samadhi and Vedantic Samadhi

There is a difference between the *Nirvikalpa* state of a Yogi and the *Nirvikalpa* state of a Vedantin. The former concerns with the mind. The latter concerns with the pure Atman or Brahman only. In Yogic *Samadhi*, the object of Meditation (*dhyeya*) remains. In Vedantic *Samadhi*, Existence (*Asti*) alone remains.

Through Bhakti Yoga

The practices of Hatha Yoga and Raja Yoga are not suited to the majority of people in this age. A vast majority of persons have no good physique and robust constitution. Bhakti Yoga is, on the other hand, easy and safe. Anyone can repeat the name of God. Anyone can sing His glory. When Bhakti is fully ripe, Knowledge of God (*Brahma-jnana*) dawns.

Every *mantra* is very powerful. It purifies the mind. It induces dispassion (*vairagya*). It causes inward manifestation. It has a seed, a significant word, which gives it a special power, and a vibration form set up by its sound. By constant and prolonged repetition of the *mantra* with feeling and Concentration, the *Mantra*-Consciousness is awakened. Then the Sadhaka gets *Mantra-Siddhi*. There is a spiritual current in every *mantra*. It takes the devotee's soul first to one center and then to another and so on, till access is gained to the goal. Dhruva had vision of Lord Hari by repeating the *mantra* "*OM Namo Bhagavate Vasudevaya*" given by Rishi Narada. Prahlada had vision of Mahavishnu by repeating the "*Narayana*" *mantra*. Valmiki realized God by repeating "*Mara-Mara*" (which becomes Rama-Rama during the course of repetition). Tukaram became one with Lord Krishna by chanting always "*vittala-vittala*'" the name of the image of Sri Krishna at Pandharpur.

Devotees (Bhaktas) like Lord Gouranga, Tukaram, Tulsidas identified themselves with their causal body and had a normal causal-body consciousness. A bhakta of causal-body consciousness is one with Brahman even when living in physical body.

Samadhi Through Vedanta

Purify the mind by *Japa*, *Pranayama*, *Satsanga*, self-study, charity, sacrifice, austerity and selfless service. Develop determination and discrimination and unite the current of the mind with the spiritual current. Give up the idea of "I", "he", "thou", i.e., the idea of duality. Cultivate *Brahma-Bhavana* (mood) instead. Then *Samadhi* will supervene automatically.

There are four ways of destroying ego: Positive and Negative Advaitic methods, Devotional method of Absolute Self-surrender and the complete Self-sacrifice of Selfless Karma Yoga.

The Negative Vedantic method is denial: "I am not the body, I am not the mind. Brahman alone is real. The world is unreal. *Jiva* is identical with Brahman.: World includes the body. Meditate on this idea. The "sense of I" will vanish. The Positive method is that everything is Self only. "All is Brahman. There is nothing but Brahman."

Mental Transformations in Higher Yoga

Three fundamental types of mental transformations are involved in the practice of higher Yoga. They represent not static, but dynamic conditions. In the progressive process of Self-realization through *Samadhi* the mind can pass from one stage to another through three kinds of transformations that are sequentially related one to another. The ordinary transformations of the mind take place according to the laws of association or reasoning or according to the stimuli applied by the external world through the sense-organs. The three kinds of transformations under consideration are of a special kind. They take place only in the higher Yoga after the yogi has acquired the capacity of passing into the *Samadhi* state at will.

1. *Nirodha Parinama* (Modifications of control). This first transformation results in the restraint of mental modifications (*chitta-vrtis*). As Yoga is described by Patanjali as the restraint of mental modifications (*Yoga Sutras*, 1.2), the importance of *Nirodha Parinama* needs no emphasis. When control of mind begins, *Nirodha* comes into play. The word *Nirodha* means "restraint or control." The efforts at control of the mind beginning with Concentration (*Dharana*) involve *Nirodha*. The distractions in mind are restrained by substituting in their place the object of Meditation. In each of these efforts there is a momentary state in which neither the distraction nor the chosen object is present and the mind is really without any seed (*pratyaya*), just as when the direction of a moving object is suddenly reversed there is a moment when the object is at rest without any movement. The object of *Nirodha* is to produce at will this momentary state and gradually extend it, so that the mind can exist for a considerable duration in this unmodified state. (*Yoga Sutras*, 3.9). The yogi should be able

to maintain this unmodified (*niruddha*) state for a sufficiently long time to enable consciousness to pass through the "cloud" or void and emerge into the next plane. *Asamprajnata Samadhi* (*See* previous Chapter) is nothing but the state of the mind in which the *pratyaya* or "seed" has been made to disappear by the practice of *Nirodha*. This condition of *Nirodha* is not a state of mental vacuum, but a state of *Samadhi*. The tendency of the "seed" to emerge again into consciousness is strong. The repetition of the effort at restraint makes it slightly easier every time to bring about the *niruddha* state. Continued practice of this kind gradually increases the tendency of the mind to remain in the *niruddha* state. The flow of this *niruddha* state becomes, after sufficient practice, easy and peaceful.

The resistance encountered from the mind is due to the past impressions (*samskaras*) still hidden within the mind. If these have been removed by dispassion (*vairagya*), the passage from one condition to another can take place without much resistance.

2. *Samadhi Parinama* (Modification of Samadhi). This mental transformation takes place in the different stages of *Samadhi*. When the distractions of the mind disappear and the state of one-pointedness appears, the mind is said to undergo the modification of Samadhi.(*Yoga Sutras*, 3.11). This transformation begins with the practice of Concentration and continues until the one-pointedness state is reached. First the distractions in the mind are replaced by the chosen object of Meditation. When Meditation is perfected all distractions are completely eliminated. Then begins a new transformation of the mind in which consciousness begins to move in depth; the object of Meditation is denuded of its coverings or non-essential elements like name or form in order to get at the core, its real nature. When this process has been completed and the object shines in the mind in its real nature, the *Nirvitarka* stage is reached. Then the next transformation begins.

3. *Ekagrata Parinama* (Modification of One-pointedness). This transformation is the consummation of the *Samadhi Parinama*. The same object (*pratyaya*), rises in the field of consciousness again and again and produces the impression as if a single fixed unchanging object is occupying the field. (*Yoga Sutras*, 3.12).

As the impressions of the first three states of restlessness (*ksipta*), torpididity (*mudha*) and distraction (*viksipta*) continue to be replaced by that of one-pointedness, a state is reached in which the thought-waves of the mind flow from similar to similar, like the oil poured from one vessel to another, or like the form of a candle flame which appears the same but is always changing from similar to similar. Here the first three states of the mind have subsided altogether and the mind is said to have undergone the modification of one-piontedness. The interval is so small that it appears to be a continuous phenomenon. We see a continuous glow in an electric bulb with an alternating current but we know that the glow is discontinuous and periods of illumination follow periods of darkness alternately at very short intervals. It is not only in *Samadhi* that this discontinuity occurs in the perception of the object; but also it is present in all perceptions. Wherever there is manifestation, there must be discontinuity or succession.

The projection of a cinematographic picture on a screen may illustrate the difference among the above three *Parinamas*. The moving picture on the screen is produced by a succession of dissimilar images falling on the screen at intervals of less then 1/10th second. This produces an illusion of continuity while there is actual discontinuity in the projection. If all the pictures on the film roll are made exactly similar there will be one stationary and unchanging image produced on the screen. But we know that the appearance of such a stationary and unchanging image is an illusion. What we see as an unchanging image is composed of a number of similar images following each other so rapidly as to be indistinguishable. If we slow down the speed of projection sufficiently, the illusion will disappear and we shall be able to see similar images following each other at regular intervals. In the same way the object (*pratyaya*) of *Ekagrata Parinama* remains apparently the same but in reality it is composed of a series of similar *pratyayas* following each other at inconceivably high speed. It is because the phenomenon is dynamic and not static, that it is called a *parinama* (transformation). The suppression of the impression of *Ekagrata Parinama* by means of *Nirodha* (controlled state) does not produce the illumination of Reality. It is only when the *pratyaya* of the last plane (Atmic) is dropped that the illumination of Reality or Consciousness of the Self (*Purusha*) dawns.

4.20: Liberation

The state of Superconsciousness or Self-realization is a state of Liberation or Freedom from Karmic bondage and suffering. In this state, the ideas of bondage and freedom have no meaning. When there is only One Thing, the All-pervading Consciousness or Brahman and nothing else, who can bind whom? This final stage of Liberation (*Kaivalya*) is reached when the Yogi attains what is called *Dharma Megha Samadhi*. "*Dharma Megha*" means "Cloud of Virtue." Just as·cloud pours rain, this *Samadhi* pours the highest virtue of success in attaining the ultimate Reality.

Dharma Megha Samadhi

As stated in the Chapter 4.8 Samadhi: Meaning and Kinds (*See above*), when a Yogi advances in *Sasmita Samadhi*, which is the highest limit of the lower (*Samprajnata*) *Samadhi*, he experiences Discriminative Discernment or Intuitive Knowledge (*Viveka Khyati*) due to the increasing purity of the mind. If this Intuitive Knowledge is maintained ceaselessly and without any obstruction, the Yogi develops Supreme Dispassion (*Para Vairagya*). Then he begins to see his Self as distinct from his mind, and therefore, he develops a mystic inclination to turn away from the mind (*chitta*) itself.

This state has two aspects. First, the flow of Intuitional Knowledge becomes firm. Second, the impression of *Asamprajnata* (or *Nirodha*) *Samadhi*, the highest form of Superconsciousness is developed. This impression destroys all other impressions, and it is figuratively described as *Dharma Megha* (Cloud of Virtue), which rains down the nectar of Immortality or

Liberation (*Kaivalya*). The Yogi, who is dispassionate even towards Intuitive Knowledge and the overpowering attraction of the high state of illumination and bliss through its ceaseless flow, attains *Dharma Megha Samadhi.* (*Yoga Sutras,* 4.29). It marks the end of all afflictions, thus leading the Yogi to Liberation.

Saint Thirumoolar says, "Even with God, please be without desire." This means that desire itself is a bondage. First, the desire for sense-objects and worldly pleasures is eliminated by replacing or transforming them by an intense desire for attaining God or Self-realization. When will that desire go? When you attain God. The fulfillment of this desire and becoming desireless happen simultaneously.

As the result of *Dharma Megha Samadhi* the five afflictions (*Klesas*) and their effects, the effects of three types of Karma (good, bad and mixed), and the seeds of all impressions (*Samskaras*) of the mind are destroyed. (*Yoga Sutras,* 4.30). The Yogi becomes established in the Self, and he attains freedom from sufferings and bondage. In *Nirbija* (seedless) or *Nirodha Samadhi* that is practiced in this final stage, the consciousness of the Yogi frees itself from the last veil of illusion and merges into the Light of Reality itself. That is, the consciousness of the Yogi leaves the world of manifestation in which *Gunas* and their combinations operate, and merges in the Ocean of the Light of Reality. The Yogi's condition may be compared to the condition of a pilot in an airplane, who comes out of a cloud bank into bright sunlight.

As the result of *Dharma Megha Samadhi*, when all the veils of illusion are lifted, the knowledge of the Yogi becomes limitless, while the knowable is rendered insignificant. (*Yoga Sutras,* 4.31). As long as a Yogi has not experienced Intuitive Knowledge, his knowledge is conditioned by ignorance. During the state of ignorance, the knowable – the objects of the world – is limitless before his vision. And in his vain effort to know these objects, he continues to go through numerous embodiments.

In *Yoga Vaishta* there is a parable about three princes, the sons of a great king, who decided to measure the extent of the universe. They practiced intense austerity with the desire of gaining the possibility to travel at immense speed in order to be able to reach the utmost limits of the universe. As a result of their austerity, they were granted the highest speed. Then with their immense speed they began to roam through creation. Even though thousands of years have rolled on, those princes have not yet covered even a small portion of creation.

Though the extent of the world of knowable objects is so immeasurable, yet when a Yogi ascends the heights of wisdom through *Samadhi,* the world begins to shrink before his vision. And when his Intuition blooms fully, the world of knowable things becomes insignificant. In other words, he transcends the relative world-process, and he has nothing more to know. His Intuitive Knowledge shines like the midday sun in a cloudless sky. Before its effulgence all intellectual forms of knowledge, like the stars of the sky, pale into insignificance.

How is it then that the ever-changing *Gunas* do not overpower the Enlightened Yogi? For the Yogi who has experienced *Dharma Megha Samadhi*, the *Prakriti,* consisting of the three *Gunas,* has accomplished its purpose, and so the series of modifications of the *Gunas* cease to exist in the Yogi. (*Yoga Sutras*, 4.32).

Devoid of serving any purpose for the Enlightened Yogi's soul, the *Gunas* return to their source (*Prakriti*), and the *Purusha* becomes established in its essential nature (the Self) and becomes free from the cycle of births and deaths. (*Yoga Sutras,* 4.34). Thus is accomplished the goal of life.

The entry through *Dharma Megha Samadhi* completes the evolutionary cycle of the individual and by destroying ignorance (*Avidya*) completely and forever, brings about the end of union of *Purusha* and *Prakrti*. Then the *Purusha* attains full Self-realization. This process is irreversible and after reaching this stage, it is not possible for the *Purusha* to fall again into the realm of *Maya* from which he has obtained Liberation.

When Intuitive Enlightenment is fully attained, the function of the mind ends. Liberation in the form of complete cessation of the mind cannot take place so long as awareness of the intellect remains. Thus in Liberation there is neither discrimination nor misconception nor ignorance. Misconception is destroyed by Discriminative Knowledge. Then the function of the mind ends. That is, Intuitive Knowledge destroys its own base, mind, as fire destroys its fuel.

The experience of Reality. is beyond description and our comprehension. Patanjali knowing the futility of such a task has not even attempted it.

The Effects of Liberation

The first result of attaining Liberation (*Kaivalya*) is freedom from sufferings and *karmas*. (*Yoga Sutras*, 4.30). The ignorance, which is the root cause for *karmas* and sufferings is itself destroyed. The Yogi then becomes a *Jivanmukta*, i.e., liberated though alive. The *Jivanmukta* cannot again fall into ignorance and start generating *karmas* that bind. All actions in the State of Liberation are necessarily done in complete identification with the Divine Consciousness without even the slightest identification with the individual ego, for, ego and other causes for sufferings have been destroyed by the Intuitive Knowledge. That is why no result accrues to the *Jivanmukta*.

The second consequence of attaining Liberation, as explained above, is the sudden expansion of consciousness into the realm of Infinite Knowledge. (*Yoga Sutras*, 4.31). When the last veil of illusion is removed in *Dharma Megha Samadhi*, the Enlightenment that blossoms is of an entirely new kind. In the different stages of *Sabija Samadhi* the knowledge that comes at each successive expansion of consciousness into a higher realm of mind-stuff appears tremendously greater than in the preceding stage. But even the transcendental knowledge of the Atmic plane sinks into insignificance when compared with Discriminative or Intuitive Knowledge that comes in the state of Enlightenment or Liberation. In the realm of Infinity, there is no realm of magnitudes at all. So the *Jivanmukta* is not really in the realm of knowledge but has transcended knowledge and passes into the realm of pure Consciousness.

The three *Gunas* having fulfilled their object, their ever-changing modifications come to an end. (*Yoga Sutras*, 4.32). The purpose of bringing together *Purusha* and *Prakrti* having been fulfilled through the destruction of ignorance (*avidya*) and attainment of Liberation, the compulsory association of *Purusha* and *Prakrti* dissolves automatically, and with this dissolution the transformations of the *Gunas* come to an end.

Liberation (*Kaivalya*)

Liberation is the ultimate state of Enlightenment. Patanjali defines it as "the state of Enlightenment which follows the re-absorption of the *Gunas* into *Prakriti*. In this state the *Purusha* is established in his Real nature which is pure Consciousness." (*Yoga Sutras*, 4.34). The nature of Consciousness in the state of *Kaivalya* is beyond description. In the words of Swami Vivekananda, "Nature's (*Prakriti*'s) task is done, this unselfish task which our sweet nurse, Nature, had imposed upon herself. She gently took the self-forgetting soul by the hand, as it were, and showed him all the experiences in the universe, all manifestations, bringing him higher and higher through various bodies, till his lost glory came back, and he remembered his own nature. Then the kind Mother went back the same way she came, for others who have also lost their way in the trackless desert of life. Thus is she working without beginning and without end. And the infinite river of souls is flowing into the Ocean of Perfection, of Self-realization."

4.21: *Jivanmukta*

The sage who comes down from the state of *Nirvikalpa Samadhi* and continues to live in this world is called a *Jivanmukta*, i.e., liberated while alive. A *Jivanmukta* does see the world and its multifarious objects, but in a quite different way. His angle of vision is different. He sees Brahman behind every name and form and the same Brahman as his own Self. No doubt, his body, senses, mind, ego and intellect function in a normal way; but the attachment to them is extinct. The mind is fully detached from the senses and their objects. The major portion of the mind always lives in Brahman. The vision of Brahman is never out of sight even for a single second. He is conscious of his real nature always. He surpasses waking, dream and dreamless sleep states. He lives in *turiya* state all the twenty-four hours and in him only real intuition works.

The Characteristics of a *Jivanmukta*

What are the signs or characteristics of a *Jivanmukta*? How he conducts himself? A *Jivanmukta* is beyond the ego, beyond the three *Gunas*, beyond the conventional codes of conduct and beyond the duties of station of life. Yet he is full of love, compassion and spirit of service. The characteristics of a Sage of Steady Wisdom described in the verses 2.55–76, the description of a Realized Devotee given in the verses 12.13–20, and the characteristics of *Trigunatita* Sage (one who has gone beyond the three *Gunas*) described in the verses of 14.22–26) of the *Bhagavad Gita* are applicable to a *Jivanmukta*.

Purity. As a freed soul, a *Jivanmukta* is fettered neither by evil tendencies nor by conventional moral codes. Purity has become his essential nature so that he does not have to bind himself by rules of conduct.

A *Jivanmukta* is always compassionate, forbearing, truthful, loving, pure and perfect. He is beyond pleasure and pain and all other pairs of opposites. He is beyond all grief. This does not mean that he has no sympathy for the miseries of others. How can a *Jivanmukta* who has transcended ego and who feels the whole world as himself be indifferent to the miseries of others? It is impossible for him not to sympathize with others in their miseries. His heart is full of compassion. That is real Divine compassion.

Nothing can tempt a *Jivanmukta*. He is always established in perfect celibacy in thought, word and deed. Even if he lives amidst most beautiful and youthful company of opposite sex, he lives without the least bit of any carnal appetites. He is always the same in both pleasure and pain. (*Bhagavad Gita*, 12.13). To him a clod of earth, a piece of stone or a lump of gold is the same. (*Bhagavad Gita*, 14.24). He maintains a balanced state of mind in honor and dishonor. He is the same to friend and foe. (*Gita*, 14.25).

Free from Ego or Body Consciousness. The *Jivanmukta*, as the knower of Brahman, becomes Brahman Itself. For, the mind is a very subtle force and it takes the form and color of the thought-object. As a *Jivanmukta* is one, who has attained *Nirvikalpa Samadhi* and has come down to the realm of the relative consciousness, his mind constantly lives in the thought of Brahman. And, as such, it becomes Brahman. The scriptures say that a *Brahma-Jnani* or *Jivanmukta* has no body. It means that since he always identifies himself with Brahman, he has no body or ego idea. He does not identify himself either with the body or with the senses and mind. When he uses the word "I," he always means Atman or Brahman. So it is said that he has no body. "With the attainment of the Superconsciousness state all the knots of the heart and the angularities of the mind are cut asunder." (*Mundaka Upanishad,* 2.2.8). The *Katha Upanishad* also says, "When all knots that fetter here the heart are cut asunder, then a mortal becomes immortal." (2.3.5).

Inaction in Action. A *Jivanmukta* does nothing even while doing all actions. It means that he performs actions without the least ego idea and without any idea of "I" and "Mine," attachment and hankering after the fruits of his actions. His actions are selfless and they are performed without the sense of doership. Therefore, they do not bind him. His actions are like a burnt rope. A burnt rope does possess the form of a rope but it cannot be used for binding. Thus the actions of a *Jivanmukta* cannot bind him. This does not mean that he can do anything even sinful or evil. That is impossible. To attain *Nirvikalpa Samadhi*, the mind must be thoroughly pure and sinless and even without a trace of desire. Therefore the *Jivanmukta* who has attained *Nirvikalpa Samadhi* can never do any sinful act. Whatever he does, it is for the good of others. But it is not done with the awareness that he is doing good to others. The sun does not give light with a view to making us happy. Illumination is sun's nature. We take advantage of it and are happy. So also the actions of a *Jivanmukta* are spontaneous. He is loving and serving everybody, because it is his nature, not that he does anything deliberately. The sun can give only light, not darkness, so also a saint lives only for the good of others. His actions are the outflow of Divine energy in and through him.

Equal Vision. A *Jivanmukta* is a sage of equal vision. He realizes that all beings and all things are the manifestations of Brahman. In this supreme vision of unity and equality, all senses of diversity and differentiation are dissolved. This vision lifts the *Jivanmukta* from the meshes of *Gunas* and fixes him in the ever pure and unchanging truth of his existence. He sees the same truth in all beings. The distinctions of caste, creed, color and race have no meaning to him. He looks upon the learned brahmin and the so-called untouchable with the same vision of equality. He beholds the entire universe as the one image of the supreme Brahman.

Desirelessness. A *Jivanmukta* has no selfish desires. Desires arise from a sense of imperfection. The feeling of imperfection is possible only when one finds something outside oneself, an object of seeking. But the perfect sage is not aware of anything other than Brahman, his own Self. Hence desires have no place in him.

The question may arise here why desirelessness is mentioned as a special mark of the *Jivanmukta*, when it is the accepted creed of all spiritual disciplines that non-attachment for the objects of the world is a pre-requisite of all spiritual seekers. There is a difference in the quality of dispassion of the spiritual aspirant and that of the perfected one who has attained the goal. As the *Jivanmuktiviveka*, a scripture in Sanskrit, notes, "at the stage prior to the realization of the goal, the seeker of God is free from cravings, as a result of his vigilant practice of self-control and other virtues; the desires still persist, and are held in control only with some effort, whereas, after realization, there being nothing like the transformation of the mind, desires cease altogether. ...... He is pure within as the sky which remains pure. The *Sreyomarga,* an ethical scripture, also says, "All that precede the attainment of realization are means which are brought about by effort, but they are inherent in a perfect person." The aspirant will always be yearning for liberation that is a form of desire, though exalted, but in a perfect sage no selfish desire remains. The ocean is not affected by the river waters flowing into it from all sides. Likewise, no reaction of desires is produced by the objects of enjoyment, which a *Jivanmukta* happens to come across. (*Gita*, 2.70). The worldly pleasures are worthless to him. For he is ever content and satisfied in the Self. (*Gita,* 2.55)

However, a *Jivanmukta* may retain his higher ego to undertake spiritual service as God's service. He is not satisfied with his individual salvation, but works for the salvation of others. This is illustrated by the lives of the greatest men of God like Buddha, Christ, Mohammed and Sri Ramakrishna.

Fearlessness. A *Jivanmukta* is free from fear. Most people live like haunted criminals; they are so attached to their possessions, position, name and fame that they always have the fear of losing them and above all the fear of death. They cannot sit in peace or move about fearlessly. But a *Jivanmukta* doe not hanker after pleasure, and has no attachment to anything and so has no fear of losing anything. (*Gita*, 2.56). He has nothing to hide and so he is fearless. Even when he moves among sense-objects, he is free from attraction and aversion. He has attained the peace of the Eternal. (*Gita*, 2.64)

Free from hatred and anger. The realized sage is free from hatred. Hatred is directed toward some object or person that causes pain or injury to oneself or obstructs one's desire. It is the obstructed desire that reappears in the guise of hatred and anger. So how can a desireless sage hate anything or anyone? How can one, who perceives his own Self in the Self of every being, hate anyone? (*Isavasya Upanishad,* 6).

How would a *Jivanmukta* react when someone hurts or insults him? The best illustration of that is given in the "Song of the Mendicant" in the *Bhagavatam*. The mendicant was badly hurt and insulted by some ignorant people. And he walked on, saying to himself, "Even if thou dost think another person is causing thee happiness or misery, thou art really neither happy nor wretched, for thou art the Atman, the Changeless Spirit. Thy sense of happiness or misery is due to a false identification of thy Self with the body, which alone is subject to change. Thy Self is the real Self in all. With whom should thou be angry for causing pain if accidentally thou dost bite thy tongue with thy teeth?" This is the attitude of the realized sage who has become one with all creation.

Relinquishes both Joy and Sorrow. A *Jivanmukta* does not rejoice over anything. He is beyond worldly fleeting pleasures and pain. He is always immersed in the higher joy of Supreme Bliss. How he would discard that eternal joy and revel in fleeting things? (*Vivekacudamani*, 522). He is everywhere unattached, not pleased at receiving good, nor vexed at evil. (*Gita*, 2.57). As Plotinus says, "They are no more two, but one; the soul is no more conscious of the body or mind, but knows that it has what it desired, and that it is where no deception can come, and it would not exchange that bliss for all the heaven of heavens."

Contentment. The realized sage is contented. This contentment is not the kind of satisfaction that comes when some desire is fulfilled; it is an absolute satisfaction arising from the absence of all desires. Will such a perfect soul lapse into inactivity? No. Though he has achieved the highest, he does not remain inactive, but works for the spiritual development of others in a spirit of service. Having merged his individuality in Brahman, the realized *Jivanmukta* is not conscious of doing anything of his own accord or for his own sake. He feels like a dry leaf at the mercy of the wind; he is made use of by the Lord Himself as His instrument to carry out His inscrutable purpose in this world. Even when he is active externally, he is internally calm and quiet.

Life becomes One Yajna (Sacrifice). As the *Jivanmukta* sees the whole world as a manifestation of the Brahman, his entire life becomes one *Yajna* (sacrifice). As he has established in Brahman, he always thinks and talks of Brahman, hears and sees the Brahman only. He thinks of nothing else, he talks of nothing else, he sees and hears nothing else. The *Chandogya Upanishad* says, "Where one sees nothing else, hears nothing else, knows nothing else, that is the state of Infinite Bliss. ..... In that which is Infinite therein lies Immortality . . ." (7.24.1)

The Behavior of a *Jivanmukta*

No uniform standard of behavior can be expected of a realized sage. He is always immersed in the bliss of Self-realization and the service of the Lord. To all external appearance, however, he may sometimes behave just like any ordinary person, discharging all the duties pertaining to his station in life, and thus set an example to ordinary people. Often he may be seen to override the accepted codes of social customs and conventions. At other times he may appear to be inactive, being immersed in the bliss of *Samadhi*, and appear dead to his surroundings like a stone.

Sri Ramakrishna described the behavior of a perfect soul in the following way: "Sometimes he will act like a five-year old child or he may seem intoxicated or mad. Or he may be apparently inert – silent and motionless. He is not bound by any code or law, but nothing he does will be immoral and unethical. His actions are selfless without his trying to be selfless, just as a flower emits fragrance."

The Glory of a *Jivanmukta*

A *Jivanmukta* is the walking God upon the earth; his body is the true temple of the Lord. He knows it not, but it is his presence that sanctifies the places, glorifies action, and lends authority to the scriptures. The places where he lives or lived become holy and sanctified. In such a living sage all fathers of the spiritual culture, the great saints of the past find their fulfillment. Their collective activities, their spiritual contributions, their personal sacrifices have all been fulfilled in the realized sage, and the world gets a savior. Only a real saint can save the world. All others are interested only in seeing that the world caters to their own self-aggrandizement and enjoyment. They never have the welfare of the world at heart. Their interest in the world is like that of a peasant in his cattle. It is only the loving service of the selfless saints that really leads human beings to their destination. It is they who bring to the earth the light that dispels the gloom and darkness in the bosom of human beings.

4.22: References for Section–IV

1. Agnihotri S.N., and Justin O'Brien, ed., *Faces of Meditation*, Honesdale: The Himalayan International Institute of Yoga Science and Philosophy, 1978
2. Arya Vsharbudh, *Superconscious Meditation,* Honesdale: The Himalayan International Institute of Yoga Science and Philosophy, 1985
3. Ballentine, Rudolph M., *The Theory and Principles of Meditation*, Honesdale: The Himalayan International Institute of Yoga Science and Philosophy, 1986
4. Davis, Roy Eugene, *Our Awakening World,* Lakemont: CSA Press, Publishers, 1987
5. Dean Ornish, *Stress, Diet and Your Heart,* New York: Signet Book, 1982
6. Eliade, Mircea, *Yoga, Immortality and Freedom*, Princeton: Princeton University Press, 1973
7. Funderburk, James, *Science Studies Yoga,* Honesdale: The Himalayan International Institute of Yoga Science and Philosophy, 1977
8. Gardner, Adelaide, *Meditatiom—A Practical Study*, Wheaton: The Theosophical Publishing House
9. Goleman, Daniel, *The Meditative Mind,* Los Angeles: Jeremy P. Tarcher, Inc. 1988
10. Hari Prasad Shastri, *Yoga*, London: W & G, Foyle Ltd., 1958
11. Harish, Johari, *Chakras*, Vermont: Destiny Books, 1987
12. Holmes, Ernest, *The Science of Mind*, New York: Dodd, Mead and Co., 1938
13. Mishra, Ramamurti S., *Fundamentals of Yoga,* New York: Harmony Books, 1987
14. Misra L.K., *The Art and Science of Meditation,* Honesdale: The Himalayan International Institute of Yoga Science and Philosophy,

1977

15. Monks of the Ramakrishna Order, *Meditation*, Madras: Sri Ramakrishna Math, 1986
16. Mouni Sadhu, *Meditation*, Hollywood: Melvin Powsers Wilshire Book Co., 1973
17. Nuernberger, Phil, *Freedom from Stress—A Holistic Approach,* Honesdale: The Himalayan International Institute of Yoga Science and Philosophy, 1983
18. Naranjo, Claudio, and Robert E. Ornestein, *On the Psychology of Meditation,* New York: An Essalen Book, 1972
19. Suzuki, D.., *Zen Meditation,* New York: Doubleday Anchor Books, 1956
20. Swami Abhedananda, *How to Be a Yogi,* Calcutta: Ramakrishna Vedanta Math, 1971
21. Swami Abhedananda, *Yoga: Its Theory and Practice,* Calcutta: Ramakrishna Vedanta Math, 1967
22. Swami Abhedananda, *Spiritual Unfoldment,* Calcutta: Ramakrishna Vedanta Math, 1969
23. Swami Hariharananda Aranya, *Yoga Philosophy of Patanjali,* Albany: State University of New York Press, 1983
24. Swami Janakanda, *Yoga, Tantra and Meditation,* New York: Ballantine Books
25. Swami Jothirmayananda, *Concentration and Meditation,* Miami: Swami Lalitananda, 1971
26. Swami Jothirmayananda, *Raja Yoga: Study of Mind,* Swami Lalitananda, 1970
27. Swami Nikhilananda, tr., *Vedantasara*, Calcutta: Advaita Ashram, 1968
28. Swami Paramananda, *Concentration and Meditation,* Cohasset: The Vedanta Center, 1974
29. Swami Prabhavananda, and Isherwood, Christopher, *How to know God -The Yoga aphorisms of Patanjali* , Hollywood: Vedanta Press, 1981
30. Swami Rama, et al., *Faces of Meditation,* Honesdale: The Himalayan International Institute of Yoga Science and Philosophy, 1978
31. Swami Rama, *Lectures on Yoga,* Honesdale: The Himalayan International Institute of Yoga Science and Philosophy, 1983
32. Swami Rama, *Path of Fire and Light—Advanced Practices of Yoga*, Honesdale: The Himalayan International Institute of Yoga Science and Philosophy, 1990
33. Swami Rama, et al., *Yoga and Psychotherapy—The Evolution of*

Consciousness, Honesdale: The Himalayan International Institute of Yoga Science and Philosophy, 1981

34. Swami Satchidananda, et al., *Living Yoga*, New York: Gordon and Breach Science Publishers, 1977
35. Swami Satchidananda, *Meditation*, Yogaville: Integral Yoga Publications, 1975
36. Swami Satchidananda, *Sutras of Patanjali*, Yogaville: Integral Yoga Publications, 1990
37. Swami Satyananda, *Meditation*, Monghyr (India): Bihar School of Yoga, 1977
38. Swami Sivananda, *Concentration and Meditation*, Shivanandanagar: Divine Life Society, 1975
39. Swami Sivananda, *Mind—Its Mysteries and Control*, Shivanandanagar: Divine Life Society, 1983
40. Swami Vivekananda, *Meditation and its Methods*, Hollywood: Vedanta Press, 1946
41. Swami Vivekananda, *Raja Yoga*, New York: Ramakrishna Vivekananda Center, 1982
42. Swami Yatiswarananda, *The Divine Life*, Madras: Sri Ramakrishna Math, 1972
43. Taimni, I.K., *The Science of Yoga*, Wheaton: The Theosophical Publishing House, 1975
44. Venkateswaran, P.S., *Yoga for Healing*, Bombay: Jaico Publishing House, 1981
45. White, John, ed., *What is Meditation?* New York: Anchor Books, 1974
46. Wood, Ernest, *Concentration: An Approach to Meditation*, Wheaton: The Theosophical Publishing House, 1968
47. Wood, Ernest, *Practical Yoga*, Hollywood: Wilshire Book Co., 1976
48. Woodroffe, Sir John (Arthur Avalon), *The Great Liberation (Mahanirvan)*, Madras: Ganesh and Co.
49. Woodroffe, Sir John, *The Principles of Tantra*, Madras: Ganesh & Co.
50. Woodroffe, Sir John, *The Serpent Power*, Madras: Ganesh and Co.
51. Yogashakti Saraswati, *Yoga Sadhana*, Bombay: Wilco Publishing House, 1972
52. Zorn, Yogi William, *Yoga of the Mind*, New York: Paperback Library, 1970

Questions

Section I

1. What is Yoga? Is it a science? Justify your answer.
2. What are the various Paths of Yoga? Are they mutually exclusive? Justify your answer.
3. Analyze the connection between Yoga and (1) religion, (2) *tapas* and (3) renunciation.
4. What is the ultimate goal of life? How does it differ from the general aims of worldly life?
5. Identify your goals and examine whether they can give you eternal peace and joy.
6. How can one know oneself? Why?
7. "Thou art That." Explain this statement.
8. Is Yoga an ancient one? Justify your answer with evidences.
9. What aspects of Yoga are emphasized in the *Vedas* and *Upanishads*?
10. How do Upanishads describe the Self or Atman?
11. What is Brahman? How can one realize It? What is the connection between Brahman and Atman?
12. How does the *Bhagavad Gita* harmonize the different Paths of Yoga?
13. Discuss the contribution of Patanjali to the science of Yoga.
14. Examine the relevance of India's Epics, *Puranas* and *Bhagavatam* to Yoga.
15. Is Yoga universal? How?
16. What is Vedanta? How do the different schools of Vedanta differ from one another?

17. As one thinks, so one becomes. – elucidate.
18. Discuss the similarities and differences between Samkhya Philosophy and Yoga Philosophy.
19. Examine the involvement of the soul in the worldly life and the process of its Liberation.
20. What are the characteristics of the three *gunas*? Why should they be transcended? How?

Section II

1. Trace the Yoga Psychology's inroad into the West.
2. Are the mind and body two independent parts of the human structure? What is the connection between them?
3. What is the true nature of the mind? How does a strong mind influence a weaker mind?
4. Why does an object appear different to different minds? Is it possible to get a true impression of an object? How?
5. Why should the mind be purified? How?
6. Is Yoga an internal research? Why is it more difficult than an external research?
7. Is our mind a multiple unit? Describe the four aspects of the mind.
8. Examine the functions and powers of the human mind.
9. Differentiate knowledge from will. How can you develop will-power?
10. What is the primary cause of diseases and evils? How can it be removed?
11. Why should senses and mind be controlled? And how?
12. Explain the cause of human suffering.
13. Why should the afflictions be destroyed? And how?
14. Is it possible to avoid human misery? What is the permanent remedy to it?

Section III

1. Briefly describe the eight stages or steps of Raja Yoga. Why

are the first five stages very important?

2. What is the need for a *Guru* in Yoga? What are the qualifications and qualities of a true *Guru*?
3. Examine the *Guru's* role in Yoga.
4. What are the three categories of disciples? What is the nature of each of them?
5. What are the qualifications of a disciple?
6. Examine the importance of devotion and faith in the *Guru*-disciple relationship.
7. Discuss the meaning and significance of five *Yamas.*
8. State the meaning and significance of five *Niyamas.*
9. Are morality and self-discipline indispensable for spiritual progress?
10. On the basis of your study of ethical literature identify other moral restraints and observances besides five *Yamas* and five *Niyamas*.
11. Why should Yoga *asanas* be practiced? what are their essential features?
12. What type of posture does Meditation require? And why?
13. What are *Mudras*? Why are they important?
14. What are *Bandhas*? Why are they performed?
15. What is *prana*? What is its role in the human body? Why should *prana* be regulated?
16. Can the autonomous nervous system be brought under conscious control?
17. How can sickness be controlled through *Pranayama*?
18. Describe the aims and benefits of *Pranayama.*
19. Discuss the techniques and importance of *pranic* healing.
20. What preparations are required for *Pranayama*?
21. What are the general instructions pertaining to the practice of *Pranayama*?
22. Why is *pratyahara* necessary? How is it possible to attain it?
23. Why is mind restless and wandering?

Section IV

1. What is concentration? How does Yogic Concentration differ from ordinary external concentration? Distinguish between external and internal Yogic Concentration.

2. What are the six main objects on which one can concentrate? Is it easy to focus the mind on the chosen object of Concentration? Why or why not?
3. On what *charkas* can the mind be focused? Why?
4. What are the requirements of Concentration?
5. How would you prepare for Concentration?
6. Examine the process and benefits of Concentration.
7. What is Meditation? What are the subtle aspects of Meditation in different kinds of Yoga?
8. Describe the meaning and the process of *Japa* and *Ajapa Japa*.
9. What are the distinctive features of Buddhist Meditation and Meditation in Jainism?
10. What are the special features of Zen Meditation and Meditation in Sufism?
11. What are the important obstacles to Meditation? How can they be overcome?
12. Describe the preparation for, and process of Meditation.
13. Examine the importance and effects of Meditation with a *mantra*.
14. Describe the process and progress of your Meditation.
15. What is meant by Meditation in Action? Give a schedule of Meditation in Action that you propose to follow.
16. What are the specific benefits derived from the practice of Meditation?
17. How does stress arise? Examine the role of Meditation in stress management.
18. How does Meditation work? What does happen during it?
19. What are the various possibilities of Yoga therapy?
20. What is *Kundalini* Yoga? What is its aim?
21. Describe the location and other aspects of the higher five charkas.
22. How is *Kundalini* awakened? Why should *Kundalini* be not awakened prematurely?
23. Differentiate *Asamprajnata* Samadhi from *Samprajnata* Samadhi.

24. What are the characteristics of Samadhi and the connection between it and the state of the mind?
25. What is *Samadhi Parinama*? How does it take place?
26. What is Liberation? What are the effects of attaining it?
27. What are the characteristics of a *Jivanmukta*?